CREATIVE HOMEOWNER®

ULTIMATE GUIDE TO Crown Molding

CREATIVE HOMEOWNER®

ULTIMATE GUIDE TO

Crown Molding

PLAN ■ DESIGN ■ INSTALL

Neal Barrett

CREATIVE HOMEOWNER®, Upper Saddle River, New Jersey

CREATIVE
HOMEOWNER®

A Division of Federal Marketing Corp.
Upper Saddle River, NJ

ULTIMATE GUIDE TO CROWN MOLDING

MANAGING EDITOR Fran Donegan
PHOTO RESEARCHER Robyn Poplasky
EDITORIAL ASSISTANTS Jennifer Calvert, Nora Grace
INDEXER Schroeder Indexing Services
COVER DESIGN David Geer
ILLUSTRATIONS Mario Ferro, Robert LaPointe (pages 12, 18, and 19)
COVER PHOTOGRAPHY Neal Barrett

CREATIVE HOMEOWNER

VICE PRESIDENT AND PUBLISHER Timothy O. Bakke
PRODUCTION DIRECTOR Kimberly H. Vivas
ART DIRECTOR David Geer
MANAGING EDITOR Fran J. Donegan

Current Printing (last digit)
10 9 8 7 6 5 4 3 2 1

Ultimate Guide to Crown Molding, First Edition
Library of Congress Control Number: 2006937269
ISBN-10: 1-58011-346-X
ISBN-13: 978-1-58011-346-5

CREATIVE HOMEOWNER®
A Division of Federal Marketing Corp.
24 Park Way
Upper Saddle River, NJ 07458
www.creativehomeowner.com

photo credits

All photography by Neal Barrett, unless otherwise noted.

page 11: Todd Caverly **pages 12–14:** Gary David Gold/CH **page 15:** Brian Vanden Brink **page 16** Index Open **pages 18–20:** Gary David Gold/CH **page 21:** Gary David Gold/CH **page 21:** Jessie Walker **page 22:** *left* Index Open; *right* Gary David Gold/CH **page 23:** Brian Vanden Brink

Metric Equivalents

Length

1 inch	25.4mm
1 foot	0.3048m
1 yard	0.9144m
1 mile	1.61km

Area

1 square inch	645mm²
1 square foot	0.0929m²
1 square yard	0.8361m²
1 acre	4046.86m²
1 square mile	2.59km²

Volume

1 cubic inch	16.3870cm³
1 cubic foot	0.03m³
1 cubic yard	0.77m³

Common Lumber Equivalents

Sizes: Metric cross sections are so close to their U.S. sizes, as noted below, that for most purposes they may be considered equivalents.

Dimensional lumber	1 x 2	19 x 38mm
	1 x 4	19 x 89mm
	2 x 2	38 x 38mm
	2 x 4	38 x 89mm
	2 x 6	38 x 140mm
	2 x 8	38 x 184mm
	2 x 10	38 x 235mm
	2 x 12	38 x 286mm
Sheet sizes	4 x 8 ft.	1200 x 2400mm
	4 x 10 ft.	1200 x 3000mm
Sheet thicknesses	¼ in.	6mm
	⅜ in.	9mm
	½ in.	12mm
	¾ in.	19mm
Stud/joist spacing	16 in. o.c.	400mm o.c.
	24 in. o.c.	600mm o.c.

Capacity

1 fluid ounce	29.57mL
1 pint	473.18mL
1 quart	0.95L
1 gallon	3.79L

Weight

1 ounce	28.35g
1 pound	0.45kg

Temperature

Fahrenheit = Celsius x 1.8 + 32
Celsius = Fahrenheit - 32 x 5⁄9

Nail Size and Length

Penny Size	Nail Length
2d	1"
3d	1¼"
4d	1½"
5d	1¾"
6d	2"
7d	2¼"
8d	2½"
9d	2¾"
10d	3"
12d	3¼"
16d	3½"

safety

Although the methods in this book have been reviewed for safety, it is not possible to overstate the importance of using the safest methods you can. What follows are reminders—some do's and don'ts of work safety—to use along with your common sense.

- Always use caution, care, and good judgment when following the procedures described in this book.
- Always be sure that the electrical setup is safe, that no circuit is overloaded, and that all power tools and outlets are properly grounded. Do not use power tools in wet locations.
- Always read container labels on paints, solvents, and other products; provide ventilation; and observe all other warnings.
- Always read the manufacturer's instructions for using a tool, especially the warnings.
- Use hold-downs and push sticks whenever possible when working on a table saw. Avoid working short pieces if you can.
- Always remove the key from any drill chuck (portable or press) before starting the drill.
- Always pay deliberate attention to how a tool works so that you can avoid being injured.
- Always know the limitations of your tools. Do not try to force them to do what they were not designed to do.
- Always make sure that any adjustment is locked before proceeding. For example, always check the rip fence on a table saw or the bevel adjustment on a portable saw before starting to work.
- Always clamp small pieces to a bench or other work surface when using a power tool.
- Always wear the appropriate rubber gloves or work gloves when handling chemicals, moving or stacking lumber, working with concrete, or doing heavy construction.
- Always wear a disposable face mask when you create dust by sawing or sanding. Use a special filtering respirator when working with toxic substances and solvents.
- Always wear eye protection, especially when using power tools or striking metal on metal or concrete; a chip can fly off, for example, when chiseling concrete.
- Never work while wearing loose clothing, open cuffs, or jewelry; tie back long hair.
- Always be aware that there is seldom enough time for your body's reflexes to save you from injury from a power tool in a dangerous situation; everything happens too fast. Be alert!
- Always keep your hands away from the business ends of blades, cutters, and bits.
- Always hold a circular saw firmly, usually with both hands.
- Always use a drill with an auxiliary handle to control the torque when using large-size bits.
- Always check your local building codes when planning new construction. The codes are intended to protect public safety and should be observed to the letter.
- Never work with power tools when you are tired or when under the influence of alcohol or drugs.
- Never cut tiny pieces of wood or pipe using a power saw. When you need a small piece, saw it from a securely clamped longer piece.
- Never change a saw blade or a drill or router bit unless the power cord is unplugged. Do not depend on the switch being off. You might accidentally hit it.
- Never work in insufficient lighting.
- Never work with dull tools. Have them sharpened, or learn how to sharpen them yourself.
- Never use a power tool on a workpiece—large or small—that is not firmly supported.
- Never saw a workpiece that spans a large distance between horses without close support on each side of the cut; the piece can bend, closing on and jamming the blade, causing saw kickback.
- When sawing, never support a workpiece from underneath with your leg or other part of your body.
- Never carry sharp or pointed tools, such as utility knives, awls, or chisels, in your pocket. If you want to carry any of these tools, use a special-purpose tool belt that has leather pockets and holders.

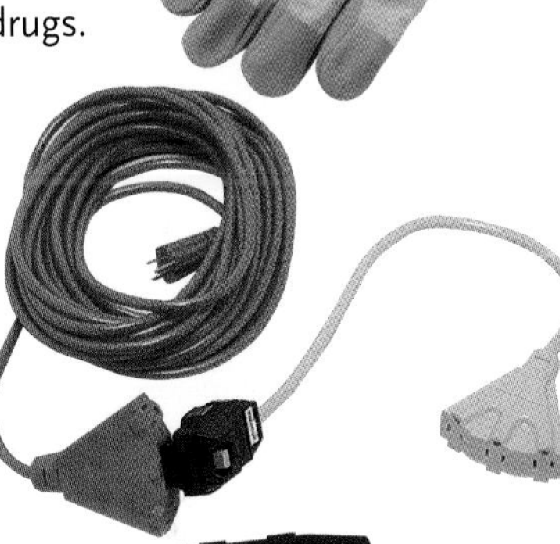

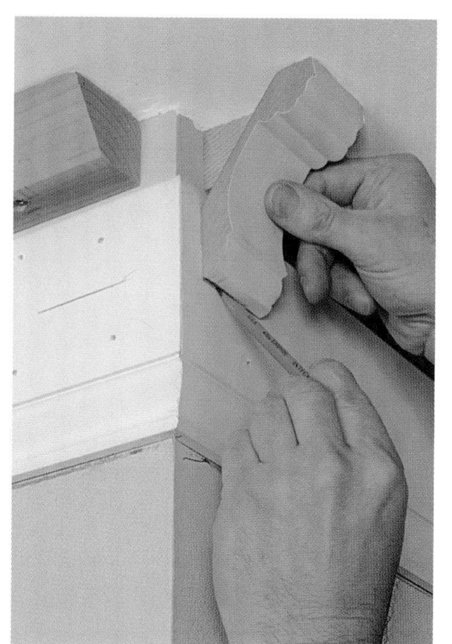
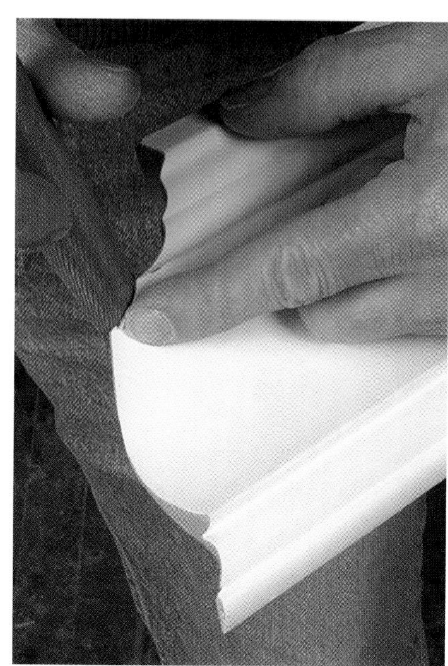

contents

introduction

Ceiling moldings have endured as one of the most popular forms of architectural embellishment, despite the fact that they are omitted from most new home construction. This curious fact is a testament to the charm of this type of ornamentation and the potential it has to shape the environment of a room, creating a sense of sophistication and personality. Of course, surface decorations, such as paint and wallpaper, and room furnishings can go a long way toward creating an individualized atmosphere, but the architectural details of a room provide a more profound sense of the spirit of the building. Ceiling moldings are particularly powerful in this regard. It may be that much of their appeal stems from the

CREATE CORNICE DESIGNS like this by combining stock lumber and molding profiles in a built-up assembly.

GUIDE TO SKILL LEVEL

Easy. Made for beginners.

Challenging. Can be done by beginners who have the patience and willingness to learn.

Difficult. Can be handled by most experienced do-it-yourselfers who have mastered basic construction skills. Consider consulting a specialist.

sense that they are, most often, purely decorative. Unlike other architectural millwork, ceiling moldings do not support the structure and operation of a window or door like casing or seal the gaps between walls and floor like baseboard. The singular nature of their function allows a unique freedom of design and, in practice, this has been freely interpreted. Historical examples of these moldings range from simple and austere to extremely elaborate and playful.

Most people associate the presence of ceiling molding in a room with a sense of elegance. Molding creates a transition between the wall and ceiling surfaces, eliminating the sharp corners and providing a focus that helps to reinforce the style of a room. These treatments include wood, composite, plastic, and pre-cast plaster moldings, ceiling medallions, and pressed tin panels. The variety of configurations is almost endless, offering you the ability to either select or design your own pattern to grace any room.

Although the idea of adding ceiling moldings to your home may be appealing, there is a popular notion that the installation process is beyond the scope of the average homeowner—especially for a more complex design. But if you are a home-improvement enthusiast who doesn't mind creating some dust, you can certainly consider these projects.

In this book, you will find instructions for installing a wide variety of ceiling moldings with a comprehensive discussion of the skills you'll need for a professional-looking job. Even with limited carpentry experience, the step-by-step details of these projects will enable you to approach them with the expectation of success. The nature of ceiling molding can present certain challenges for any installer, whether professional or amateur. Of course you need to work overhead, and this necessitates standing on ladders or building scaffolding. In addition, the often complex shapes of the molding profiles and their angled orientation demand patience and the application of some techniques that are not always intuitive. But with an understanding of the basic layout, cutting, joining, and installation techniques, you can gain confidence in your ability to tackle any ceiling molding job.

- **Covering the Basics.** The first four chapters of *Ultimate Guide to Crown Molding* deal with selecting the tools and materials you will need to complete the projects. A chapter on techniques covers the procedures involved with cutting and installing cornice molding.
- **The Projects.** The rest of the book gives directions for installing 30 original cornice designs. The projects range from easy to quite challenging—providing something for every skill level.

EACH PROJECT in the book contains a sequence of photos like those shown below. Starting with laying out the design (left), you will learn to install blocking for extra nailing surfaces if needed (middle) and follow through with cutting and fitting the molding sections (right).

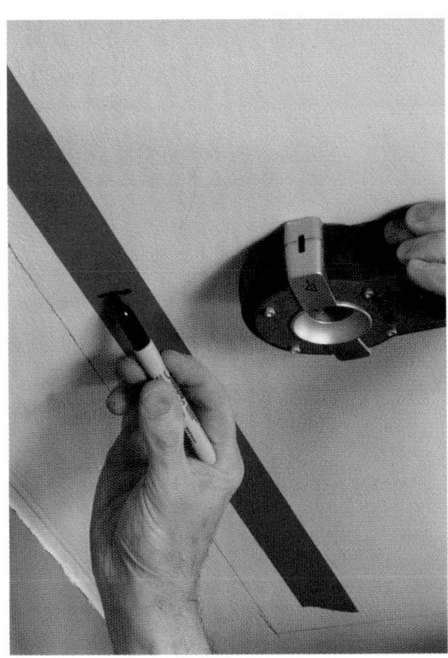

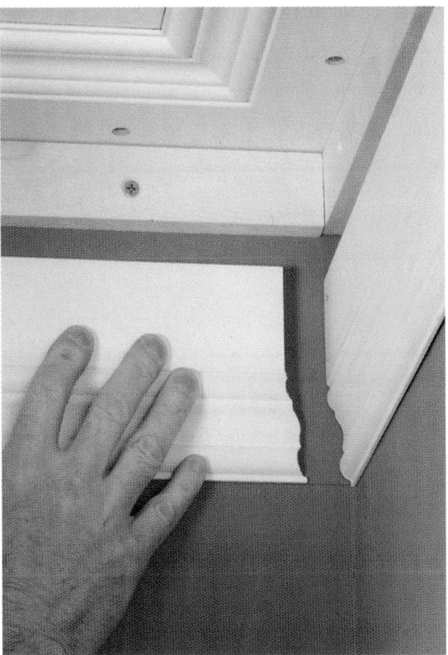

1 cornice design

The architectural details of a home are the features that define its style. They color the way that we feel about the building because each detail imparts an emotional and aesthetic reaction to what we see. The overall structure of the home, including its materials, layout of the rooms, and window placement present an initial impression. But it is largely the trim and finish of the building, including moldings and wall treatments, that shape the way we experience the interior space. They influence how our eyes move around a room, whether our gaze lingers over a doorway, focuses in the center of the ceiling, or is drawn to an elaborate mantle. In the most successful instances, the trim elements work together to form a consistent and pleasing environment.

THE EVOLUTION OF CORNICE MOLDING

Much of our modern concept of ceiling moldings derives from the use of a cornice in classical Greek architecture. In this tradition, the vertical building supports, columns, or pilasters are capped by an *entablature*. The entablature is a horizontal assembly of moldings and bands that rests directly on, and spans the space between, the column *capitals*. Depending on the particular classical order, an entablature can take various forms; however, it is always divided into three portions. Immediately above the columns or pilasters is the *architrave*.

The *frieze* is the next horizontal band and is often decorated with carvings. The topmost portion is the cornice, which consists of a set of projecting moldings with the uppermost element being the crown molding, or *cymatium*. This particular molding was often based on the *cyma recta* profile, with a convex lower half and concave upper half. The profile has survived today as the ogee shape that is included in many popular moldings. The cornice was designed for both decorative effect and to fulfill practical functions, including directing rainwater away from the face of the building and helping support the roof structure.

■ **Interior Ornamentation.** In many ancient examples, the cornice was primarily an exterior feature of a building; however, by the time of the Renaissance, elements of classical architecture were being applied to interiors as well. Cornice moldings have maintained their popularity to this day and have been freely adapted for the most popular design schemes, including Colonial, Georgian, Federal, Neo-Classical, Victorian, Arts and Crafts, Art Deco, and even some Contemporary styles.

classical column styles

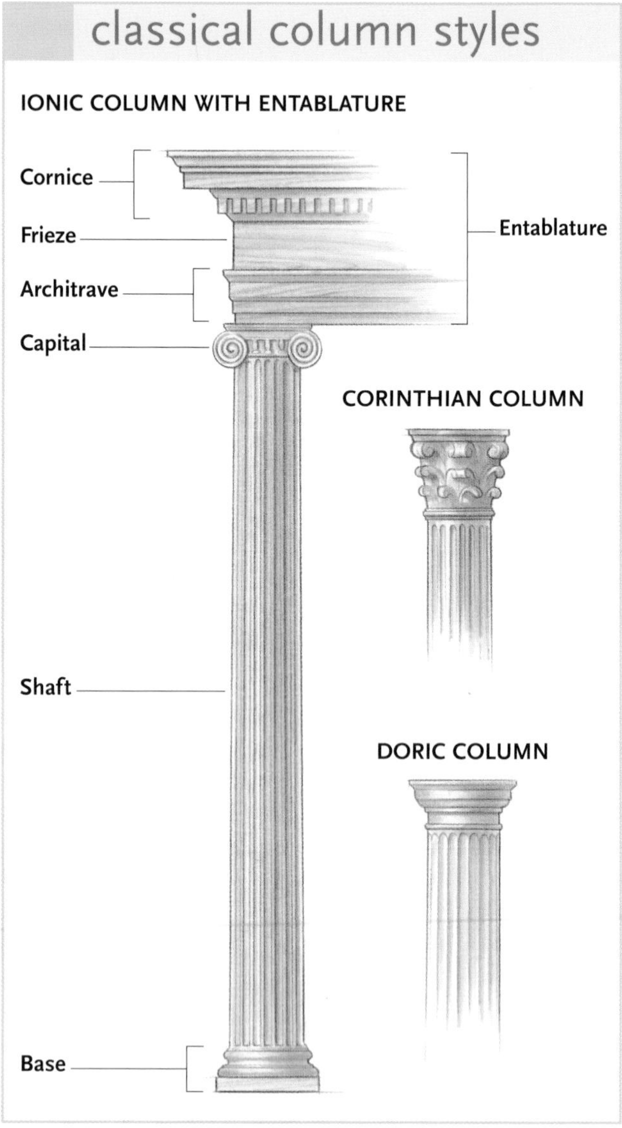

LEFT Crown or cornice moldings are not only used to decorate the junction of wall and ceiling, but they can also be copied on cabinetry and door casings.

OPPOSITE The basic designs of cornices were first used on the exteriors of buildings. Compare the parts of this cornice with the entablature shown above.

CROWN VERSUS CORNICE

THE TERMS "CROWN MOLDING" AND "CORNICE" are often used interchangeably to describe the ceiling molding at the top of a wall or used above a door or window. And, while it is unlikely that anyone would protest the use of either term, they are not technically synonymous. Most millwork suppliers use "crown molding" to refer to a particular family of profiles that are derived from the Greek *cyma recta* moldings. These moldings are often referred to as "sprung" moldings because they sit at an angle between the wall and ceiling. In common use, the term "crown molding" is applied to a variety of moldings that include ogee, bed, and cove profiles. These individual moldings span a range of sizes from 1 to over 8 inches wide. Crown moldings are used to cap door and window casings, decorate mantles, embellish furniture and cabinets, and also to form part of a cornice assembly.

A "cornice" is a single molding or assembly of different moldings that is applied at the junction of a wall and ceiling. Most cornice designs include some type of crown molding as part of the assembly (sometimes as the only element), but this is not absolutely necessary. A cornice can also be constructed of a single flat molding or layered combination of flat moldings; it is not unusual for moldings designed for other applications to be incorporated into a cornice design. Baseboard, chair-rail, and panel-molding profiles are frequent additions to these assemblies.

So, even though crown molding is a name that is loosely applied to many types of ceiling molding applications, cornice is a more comprehensive term.

Cornices Today

It is quite rare for a builder of tract homes to include cornice molding in new construction. This remains one of the accepted places to exercise some cost-cutting measures and, in fact, there is no longer a general expectation to see these features in new homes. Custom home builders will sometimes offer a cornice as an option in one or two rooms—a dining room or formal entry are typical—but it would be surprising to see this type of trim throughout the house. And in most cases, any cornice offered would be a relatively simple, one- or two-piece installation using stock profiles.

■ **Upscale Designs.** At the luxury end of residential construction, when an architect and/or interior designer is involved directly with the owner, cornice moldings are often used to complement the decor of a particular room or even the entire home. In these houses, cornices are sometimes coordinated with a ceiling medallion or used to accent beamed or coffered ceilings. In rooms with extensive built-in cabinetry, such as a library or family room, cornice molding is frequently used to make the transition between the casework and ceiling. For this type of project, it is not uncommon for moldings to be made to order by a millwork shop, often with a custom profile and in one of the hardwood species.

But while you may correctly associate the presence of cornice molding with an upscale and elegant home decor, it would be wrong to conclude that you cannot include it in your own home, even if you prefer a more informal style. Moldings are available in a wide range of materials and styles, and there is a product and technique to suit almost any budget. For those who are willing to invest in some basic tools and who are prepared to master the fundamental skills, including a good dose of patience, the reward can be a truly remarkable transformation of your home.

TOP Crown-molding treatments are often incorporated with other trim elements, such as the window cornices shown here.

ABOVE While many builders of new homes do not install distinctive trim treatments, builders of custom homes often include these details.

OPPOSITE Older homes, especially grand older homes, often include one-of-a-kind crown-molding treatments.

MOLDING CONFIGURATIONS

Cornice trim can take many forms, ranging from very simple to extremely ornate and complex. The most elemental cornice trim would consist of one or more flat moldings applied at the top of the wall. As previously mentioned, a frieze can be an integral part of many different cornice treatments. And a frieze can serve as the base layer for other flat moldings to comprise a built-up cornice design. For example, you could install a frieze of inverted baseboard stock and then apply a chair rail or panel molding over it. Or, for an Art Deco-inspired theme, you might layer two or three flat boards to create a stepped cornice.

Combining Molding Types

A multipiece cornice offers the ability to really customize your room trim. One of the more straightforward treatments might involve installing a baseboard molding to both wall and ceiling and then mounting a cove or ogee profile between them. But there is no limit to the possible options for this type of cornice, and elaborate assemblies of five or six separate elements are not unusual.

It is important to keep your design in reasonable proportion to the scale of the room, but with careful planning, a built-up cornice can completely transform a room. Even though a multipiece cornice can appear to be an extremely complicated project—and, in fact, that is often the intended impression—the basic techniques involved are the same ones used for a simple installation. Once you've mastered them, you can tackle a project of considerable complexity. Planning and careful layout are key elements for success in this type of job and, as in any demanding craft, you need to exercise a good measure of patience and attention to detail.

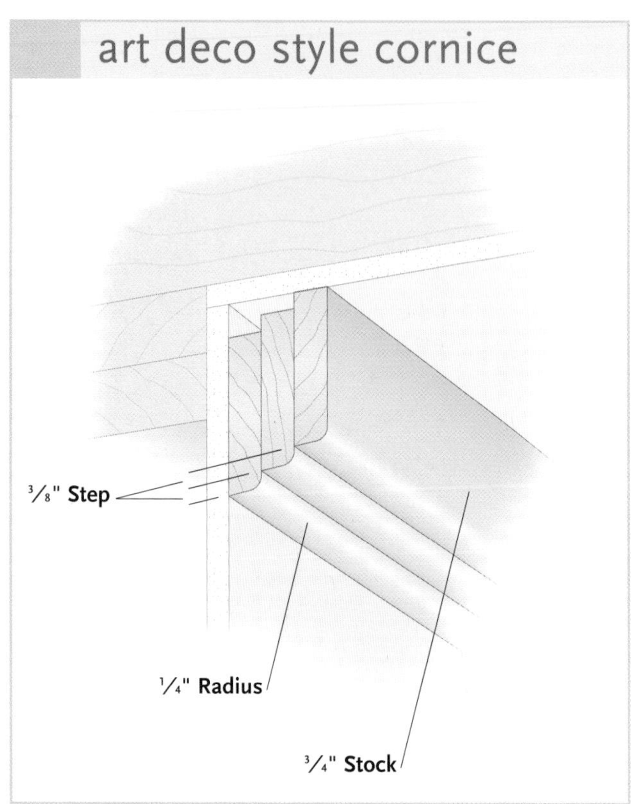

LEFT Distinctive crown-molding treatments are often used in the more public rooms of a house, such as the living room, dining room, and foyer.

SPRUNG MOLDING

SPRUNG MOLDING refers to a molding that sits at an angle between the wall and ceiling; it derives from the concept of "spring angle," which describes the angle between the back surface of a molding and the wall. Most commonly used moldings feature a spring angle of either 45 or 38 degrees, but in practice, it is always a good idea to check with an angle gauge because it's common for moldings to vary from the standard. The spring angle is an important concept in cornice work, as it determines how the molding gets cut for corner joints. The most common single moldings used for simple cornices are bed, coves, and ogee profiles, but there are hundreds of different profile shapes available that combine these basic elements or add others such as beads, rabbets, dentils, or carving.

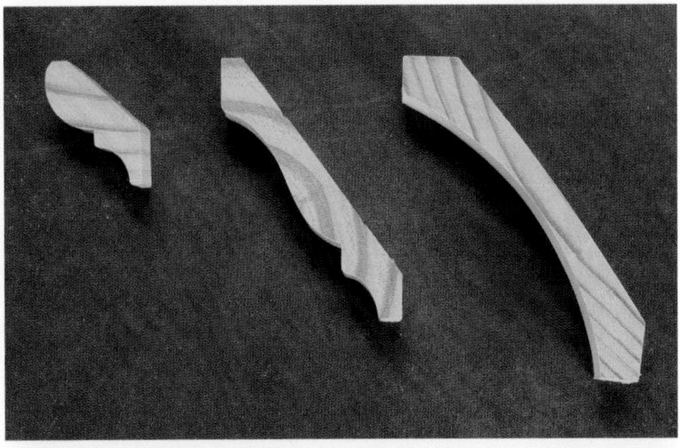

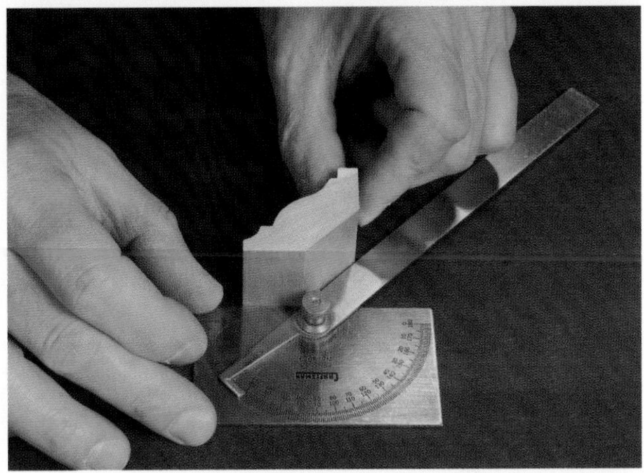

COMMON MOLDING PROFILES that sit at an angle between the wall and ceiling include bed, crown, and cove moldings, top. Each has a unique profile and are often used with other profiles in built-up assemblies. When installing sprung moldings, check the angle using an angle gauge, bottom.

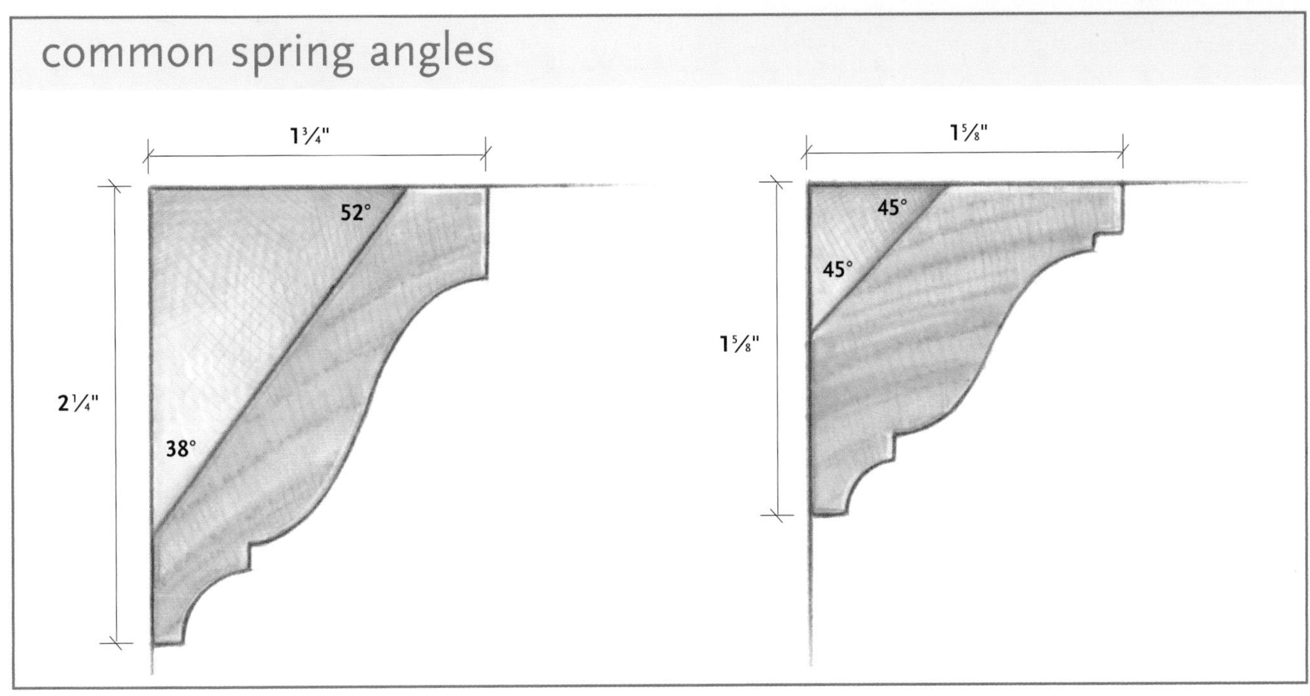

Designing Cornice Trim

There are no hard and fast rules for designing cornice trim, but there are definitely some things that you should keep in mind when planning your job. First among these is the scale of your room; this includes both the overall size of the room and, most important, the height of the ceiling. A small space, or one with a low ceiling, can easily be overpowered by a cornice that is too large; similarly, a large room, or one with a high ceiling, would look foolish with a small ceiling molding. Of course, the specifics of your particular design will be the most compelling factor. (See "Cornice Height Guidelines," below.)

Keep in mind that a smaller cornice may work well for a high ceiling if it features heavy, boldly carved details. It's also important to try to maintain a sense of proper proportion between the height of a cornice and that of the baseboard in a room. If you are adding a large cornice assembly to a room with existing 3- or 4-inch base trim, you may eventually want to install some taller baseboards.

The overall shape of your molding or built-up assembly also colors how the cornice affects the room. A large cove molding, for example, softens the transition between walls and ceiling, creating a rounded, informal appearance; a stepped, multipiece assembly that projects farther into the room appears more formal.

Although the style of your home and its furnishings are important considerations when planning a cornice, they need not be defining factors. You certainly want a new cornice to feel like it belongs in the home. However, unless your cornice design is a reflection of a very specific design theme, something with readily identifiable features—an Art Deco motif, for example—you have considerable latitude in the elements you might include.

ABOVE When adding a cornice, try to establish a relationship between the cornice and baseboard treatments.

OPPOSITE Crown molding sizes should relate to the size of the room and other trim treatments.

smart tip

CORNICE HEIGHT GUIDELINES

THERE ARE NO HARD AND FAST RULES REGARDING THE SIZE OF A CORNICE, BUT HERE ARE SOME SUGGESTIONS TO GET YOU STARTED.

Height of Ceiling	Height of Cornice
8 TO 9 FEET	2½ TO 4½ INCHES
9 TO 10 FEET	5½ TO 7½ INCHES
10 TO 12 FEET	7½ TO 12 INCHES

typical cornice profiles

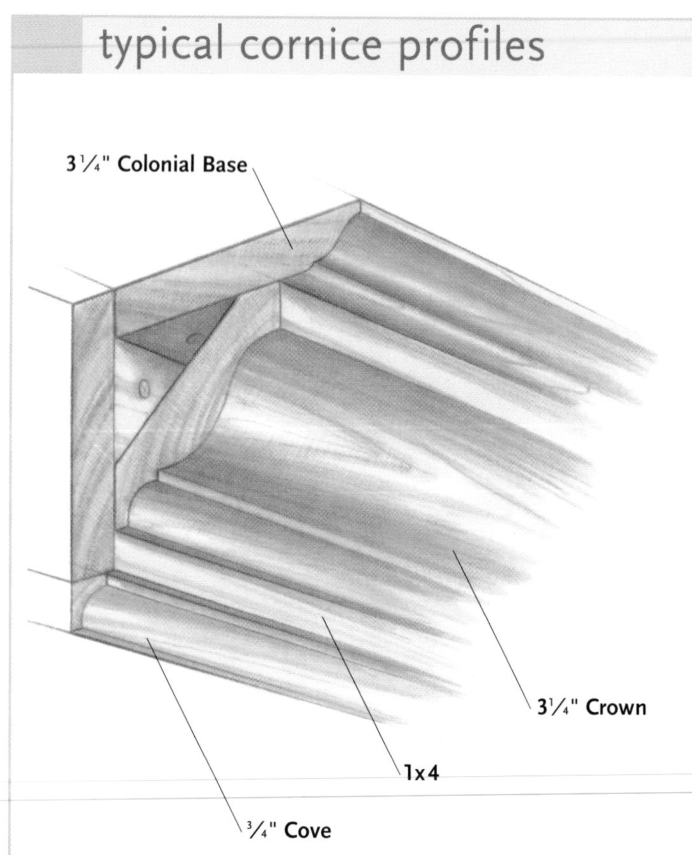

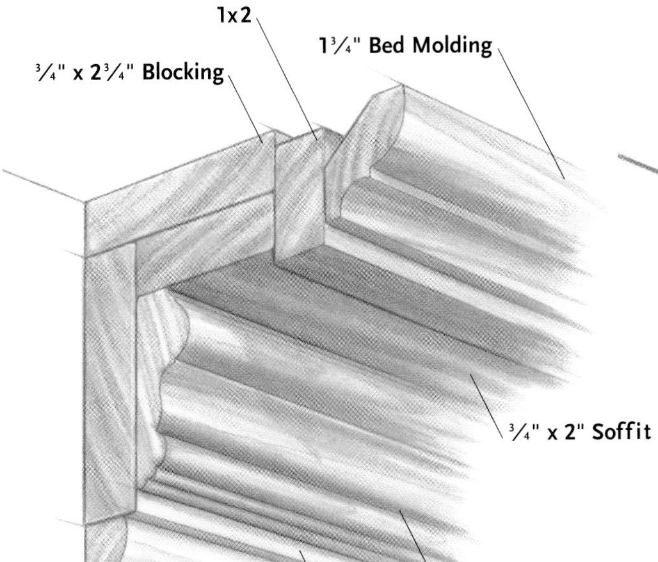

1x2
1¾" Bed Molding
¾" x 2¾" Blocking
¾" x 2" Soffit
2 7/16" Chair Rail
1x4
Shoe Molding

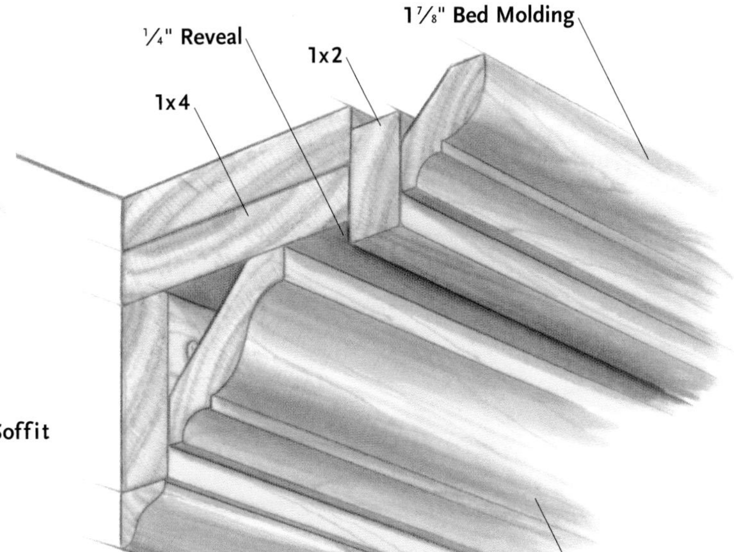

1⅞" Bed Molding
¼" Reveal
1x2
1x4
2¾" Crown
¾" Cove
1x3

■ **Materials and Design.** Your choice of molding materials plays a large part in determining the ultimate appearance of your cornice; conversely, the look you want to achieve will largely determine which materials you can choose. Of course, for painted trim, you have many material choices, but for a clear or stained finish, your best options are clear pine or hardwood stock.

When you plan a painted finish, you will need to make some design decisions that will, literally, color the way you view the cornice. If you paint the trim the same color as the ceiling or walls, it will become a less visually demanding feature in the room. You could decide to use a bold color for the cornice—something that echoes the colors in some room furnishings—to cause the trim to be extremely prominent. Or, you might opt to use a color that is just a shade or two darker or lighter than the wall color, which is usually enough difference to make the trim distinct but not overly dominant.

■ **Clear Finishes.** If you decide to install a stained or clear-finished cornice, it will inevitably contrast with the wall and ceiling finishes and, as a result, will draw your eye more aggressively. The variations of color and grain offered by a natural finish have a great appeal, but this type of treatment is not for every situation. You will also need to consider the additional cost, both in materials and labor, that a clear finish mandates. The raw material cost of hardwood stock is at least two to three times that of paint-grade alternatives and, for the more exotic species, the cost can be much higher. And whenever you are planning a clear or stained finish, the time required for installation is easily two to three times more than what would be needed for a paint-grade job.

BELOW Selecting a painted finish allows you to use pine or less-than-perfect material for trimwork.

OPPOSITE Natural finishes allow the grain and look of the wood to show through, so a clear native hardwood or an imported wood are usually the choices here.

FUNCTIONAL USES FOR CROWN MOLDING

Even though cornice molding is primarily a decorative element, it can also have a functional aspect that affects your decision as to what kind of trim you will install. For example, one of the most traditional cornice treatments includes a picture molding as one of the elements—used as a direct component of the cornice or mounted 12 to 18 inches down the wall—creating a decorative frieze. The profile of this type of molding is specifically designed to support the use of clips to hang paintings or photographs—hence the name. This eliminates the need for individual picture hooks nailed into the wall surface and provides infinitely flexible spacing for your artwork.

■ **Problem Solver.** Most often, you'll consider adding a cornice molding to dress up a room, but there are situations where the molding can also solve a construction problem. After many years, the plaster ceilings in older homes can develop cracks; sometimes these can be easily patched, but in severe cases the ceiling needs more serious repair. One of the most direct means of addressing this problem is to cover the old ceiling with a new layer of

LEFT Formal, traditional rooms cry out for a distinctive cornice treatment.

ABOVE Casual spaces usually look best with simple crown molding treatments, such as a one-piece crown molding or a basic two-piece design.

MOLDING AND LIGHTING

LIGHTING IS A KEY ELEMENT in creating a desired character in a room. In fact, the type of lighting in a room can do as much as the paint and wallpaper to set the mood and complement the furnishings; this is particularly valuable in rooms that are used for entertaining guests, such as the dining room or living room. Interior designers have long maintained that mixing different types of lighting is the best way to create a layered sense of atmosphere in a room.

Standard options such as table lamps and ceiling fixtures can go a long way in this regard, but with a cornice you have the additional option of providing concealed, indirect lighting at the ceiling level for a very dramatic effect. For this type of use, a cornice is mounted lower on the wall, so that the light can be reflected off the ceiling. A wide variety of lighting options can be used for this type of installation, including traditional incandescent and fluorescent fixtures, halogen or xenon lights, and LED (light-emitting diode) illumination. And for maximum effect, you can control these lights with a dimmer. When designing this type of cornice, you should always consult with a licensed electrician so that you can provide proper support and clearance for the type of lighting you want to use, and also arrange to have the necessary wires run, in advance, for a safe and easy installation.

USE CORNICE TREATMENTS to hide the light fixtures when adding light shelves.

drywall. Of course this process includes taping many joints, which is clearly the most tedious and difficult part of the job, especially for the amateur. The most challenging joints are those between the wall and ceiling, and here is where a cornice can provide some relief. Because the cornice molding covers the joint between the wall and ceiling, taping those perimeter joints becomes unnecessary. Should some future homeowner wish to remove the cornice in their own remodeling frenzy, they can then take on the job of taping those joints.

One of the most impressive ceiling treatments involves the installation of a *beamed* or *coffered* ceiling. These features can completely transform a room, creating a strong sense of place that can range from rustic to extremely formal. The process of fitting a series of beams to a ceiling can be an extremely rigorous process, especially if each piece must be individually scribed to fit tightly to an irregular ceiling. Here is another situation where the use of a cornice molding can make your installation go more smoothly. By covering the joints between ceiling and beams, a cornice molding eliminates the need to scribe the beam stock: a small, flexible molding can usually be "cheated" up and down to follow an irregular ceiling surface. And if the ceiling has some extreme dips and humps, you can caulk the gaps between the molding and ceiling. Of course, adding cornice trim to a beamed or coffered ceiling does more than solve some practical problems. A properly designed cornice can add another dimension to the project, creating an elegant and layered installation.

2 tools

If you're the type of individual who is considering a do-it-yourself cornice project, it's likely that you're also someone who is attracted to tools. This is not a rare affliction, as illustrated by the generous tool departments in every home center and the many tool catalogs that arrive by mail. For many people, tools are just irresistible, whether or not any particular work is planned. However, if you are actually planning to install some cornice trim, it's important that you have the right tools for the job because they can make the difference between a project that is fun and satisfying and one that leaves you both frustrated and disappointed. If you have little experience, begin with a small collection of basic tools and master their uses, and then purchase additional items as your projects become more advanced.

WARNING

MEASURING, MARKING, AND LAYOUT

Accurate measurement and layout provide the basis for a successful trim job. From the rough measurements required for material estimation to the precise angles required for tight miter joints, these are critical elements of your project. There are many of these tools available, and the particular ones you select will depend more on personal preference than any arbitrary standards. Just keep in mind that measuring tools should be easy and clear to read, layout tools should be accurate, and marking tools need to be clear and precise.

Marking and Layout Tools

The utility of any measurement is limited by your ability to transfer that measurement to your work piece and, then, your ability to cut it accurately. When your job requires that you cut some stock to rough length—within a few inches of the final dimension—it isn't critical that you have a particularly accurate mark. For this type of job, the traditional carpenter's pencil is a perfect choice. These flat pencils have a thick, soft lead that you can easily sharpen with a utility knife. They are not particularly fragile, and their marks are thick, dark, and easy to read. At one time, these pencils were freely given away with any purchase at a lumber yard, but those days are now past. While still available for purchase, they are sometimes hard to find, so a good substitute would be a wide, felt-tipped marker.

CHALK-LINE BOX

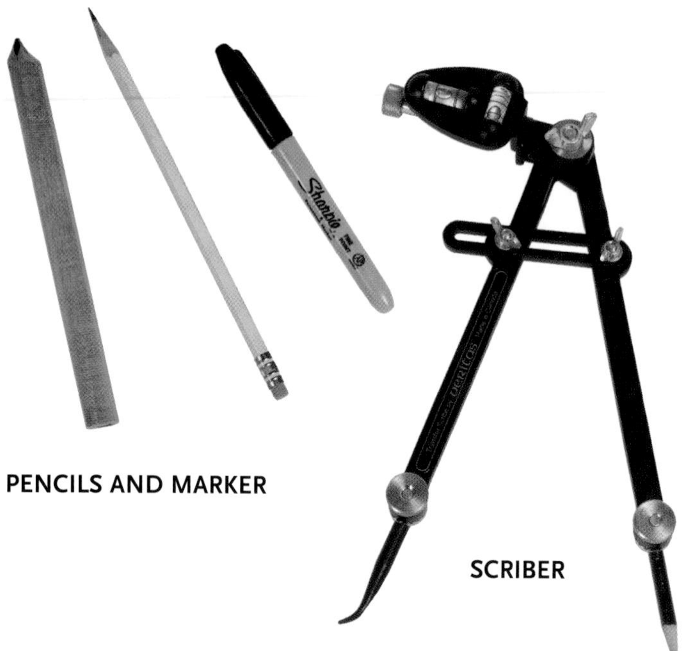

PENCILS AND MARKER

SCRIBER

IF YOU ARE WORKING with an uneven ceiling, use a scriber to get the best results. Note the assembly at right. The piece to be trimmed is resting on nails in the base piece. The exposed section of the base should be uniform along the entire wall. Scribe the profile of the ceiling on the molding, and trim as needed.

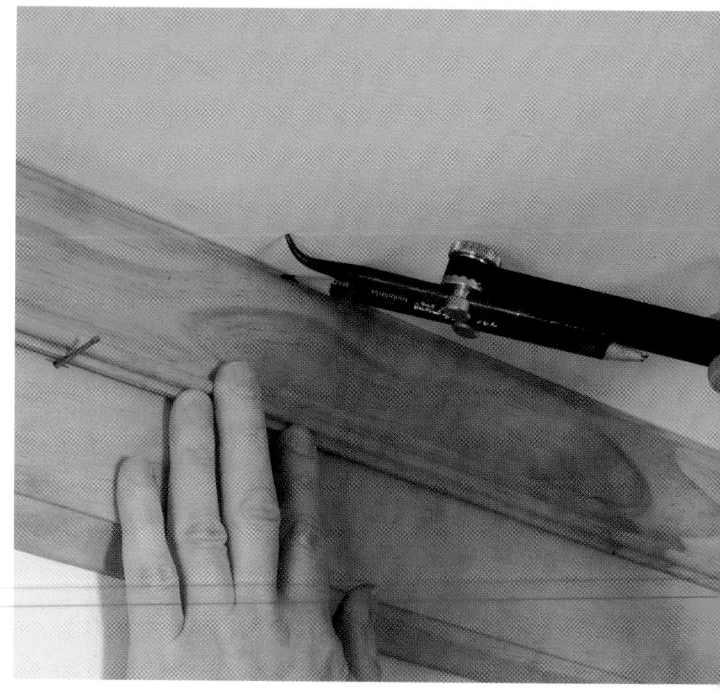

ELECTRONIC STUD FINDERS

EVEN THOUGH CORNICE TRIM is not a structural element in a house, it still must be securely fastened in place—and that usually involves using nails or screws to attach it to the wall or ceiling framing. Because the studs and ceiling joists are hidden behind a layer of drywall, you need to do a bit of detective work to locate them. Of course, you can drill small holes in an area that will be covered to find the framing. However, a much simpler and less messy approach is to use an electronic stud finder. Early models of stud finders used magnets to locate the nails or screws driven into the framing members. The newer models use sensors to detect difference in capacitance to find the studs, and some even use a type of radar technology to locate the framing. Most models feature a combination of sounds and lights to alert you when the tool is over a stud.

IF YOU ARE WORKING in a room with finished walls, place a strip of masking tape on each wall so that you can mark the stud locations on it instead of on the wall. Turn on the electronic stud finder and hold it against the wall near a corner. When the "ready" indicator on the tool lights up, slide it along the wall until the audible or visual alarm detects a stud. Place a mark on the wall or tape to indicate the center of each stud.

When your job starts to get serious, and your measurements start approaching the nearest 1/16 of an inch, it is time to switch to a more precise marking tool. Fortunately, you do not need to get too exotic with your selection, as a normal hard pencil with a #3 lead is perfect for the job. These pencils will take a very fine point and, if you keep them well sharpened, they will allow you to make very accurate layout marks.

■ **Scribers.** These are V-shaped tools that has a marking pencil on one side and a metal point on the opposite side. The legs of the tool are adjustable so that the space between the ends can be changed to fit a wide range of situations. Some models have a built-in level for more accuracy. This tool is extremely useful in those situations when you must fit a board or piece of molding to an irregular surface, such as another molding or a brick or stone fireplace. You will find scribers that sell for less than $5 and some models that approach $100; for most uses, the inexpensive tool will be perfectly adequate.

■ **Chalk-Line Boxes.** This is a very basic tool with a simple purpose: to mark a straight line between two distant points. The tool consists of a small container with a reel that holds a cotton string with a hook on its free end. Pour powdered chalk into the box, and then stretch the string between two points. Holding the string taut, gently lift and release the line, allowing it to snap against the surface to create a mark. This tool can be extremely handy to mark the outer limits of cornice trim boards on either the wall or ceiling. However, if the room is painted before the trim installation, it's best not to use the chalk line, as the color chalk marks can be difficult to remove from a finished surface.

Measuring Tape and Stick Rule

■ **Retractable Steel Tapes.** This will be your primary tool for measuring on a trim job. These tapes commonly have $\frac{1}{16}$-inch graduations down their entire length, and some provide $\frac{1}{32}$-inch markings for the first foot. A good tape will feature each "foot" marking clearly emphasized by contrasting colors or larger numbers and arrows or some other indication of 16-inch spacing for easy location of wall studs and ceiling joists. Tapes come in a wide range of sizes, but a model that has a 1-inch-wide blade and 25-foot length is a good choice for trim use. Make sure that any tape you select has a belt clip and locking lever that allows you to keep the blade extended.

■ **Stick Rule.** A folding stick ruler is another useful measuring device, and one with a long history. Comprised of a series of $\frac{1}{8}$-inch-thick x 8-inch-long slats that are hinged together, this type of ruler provides a rigid measuring device that can also fold into a compact package. Folding rules are available in 6- and 8-foot lengths, and most models include a sliding metal extension at one end. This feature makes this a particularly valuable tool for taking accurate inside measurements—something that is difficult to do using a retractable tape.

Squares

The concept of "square" is one of the foundations of carpentry. Two surfaces are considered to be square to one another when the angle between them is exactly 90 degrees. Appropriately, the device used to test that condition is also called a square.

■ **Framing Squares.** A framing square is constructed of either steel or aluminum and has two arms, one 24 inches long, called the blade, and one 16 inches long, called the tongue. This type of square is designed to be used in house framing, and it always features a chart that provides dimensions for rafter calculations. However, it is also extremely useful for checking if inside and outside corners are square and also for use as a straightedge.

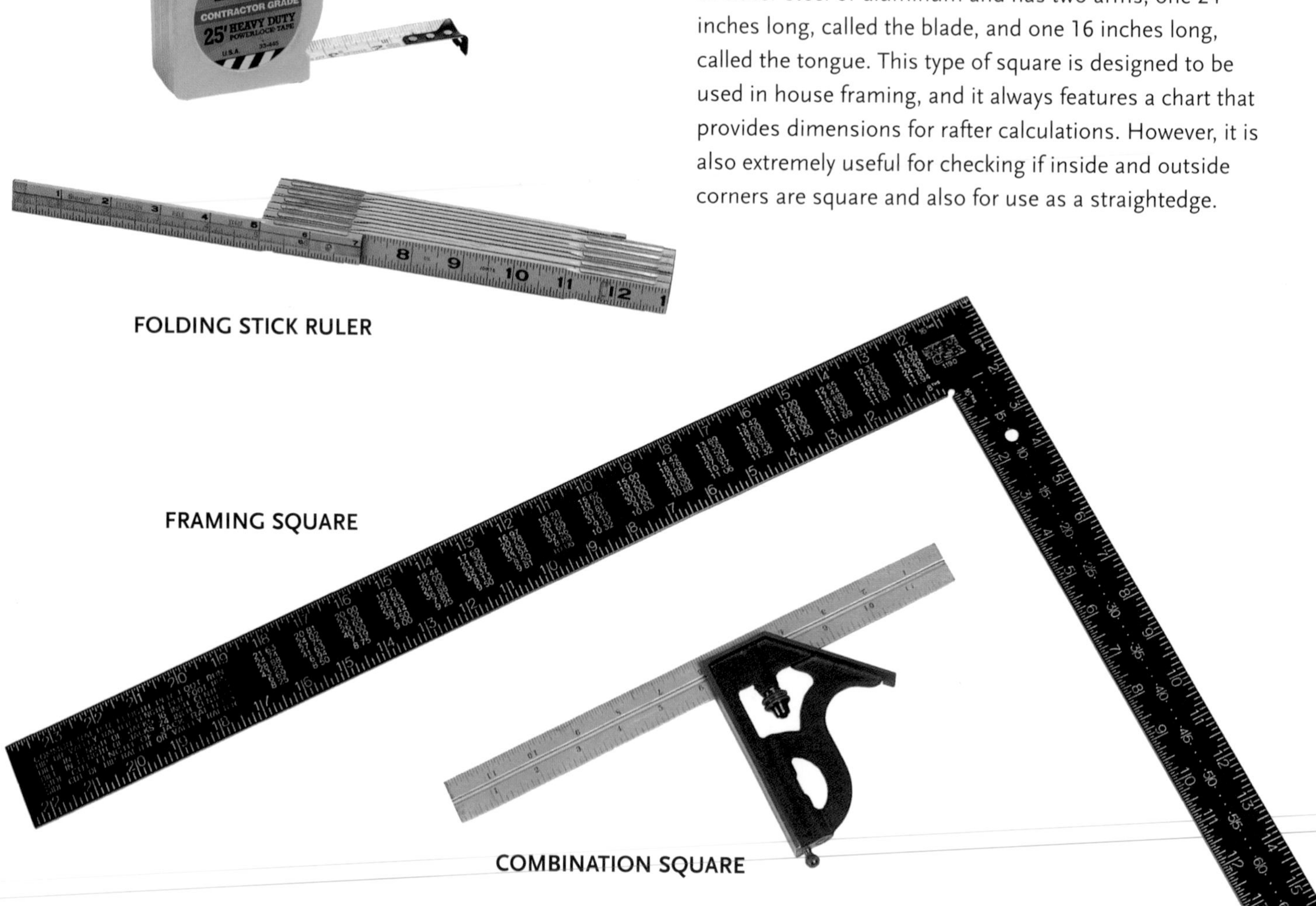

MEASURING TAPE

FOLDING STICK RULER

FRAMING SQUARE

COMBINATION SQUARE

■ **Sliding Combination Squares.** This tool has a 4½-inch-long body that can slide along a 12-inch blade and lock in place. This allows you to use it as either a depth or marking gauge as well as a square. In addition, the body has a milled edge that sits at 45 degrees to the blade, which can be used to check miter cuts.

Levels

In general carpentry, the concepts of plumb and level are extremely important, and the spirit level is the tool that you would use to test these qualities. For cornice work, it usually is not much of a concern whether the ceiling is level, as the trim will follow it in any case. Of course, if the ceiling in a room slopes a few inches from one side to the other, you might need to make some adjustments to avoid feeling like you are in a fun house. But in most installations, this won't be necessary. A 4-foot level, however, can still be a handy tool to test the ceiling and walls for bumps and hollow areas. In this type of use, the level is really being used just as a straightedge, so if you do not happen to have one, a straight board or piece of aluminum angle could also be used.

Measuring Angles

■ **Angle Gauges.** The most demanding part of a cornice project is fitting the joints at inside and outside corners. In theory, most of these corners should be perfect 90-degree angles, but this is often not the case. Sloppy framing and built-up drywall compound can easily contribute to corners that aren't square, and many times there are corner joints that are intentionally created at different angles, such as walls for bay windows. To cut molding joints to follow these walls, you need to be able to measure the true angle of the corner, and that's where an adjustable angle gauge comes in. While there are many different designs of this basic tool, most have two legs that can be held against the two sides of a corner and give a measurement of the angle. The appropriate miter angle for the trim is then one-half of that reading.

■ **Adjustable Sliding Bevel.** An adjustable sliding bevel gauge is a similar tool, but with shorter legs and no graduations for angle measurement. This tool is used to simply copy an existing angle and allow you to transfer it directly to a piece of trim or to a scrap board for bisecting with a divider or protractor. To use the tool, loosen the nut, and then hold the body against one side of the angle. Allow the blade to rest against the opposite side of the angle, and tighten the nut to maintain the setting.

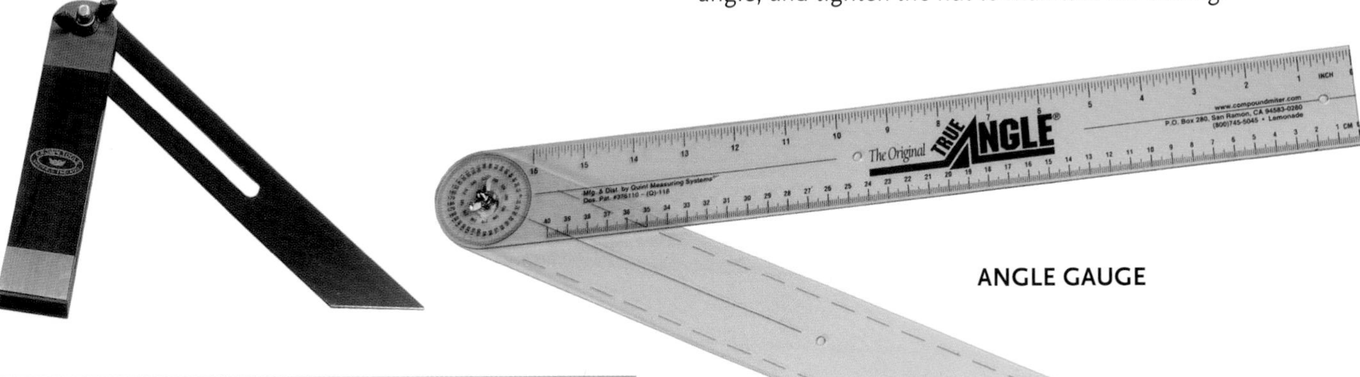

ADJUSTABLE SLIDING BEVEL GAUGE

ANGLE GAUGE

IN MANY ROOMS, CORNER ANGLES are not true 90-deg. angles due to sloppy construction or a glob of drywall compound. In these cases, you will need to know the angle of the corner in order to cut a miter that fits. Hold the angle gauge on the corner, and read the true angle. The miter angle is one-half the total angle.

CUTTING TOOLS

Every piece of trim in a house needs to be cut to size, often with provision for one or two complex joints. A natural corollary of that requirement is that you will need some reliable tools to achieve those cuts. Many cuts that you will make are simple, square crosscuts, but many others will require you to maintain exact miter and/or bevel angles or to form complex coped profiles. These jobs demand an array of cutting tools that is complete and flexible enough to take on a range of tasks. Every part of a cornice project can be executed solely with hand tools, but your job will be infinitely easier, and will proceed more quickly, if you take advantage of some powered alternatives.

Handsaws

A properly sharpened handsaw can be a joy to use, and it can be one of the most efficient tools for executing some particular jobs. In particular, when installing wooden cornice trim, coped or fitted joints are the recommended treatment at most inside corners.

■ **Coping Saws.** While there are other alternatives, a coping saw is the first tool that most carpenters would choose for coped joints. This tool has a wooden handle attached to one end of a C-shaped frame. A thin blade is held in tension between the ends of the frame, with mounting fixtures that allow the user to orient the cutting teeth on the blade in different directions. You also have the ability to mount the blade to cut on either the "pull" or "push" stroke, although most carpenters prefer the

THE THIN, FLEXIBLE BLADE of the coping saw allows you to follow the profile of the molding.

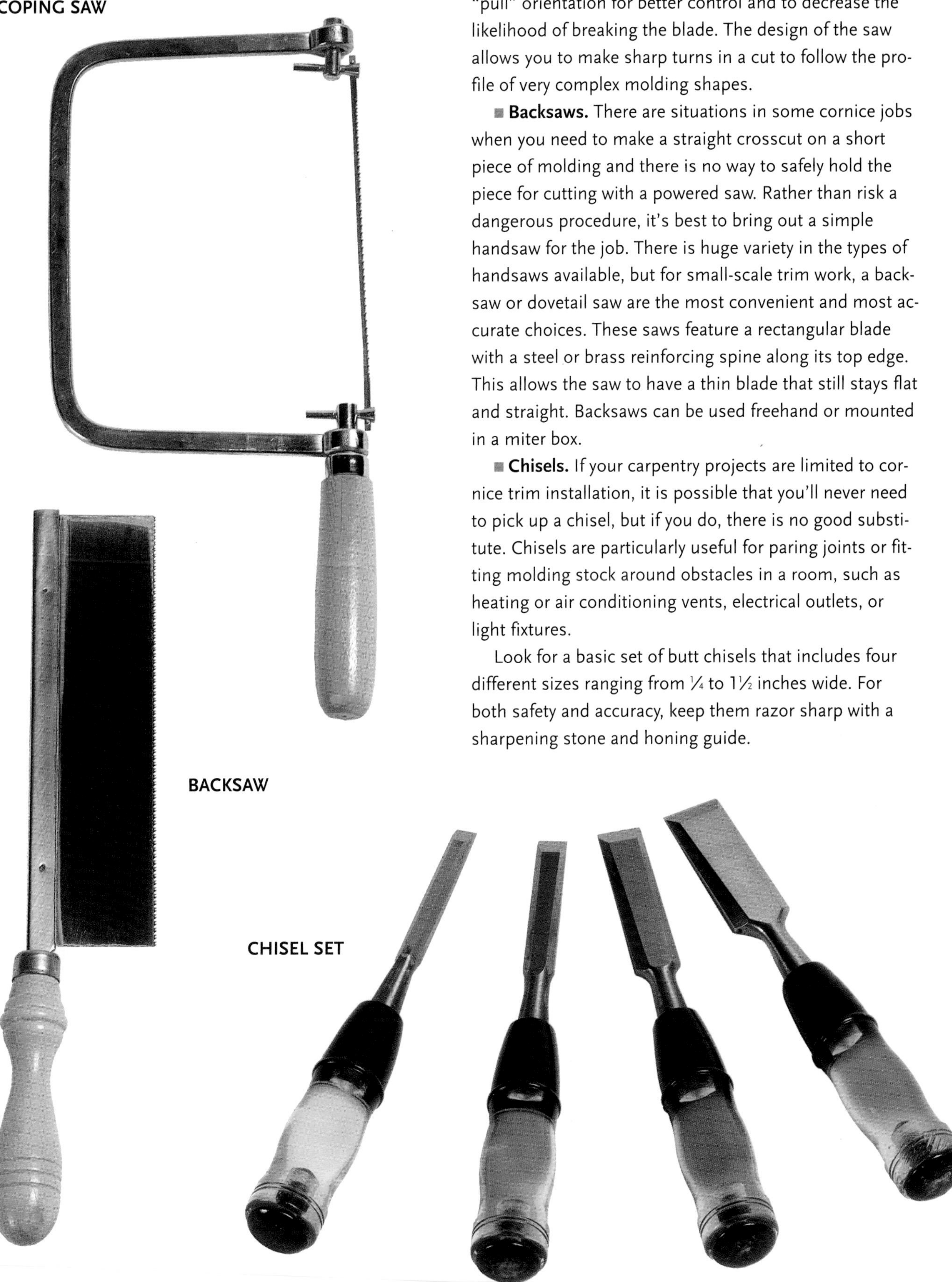

"pull" orientation for better control and to decrease the likelihood of breaking the blade. The design of the saw allows you to make sharp turns in a cut to follow the profile of very complex molding shapes.

■ **Backsaws.** There are situations in some cornice jobs when you need to make a straight crosscut on a short piece of molding and there is no way to safely hold the piece for cutting with a powered saw. Rather than risk a dangerous procedure, it's best to bring out a simple handsaw for the job. There is huge variety in the types of handsaws available, but for small-scale trim work, a backsaw or dovetail saw are the most convenient and most accurate choices. These saws feature a rectangular blade with a steel or brass reinforcing spine along its top edge. This allows the saw to have a thin blade that still stays flat and straight. Backsaws can be used freehand or mounted in a miter box.

■ **Chisels.** If your carpentry projects are limited to cornice trim installation, it is possible that you'll never need to pick up a chisel, but if you do, there is no good substitute. Chisels are particularly useful for paring joints or fitting molding stock around obstacles in a room, such as heating or air conditioning vents, electrical outlets, or light fixtures.

Look for a basic set of butt chisels that includes four different sizes ranging from ¼ to 1½ inches wide. For both safety and accuracy, keep them razor sharp with a sharpening stone and honing guide.

Rasps, Files, and Knives

To efficiently execute the complex, shaped joints that can arise in cornice work, you will often need to use a variety of tools. It's highly unlikely that you can achieve a perfectly fitted joint by cutting it with a saw—it is just too difficult to control the tool in the subtle ways required to follow every nuance of shape. So when adjustment in a cut is needed, you can first try to simply pare the part using a knife. The particular type of knife you select is not important, as long as the blade is razor sharp. Utility knives have the attractive feature of replaceable blades, so sharpening is not an issue, but a small paring knife may be easier to manipulate.

■ **Files and Rasps.** For another approach, you can assemble a variety of files and rasps to shape these joints. You will find an impressive range of shapes and tooth styles—some for aggressive cutting and some for final smoothing. Often these provide the perfect way to remove that last bit of stock that keeps a joint from closing tightly. To keep your files and rasps working at peak efficiency, purchase a file card to keep the teeth clear of wood debris. The card features a surface of short, thin wires that you can use to brush away the waste.

■ **Block Planes.** When you install cornice trim, you often literally come face to face with the imperfections in the walls and ceiling. Bumps and hollows that you otherwise wouldn't see can become glaring defects when you

are trying to get the molding to fit tightly to those surfaces. Sometimes, the best you can do is to get close and apply caulk to the joint or skim-coat the wall with joint compound to fill a hollow, but in many situations you can scribe the trim to fit more closely to the irregular surface. The tool for this job is a block plane. Block planes feature a cutting iron that is about 1½ inches wide, mounted with its bevel facing up at a low cutting angle. The body of the plane is usually about 6 inches long, making it easy to hold in one hand. As with all cutting tools, it is important that you keep the cutting iron razor sharp for best results.

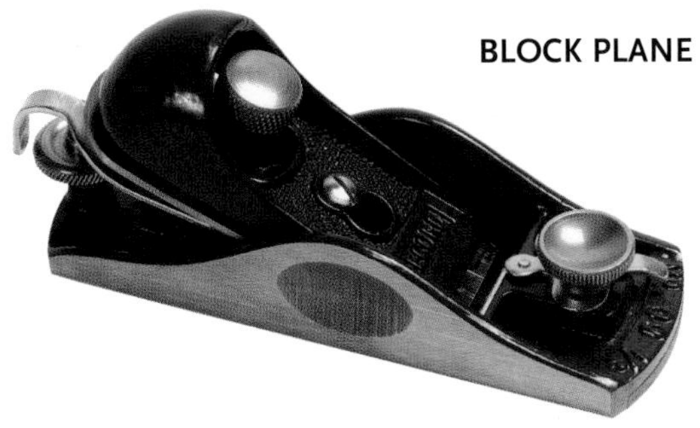

BLOCK PLANE

■ **Jigsaws.** The portable jigsaw (also called a saber saw) is an extremely useful tool for making both shaped and curved cuts. Most of the major tool manufacturers offer at least one style of saw, and some offer several designs with various motor and body configurations. Look for a model that features a tilting base for bevel cuts and a switch that allows the blade to operate in either an orbital or straight, reciprocating movement. These saws accept a variety of blades that can cut wood, plastic, and metal.

A jigsaw can also be a valuable tool for cutting coped joints for inside corners. By using an aftermarket accessory base, the Collins Coping Foot, you can maneuver the saw through the intricate cuts required for these often tricky joints. (See "Using a Collins Coping Foot," page 74.)

JIGSAW

BLOCK PLANES help you deal with minor imperfections in walls and ceilings by allowing you to trim particular areas or thin slivers of wood. This lets the trimwork fit snugly to the surface. Planes are designed to shave rather than cut the wood. It may take several passes to remove the desired amount of material.

Routers

A router gives you the ability to manufacture your own molding. Of course, you cannot expect to duplicate the elaborate, large profiles that a millwork house can produce, but there are a wide selection of molding cutters available that will allow you to create a variety of cove, bead, ogee, and fluted shapes.

A router is essentially a motor that is vertically mounted in a frame; at the bottom end of the motor is a tool-holding collet with a locking nut. Routers come in all sizes, from small trim models to large, heavy 3-horsepower production machines, but for most casual jobs you can look for one with a 1½ to 1¾-horsepower motor. You will find two basic configurations. A fixed base model requires that you set the depth of cut by rotating an adjusting ring on the base. With this type of router, you must make this setting before turning on the machine. A plunge-base model lets you lower a spinning bit into the work so that you can start a cut in the center of a board—not a particular advantage when making molding, but it can be very handy for other types of woodworking projects, including general trim carpentry and cabinetmaking.

ROUTER

EDGE GUIDE

Some routers are sold in a kit that includes a carrying case and accessory edge guide. If the tool you buy does not come with a guide, it's worth considering the purchase as an add-on. Many edge-shaping bits come with an integral ball-bearing pilot to guide the tool, but there are also quite a few without a pilot. An edge guide on the router will allow you to use any cutter to shape an edge and also give you the ability to modify the depth of cut on those bits that do have a pilot.

When using a router for edge-shaping, move the tool against the direction of bit rotation. In practice, this means that, when facing a work piece, you will guide the router from your left toward your right. A spinning bit is extremely powerful, so it is also very important that you clamp the work piece firmly to a table or bench before beginning any cutting procedure.

ROUTER TABLES

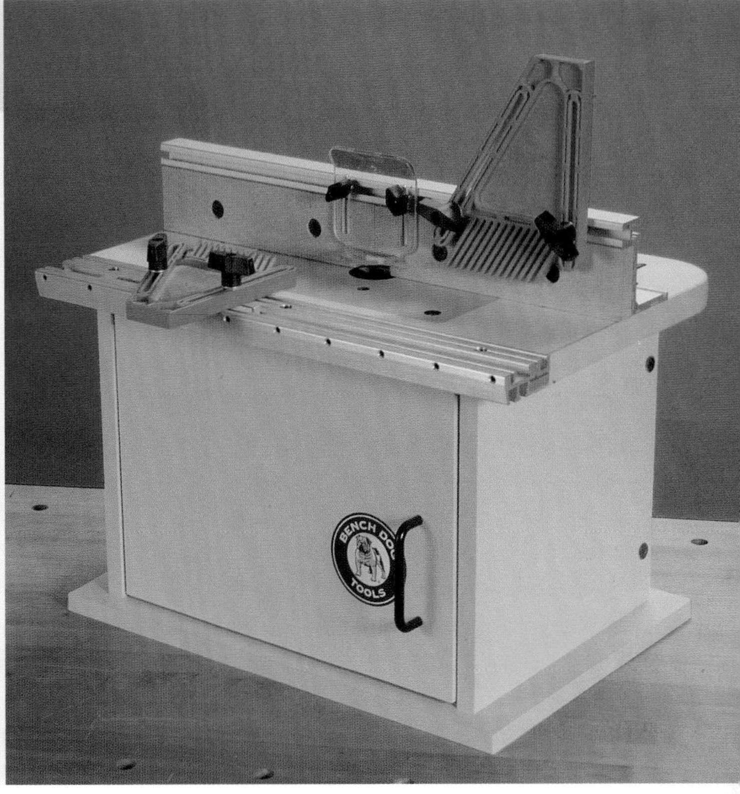

AS YOU GAIN EXPERIENCE with your router, you will find that there are certain jobs that are awkward to accomplish when holding the tool by hand, such as cutting a shaped edge on a short or narrow board, or making a large quantity of molded stock. An alternative approach is to mount your router upside down in a router table. There are quite a few commercially manufactured router tables available, some with a tabletop design and others that have freestanding bases, but they all function in basically the same way.

When using a router table, the cutting bit is exposed, so you will need to take added precautions for safety. Always use the guide fence that is provided, and adjust it so that no more than one half of the cutting bit is exposed. Whenever possible, use hold-down jigs and guards so that your hands can be kept far from the cutter.

A ROUTER EDGE GUIDE provides the flexibility to use the router to shape the edge of a board.

Miter Saws

If you are planning a cornice trim project, no matter how simple, a miter saw is a necessary part of your tool arsenal. These saws come in many different incarnations, from hand-powered models costing less than $100 to extremely sophisticated, sliding compound saws for over $600.

■ **Hand Miter Saws.** A hand miter saw consists of a saw with a thin, fine-tooth blade that is held in a guide to keep the blade cutting in a straight line. Some hand models use a large backsaw as the cutting tool, and some models use a saw that is designed much like a hacksaw, with the blade held in tension between the ends of a frame. The blade carriage is adjustable and can cut any angle from 45 degrees left to 45 degrees right.

You can certainly use a hand miter saw for most cornice trim work. If the saw is sharp and the angles adjusted accurately, your results can be exceptionally good. But for a large job, it can be quite tiring to cut all of the joints by hand. Because each cut proceeds quite slowly, it can require considerable energy to hold the molding in the proper position, and a slip can result in a costly error. In addition, these saws do not have the ability to shave a tiny amount from a piece that has already been cut, providing you with limited adjustment options.

■ **Power Miter Saws.** A power miter saw can make your cutting jobs go quite smoothly and quickly. These saws feature a circular saw blade that is mounted on a pivoting stand. The motor and blade can swing over the table and can be locked at the desired angle of cut. Most power saws of this design can cut moldings up to 3½ or 4 inches wide.

The most sophisticated tools in this category are called sliding compound miter saws. With this type of saw, you gain the ability to tilt the cutting blade to cut a bevel angle as well as the miter angle. The design also provides a guide rail support for the cutting head that allows the blade to slide toward the operator, which gives you the ability to cut compound angles on molding with the stock held flat on the saw table. These tools come in a variety of sizes, with blades that range from an 8-inch diameter to a 14-inch diameter. Some saws are designed to tilt only to one side, but the most feature-intensive models have the ability to tilt either to the right or left.

HAND MITER SAW

POWER MITER SAW

SLIDING COMPOUND MITER SAW

TRIM BLADE

making a miter-saw bench

ON MOST CORNICE PROJECTS, the miter saw is the one tool you'll come to for every piece of molding. Because it is so central to the job, it is important that you keep it in a spot that is easily accessible, comfortable to use, and that promotes safety. Placing the saw on the floor, or on a shaky folding table, can be dangerous and can also lead to cutting errors. There are a variety of commercial saw stands available, and these are excellent alternatives, but it is also quite simple to construct a support bench using saw horses, 2x4 lumber, and some construction-grade plywood. You can easily modify the size of the bench top to suit your particular saw and site requirements. And the system can be broken down into parts that you can store easily until your next project.

1 A bench 60 in. long x 18 in. wide is a good size. Cut 2x4 lumber to size. Drill and countersink pilot holes for screws. Assemble the frame.

2 Use a circular saw to cut a ¾-in.-thick plywood panel to size, and then position it on the 2x4 frame.

3 Screw the plywood panel to the frame. Make sure that you countersink the screw heads so they are flush with the plywood surface.

4 Set the saw platform on a pair of saw horses, and apply clamps to keep the stand from moving.

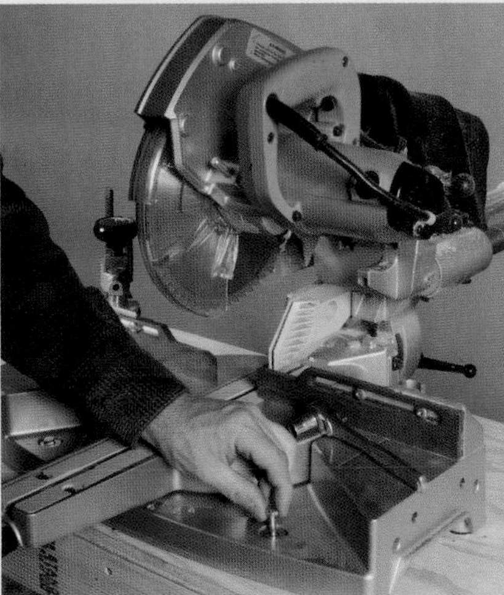

5 Use lag screws to mount the miter saw to the bench top.

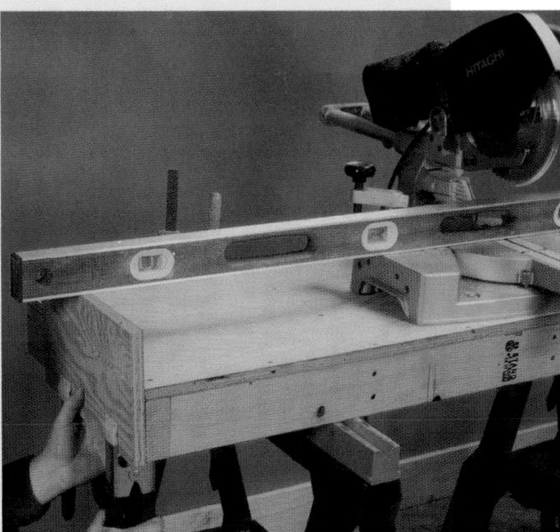

6 Use a level, or a piece of straight lumber, to help you position outboard supports at each end of the bench. Spring clamps can be used to temporarily hold the supports in place while you screw them to the 2x4 frame.

making power miter-saw adjustments

EACH MITER SAW MANUFACTURER has its own proprietary design for adjustment mechanisms, but the basic theory and approach is usually similar. As you might expect, as the saws become more complex and offer more features, the number of possible adjustments also increases.

1 Most saws have a locking feature that allows you to keep the miter saw arm in a lowered position for transporting the saw. On this saw, you pull the locking button to free the saw arm for use; with the arm lowered, you push the button in to lock it.

2 When you wish to change the saw blade, the first step is to remove the blade cover and swing-away guard. A simple wing nut holds the cover to the saw body.

3 This saw requires two wrenches to change a saw blade. Use an Allen wrench to immobilize the arbor while you remove the blade nut with an open-end wrench. Many saws have arbor locking buttons so that only one wrench is needed.

4 As a safety measure, most saws have a release button that must be held down to operate the saw. The button is conveniently located on the saw handle.

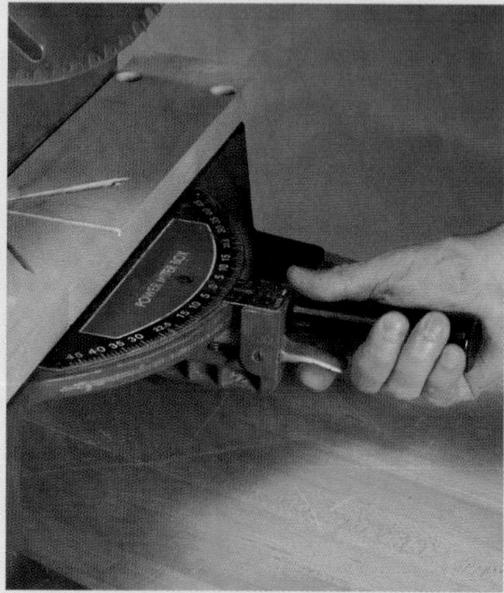

5 You will generally find that the most common miter angles are marked with detents that stop the rotation of the cutting arm. On this saw, there is a trigger release to move the blade past each detent.

6 To set the saw to cut a miter angle other than one with a detent, simply move the indicator to the desired angle setting on the saw table, and twist the handle to lock it in position.

making sliding compound miter-saw adjustments

BECAUSE YOU CAN DO MORE with a sliding compound miter saw than you can with a standard miter saw, there is more to adjust on these models. Fortunately, manufacturers have improved upon some of the basic features, such as changing blades, and made them easier to accomplish.

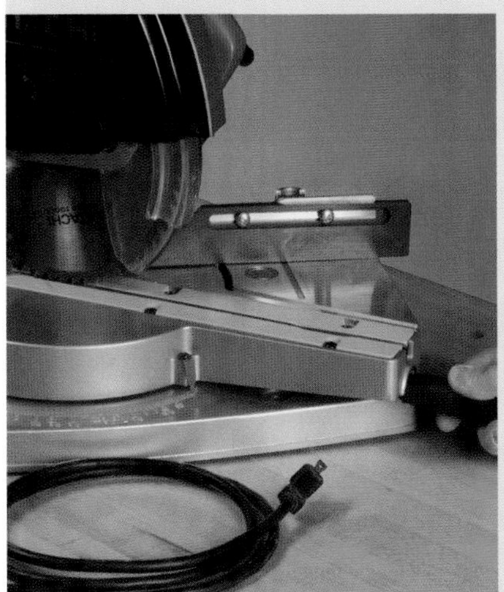

1 Twist the locking handle to release the saw table and allow it to rotate to the desired miter angle.

2 A locking pin holds the cutting arm in the "down" position for safe transport of the saw. Simply pull the pin to release the arm (top). Loosen the slide locking knob on the back side of the carriage to free the blade assembly for sliding cuts (bottom).

3 To change the blade on the saw, depress the arbor lock and loosen the blade nut using a wrench. You do not need to remove the entire blade cover, just a small access panel on the left side of the housing.

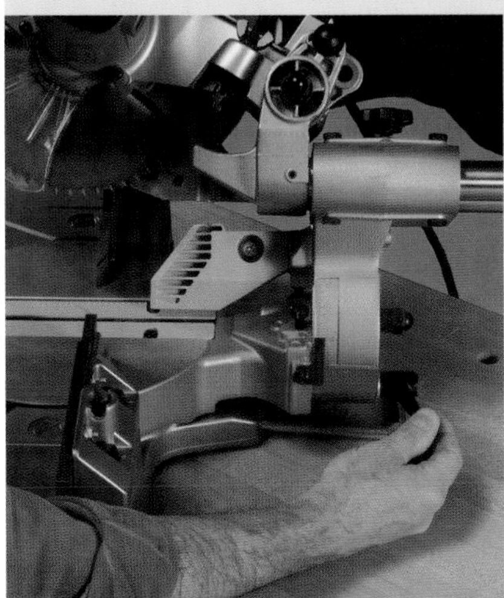

4 The locking lever for the bevel angle is located on the back side of the saw. Simply lift the lever to release the lock, and allow the saw carriage to tilt to the desired angle; then tighten the lever to hold the setting.

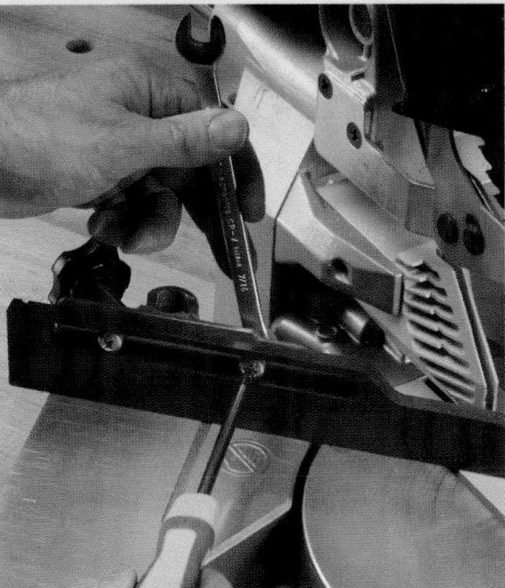

5 Adjust the sliding fence to provide maximum support for the stock near the blade. The position of the fence will change depending on the miter and bevel angles.

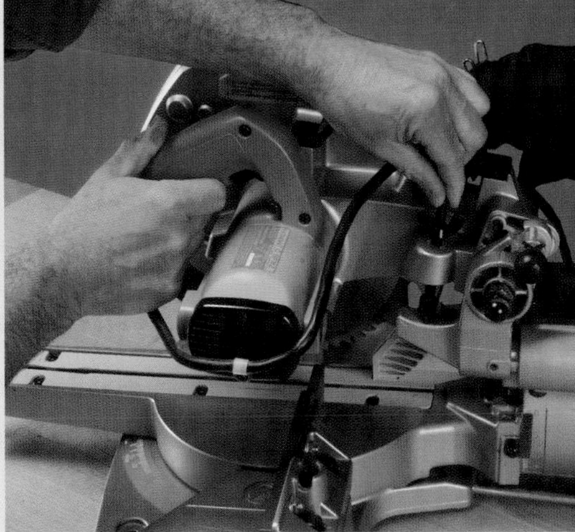

6 You can limit the depth of cut on the saw by adjusting a stop, which is particularly useful for cutting grooves or making dentil molding.

INSTALLATION TOOLS

Hammer and Nail Set

■ **Hammers.** A hammer is the primary tool of the carpenter, used for driving and pulling nails. Even though it might seem to be a crude implement, with practice it can also become an instrument of quite subtle persuasion. Hammers come in a variety of styles and weights, but most people prefer a 16- or 20-ounce claw hammer for trim use. When looking for a hammer, always make an attempt to test it in use. You will find hammers with shafts of wood, fiberglass, or steel; and claws that are straight or curved. Although each has its advocates, no particular configuration is generally acknowledged to be best. Because different style grips and shaft materials make a big difference in how a hammer feels, you will find that some combinations are much more comfortable than others—in this instance, personal preference should be the key factor in which you choose.

■ **Nail Sets.** A nail set is a hardened steel tool that is used to drive a finishing nail below the wood surface. One end of the set is tapered to a specified diameter that fits into a recess in the nailhead. Sets are made to fit different size nails, so always select the appropriate tool for the nails you are using—a set that is too large or small can easily slip off the nailhead and damage the molding.

Nail Guns and Compressors

For a large cornice project, or one that involves hardwood or MDF molding, a pneumatic nail gun is definitely worth considering. This is a tool that can make your job go more quickly and also give better results than nailing by hand. When driving nails by hand into hardwood or MDF, you need to drill pilot holes to avoid splits and bent nails. A gun eliminates that task entirely. By efficiently focusing great pressure on a single nail, it can drive the fastener home in one quick step. Using a nail gun also frees up one hand to hold or guide a piece of molding in place. When you nail by hand, both hands are occupied—one holding the nail and one holding the hammer.

The nails that are driven by a gun are also of smaller diameter than traditional finishing nails, and unlike normal nails, their diameter stays the same even as their length increases, which makes it less likely that the fastener will cause a split in a delicate molding. Tools are divided into two categories: those that drive 15- or 16-gauge finishing nails are called nail guns, and those that drive 18-gauge brads are called brad guns. You can select the appropriate tool and fastener for any situation—nails for tougher fastening jobs in heavy stock and brads for holding smaller, fragile molding.

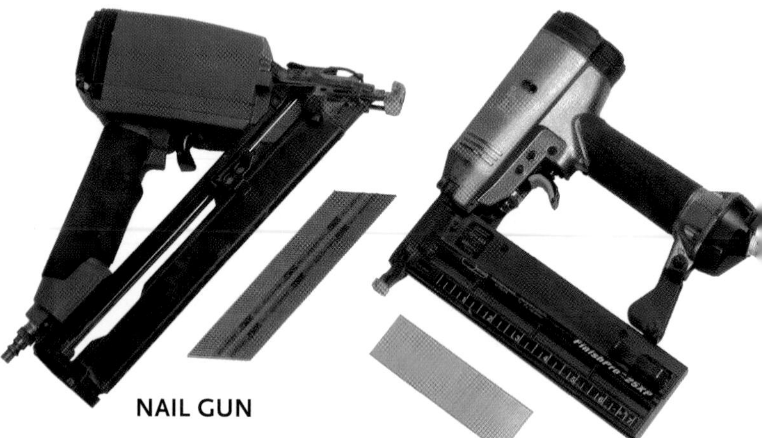

NAIL GUN

BRAD GUN

HAMMER AND NAIL SETS

COMPRESSOR

using a nail or brad gun

1 Load nails into the gun magazine by sliding them through an opening at the back end of the gun. Release the spring catch that applies pressure to the back side of the nail clip.

2 Hold the gun perpendicular to the face of the molding, and press the safety release at the nose of the gun against the wood surface. Pull the trigger to drive the nail.

3 To load brads, open the magazine by releasing the locking lever and pulling back on the cover. Lay the brads in the gun, and slide the cover forward until it clicks shut.

4 You can adjust the countersink depth on both nail and brad guns by turning a knurled wheel behind the nose of the gun.

Most new nail and brad guns have an adjustment that allows you to determine how deep a nail is driven into the wood, eliminating the additional step of countersinking the nail heads with a set. If your gun lacks this type of adjustment device, you can vary the air-pressure setting to achieve the same result.

A nail gun is useless unless you have an electric compressor to provide the air pressure that drives the nails. Compact models are available with motors rated between ¾ and 2½ horsepower in both oil-less and oil-lubricated designs, and either system is fine for trim installations. You will also need an air hose to connect the compressor to your gun. A ¼-inch diameter x 25-foot hose is fine for this type of work. If your hose is too short, you will waste much valuable time moving the compressor.

If your cornice project is small, and you do not want to make the investment necessary for a nail gun and compressor, these tools are also available from rental companies.

Pry Bars and Putty Knives

It's not always simple to accurately fit a piece of molding, and some coaxing and prying are often a necessary part of the process. While some adjustments can be made with just your hands, there are times when some additional implements are required, and pry bars and putty knives are the perfect tools for the job. When shopping for pry bars, look for small models with flat ends—two or three different bars varying in size from 4 to 8 inches will serve you well. And it's always handy to have a small putty knife that you can use for light prying and coaxing a piece into position.

Locking Pliers and End Nippers

Some cornice jobs require that you remove an old molding before starting to install a new one, and it's common to put up and remove some stock a few times before you are satisfied. In either situation, you will need to remove nails from the molding, and the best tools for this job are end nippers or locking pliers.

Drill and Screwdriver

A cordless, combination drill/screwdriver is an extremely important tool for any trim installation; you will use it often for drilling pilot holes and driving screws to hold both trim and blocking. Corded drills and screw-guns are perfectly fine tools, but the great convenience of the cordless models gives them the clear advantage over their wire-tethered cousins. Corded tools are usually separated into dedicated drills and dedicated screwdrivers, but just about all cordless models are combination tools with a fixed clutch setting for drilling and an adjustable clutch for driving screws. In addition, keyless chucks are standard on all models, allowing quick tool changes without an easily misplaced chuck key. For most situations, select a model rated at 12 or 14.4 volts.

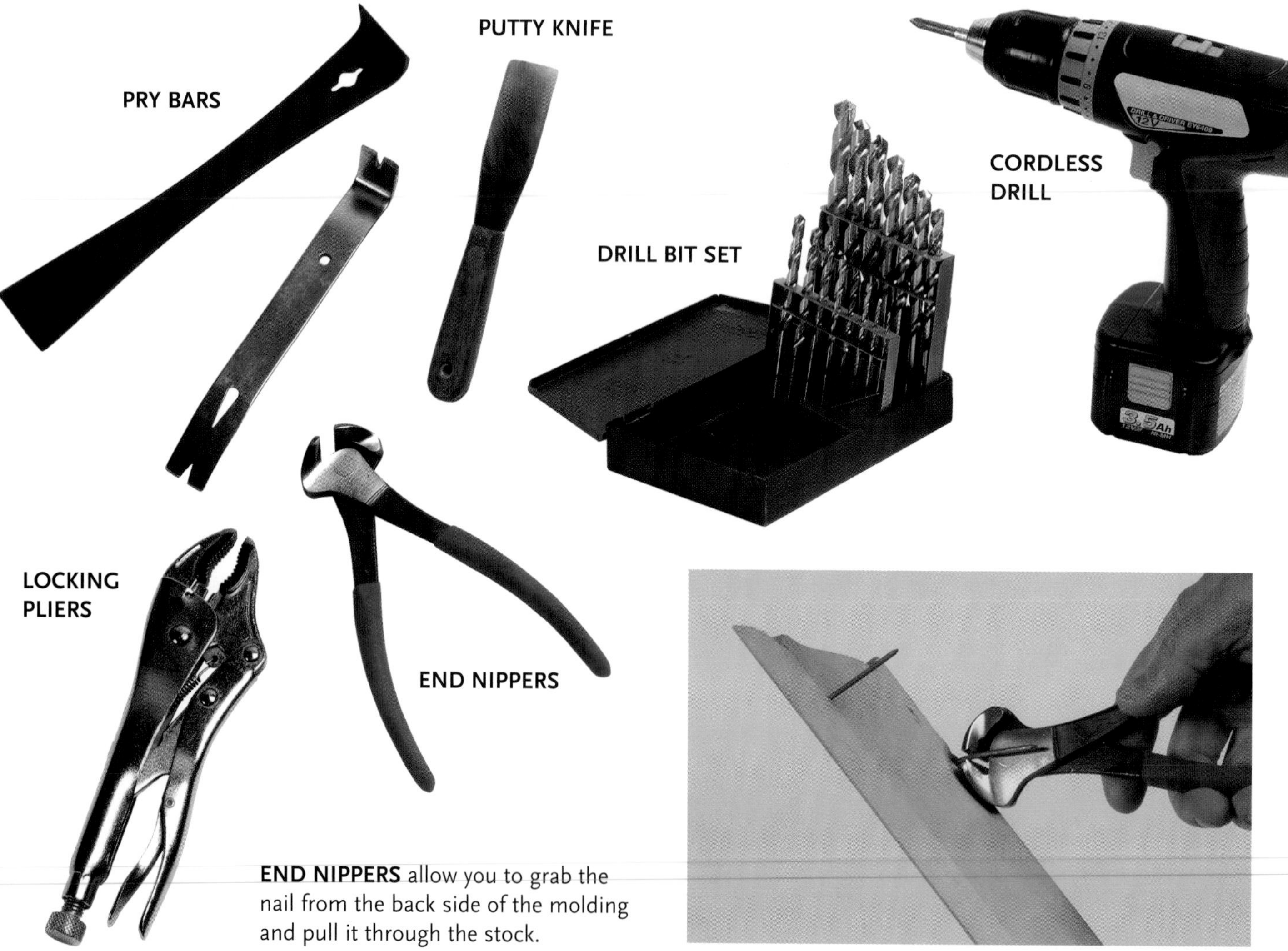

END NIPPERS allow you to grab the nail from the back side of the molding and pull it through the stock.

SANDPAPER

SANDPAPER is an important part of the trim carpenter's tool kit, although it is rarely the favorite part. Sanding is tedious work, but when it is incorporated into the job in manageable portions, it can be much less imposing than when left to the end of a project.

To avoid an unpleasant surprise at the finishing stages of your job, it's best to lightly sand each piece of molding just before installing it. For most finishes, sanding with 120- and 150-grit sandpaper is sufficient preparation.

Sanding is also necessary to remove any surface residue from fillers used in nailholes or open joints. If a scarf or corner joint is slightly uneven, a judicious use of sandpaper can bring the surfaces flush.

Because cornice trim is mostly involved with molded stock, you will find that a variety of shaped backers, such as dowels of varying diameter and small pieces of wood and molding scraps, will be extremely helpful when sanding profiled stock.

Sandpaper comes in 9 x 11-inch full sheets and also in half and quarter sheets. You will find a variety of different abrasives and backing materials, as well a range of grits. Lower grit numbers indicate coarser abrasives, and products are available in papers rated between 40 to 1800 grit. For most trim jobs, look for garnet or aluminum oxide abrasives with an "A"-weight paper backing; this is the lightest weight backer and will best conform to intricate molding profiles.

WORK SPACE LOGISTICS AND WORK SUPPORT

WHEN YOU GET INVOLVED in a cornice project, or any trim job, it is important that you set up a work space that is convenient to the area where the installation will take place. Because these jobs involve many individual measurements and trial-and-error fitting of joints, it only makes sense to limit unnecessary travel between rooms or to a remote basement workshop. It's surprising how the likelihood of mistakes increases with the distance you travel between tasks.

Because all cornices involve considerable overhead work, try to arrange to have two ladders available for your job. Long molding pieces require a second set of hands for fitting and installation, and your helper will need a place to stand. And accurate measurement and cutting demand good lighting, so invest in a few inexpensive work lights.

Much of the work in putting up a cornice is preparatory in nature—cutting and fitting each joint takes place away from the walls and ceiling where the molding will eventually be mounted. Often, more than one step is involved in this preparation, and sometimes the process can get pretty fussy, involving multiple adjustments to a joint before it fits properly. All of this work requires support, and an old, sturdy table about 36 inches high can serve as a perfect work center. Also provide plenty of quick-action clamps as part of the work area.

SPRING CLAMPS

SMALL BAR CLAMPS

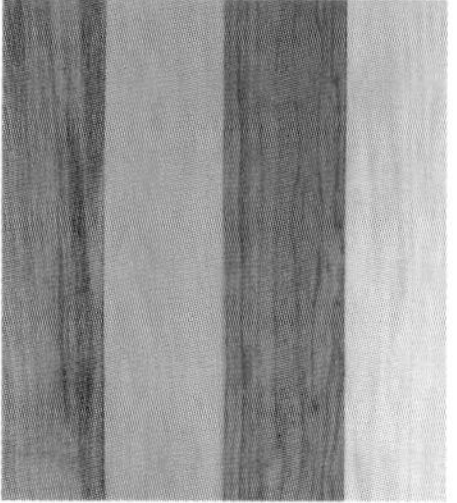

3 materials

Because cornice molding is a decorative item, appearance is the primary guide when selecting material. Of course, cost is also an issue, both in terms of out-of-pocket expenses and time to do the actual job. Some materials are much more installer-friendly than others. For example, if your job is to be painted, you can select one of the less expensive material options, and you also have the luxury of using caulk to fill open joints or gaps at edges of the molding. On the other hand, if you intend to install a hardwood molding with a clear or stained finish, each joint must be nearly perfect and the stock may need to be scribed to fit tightly to the walls and ceiling. In this case, the labor involved for installation could easily be two or three times that for a painted molding.

MOLDING PROFILES

The degree of complexity of your cornice profile can also be a factor in material selection. While it is certainly possible to create a complex cornice from several wood moldings, some results, including elaborately carved surfaces, can be quite expensive and difficult to execute in wood. Fortunately, there are alternative materials that are precast in a dazzling array of detailed patterns to suit almost any room decor.

If you limit your molding search to the local home center, you'll likely find 15 or 20 different profiles that you can use for cornice trim. But if you expand your search to include some specialty millwork suppliers, you will have an almost endless selection of moldings in wood, MDF, plaster, and synthetic materials. These choices range from simple to elaborate profiles, allowing you to coordinate cornice designs with chair-rail and baseboard treatments, see below and opposite. In addition, many suppliers that offer their products on the Internet.

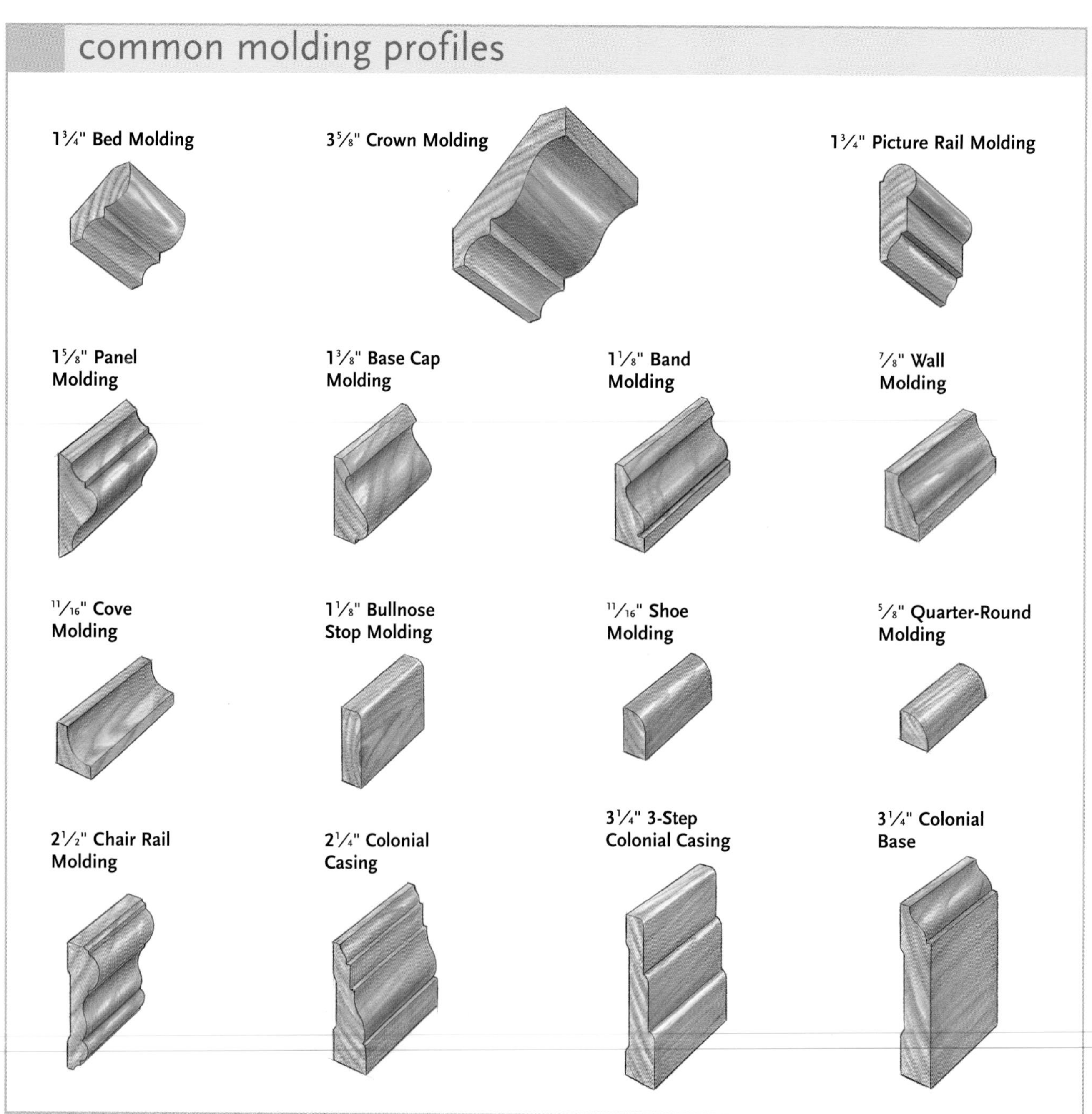

smart tip

BUYING MOLDING

When you decide on a particular molding profile that you want to use for a job, it is always best to make sure that you purchase plenty of material to finish the project—and that you get it from one supplier. Moldings from different millwork manufacturers may have the same descriptive name and size specification, but that is no guarantee that they will be identical. Local millwork shops can order their cutting knives from a wide range of sources, and some have the capability to grind their own knives; these are unlikely to match those of the shop down the road or a large national retailer.

built-up molding profiles

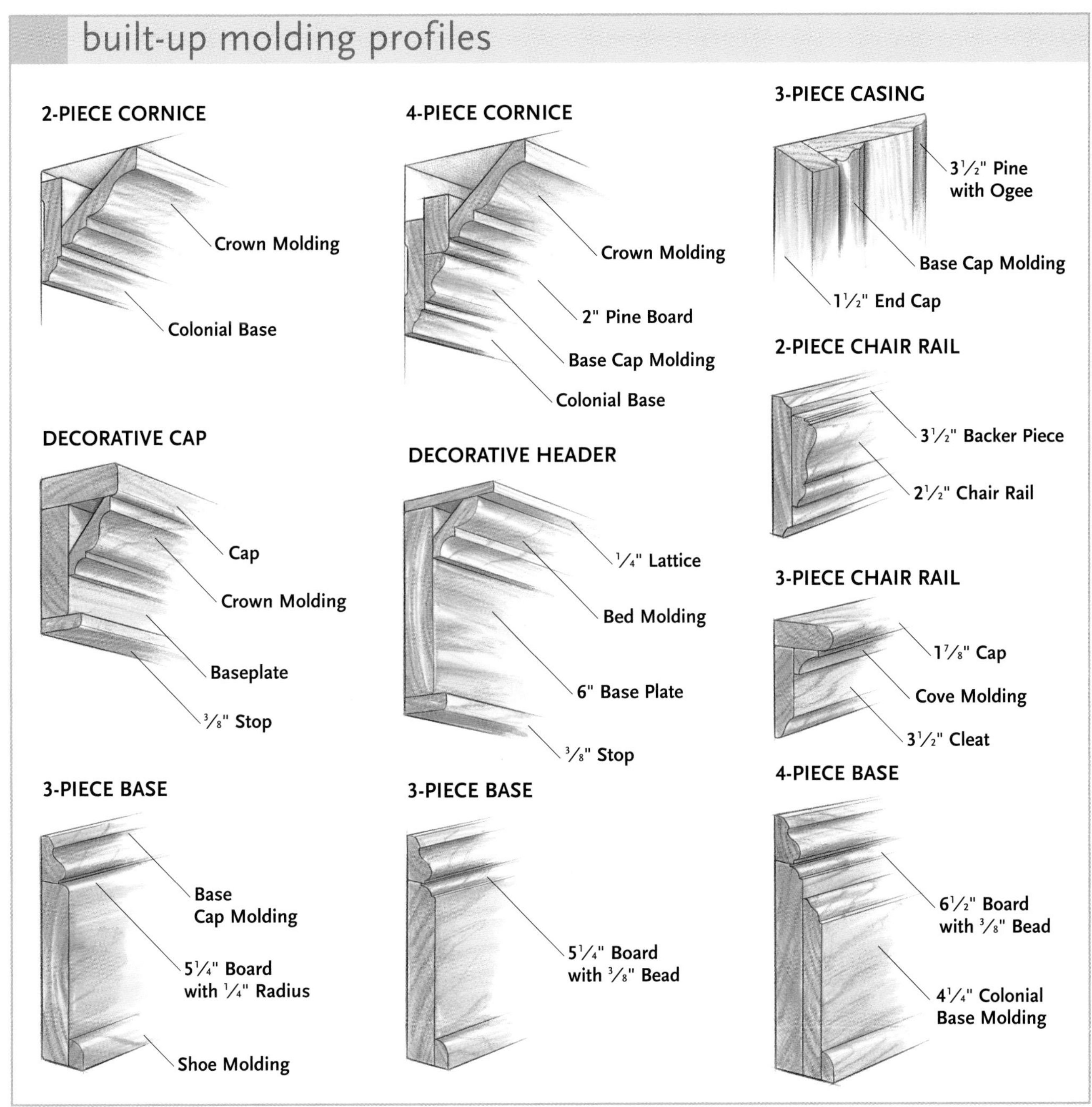

TRADITIONAL MATERIALS

Wood is the most commonly used material for cornice moldings, and it is also the easiest to find: any lumberyard or home center will offer a reasonable selection. Different species provide a range of appearance options and each is distinguished by a characteristic level of workability and cost.

Pine Molding

Clear pine lumber is the traditional choice for interior millwork of all types, and cornice moldings are certainly included in that category. From the user's point of view, pine is one of the easiest species to work with when using either hand or machine tools. And from the manufacturer's vantage point, pine does extremely well in the tree farms that are now the main source of softwood lumber. The trees grow relatively quickly, ensuring a renewable source for this popular material.

Classified as a "softwood" lumber, pine comes from a *coniferous* or cone-bearing tree. These trees generally have waxy needles, rather than leaves, which they keep all year. The lumber is high in resin content and soft enough to nail by hand without requiring pilot holes. It can be sanded easily, and it accepts clear, stained, and painted finishes relatively well. Most suppliers keep several different profiles as stock items and also offer a catalog of additional profiles that are available on a special-order basis. Keep in mind that many moldings that are intended for other uses can also be included in a cornice assembly, so the list of possible shapes is quite extensive.

■ **Finger-Jointed Moldings.** For those applications that will receive a painted finish, finger-jointed pine moldings are available in some of the same profiles as clear stock. Some suppliers who specialize in architectural millwork offer only finger-jointed material, and their catalogs of profiles are quite extensive.

To create finger-jointed material, short lengths of lumber are glued together, end to end, with an interlocking "finger-like" joint. The resulting stock is then milled to shape in the same way as clear lumber. This process allows manufacturers to make efficient use of stock that might otherwise be rejected for defects such as knots and sap pockets, and it allows the consumer to reap considerable cost savings as well. An additional bonus for the end user is that most finger-jointed millwork is primed at the factory, eliminating the need for you to include that step in the finishing process.

OPPOSITE Pine comes in profiles that can be used as one-piece cornices or buildup designs.

CLEAR PINE MOLDING

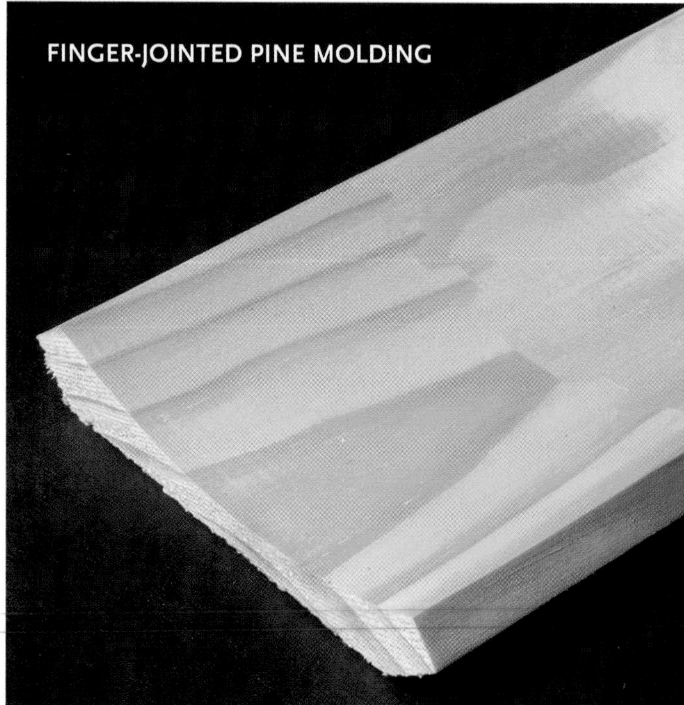
FINGER-JOINTED PINE MOLDING

PINE LUMBER DIMENSIONS

MANY CORNICE PROJECTS can be completed using only profiled stock, or moldings. But, if your design is a multipiece assembly, it is also possible that you will need some plain boards to use as a *frieze, fascia,* or *soffit.* For pine or paint-grade projects, the most accessible choices are clear or finger-jointed pine stock. This material is readily available at lumberyards and home centers, usually in close proximity to the millwork items. These boards are available in stock (nominal) sizes ranging from 1 x 2 to 1 x 12 and in lengths from 6 to 16 feet, in 2-foot increments. You will also find a smaller selection of thicker stock, called 5/4 material. When you shop for these boards it is important to keep in mind that the nominal size of the stock refers to the rough dimensions of the boards when they are first cut at the mill, and it is always greater than the actual measurement of the lumber that you buy. For example, all 1-by stock is actually 3/4 inch thick and 5/4 stock is 1 1/8 inch thick. This convention also applies to the different board widths as shown in the chart below.

NOMINAL SIZE	ACTUAL SIZE
1 x 2	3/4 x 1 1/2
1 x 3	3/4 x 2 1/2
1 x 4	3/4 x 3 1/2
1 x 6	3/4 x 5 1/2
1 x 8	3/4 x 7 1/4
1 x 10	3/4 x 9 1/4
1 x 12	3/4 x 11 1/4

Hardwood Molding

Red oak and poplar moldings are also commonly carried at lumberyards and home centers, although the selection of stock profiles is usually smaller than the pine offerings. While both of these species fall in the "hardwood" category, their appearance is very different.

■ **Painting Hardwoods.** Poplar moldings are often a good choice when you intend to paint the molding. The natural color of poplar can range from cream to green and even purple, making it largely unsuitable for clear finishing, but if the material is selected carefully, poplar can be used for jobs that will be stained. It is soft enough to nail either by hand or by nail gun with no worries about drilling pilot holes; it sands easily; and it has a uniformly smooth surface that accepts a finish well. In addition, poplar is one of the least-expensive hardwood species. In fact, millwork shops generally choose poplar as the best material for their custom, paint-grade moldings. The raw lumber is readily available to manufacturers and the stock is usually quite wide and long, providing good yields with little waste.

■ **Natural Finishes.** For those projects intended to receive a natural finish, red oak has become the default hardwood species for stock molding profiles. Many of the same profiles available in pine are also carried in red oak and, as with pine, you can usually buy from a larger catalog on special order. Red oak is an open-grained hard-

LEFT Applying a clear finish over red oak trimwork adds a traditional touch to a cornice design.

HARDWOOD SPECIES

HARDWOOD LUMBER comes from *deciduous* trees, those that lose their leaves at the end of each growing season. In most instances, hardwood lumber is, in fact, harder than softwood lumber, but this is not always the case. Some hardwood species—basswood, balsa, and poplar are three examples—are quite soft.

The most popular and common domestic hardwoods—maple, birch, poplar, cherry, ash, oak, and walnut—are widely used for furniture and cabinets as well as for molding stock. Within the broad hardwood umbrella, hardwood species are divided into two descriptive categories—*open-grained* and *closed-grained* (also called *close-grained*) woods. Open-grained woods are those that display alternating areas of relatively dense and porous material; these are also called ring-porous woods. Examples of species that feature an open-grained pattern are oak, ash, walnut, and mahogany. Typically, when an open-grained wood is stained, the pigment is absorbed much more readily in the porous areas, creating a distinct contrast and very visible grain pattern. Closed-grained hardwoods display a relatively even texture and much more uniform surface. Cherry, maple, birch, and poplar fall into this group.

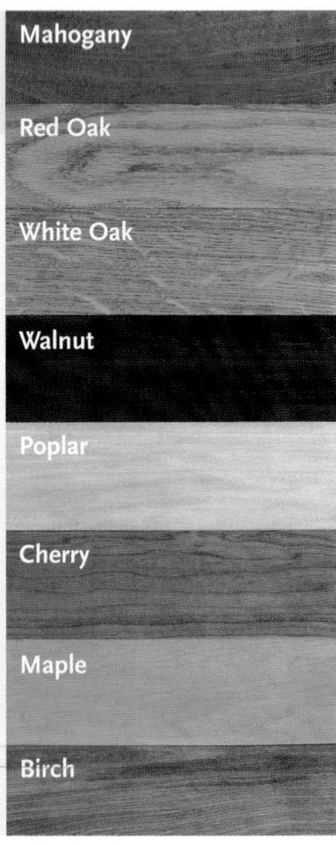

wood and displays characteristic grain patterns of alternating porous and dense areas that can be quite bold. With a clear finish, the material displays a natural reddish-brown color that is compatible with many color schemes, but it also accepts stain very well. Oak is quite a bit harder than poplar lumber and requires a different approach for nailing. If you have access to a pneumatic nail gun, fastening this material will certainly present no problems, as the gun will drive fasteners through most any wood species. But if you plan to nail by hand, you will need to drill a small pilot hole for each nail to avoid either bending the fastener or splitting the wood.

PILOT-HOLE DIAMETERS FOR FINISH NAILS

IF YOUR JOB INCLUDES hardwood or MDF moldings, you will need to drill a pilot hole for each nail that you drive by hand. Use the chart below as a guide for the proper pilot-hole size. But keep in mind that the "hardness" of the material can make a difference in the appropriate size of the holes. Harder species require holes closer in size to the shaft of the nail, while softer species can tolerate smaller pilot holes. Start with the suggested pilot hole dimension and drive a few nails to check if you need to modify the bit size for the rest of the job.

NAIL SIZE	LENGTH	PILOT HOLE DIAMETER
4d	1½"	1⁄16"
6d	2"	5⁄64"
8d	2½"	3⁄32"
10d	3"	7⁄64"
12d	3¼"	⅛"

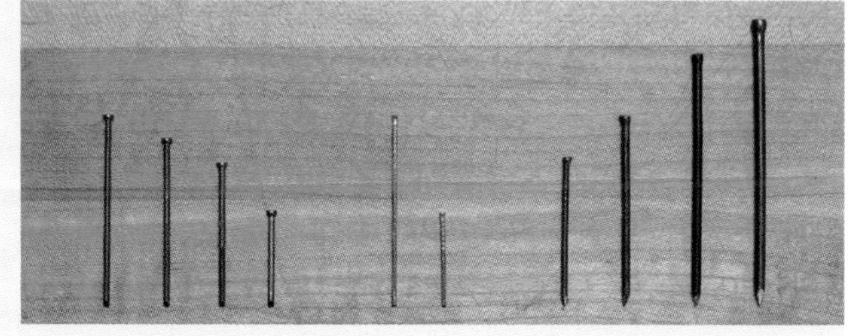

HARDWOOD LUMBER DIMENSIONS

IF YOUR PROJECT INCLUDES either red oak or poplar moldings, you may also need some plain board stock for friezes or soffits. Often, you can find these boards in the home center in the same size selection as pine stock. Because these two species are so popular, suppliers have made an effort to provide a ready supply of material in familiar dimensions. However, if you require board stock of another hardwood species, you will need to consider other sources and another standard of size classification.

Hardwood lumber is usually sold by specialty lumberyards and, because many of the customers for this material are cabinet shops and furniture makers, it is often warehoused in its rough state, as it comes from the mill. Most of these dealers will gladly surface the lumber for a customer who lacks their own planing facility. For hardwood, the thickness of a board is described by its rough measurement in quarters of an inch; so a board that is 1 inch thick would be called 4⁄4 stock and one 1½ inch thick would be 6⁄4 . When hardwood lumber is planed to standard thickness dimensions, these specifications are different than those used for pine boards. 4⁄4 stock is typically planed to 13⁄16 inch thick and 5⁄4 stock actually measures 1 1⁄16 inch. In most cases, hardwood lumber is also sold in boards of random width and length, so it is important that you plan for additional waste when computing the amount of material you will need for a job.

MODERN MATERIAL CHOICES

Wood is still the most popular material used for molding and trimwork projects, including crown and cornice moldings, but it is not the only material. Some newer products are made from wood waste; others are made from plastic materials.

MDF

MDF is an acronym for medium density fiberboard, a composite of fine sawdust and glue that is heated and compressed into an extremely uniform and very stable material. The manufacturing process uses wood of almost any species and in any form, from small tree branches to waste from a mill, so it is a highly efficient use of all types of wood waste. Manufacturers have long used MDF as a core material for architectural and furniture panels, which are then faced with either veneers or plastic laminates.

Because of its uniform density, MDF machines extremely well. It can be shaped, cut, drilled, nailed, glued, screwed, and routed much like solid wood, and it is an excellent substrate for a painted finish. So it was only a matter of time before architectural moldings were made from this versatile material. Now MDF moldings are available in a wide selection of profiles and sizes, many with intricate details that suggest the elaborate patterns of carved wood or plaster molding. These profiles are sold with a factory-applied coat of primer, so they are ready to paint. And when compared to solid wood, MDF moldings are generally much less expensive.

■ **MDF Installation.** Installing a cornice from MDF is much like working with wood. You can use the same fasteners and glue but, if you are nailing by hand, pilot holes will be necessary. One particular characteristic should be kept in mind when planning a job with MDF moldings: while it is perfectly fine to nail the material through its face for fastening, it does not respond well to nails being driven through the edge or end of the stock.

MDF MOLDING has many of the same qualities of solid wood, including its workability. You can nail and cut MDF just as you would pine, top. Painting is the only finishing option available, bottom. But most MDF moldings come preprimed.

Polyurethane and Polystyrene

Polyurethane and polystyrene moldings are synthetic alternatives for cornice trim, and they are definitely worth considering for paint-grade projects. Both of these materials can be cast in an infinite variety of molded profiles, suggesting intricate plaster or wood moldings. They are a particularly competitive choice when considering large cornice assemblies because, in these projects, the savings in material cost and installation time can be substantial. While the price of the individual molding sections can, at first glance, seem high, when you consider the ease of installation against the labor involved in running multiple wood profiles to achieve a similar appearance, these become an attractive option.

■ **Easy Joints.** The large profiled moldings are lightweight and easy to work with. In contrast to wood or MDF moldings, these products do not require *coped joints* at inside corners or *scarf joints* when joining pieces end to end. Instead, inside corner joints can be mitered and end joints can be cut square—any gaps in these joints are simply filled with caulk or joint compound. For an even simpler alternative, many suppliers offer decorative blocks that can be used for inside and outside corners, and also butt joints so that your installation requires only simple 90-degree cuts. These resin products are installed with a combination of adhesive and nails or screws, so no special tooling is required.

Some manufacturers also offer a line of flexible polyurethane moldings for use in curved applications on either concave or convex walls. If your cornice incorporates a flat profile, these moldings can easily be bent to conform to the shape of the wall, eliminating the need for costly custom moldings. If you want to include a more traditional molding, one that sits at an angle between the wall and ceiling, then you can specify the radius of the wall and have the molding cast to fit.

All of these resin products are excellent paint-grade surfaces and require no extra preparation for finishing. Some polyurethane moldings come in a neutral beige color that can also accept a stained finish to match wood trim elsewhere in the room.

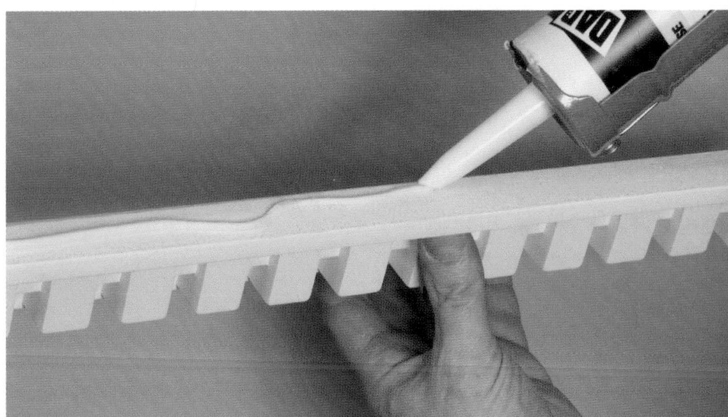

POLYURETHANE AND POLYSTYRENE MOLDING are becoming more and more popular. The systems come with corner blocks, so there is no coping of joints, top. They are installed using adhesive, middle. From the floor, they look almost identical to painted wood molding.

making molding

MILLWORK SHOPS use large and sophisticated equipment to manufacture the wide variety of moldings that we can buy at home centers or other retail outlets. Large planers, shapers, molders, and profile sanders are all key tools in the production process, and it would be foolish for someone at home to try to turn out a similar product in their basement or garage. This is particularly true for *sprung moldings,* those that sit at an angle between the wall and ceiling. However, many cornice designs incorporate flat stock with simple molded profiles as part of the assembly—frieze boards, panel moldings, cove profiles, and ogee profiles, for example. These items could be shaped with a relatively simple setup in a home shop. And some router bit manufacturers offer cutters that are designed to shape crown moldings up to 2½ inches wide.

■ **Molding Bits.** If you browse the router bit selection at your local tool outlet, or glance through one of the many available woodworking supply catalogs, you will get an idea of the possible profiles that you can create with nothing more than a router. Many of these bits feature a ball-bearing pilot to guide the cutter along the edge of a board; others require that you use an accessory edge guide to limit the depth of cut. Large-scale profile bits generally have a ½-inch-diameter shank and require the use of a heavy-duty router with variable speed control, but many bits are available with ¼-inch-diameter shanks.

For small quantities of molding, use a hand-held router to shape the molding. Install the bit according to the router manufacturer's instructions, and adjust the depth of cut. Clamp a scrap board to your worktable, and test the cut before proceeding with your finished material. If you are making a narrow molding, it is always best to cut the molded profile on the edge of a wide board, and then use the table saw to rip the shaped piece to desired width. Then you can repeat the process to yield as many pieces as you need.

■ **Large Jobs.** When your job calls for a large quantity of molding, or if you are using a large cutter, a router table is the better choice for shaping the stock. If you mount the router in a table—either a commercial model or one that you fashion yourself—you can easily control the feed rate of the cut, and you eliminate the need to clamp each piece before routing. You also gain the ability to mount one or more hold-down jigs on the table to maintain even pressure against the bit, which will lessen the chance of burn and chatter marks on the shaped edge. A router table also gives you the flexibility to run the stock vertically, with the face of the stock against the fence, or horizontally, with the face flat on

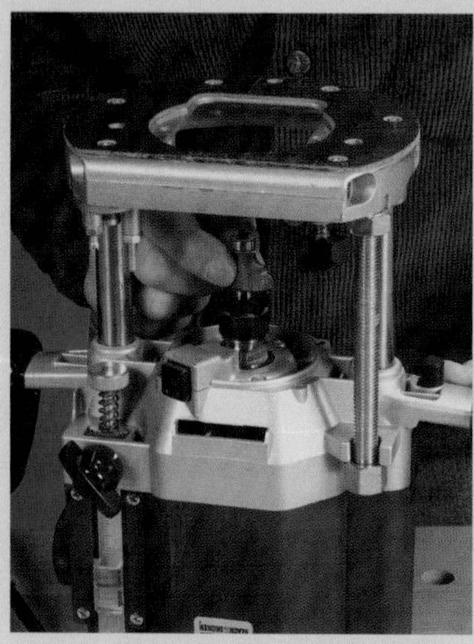

1 To prepare your router, first insert the shank of the cutting bit into the collet. Many manufacturers offer bits designed for shaping moldings.

2 Use the wrench that came with your tool to tighten the bit in place. Adjust the depth of cut on the router.

3 Test the setup by working on a scrap board clamped to your worktable. As a rule, you should move the router against the direction of rotation of the bit.

the table, increasing your design options.

If you have a heavy-duty router, some manufacturers offer large bits that can cut crown-molding profiles. Of course, these bits can only be used in a router table and often require that you fabricate a special fence to accommodate the extra height of the cutter.

Install the cutting bit in the router before mounting it in the table. Adjust the height of the cutter, and set the fence to expose the appropriate amount of the bit. Even if the bit has a pilot guide, it is best to use the table fence; it serves an important safety function and also provides a way to use hold-down jigs and a guard to cover the bit. For small moldings, it is still best to shape the edge of a wide board and then to rip narrow molded stock off the edge. Remember to always use a push stick to guide the material at the end of a cut.

4 **Many bits have a ball-bearing pilot to guide the cutter; others require the use of an edge guide.**

5 **Attach the edge guide, and test your work on scrap lumber. The edge guide limits the depth of cut.**

6 **Heavy duty routers can accept ½-in. bit shanks. Some of these cutting bits can shape 2½-in.-wide boards.**

7 **For large jobs, use a router table. This gives you the option of using bigger cutters and hold-down jigs to better control the work.**

8 **For some jobs, it makes sense to shape a large board and then to rip it to size using a table saw. Be sure to use push sticks when working near the blade.**

9 **Here's a finished profile created with a router and a table saw.**

ADDITIONAL DECORATIVE OPTIONS

Frieze

In architectural terms, a frieze can be several things. As previously mentioned, a frieze is the wide central portion of an entablature, the structure that spans columns in classical buildings. This type of frieze can be a plain band or it can be embellished with low-relief carvings that might be purely decorative or depict figures or events. When discussing an interior, a frieze is the portion of a wall that lies between the cornice and picture molding. Sometimes this type of frieze can be left unadorned, but it can also be emphasized by contrasting wallpaper, paint, or other applied decoration. Or in a modification of the traditional form, a frieze can be a plain or carved band of wood or plaster that is directly incorporated into the cornice design. When designing your own cornice, a frieze might also offer a helpful structural component, functioning as a flat and uniform base for a subsequent layer of molding over an irregular wall surface. The frieze can provide a continuous nailing surface so that you do not need to consider the location of wall studs to fasten the subsequent layers of molding.

ABOVE Create a frieze by including a picture molding a few inches down from the ceiling.

frieze types

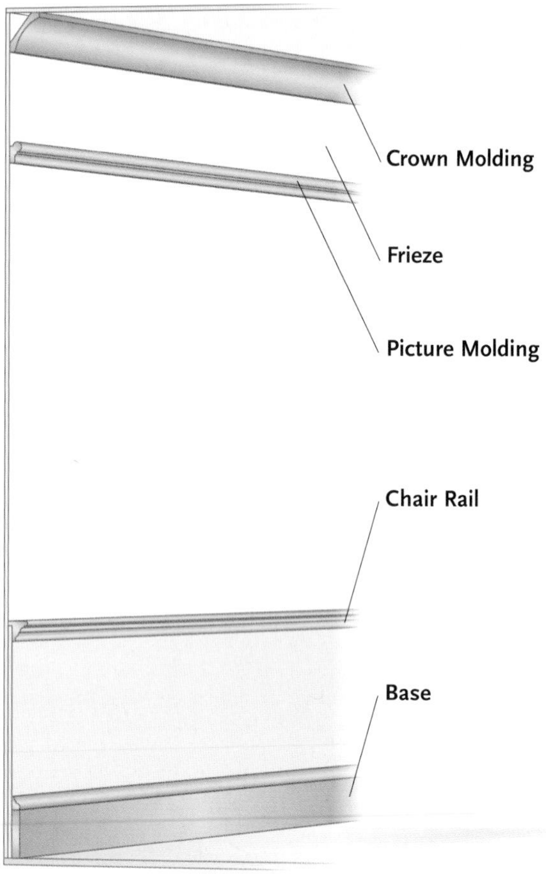

Crown Molding

Frieze

Picture Molding

Chair Rail

Base

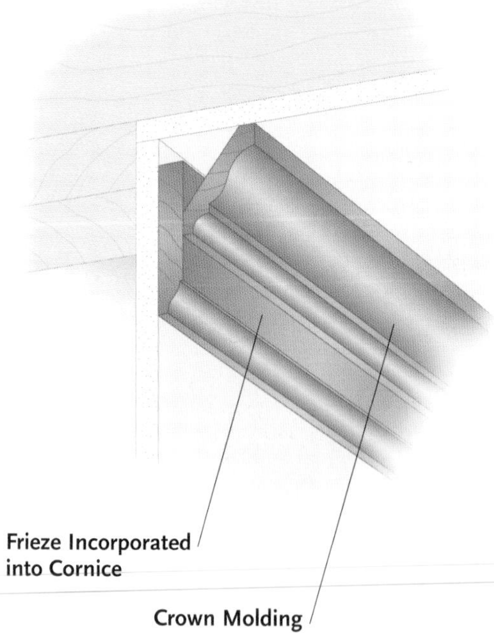

Frieze Incorporated into Cornice

Crown Molding

GLUE AND MOLDINGS

THE PRIMARY FASTENERS for most molding species are nails and screws. However, in addition to these mechanical devices, glue plays an important part in a cornice installation. For wood or MDF moldings, it is extremely important that joints are both glued and nailed together because seasonal variations in humidity can place considerable strain on those joints. Also, when you plan to install hardwood moldings that will receive a stained finish after being installed, the glue on these joints serves a secondary function. In these installations, the glue helps to seal the end grain of the wood and prevents the stain from being aggressively absorbed into those areas and leaving dark lines at the joints.

For all of these applications, you have a choice of glue types. Most professional carpenters favor either white PVA (polyvinyl acetate) or yellow (aliphatic resin) glues. These adhesives are easy to use and clean up with water before they fully set. There are a variety of available manufacturers and formulations, each with a particular setting speed and viscosity, and just about any name brand will be fine. Some manufacturers also offer brown-colored aliphatic resin glue for use with dark-colored woods. This is particularly useful when working with hardwoods such as cherry and walnut that will receive a clear finish as it reduces the visibility of the glue line.

■ **Poly Glues.** Polyurethane glues are another option for wood or MDF molding joints. These glues provide a strong bond, especially on end-grain joints, and long open time, so you do not need to rush an assembly. But polyurethane glues are messy to use and have a tendency to stain your hands, so it is important to wear gloves when working with them. As it hardens, this type of glue expands, creating a foam-like squeeze-out at the joint line that needs to be scraped off the wood surface. One of the interesting features of urethane glues is that they require moisture to cure properly; so it is often recommended that you should lightly dampen the joint surfaces with water before applying the glue.

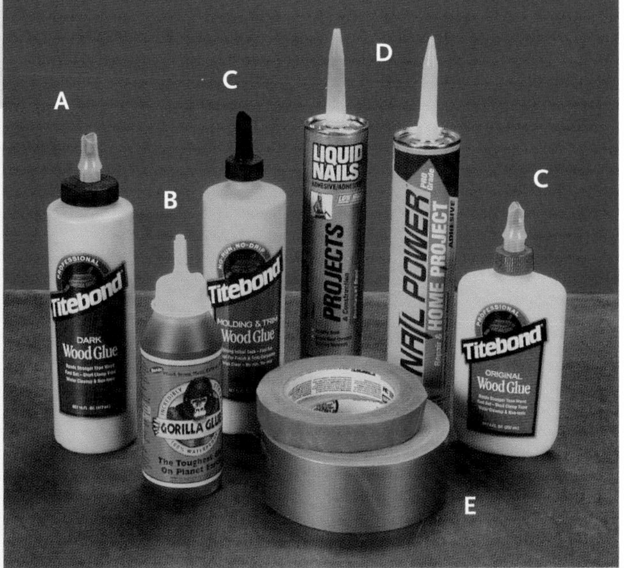

GLUING OPTIONS: A—dark aliphatic resin; B—polyurethane; C—yellow aliphatic resin; D—construction adhesive; E—duct and painter's tape

The installation process for polymer moldings involves both mechanical fasteners and adhesives to hold the molding in place. Most manufacturers recommend using a good quality construction adhesive—these come in tubes that require a caulk gun for application. Some suppliers also sell a proprietary adhesive that they recommend for assembling one piece of molding to another.

Ceiling Medallions

The ceiling medallion is yet another detail that, historically, was fashioned in plaster. Today, plaster medallions are still available, but you also have the option of selecting products made of polystyrene, fiberglass, PVC, and other polymers. These make the process of installation extremely simple—even for those with no experience in this type of work. In most cases, the design of a medallion relates to the style of cornice in the room. While it is common to use a medallion around a light fixture or ceiling fan, they can certainly be used alone. Designs are available in a wide variety of styles, shapes, and sizes. Most medallions are either round or oval, but square panels are also used, and there are even some medallions in star shapes. Small medallions start at about 6 inches in diameter and large designs can extend to over 6 feet. Many models come with a center hole to accommodate a ceiling fixture, but if you have no fixture, a rosette can be used to cover the hole.

While most of the available medallions are designed to be painted after installation, there are also some models that are sold with an ornate decorative painted finish.

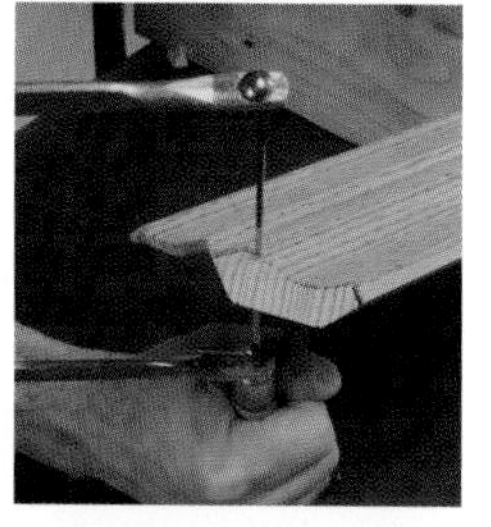

4 techniques

Cornice trim can exist in many different forms, but there are a number of basic principles and techniques that apply to almost any project. A multipiece cornice often requires the same procedures as a simple, one-piece installation—you just repeat them for each additional layer of molding. Careful planning is important in any job, so take time to assess the room's conditions, formulate a strategy, and test the design before you cut any molding. Purchase a short piece of each molding in the cornice, and assemble a small model. For a multipiece cornice, use hot glue to assemble an 18- to 24-inch length of the design and one or two nails to hold it in place while you decide if it meets your expectations. For a single molding, simply tack it in place to judge its appearance.

RELOAD
FASTENER GAUGE
18 GAUGE
Depth of Drive Thumbwheel
Countersink Drive
Flush Drive

ESTIMATING MATERIALS

Once you have decided on your cornice design, you'll need to measure the job and estimate the materials that you will require. Most types of molding stock are available in lengths from 8 feet to 16 feet in 2-foot increments. Fashioning clean, tight joints is the most difficult and time-consuming part of a cornice installation, so when possible, use a single piece of molding on each wall of a room. This speeds the installation process and lets you concentrate on the corner joints. Of course, there are times when a wall is longer than the available stock, or when it makes strategic sense to splice a length of molding. In these cases, you should plan to fashion a scarf joint where the two pieces of molding meet.

■ **Overestimate.** When a single piece of molding will cover a wall, make sure that you purchase stock that is at least 6 inches longer than the wall dimension to give you plenty of extra material for making the corner joints. If you must join two or more pieces of molding on a wall, plan on 2 feet of extra stock to make the joints. For each profile in a room, it's a good practice to purchase some extra stock, in case you make a mistake in cutting or need it for possible future repairs—a piece that will cover the longest wall in the room will provide good insurance.

Locating Studs and Ceiling Joists

In most situations, molding applications rely on using nails or screws to fasten the stock to the wall studs and top plates, and ceiling joists—the framing members that provide the basic structure of the building. You can usually expect to find wall studs spaced every 16 inches around a room, as well as at inside and outside corners. However, ceiling joists typically run in one direction only, and for those walls parallel with the joists, it is unlikely that they will fall just where you need them for fastening the ceiling trim. Even for those walls where joists are available, there are often situations where you need nailing where there is no joist, and then you will need to provide blocking. (See "Blocking," page 62.) So, in anticipation of the installation, spend some time locating these framing members, and also formulate a plan for fastening where they are missing or where a better means of attachment is prudent. Of course, if you intend to install a single bed molding as your cornice trim, it is small enough so that you can nail it exclusively to the wall plates, and these can be found at any spot along the room perimeter. A flat, band, or frieze molding can also be fastened solely to the wall framing and, once installed, can serve as a nailing base for subsequent layers of molding—at least on the wall side. A similar band can also be applied to the ceiling, fastening it to ceiling joists when possible and using hollow-wall fasteners when necessary. (See "Hollow-Wall Anchors," page 63.)

To locate the studs and joists, run an electronic stud finder over the walls and ceiling close to the corners where they meet. If you are working in a room that is unfinished, you can place a light pencil mark on the surfaces to indicate the centers of framing members. When the walls have been painted or are covered with wallpaper, run a strip of painter's blue masking tape down the walls and ceiling, just beyond the outer extremes of the cornice profile. You can then use a soft pencil or marker to indicate the stud and joist centers on the tape.

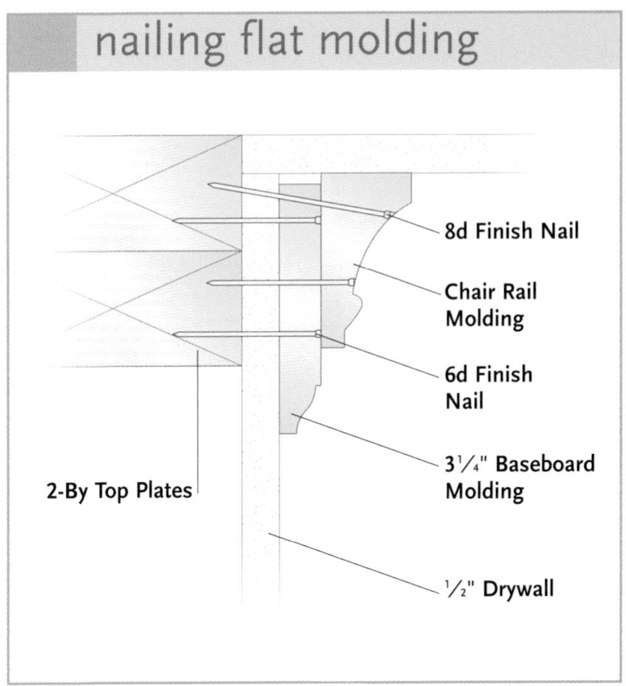

TO SECURE TRIMWORK TO THE WALL, left, begin by marking the locations of the studs.

CONTINUOUS BLOCKING, below, ensures a firm surface for fastening trimwork.

blocking

CEILING MOLDING needs to be firmly fastened to withstand the stresses that are imposed by changes in humidity and the inevitable settling and movement that occur over time in any home. For moldings that span the joint between walls and ceiling, this normally means that nails are driven at both the top and bottom edges of the material. As previously discussed, the bottom edge of most profiles can be nailed to either the wall framing or frieze board stock and, sometimes, the top edge can be nailed to the ceiling joists. However, when good nailing is absent, the best solution is to provide solid blocking that can accept the nails at the ceiling level. Many professional carpenters install blocking along all walls, just so that they can be sure that they will always have a place to fasten the molding.

■ **Blocking Materials.** Blocking can be made from almost any type of stock—remember that its only function is to hold your ceiling molding in place and that it will not be visible—but 2x4 or 2x6 material is an excellent choice. First, it is a relatively inexpensive and convenient material to buy; and second, its 1½-inch thickness provides a good nailing surface to hold even heavy molding in place. Each cornice profile requires its own type and size of blocking, so it's not possible to recommend a configuration for every case. But for the particular projects described in this book, blocking is always specified where it is necessary.

■ **Sizing Blocking.** To determine the size of the blocking for a single, sprung molding, draw a cross-section of your molding profile as it will be installed and measure the distance from the wall to the back side of the molding at the ceiling line. Subtract ⅛ to ¼ inch from that dimension, and rip the backing stock to size at the appropriate spring angle for your molding. By sizing the blocking to leave a space behind the molding, you will allow yourself a bit of adjustment room to adjust the stock up and down to accommodate small variations in the wall and ceiling surfaces.

For more complex cornice designs, it's also a good idea to make a drawing of the cross-section of the entire profile; then you can determine the appropriate type of blocking. Sometimes an L-shaped assembly made from common pine or construction-grade plywood is appropriate, and other times two or three individual pieces are necessary.

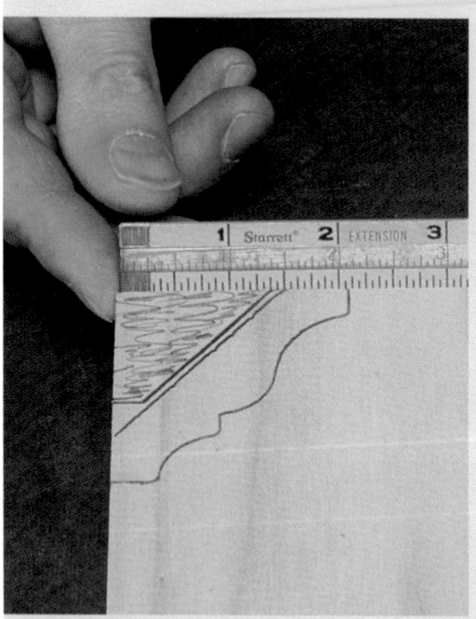

1 **Determine the size of blocking by drawing a cross-section of the molding and measuring from the wall line to the back side of the molding at the ceiling line. Subtract ⅛ in. from that dimension, and rip blocking stock to width at the appropriate spring angle.**

2 **Adjust the table saw bevel angle to match the spring angle of your molding; then rip blocking strips from 2x4 stock. Always use a push stick at the end of the cut so that your hands stay far from the blade. (Guard removed for clarity.)**

3 **Screw blocking strips to the top plate of the wall framing. Drill and countersink pilot holes for screws so that the heads do not protrude beyond the angled face of the strips.**

hollow-wall anchors

HOLLOW-WALL ANCHORS can provide a means of firmly fastening blocking to the ceiling when there are no conveniently located ceiling joists. For many years, toggle and molly bolts were considered the standard anchors for plaster or drywall surfaces. While molly and toggle bolts are considered to be the strongest type of anchors, they can be somewhat awkward to install and are hard to position accurately. Because cornice molding is not a structural or functional element, it is not critical that the blocking be able to support a great amount of weight.

An excellent alternative is to use a spiral anchor. These anchors, commonly sold under the names Zip-It and E-Z Anchor, are available in both metal and nylon, but the metal variety is considerably stronger and more reliable. To use a spiral anchor, drill a small pilot hole to indicate the desired location, and then use a hand screwdriver to turn the anchor into the drywall until the wide head is flat against the surface. You can then drive a screw through the blocking into the anchor. For an even stronger installation, you can also spread some construction adhesive on the upper surface of the blocking to bond with the drywall.

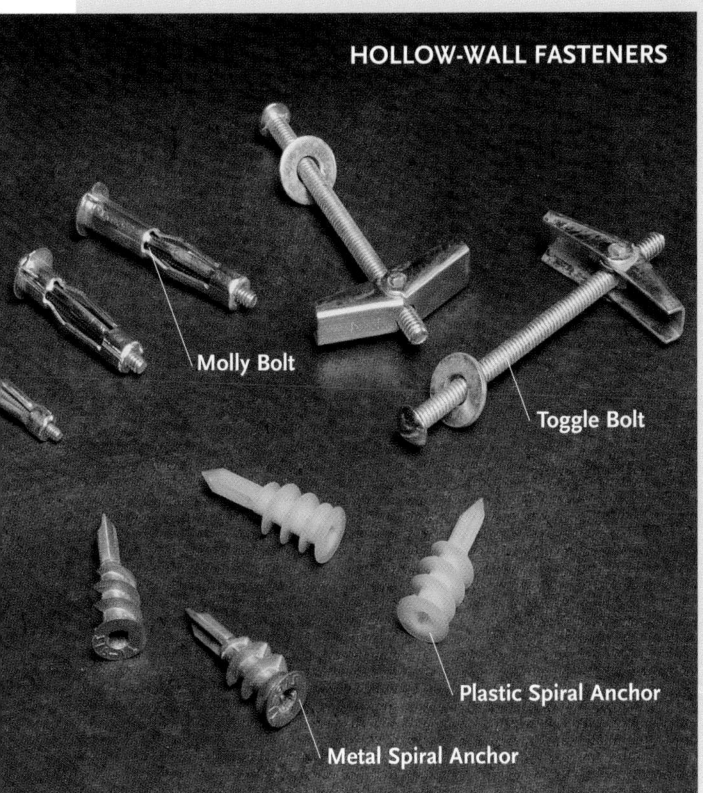

1 **Hold a piece of blocking in place, and drill pilot holes through the blocking to mark the location of anchors in the ceiling.**

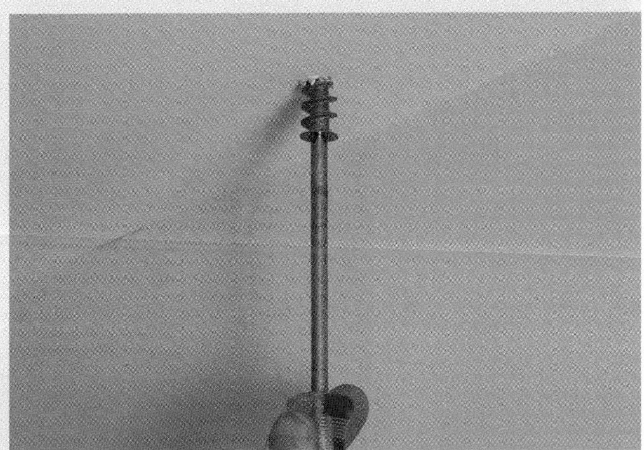

2 **Install spiral anchors using a screwdriver. Turn the anchors until the head sits flush with the drywall surface.**

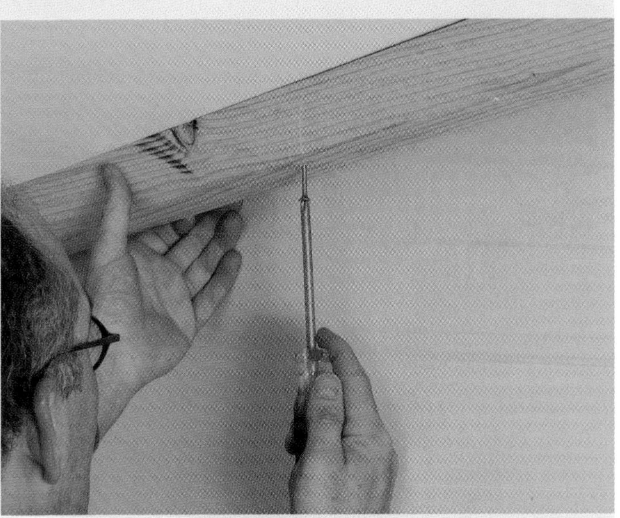

3 **Drive screws through the blocking so that they engage the spiral anchors in the ceiling.**

outside corner joints

AS A GENERAL RULE, moldings that meet at outside corners must be cut to form a miter joint. For flat stock such as friezes, chair rail, and picture molding, these miter joints are relatively simple: pieces that are mounted to the wall are cut with a bevel cut (through the thickness of the stock) and those that mount to the ceiling are cut with a flat miter (across the width of the stock). In both cases, the angle cut on each piece is equal to one-half of the total corner angle. For example, if two walls meet at a corner that measures exactly 90 degrees, each piece of molding will be cut at a 45-degree angle; if the corner is 86 degrees, each side must be cut at a 43-degree angle.

To fashion a tight miter joint, it is important that you know the exact angle of the corner. Even though a corner is supposed to be 90 degrees, there are plenty of reasons why this is often not the case.

For the most direct approach, use an angle measuring gauge to get a reading of the corner angle. Then simply divide the total angle in half for your miter setting. As an alternative, you can cut a 45-degree miter on the ends of two scrap boards and hold them in place to test if they fit tightly together. If the joint is open at the outside edge, the angle is greater then 90 degrees; if it is open along the wall, it is less then 90 degrees. In either case, re-cut the angles on both of the scrap pieces and test again. With a little trial and error, you will arrive at the proper miter setting. Remember that both sides of the miter must be cut at exactly the same angle for a proper joint.

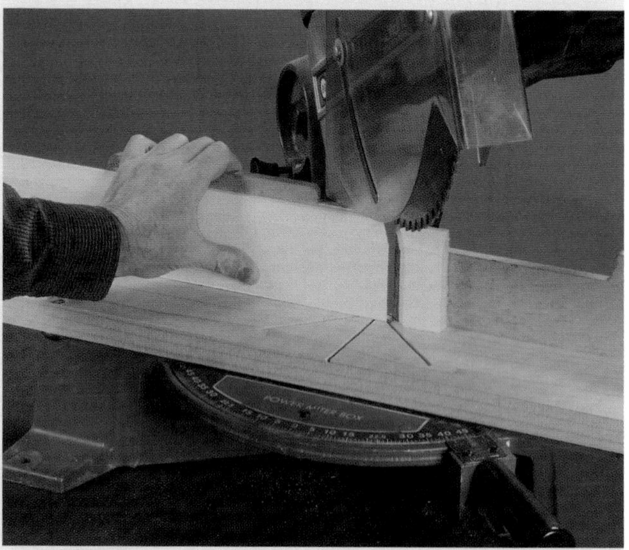

1 **To make a bevel cut on a flat molding, hold the molding against the fence and rotate the saw to the desired bevel angle.**

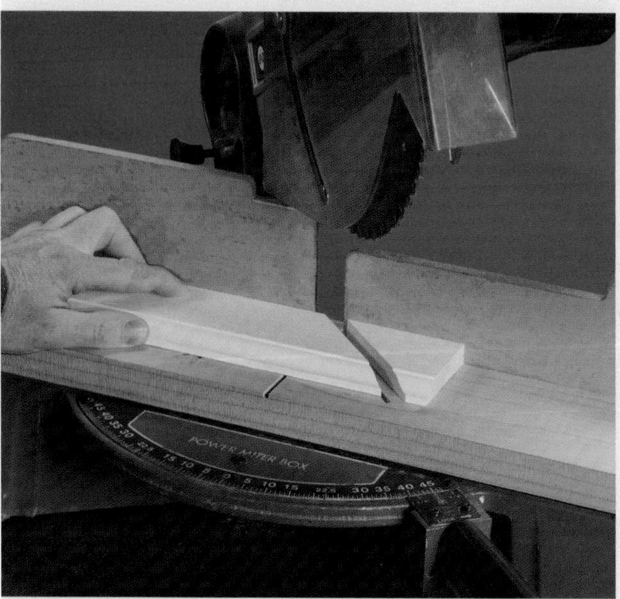

2 **To make a miter cut on a flat molding, hold the molding flat on the saw table.**

3 **The most direct method of determining the angle of a corner is to use an angle gauge. Hold the legs of the gauge against the walls and read the angle. The miter angle is one-half of the total measurement.**

calculating the right angle

YOU CAN USE GEOMETRY to determine the proper miter angle. Begin by taking a reading of the angle using an adjustable bevel gauge. Transfer the angle to a piece of scrap cardboard or plywood. Then use a set of dividers to mark out equal distances from the apex of the angle along each leg. Place the dividers on each of those marks and, using the same distance setting, make two intersecting arcs in the center of the angle. Draw a line from the apex of the angle through the intersecting point to indicate an angle that is one half of the original. Use an angle gauge to measure the resulting angle.

1 To bisect the angle of an outside corner, use an adjustable sliding bevel gauge to copy the angle.

2 Transfer the corner angle to a piece of scrap plywood or cardboard.

3 Use a set of dividers to mark out equal distances from the apex of the angle down each leg.

4 Place the dividers on each of the previously established marks, and using the same setting, scribe two intersecting arcs in the center of the angle.

5 Draw a line that connects the apex of the angle with the intersection of the two arcs. This line divides the original angle into two equal parts.

6 Use an angle measuring gauge to determine the desired miter-saw setting.

cutting sprung moldings with a simple miter saw

MOLDINGS that sit at an angle between the wall and ceiling must be cut with a compound miter, which includes both a bevel and miter. With a simple miter saw, you can accomplish these cuts by holding the molding in the saw at its appropriate spring angle; you only need to set the miter angle and the bevel angle will automatically be correct. To hold the molding in the right position, cut it upside down in the saw—the saw fence represents the wall and the saw table represents the ceiling.

1 Create a positioning jig by cutting a straight strip as long as the miter saw table. Position the strip so that it supports the molding against the fence at the proper spring angle.

2 Screw the support strip to the saw table. Keep the screws outside the range of the saw blade (top). Make cuts at 45 deg. left and right to cut through the strip; remove the portion between the cuts (bottom).

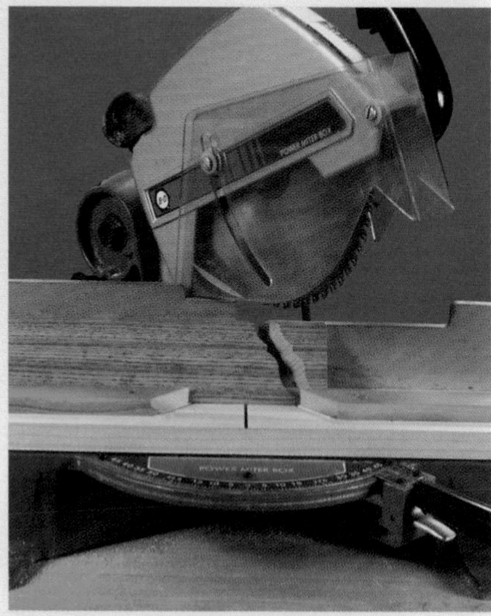

3 This is a simple miter saw setup for a left-end outside miter (right-hand side of the joint).

4 This is a simple miter saw setup for a right-end outside miter (left-hand side of the joint).

5 This is a simple miter saw setup for a left-end inside miter or coped joint (right-hand side of the joint).

6 This is a simple miter saw setup for a right-end inside miter or coped joint (left-hand side of the joint).

cutting sprung moldings with a sliding compound miter saw

A SLIDING COMPOUND MITER SAW offers the ability to cut a compound miter on a piece of molding while you hold the stock flat on the table. To do so requires you to set both a miter angle and a bevel angle. These adjustments are controlled independently on the saw, and many saw models have detents for the most common angle combinations. Because the molding is flat on the table, instead of being held at the spring angle, the angle settings are different from those used for a simple miter saw, and you must refer to a chart to find the correct settings. (Find a sample chart on page 68.) If your saw tilts only to one side for bevel cuts, you will need to flip the molding around to obtain the correct angle combinations.

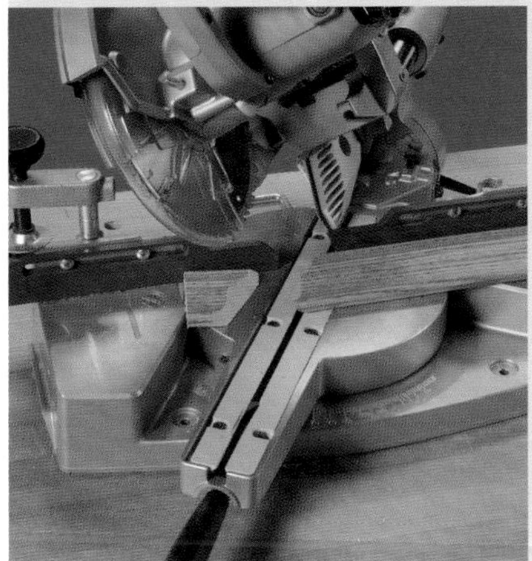

1 This is a sliding compound miter saw setup for a right-end outside miter (left-hand side of the joint). The bottom edge of the molding is held against the saw fence.

2 This is a sliding compound miter saw setup for a left-end outside miter (right-hand side of the joint). The top edge of the molding is held against the saw fence.

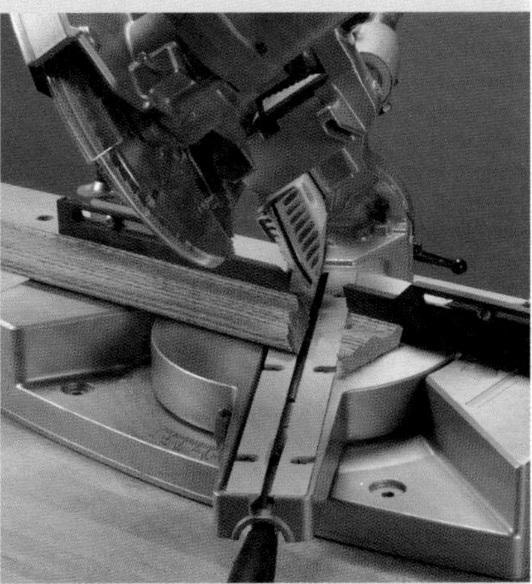

3 This is a sliding compound miter saw setup for a right-end inside miter or coped joint (left-hand side of the joint). The top edge of the molding is held against the saw fence.

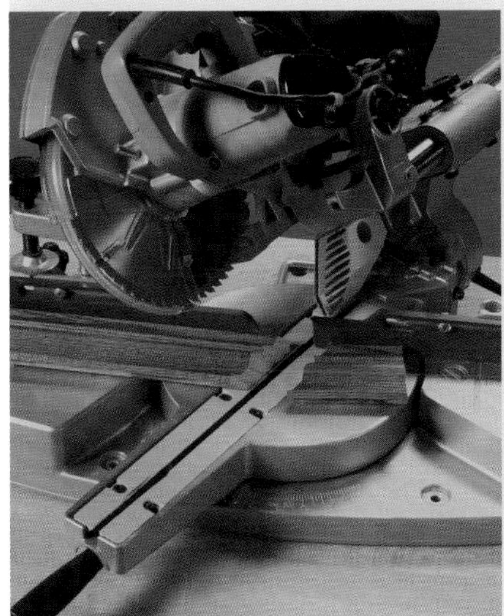

4 This is a sliding compound miter saw setup for a left-end inside miter or coped joint (right-hand side of the joint). The bottom edge of the molding is held against the saw fence.

MOLDING SAMPLES to illustrate the four basic miter cuts. It is a good idea to make samples like these and keep them for reference when adjusting the saw. It's easy to get confused as to the orientation of the molding, especially when using a sliding compound miter saw.

COMPOUND MITER SAW SETTINGS FOR CUTTING CROWN MOLDING

	52/38 Spring Angle		45/45 Spring Angle			52/38 Spring Angle		45/45 Spring Angle	
Corner Angle	Miter Angle	Bevel Angle	Miter Angle	Bevel Angle	Corner Angle	Miter Angle	Bevel Angle	Miter Angle	Bevel Angle
179°	0.31	0.39	0.35	0.35	134°	14.7	17.9	16.7	16
178°	0.62	0.79	0.71	0.71	133°	15	18.3	17.1	16.4
177°	0.92	1.18	1.06	1.06	132°	15.3	18.7	17.5	16.7
176°	1.23	1.58	1.06	1.06	131°	15.7	19.1	17.9	17.1
175°	1.54	1.97	1.41	1.41	130°	16	19.5	18.3	17.4
174°	1.85	2.36	2.12	2.12	129°	16.4	19.8	18.6	17.7
173°	2.15	2.75	2.48	2.47	128°	16.7	20.2	19	18.1
172°	2.5	3.2	2.8	2.8	127°	17.1	29.6	19.4	18.4
171°	2.8	3.5	3.2	3.2	126°	17.4	21	19.8	18.7
170°	3.1	3.9	3.5	3.5	125°	17.8	21.3	20.2	19.1
169°	3.4	4.3	3.9	3.9	124°	18.1	21.7	20.6	19.4
168°	3.7	4.7	4.3	4.2	123°	18.5	22.1	21	19.7
167°	4	5.1	4.6	4.6	122°	18.8	22.5	21.4	20.1
166°	4.3	5.6	5	4.9	121°	19.2	22.8	21.8	20.4
165°	4.6	5.9	5.3	5.3	120°	19.6	23.2	22.2	20.7
164°	5	6.3	5.7	5.7	119°	19.9	23.6	22.6	21
163°	5.3	6.7	6	6	118°	20.3	23.9	23	21.4
162°	5.8	7.1	6.4	6.4	117°	20.7	24.3	23.4	21.7
161°	5.9	7.5	6.6	6.7	116°	21	24.7	23.8	22
160°	6.2	7.9	7.1	7.1	115°	21.4	25.1	24.3	22.3
159°	6.5	8.3	7.5	7.4	114°	21.8	25.4	24.7	22.7
158°	6.8	8.7	7.8	7.8	113°	22.2	25.8	25.1	23
157°	7.1	9	8.2	8.1	112°	22.6	26.2	25.9	23.6
156°	7.5	9.4	8.6	8.5	111°	22.9	26.5	25.9	23.6
155°	7.8	9.8	8.9	8.8	110°	23.3	26.9	26.3	23.9
154°	8.1	10.2	9.3	9.2	109°	23.7	27.2	26.8	24.2
153°	8.4	10.6	9.6	9.5	108°	24.1	27.6	27.2	24.6
152°	8.7	11	10	9.9	107°	24.5	28	27.6	24.9
151°	9.1	11.4	10.4	10.2	106°	24.9	28.3	28.1	25.2
150°	9.4	11.8	10.7	10.6	105°	25.3	28.7	28.5	25.5
149°	9.7	12.2	11.1	10.9	104°	25.7	29	28.9	25.8
148°	10	12.5	11.5	11.2	103°	26.1	29.4	29.4	26.1
147°	10.3	12.9	11.8	11.6	102°	26.5	29.7	29.8	26.4
146°	10.7	13.3	12.2	11.9	101°	26.9	30.1	30.2	26.7
145°	11	12.7	12.6	12.3	100°	27.3	30.4	30.7	27
144°	11.3	14.1	12.9	12.6	99°	27.7	30.8	31.1	37.3
143°	11.6	14.5	13.3	12.9	98°	28.2	31.1	31.6	27.6
142°	12	14.9	13.7	13.3	97°	28.6	31.5	32	27.9
141°	12.3	15.3	14.1	13.7	96°	29	31.8	32.5	28.2
140°	12.6	15.6	14.4	14	95°	29.4	32.2	32.9	28.5
139°	13	16	14.8	14.3	94°	29.9	32.5	33.4	28.8
138°	13.3	16.4	15.2	14.7	93°	30.3	32.9	33.9	29.1
137°	13.6	16.8	15.4	15	92°	30.7	33.2	34.3	29.4
136°	14	17.2	15.9	15.4	91°	31.2	33.5	34.8	29.7
135°	14.3	17.6	16.3	15.7	90°	31.6	33.9	35.3	30

To set the miter angle, adjust the miter gauge on the saw. The bevel angle is set by adjusting the tilt of the saw blade.

	52/38 Spring Angle		45/45 Spring Angle			52/38 Spring Angle		45/45 Spring Angle	
Corner Angle	Miter Angle	Bevel Angle	Miter Angle	Bevel Angle	Corner Angle	Miter Angle	Bevel Angle	Miter Angle	Bevel Angle
89°	32.1	34.2	35.7	30.3	44°	56.7	46.9	60.3	41
88°	32.5	34.5	36.2	30.6	43°	57.4	47.2	60.9	41.1
87°	33	34.9	36.7	30.9	42°	58.1	47.4	61.5	41.3
86°	33.4	35.2	37.2	31.1	41°	58.7	47.6	62.1	41.5
85°	33.9	35.5	37.7	31.4	40°	59.4	47.8	62.8	41.6
84°	34.4	35.9	38.1	31.7	39°	60.1	48	63.4	41.8
83°	34.8	36.2	38.6	32	38°	60.8	48.2	64	42
82°	35.3	36.5	39.1	32.3	37°	61.5	48.4	64.7	42.1
81°	35.8	36.8	39.6	32.5	36°	62.2	48.5	65.3	42.3
80°	36.3	37.1	40.1	32.8	35°	62.9	48.7	66	42.4
79°	36.8	37.5	40.6	33.1	34°	63.6	48.9	66.6	42.5
78°	37.2	37.8	41.1	33.3	33°	64.3	49.1	67.3	42.7
77°	37.7	38.1	41.6	33.6	32°	65	49.2	67.9	42.8
76°	38.2	38.4	42.2	33.9	31°	65.8	49.4	68.6	43
75°	38.7	38.7	42.7	34.1	30°	66.5	49.6	69.2	43.1
74°	39.3	39	43.2	34.4	29°	67.2	49.7	69.9	43.2
73°	39.8	39.3	43.7	34.6	28°	68	49.9	70.6	43.3
72°	40.3	39.6	44.2	34.9	27°	68.7	50	71.2	43.4
71°	40.8	39.9	44.8	35.2	26°	69.4	50.2	71.9	43.5
70°	41.3	40.2	45.3	35.4	25°	70.2	50.3	72.6	43.7
69°	41.6	40.5	45.8	35.6	24°	71	50.4	73.3	43.8
68°	42.4	40.8	46.4	35.9	23°	71.7	50.6	73.9	43.9
67°	42.9	41.1	46.9	36.1	22°	72.5	50.7	74.6	44
66°	43.5	41.4	47.4	36.4	21°	73.2	50.8	75.3	44
65°	44	41.7	48	36.6	20°	74	50.9	76	44.1
64°	44.6	41.9	48.5	36.8	19°	74.8	51	76.7	44.2
63°	45.1	42.2	49.1	37.1	18°	75.6	51.1	77.4	44.3
62°	45.7	42.5	49.6	37.3	17°	76.4	51.2	78.1	44.4
61°	46.3	42.8	50.2	37.5	16°	77.1	51.3	78.8	44.4
60°	46.8	43	50.8	37.8	15°	77.9	51.4	79.5	44.5
59°	47.4	43.3	51.3	38	14°	78.7	51.5	80.1	44.6
58°	48	43.6	51.9	38.2	13°	79.5	51.5	80.8	44.6
57°	48.6	43.8	52.5	38.4	12°	80.3	51.6	81.5	44.7
56°	49.2	44.1	53.1	38.6	11°	81.1	51.7	82.9	44.8
55°	49.8	44.3	53.6	38.8	10°	81.9	51.7	82.9	44.8
54°	50.4	44.6	54.2	39.1	9°	82.7	51.8	83.6	44.8
53°	51	44.8	54.8	39.3	8°	83.5	51.8	84.4	44.9
52°	51.6	45.1	55.4	39.5	7°	84.3	51.9	85.1	44.9
51°	52.2	45.3	56	39.7	6°	85.1	51.9	85.8	44.9
50°	52.9	45.6	56.6	39.9	5°	85.9	51.9	86.5	44.9
49°	53.5	45.8	57.2	40	4°	86.8	52	87.2	45
48°	54.1	46	57.8	40.2	3°	87.6	52	87.9	45
47°	54.8	46.3	58.4	40.4	2°	88.4	52	88.6	45
46°	55.4	46.5	59	40.6	1°	89.2	52	89.3	45
45°	56.1	46.7	59.6	40.8	0°	90	52	90	45

INSIDE CORNER JOINTS

If you are planning to install only a flat band around the room, the inside joints can be simple butt joints. However, once your molding choices get more complex, the joinery also gets more involved. There are some molding materials, such as plaster, and a variety of synthetic cast options that are designed to be joined with miters at the inside corner joints. However, if you plan to install either wood or MDF moldings, arguably the most common materials, the best treatment for inside corners involves cutting a coped joint. A coped joint is one in which one of the intersecting pieces of molding is cut so that its end matches the face profile of the opposite corner piece. Although the process of cutting this type of joint requires more time, effort, and experience than a simple inside miter, the advantages for a quality installation are more than sufficient to justify the effort.

Coped Joints

If you have no experience in fashioning coped joints, it's a good idea for you to practice the basic techniques on some scrap molding stock before attempting your first cornice project. While not particularly difficult, the steps involved are also not exactly intuitive, and manipulating a coping saw can be frustrating at first. Although there are some basic rules that guide the coping process, it is important to remember that a certain amount of trial and error and adjustment are an expected part of most trim carpentry, and these joints will certainly illustrate that principle. In addition to your tools, bring a good bit of patience to the job to ensure the best results and a satisfying experience.

Because a coped profile is cut on the second piece of molding in any inside corner, begin by installing the first piece of stock. For purposes of this example, we'll assume that this molding has a square cut at either end and will fit between two walls. For the coped joint, measure the length of the next wall, and add 4 to 6 inches to that measurement. Begin the coped joint by cutting an open 45-degree miter joint on the end of your molding stock that will abut the already installed piece. This is the same angle you would cut for an inside miter joint, and the cut will clearly expose the molding profile that you need to follow. To make it easier to follow the molding shape, it's a good idea to run the side of a pencil lead over the edge of the cut to outline the profile.

■ **The Bottom Edge.** At this point, you have two options as to how to approach the intersection of the moldings at their bottom edges: they can be either mitered or treated with a simple butt joint. There are as many opinions on this issue as carpenters, and either method can yield perfectly satisfactory results. Because the more conservative tactic is to use a butt joint at the bottom edge, that will be your default approach. So, assuming you will cut a butt joint, use a small square to mark across the bottom edge of the molding for a straight cut, perpendicular to the back side of the stock. Use a small dovetail saw or backsaw to make the cut. It's always a good idea to clamp the molding stock to a worktable to keep it from moving around.

PREPARE A PIECE OF MOLDING for a coped joint by cutting an open miter cut to expose the profile of the molding. The molding should be cut at the same angle that you would use for an inside miter joint in the same corner.

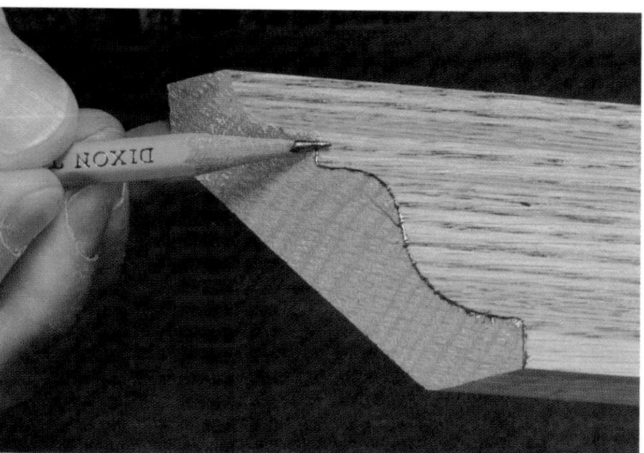

SOMETIMES it can be difficult to clearly see the cut line for a coped joint, so use the side of a pencil to outline the edge of the molding where it meets the open miter.

dealing with bottom edges of sprung molding

WHEN YOU CUT A COPED PROFILE on a piece of sprung molding, you need to make a decision about how to treat the intersection of the two pieces along their bottom edges. If you strictly follow the profile as it is exposed by the open miter cut, you will end up with a miter joint along the edge. This technique creates an elegant-looking joint, as the line of the intersecting profiles is continuous. However, there is a price to be paid for this type of detail. The thin, mitered sliver of stock at the bottom edge of the coped joint is extremely fragile and difficult to cut, the process of testing and adjusting the joint can easily damage it. In addition, this type of joint requires that you cut a shallow mortise in the adjacent molding to house the overlapping miter

For an equally acceptable and safer approach, you can make a square cut at the bottom edge of the molding. This technique simplifies the coped profile and eliminates the need to mortise the adjoining molding.

MITERED BOTTOM EDGE. To accommodate the thin angled return piece, you must cut a shallow mortise in the bottom edge of the mating molding. Use a sharp chisel to pare away the required stock. (Shown upside down.)

1 At the bottom edge of a sprung molding, it is often best to make a square cut rather than follow the angled profile exposed by the open miter. This will allow the molding to butt cleanly to the adjacent profile. Use a square to mark the cut at the molding's bottom edge.

2 Begin the coped joint by making the short square cut at the bottom edge of the molding. A dovetail saw is the perfect tool for this type of cut—it is small and easy to control.

3 This is a detail of coped inside corner joint with a square-cut bottom edge joint. (Shown upside down.)

4 This is a detail of an assembled inside corner joint with a square-cut bottom edge joint. (Shown upside down.)

cutting a coped joint

WITH THE OPEN MITER CUT, you can begin to cut along the exposed profile line. Once again, this is a process in which you will need to develop a feel for the tool and a logical approach to the joint. Most carpenters prefer to install the coping saw blade so that it cuts on the pull stroke. Because coping blades are, by necessity, quite thin, this orientation allows you to cut with minimum force, making it less likely that the blade will bind or break. It also permits you to clearly view the cut line and eliminates the risk of chipping out the molding on its face side. The action of the saw should be quite easy; if you find yourself forcing the blade, you are most likely twisting it. The teeth of a coping blade are set to create a generous kerf, creating ample room for adjustment and change of direction. Position the saw so that the angle of the cut is sharper than 90 degrees; the cut should remove more stock from the back side of the molding than from the front. This technique is called back-cutting, and it will allow the coped profile to meet the adjacent piece along a sharp edge with no interference. Back-cutting also makes it easier to adjust the profile, as you won't need to remove much stock to alter the shape.

SMART TIP

YOU CAN CUT THE MOLDING 1/16 TO 1/8 INCH LONG (DEPENDING ON ITS TOTAL LENGTH) AND SPRING IT INTO POSITION SO THAT ITS COPED END ACTUALLY DIGS INTO THE ADJACENT PIECE. THIS TECHNIQUE FORMS A TIGHT JOINT WITH THE ADDED ADVANTAGE OF CAUSING ANY SMALL GAPS IN THE JOINT TO DISAPPEAR.

1 Hold the coping saw at an angle greater than 90 deg. to start cutting the coped profile. Keep the saw blade about 1/32 in. to the waste side of the layout line.

4 Use a rasp to further refine the shape of the coped joint.

5 It is often necessary to use a variety of abrasive tools to finish shaping a coped profile. Here a round Surform tool is used on the concave portion of the joint.

Cornice molding shapes can be very complex, and it is usually not possible to cut the entire profile from one direction. Cut as far as you can along the profile, keeping the kerf approximately 1⁄32 inch to the waste side of the line. When you reach an impasse, remove the blade from the kerf and make a relief cut from the outside edge to remove some of the stock. Then proceed with the cut, working from both directions whenever necessary.

As you gain skill with the coping saw, you will find that you can follow the profile line quite closely; however, this is not a precision tool and you should not expect to cut a perfectly finished joint. Instead, use a selection of rasps and knives to refine the profile.

Hold the molding in place, and check the fit against its mating piece. Use a sharp pencil to mark any areas that need adjustment, and make the alterations.

2 **Make relief cuts as necessary to keep the saw blade from binding in the cut. It is sometimes necessary to make several relief cuts, especially for more complex molding profiles.**

3 **Continue the coped cut after removing some of the waste to free the saw blade. It is perfectly fine to cut from either edge of the molding; just remember to keep the blade angled to create a back-cut.**

6 **This is a finished coped profile.**

7 **This is the back side of a coped joint. Notice the clearance provided by the back-cut on the profiled edge. This will allow the adjacent molding to pass by the shaped end of the molding and will also make it easy to adjust the profile for a tight fit.**

using a collins coping foot

FOR PROJECTS THAT INCLUDE many inside corners, you might want to consider an alternative to the coping saw for shaping coped joints. The Collins Coping Foot is an aftermarket attachment that replaces the factory-supplied foot on a portable jigsaw. Instead of a flat surface, the coping foot features a domed shape that allows the user to pivot the jigsaw over a wide range of angles while still maintaining contact with the back side of the molding. The manufacturers of this accessory recommend that you use a coarse blade for these coping cuts to provide a wide kerf for maximum control of the tool.

As with any tool, you can expect to spend some time mastering the coping foot. Proper use requires that you build a small channel or cradle to hold the molding at its appropriate spring angle and also that you hold the jigsaw upside down to make the cuts. For some cuts you will pull the saw toward you and for others you will push it away from your body—the best orientation depends on the particular molding configuration. When practicing the use of the saw, remember to always keep the coping foot in contact with the back side of the molding. Your first few attempts will probably be a bit frustrating, but soon you will find that you can manipulate the saw to make a very precise cut. It's particularly helpful to keep both hands on the tool body for maximum control.

Begin by making an open miter cut, just as if you were using a coping saw. Next, clamp the molding in the support cradle, allowing it to overhang the end of the cradle

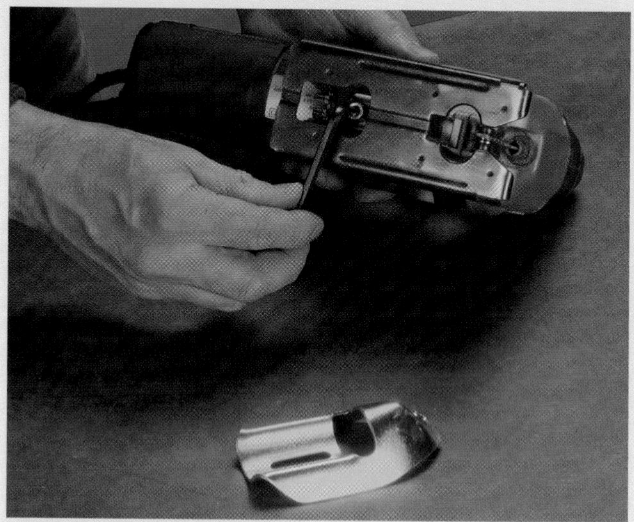

1 Remove the standard foot on the jigsaw by loosening the Allen-head screw that holds it to the saw housing.

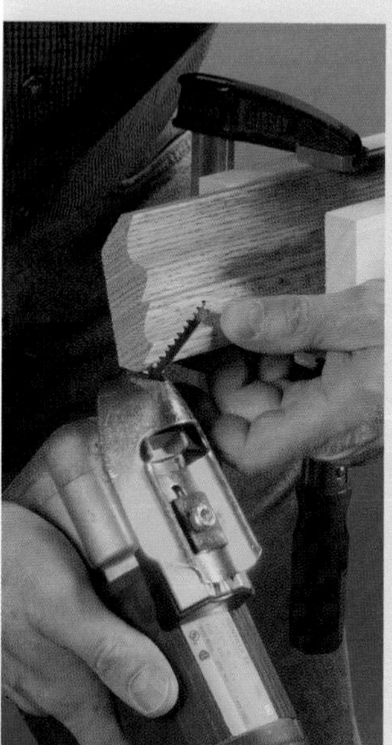

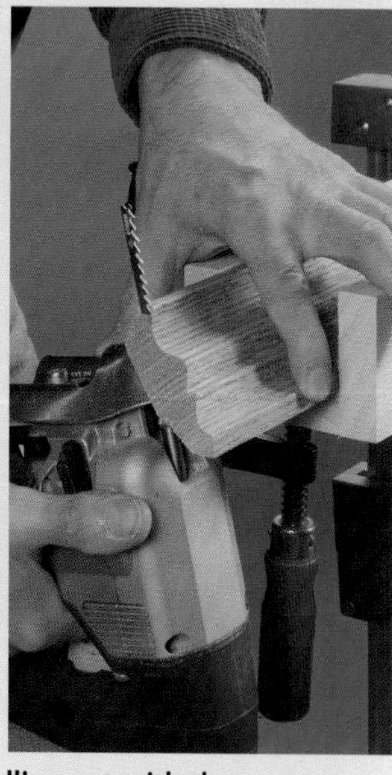

4 Begin by making a pulling cut with the saw to trim the square return at the bottom edge of the molding (left). Turn the saw around to make a pushing cut to define the top edge of the coped profile (right).

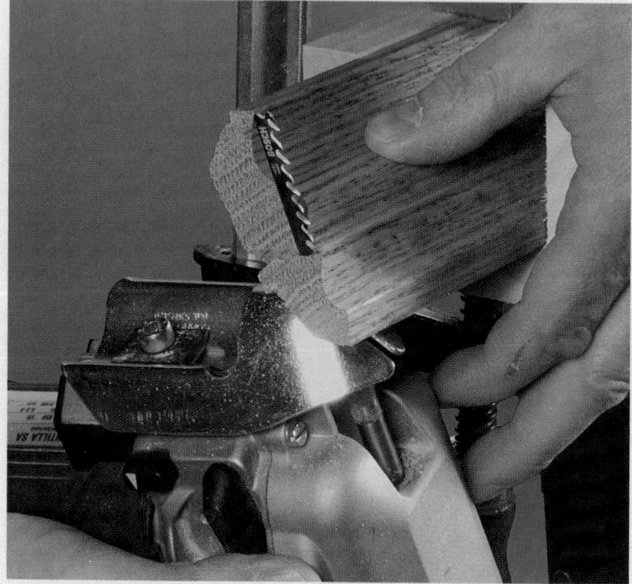

5 Make relief cuts at critical points so that the saw blade will not bind when cutting along the coped profile.

by several inches so that you can have plenty of clearance for the jigsaw body. Make short cuts at the top and bottom edges of the molding to define the ends of the profile. Then with the saw angled to form a back-cut, begin to trace the coped profile. Keep the saw kerf ⅛ to 1/16 inch back from the edge of the profile line for your first pass. With the coarse blade in the saw, you will be able to go back and use the blade like a rasp to shave small amounts of material from the edge of the cut when it comes time to test fit the assembly. To keep the blade from binding, make relief cuts as necessary to free pieces of waste stock as you work.

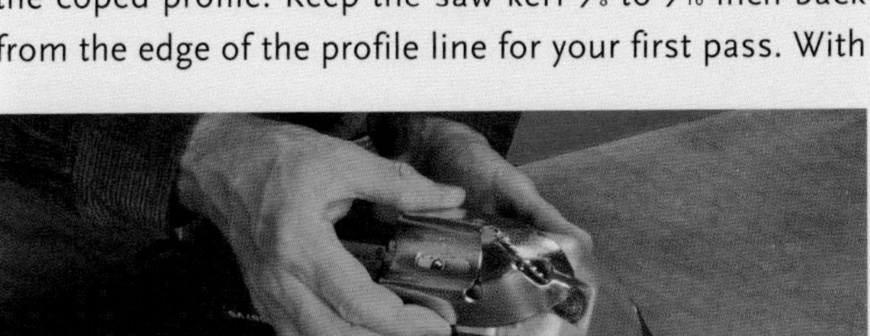

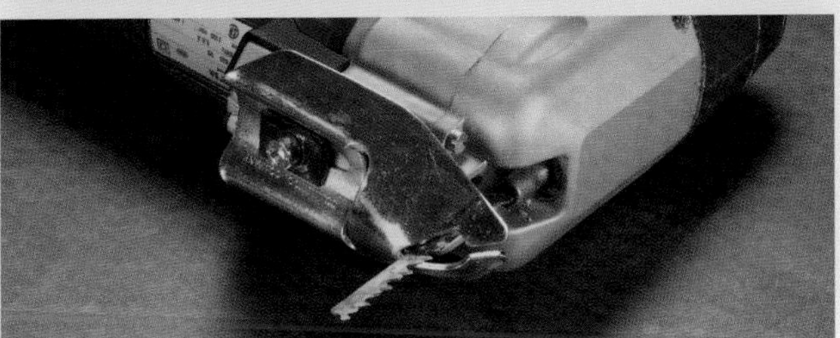

2 Install the coping foot to the saw using the same screw that held the factory foot (top). Check that there is no interference with the saw blade (bottom); readjust the position of the coping foot, if necessary.

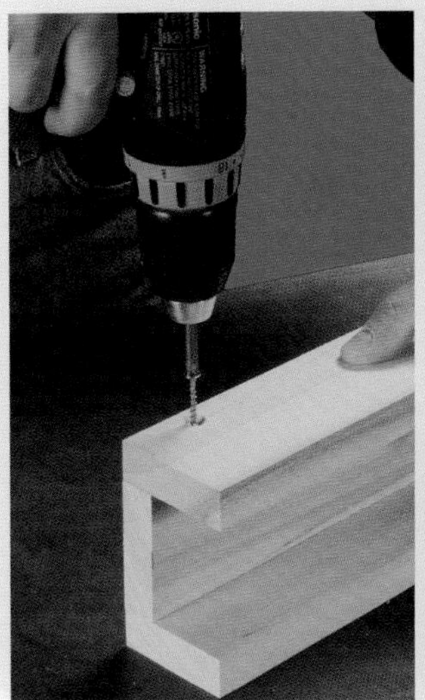

3 Create a cradle to support the molding at its proper spring angle (left). Cut an open miter on the end of the molding stock, and position it in the cradle (right). It is a good idea to clamp the cradle to a workbench or heavy table.

6 Begin cutting the shaped profile, keeping the saw angled beyond 90 deg. for a back-cut. It is important that the foot of the saw stay in contact with the back of the molding at all times.

7 Reverse the direction of the saw, as required, to finish cutting the coped joint. Refine the joint, as usual, by using rasps, files, and knives.

SCARF JOINTS

In most cases, it is to your advantage to use a single length of molding to cover a wall. However, if you have a wall that is longer than your available molding stock, a joint is inevitable. In some situations, it makes good strategic sense to include a joint even where one is not absolutely necessary. One example of this is a case in which you would need to fashion a coped joint at both ends of a molding. By creating a joint instead of a single length of molding, you have the ability to fit each coped end individually, and then easily cut each piece to exact length.

Whatever the reason, when joining two lengths of wood or MDF molding end to end, the preferred method is to fashion a scarf joint rather than a simple butt joint. In a scarf joint, the two pieces are cut in mating 45-degree angles, one open miter and one closed miter.

■ **Scarf Joint Locations.** A scarf joint eliminates the possibility of any gaps opening up due to seasonal swelling and shrinkage of the molding stock. It also provides a strong bond between the two pieces and results in a joint that is much less visible. Locate a joint in a spot that does not draw your attention.

If you want to assemble a scarf joint on the workbench, use a backer of ¼-inch-thick plywood to strengthen and align the two molding pieces. Rip the backer so that it is about ½ inch narrower than the back side of the molding to ensure that it doesn't interfere with the joints at either the wall or ceiling. Spread some glue on the mating joint surfaces, and then assemble the scarf joint. Spread glue on the backer and center it over the joint. Use ½-inch long brads or staples to fasten the backer to the molding. After the glue sets for about one hour, you can treat the joined piece just like a single length of molding.

assembling a scarf joint on the wall

TO ASSEMBLE A SCARF JOINT IN PLACE, install the open-mitered portion of the joint first. Cut the molding so that the joint falls over a stud, or in a spot that has good blocking. Cut a closed miter to match the first cut. Apply glue to the mating surfaces, and assemble the joint; drive nails through the overlapping pieces to hold the parts in proper alignment. When the glue is cured, lightly sand the joint to create a smooth transition between the pieces. If your cornice is to include multiple moldings, locate joints in subsequent layers away from the initial joint, which will make them even less noticeable.

1 **You can also assemble a scarf joint on the wall. Cut an open miter on the first piece, and nail it to both the blocking and wall studs.**

2 **Cut a closed miter on the second piece of molding, and then test the fit of the joint. When you are satisfied with the joint, apply glue to the mating surfaces, and nail the second piece to the wall.**

3 **Use brads to pin the joint together.**

preassembling a scarf joint

1 To form a scarf joint, cut matching open and closed miters on a length of molding stock.

2 Apply glue to the mating surfaces of the joint, and align the two sections of molding. Check to make sure that the outer edges remain in a straight line.

3 Spread glue on a backer of 1/4-in.-thick plywood, and place it over the back side of the joint. Use short brads (1/2 or 5/8 in. long) to fasten the backer to the molding. Take care to locate the brads so they do not protrude through the face of the molding.

4 Sand the face of the joint to eliminate any uneven spots and to smooth the transition between the two pieces. Note: If your molding requires blocking for installation, you will need to make provisions for the thickness of the backer at the scarf joint.

PLANNING THE JOB

A SUCCESSFUL CORNICE JOB depends on careful planning. Of course, there are some parts of the job that naturally occur in a certain order. For instance, blocking must be installed before the molding, and stud and joist locations must be determined before any parts can be nailed to the wall. But when it comes to the molding, the best order of installation is not necessarily obvious. As with many other trim jobs, every carpenter will develop a preference for how to best proceed on a cornice installation. Most of these decisions revolve around issues of efficiency and how best to minimize the most difficult joints. In some situations, it is important to locate a scarf joint in a spot where it will not draw excessive attention. In all cases, it is a good idea to plan the order of installation so that you can make the best use of your materials and reduce the likelihood of errors.

In almost all cases it is best to avoid circumstances in which a coped joint is required on both ends of a piece of molding. While it is not impossible to successfully negotiate this type of situation, it can be tricky to fit both joints while maintaining the exact length required. When this occurs, a good alternative approach is to separate the wall into two separate pieces; fit each coped joint separately; and then cut a scarf joint where the two pieces meet.

MITERED RETURNS

Every so often a situation arises in which a molding must be ended on an open wall instead of at a corner. This can occur at a stairwell opening, skylight shaft, or a transition from a flat to a cathedral ceiling. Whatever the reason, the best treatment for this condition is to fabricate a mitered return to terminate the molding. Mark the long point on the molding stock, and cut a 45-degree miter on the piece. Cut a matching 45-degree miter on a piece of scrap stock, and then carefully cut off just the mitered section of the molding to make the cap. Because the piece is so small, it is safest to use a handsaw to make this cut. Spread glue on the mating surfaces of the joint, and use tape to hold the parts together until the glue sets—nails, and even brads, can easily split the delicate piece. After the glue has cured, install the length of molding to the wall.

PLANNING IS THE KEY to a successful cornice or crown molding project. It is best to draw the project on paper to help eliminate cutting more coped joints than necessary.

assembling a mitered return

1 Begin a mitered return by cutting a closed miter on the end of the molding stock. Cut a matching miter on another piece of molding, and then use a handsaw to cut off just the mitered section of the molding to form a return.

2 Test the fit of the mitered return on the end of the molding. When assembled, the joint should be almost invisible.

3 Spread glue on the joint surfaces using a small brush or wooden shim (top). Use masking tape as a clamp for the delicate return (bottom). Because the piece is so small, it is best to avoid nails or brads as they could easily split the return.

4 Install the molding with the mitered return. It's best to keep the face of the return $\frac{1}{8}$ to $\frac{1}{4}$ in. back from the edge of a drywall or plaster corner.

5 projects

With so many product and layout options, selecting a cornice design for a do-it-yourself project can be an intimidating process, especially for someone without much carpentry experience. It is with this dilemma in mind that the following 30 cornice projects were developed. The projects include an assortment of materials—from the most inexpensive to some that are quite luxurious. They also represent a range of levels of complexity.

While the plans are presented from simple to more difficult, you should not feel obligated to complete the earlier installations before moving on to the more involved designs. And keep in mind that you can always utilize the relevant principles of design and layout, as well as the demonstrated installation procedures, to create your own cornice trim projects.

PINE BED MOLDING

A bed molding is one of the most common sprung molding profiles. Consisting of a combination of cove and rounded shapes, this type of molding is available in a variety of sizes ranging from 1¾ to 3¼ inches, although the smaller sizes are much more common. It is quite common to find a bed molding used as part of a complex cornice assembly, but it is also an excellent choice, used alone, for a small room such as a bathroom or an area with a low ceiling.

If you browse through the molding aisle at a home center, you will likely find versions of bed moldings offered in clear and finger-jointed pine, red oak, MDF, and urethane. This range of choices provides you with many cost and finish options, but the basic installation principles remain the same regardless of the material you select. Of course, if you are looking for a more obscure hardwood species, you may need to special order the molding.

If you are considering your first cornice project, bed molding provides a good introduction to the techniques involved in working with a sprung molding. Because of its relatively small size, it is not too challenging to install because you can nail it exclusively to the top plate, eliminating the need to locate individual studs or ceiling joists. In addition, it typically requires no special blocking and is flexible enough to conform to gentle irregularities in a ceiling or wall surface.

For a simple profile, a bed molding can work in a variety of ways to enhance a living space. Painted the same color as the walls or ceiling, the molding will provide a quiet transition between the surfaces, subtly softening the transition from vertical to horizontal. However, if you select a bold, contrasting color, the molding can be an eye-catching accent that defines and accentuates the different planes.

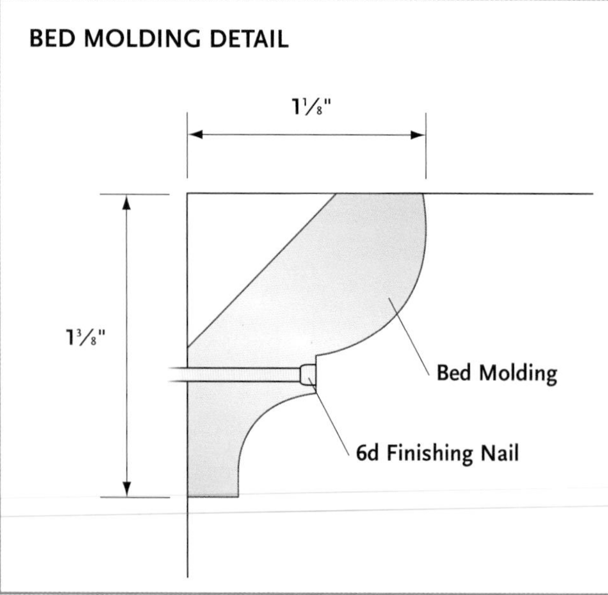

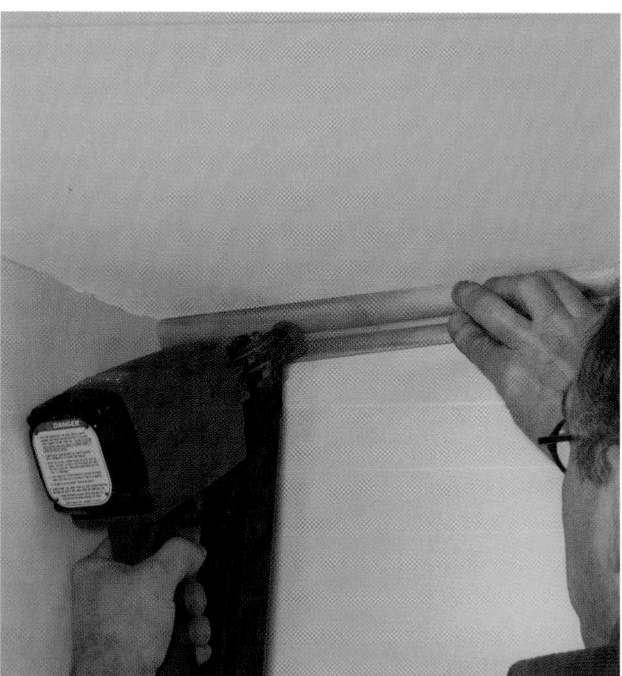

2 Use a nail gun or hammer and 6d finishing nails to fasten the molding to the top plate of the wall framing. Make sure that the molding sits tightly against both the wall and ceiling surfaces before starting to nail.

1 Install the first piece of molding with square cuts on both ends, butting tightly to the end walls. As a general rule, it is a good idea to cut the molding about $^1/_{16}$ in. longer than the wall measurement to "spring" it into position.

3 Cut an open miter to expose the profile for a coped inside corner joint. Remember that the molding must be oriented upside down on the saw table, with the fence representing the wall and the table representing the ceiling.

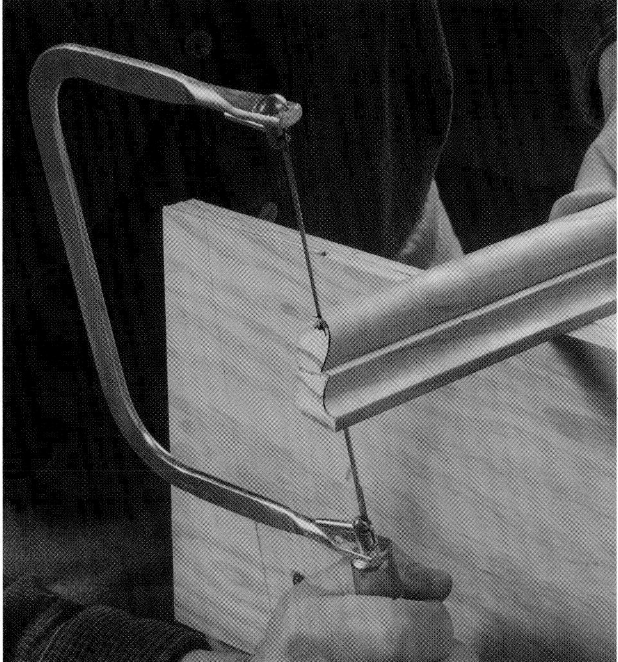

4 Use the coping saw to cut the profile for a coped joint. Angle the saw blade so that the cutting angle is slightly steeper than 90 deg., and keep the saw blade $^1/_{32}$ to $^1/_{16}$ in. on the waste side of the layout line. Finish shaping the joint by removing additional waste with a rasp or file.

5 Test the fit of the coped joint. If you find gaps in the joint, mark the molding to indicate the areas that need to be modified, and then use a rasp or knife to adjust the fit. Then trim the opposite end of the molding to length with the appropriate cut and nail it in place.

6 Here is a detail of a coped inside corner joint. Note that the small gap between the molding and ceiling can easily be filled with caulk before painting.

9 Test the fit of the outside corner joint. It's not unusual for a joint to require a bit of adjustment to achieve a tight fit.

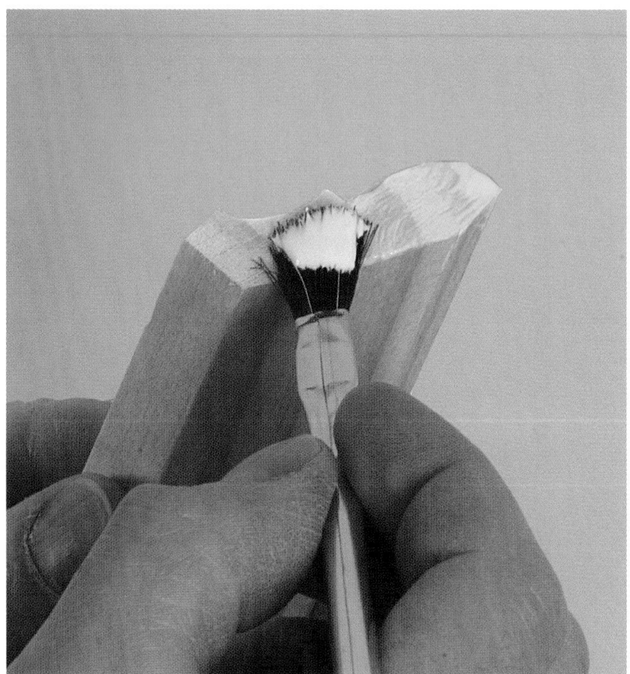

10 Use a small brush or wooden shim to spread glue on both surfaces of the miter joint before assembly. After nailing the molding to the wall, use brads to pin the miter together.

7 Cut a closed miter on bed molding for an outside miter joint. Either directly measure the outside corner angle with an angle gauge, or cut matching 45-deg. miters on scrap stock to test if the angle is correct. It is easier and more accurate to hold the molding in place and mark the length directly on the stock than to measure the wall and transfer the dimension to the molding.

8 Nail the molding for one side of an outside corner joint to the wall, but keep the nails back a few inches from the corner to allow for adjustment.

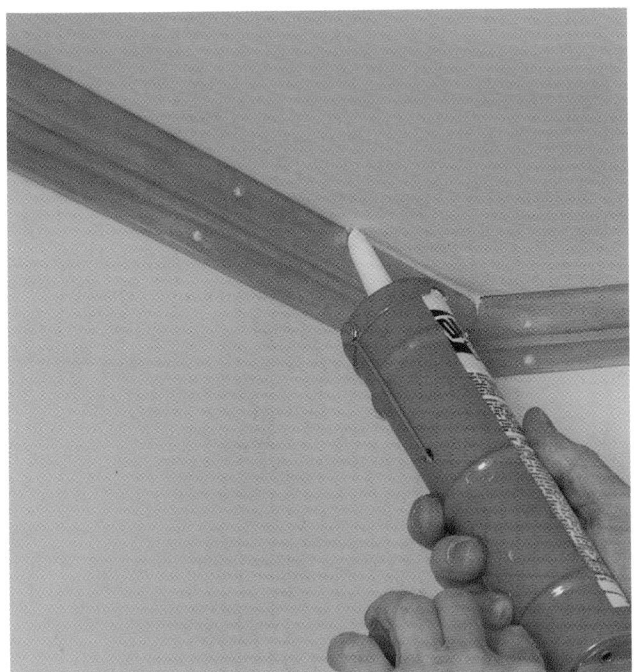

11 Fill all nailholes with either painters putty or drying filler, and sand as necessary to achieve a smooth surface. Caulk the joints between the molding and the ceiling and between the molding and the walls; then apply a good quality primer. Allow the primer to dry thoroughly, and lightly sand again before painting.

12 Here is the finished pine bed molding.

POLYURETHANE CHAIR-RAIL CORNICE

If you are looking for a simple cornice that requires minimal investment in tools and is an appropriate project for someone with no woodworking experience, here is an excellent option This design combines the ease of a flat molding installation with a polyurethane chair-rail molding that installs with screws and construction adhesive. Because the polyurethane core is too soft and fragile to support a complex coped profile, the installation employs simple miter joints for both inside and outside corners, so you do not even need a coping saw and files for this job.

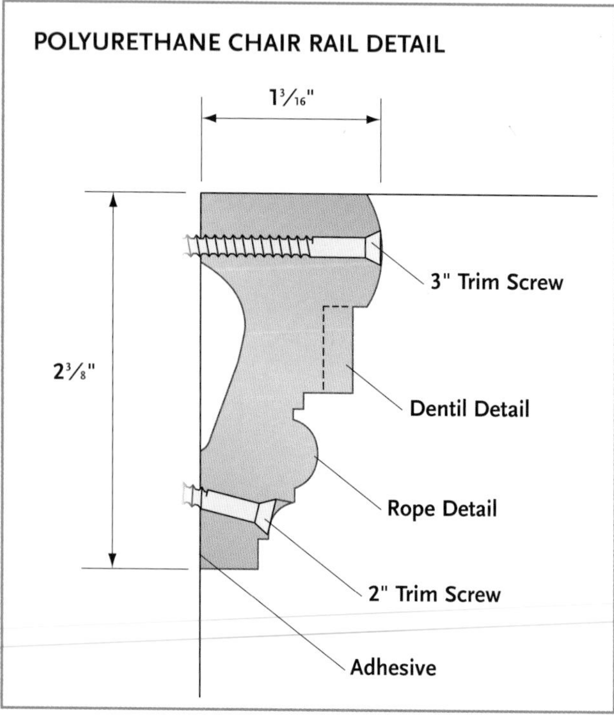

The chair-rail molding featured here is a stock profile offered by home centers. Or you can apply the techniques used in this project to many of the flat molding profiles offered by online suppliers.

While these photos show the use of a power miter saw, the molding material is so soft and cuts so easily that even a large job could be easily accommodated by a hand miter box and small backsaw.

In this cornice, the molding is mounted to the wall with its top edge pushed tight to the ceiling. The polyurethane material is certainly flexible enough to conform to gentle variations in the surface, so minor dips or hollows in your ceiling should not be a problem. However, if your ceiling has some serious sags, you can always leave a small space of 1/4 to 3/8 inch between the top edge of the molding and the ceiling to create a shadow line that will hide these irregularities.

Because the molding features a regular dentil pattern, it is best to begin your layout at the outside corners of your room. Outside corners are always the most visible areas for cornice molding, so it is important to create a symmetrical pattern on either side of these joints.

2 **Inside corners on the polyurethane moldings are joined with inside bevel joints instead of the coped joints used with wooden or MDF moldings. Remember that the wall measurement corresponds to the distance from the short side of the outside bevel to the long side of the inside bevel.**

12 Use an electronic stud finder to locate the wall studs, and place a mark to indicate the center of each on a strip of masking tape. Install the molding to one side of an outside corner; then apply glue to the mating surfaces of the miter joint. Hold the second side of the joint in position, and nail it to the wall, making sure that the joint fits tightly. Use brads to fasten the joint halves together.

15 Here is a detail of an open miter cut in preparation for cutting a coped inside corner joint. Because of the ornate decorative pattern of this molding, you should expect that it will be necessary to adjust the coped profile to achieve a tight joint.

16 Here is the finished poplar cornice with rope crown and frieze.

PINE AND POPLAR CORNICE WITH WIDE-CASING FRIEZE

This three-piece cornice combines a commonly available crown molding with a more unusual casing molding, used as a wide frieze, and panel molding. The assembly provides an interesting variation on the traditional cornice form and it shows how you can use profiles that are intended for other uses in a cornice design.

The wide frieze is formed from a Victorian-style casing that is available from San Francisco Victoriana, Inc. The profile is sold as a stock item in poplar, but it can also be manufactured in other species as a custom order. The panel molding is an item that you may be able to find at a local lumberyard; many suppliers offer a variation on this profile, often with a proprietary model number. If you cannot find it at a local supplier, you can order it from San Francisco Victoriana, Inc., as profile # 1-21, in poplar. And you can substitute another panel molding or base cap profile. The crown molding can easily be obtained, in pine, at any home center or lumberyard. If you are planning on applying a painted finish, it is not a problem to mix poplar and pine species; if you want to apply a clear finish, you can special order these moldings in the species of your choice.

This is a design that appears much more complex than it really is. Because both the frieze and panel molding are flat profiles, they are quite simple to apply. And because the blocking, frieze, and panel molding all butt tightly together, there is no need for meticulous measuring and layout for these elements.

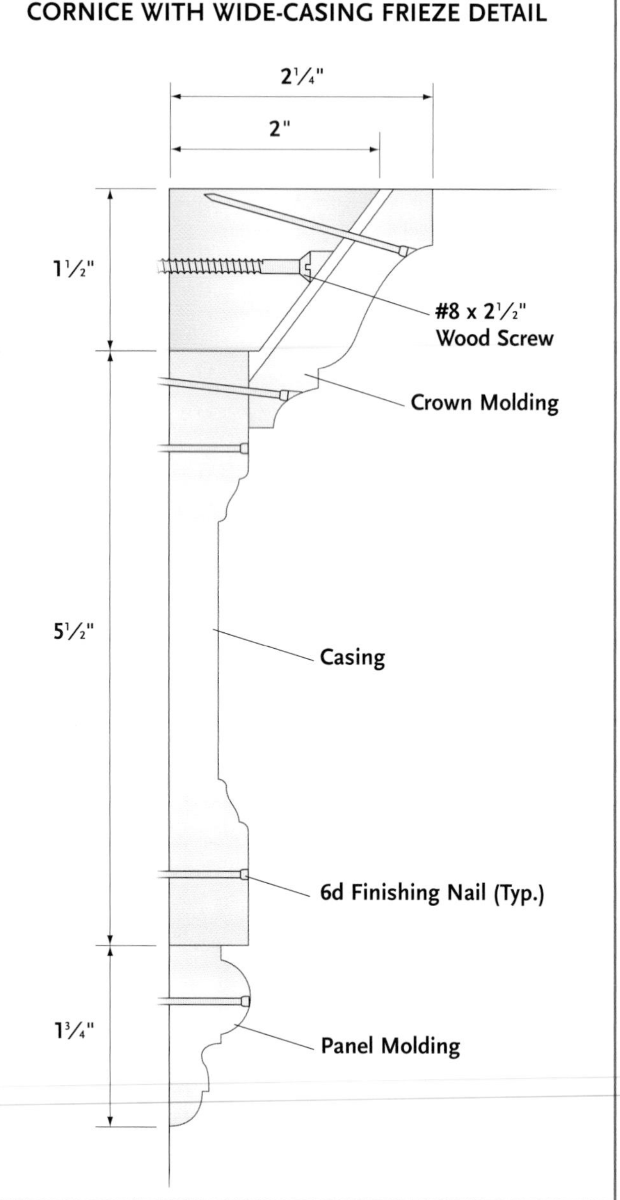

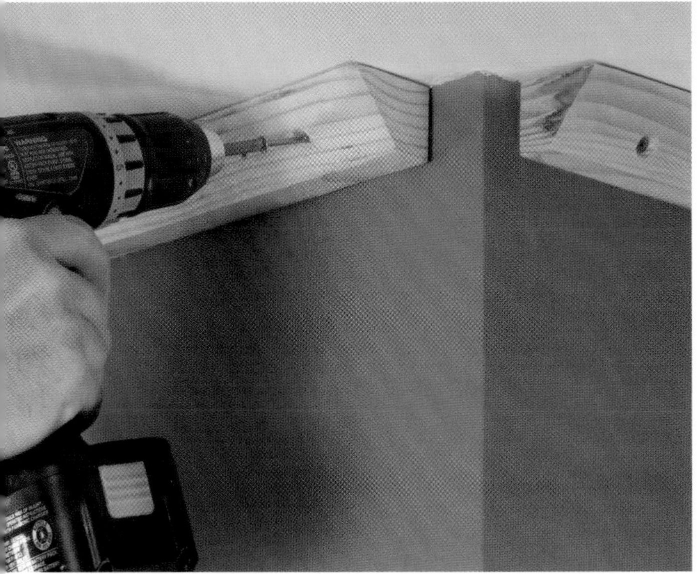

1 Rip blocking strips to an angle of 45 deg.; then drill and countersink pilot holes. Screw the strips to the top plate of the wall framing, holding the strips tight to the ceiling. If you find that the corner between the wall and ceiling is not a perfect 90-deg. angle, you may need to plane off the back corner of the blocking to get it to fit properly. Remember that the main function of these strips is to hold the nails for the crown molding, so don't be concerned with their appearance.

2 Cut a square end on a piece of frieze stock, and test its fit at the first inside corner. Because the molding is quite wide, you may find that the molding does not fit tightly along its entire end. You do not need to be overly concerned with a perfect fit, because the second piece, with a coped end, will cover the profile face and the panel molding will cover the bottom edge.

3 Set the miter saw to cut a 45-deg. bevel to expose the profile for a coped joint. Use a coping saw to cut the joint, then fine-tune the edge profile with rasps and files.

4 Test the fit of the coped joint, and note any areas that need adjustment. Normally, either a rasp or a sharp knife will be sufficient tools to make the necessary changes; it is not unusual to make several attempts before achieving a tight joint.

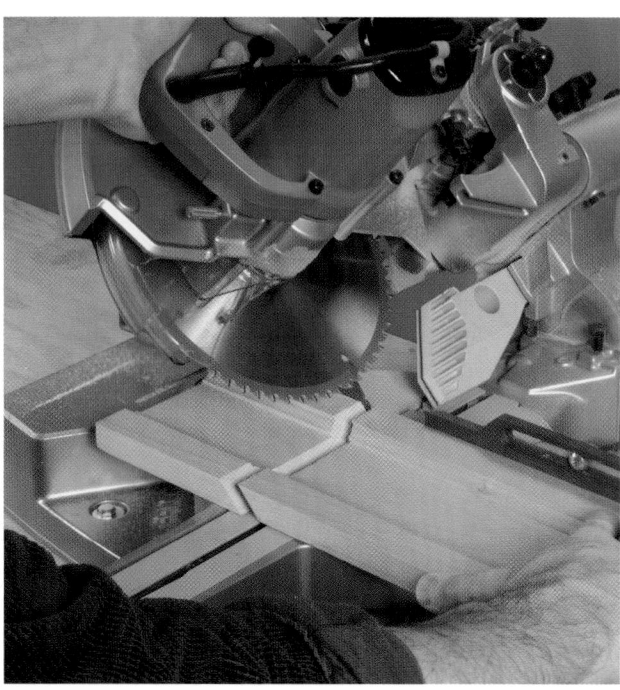

5 Hold the frieze stock in place on the wall to mark the length of pieces at an outside corner. Use the miter saw to cut a closed bevel joint on each of the pieces.

6 It can be awkward to hold two long pieces in place to test the fit of an outside bevel joint. To simplify the process, cut a short piece of the molding with an outside bevel and use it to test the fit of the joint.

9 Cut a short piece of crown molding stock, and use it as a gauge to mark the position of its bottom edge on the frieze near each corner. While the position of the molding will vary slightly along the length of a wall, the guide lines will keep you from straying too far. This is particularly important at the corners.

10 Detail of crown molding at an inside corner. Note that the first piece of crown molding butts against the face of the frieze. The blocking strip is held back to allow room for the projection of the crown.

7 Apply glue to the mating surfaces of the bevel joint; then nail the frieze stock to the wall studs and top plate. Use brads to pin the joint together.

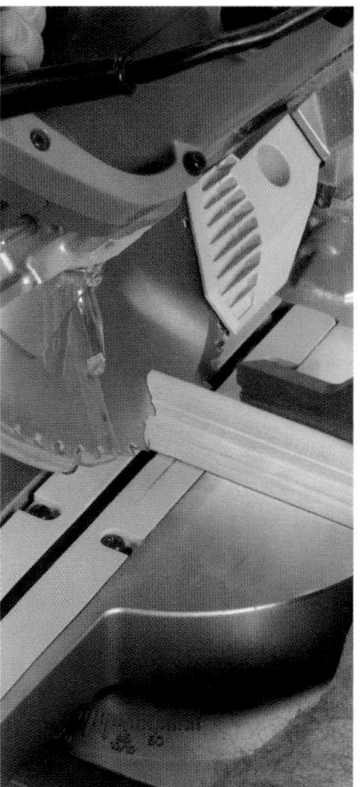

8 Set the miter saw to a bevel angle of 45 deg. (left) to cut panel molding stock for joints at inside and outside corners. Use shaped abrasive tools to fine-tune the coped profile for inside corner joints on the panel molding (right). A round rasp is perfect for shaping the large concave profile.

11 Hold the crown molding stock in place to mark its length at an outside corner. When cutting the compound angle, remember that your mark indicates the shortest point of the angle.

12 Here is the finished pine and poplar three-piece cornice.

MDF FLAT CORNICE WITH BASEBOARD AND CASING

The elegant and sophisticated appearance of this three-piece cornice would lead you to believe that its installation requires an experienced carpentry professional. However, the real story is that this assembly is quite simple, and it even makes use of a relatively inexpensive material choice—MDF moldings. The cornice shown here features a baseboard and casing profile from a supplier called Moulding & Millwork that manufactures moldings in a variety of wood species as well as in MDF. These products are widely distributed across the United States and Canada, and you should be able to access them through lumberyards and home centers. Should you wish to achieve a different look, the same design can be executed in another material. For that matter, you could take the basic concept of this cornice and substitute moldings with different profiles to personalize your installation.

The cornice design makes use of a stock baseboard molding that you apply to both the wall and ceiling. The transition between those two profiles is made by installing a molded casing over the baseboard frieze. This layered approach results in a considerable variety of shapes and surfaces that encourage light and shadow to create interesting patterns. While the cornice is probably most appropriate for a room with ceilings around 9 feet high, you could consider it for an 8-foot ceiling if the paint scheme allows the cornice to blend with the wall treatment.

When working with MDF moldings, keep in mind that the material is less resilient than solid wood. Even though it is provided with a factory-applied primer coat and seems quite tough, the surface is somewhat brittle—especially at the freshly cut edges of a joint. If you hit the molding against a sharp corner it can chip. Fortunately, as a paint-grade material, you can repair chipped or otherwise damaged areas with drywall compound or two-part fillers. On the positive side for the installer, MDF works very easily, and coped joints in particular are much easier to cut in MDF than in any wood species.

FLAT CORNICE WITH BASEBOARD AND CASING DETAIL

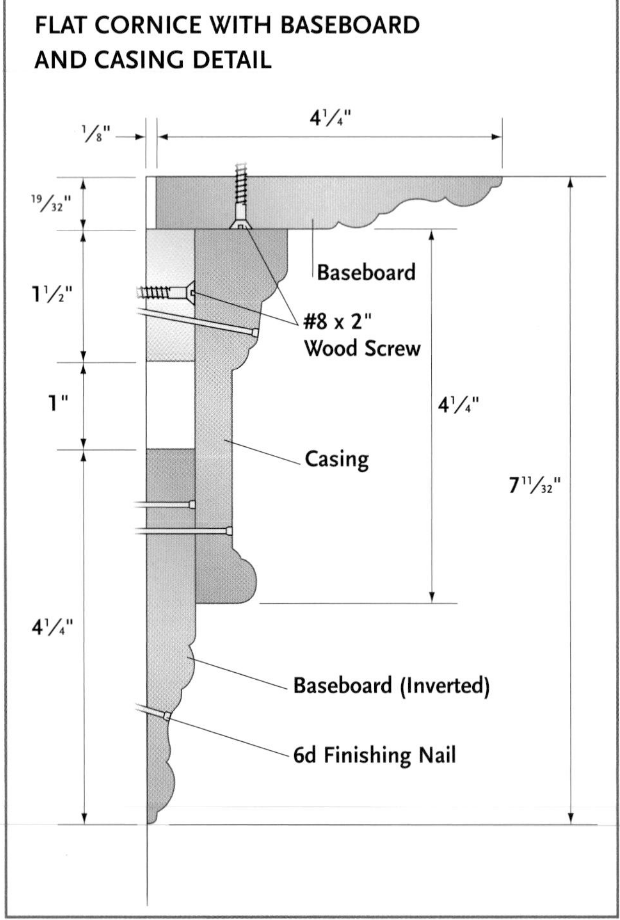

1 Start the installation process by establishing some layout lines for the ceiling and wall moldings. Cut a block of wood to a dimension of $4\frac{3}{8}$ in., and use it to mark the location of the outside edge of the ceiling molding. Place a light mark near the ends of each wall. Note that this dimension leaves a space of approximately $\frac{1}{8}$ in. between the back edge of the molding and the wall to allow for any irregularities in the surface.

2 Use a board with a straight edge as a guide to connect the gauge marks for the ceiling molding layout. You can also use a chalk line to mark the lines, but keep in mind that the chalk lines can be messy and aren't suitable for rooms that have already been painted. Repeat the layout process to establish a line for the bottom edge of the wall molding, only this time cut your gauge block to a length of $7\frac{11}{32}$ in.

3 Next, make a drawing of the room outline that you can use as a reference when cutting molding joints. Measure the actual angle measurement of each corner. Hold an adjustable angle gauge against the ceiling to get an accurate reading, and then note the measurement on your drawing. Keep in mind that irregularities in the wall surfaces can throw your readings off by a few degrees, so test-fitting of joints will still be necessary.

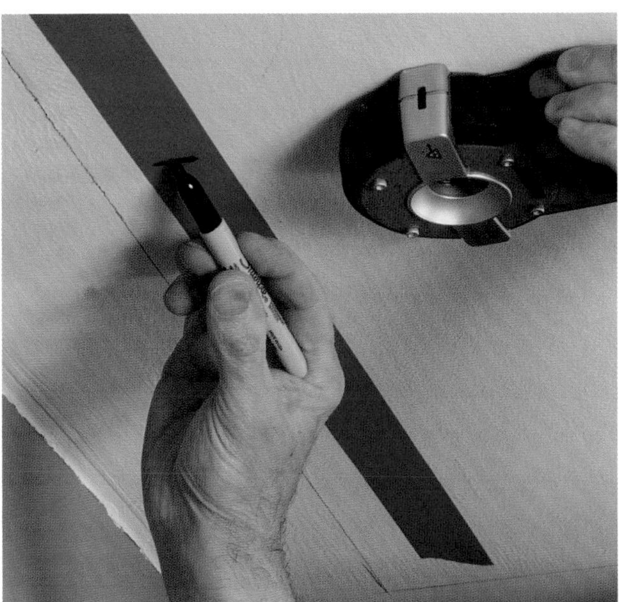

4 If you are working in a room with a finished ceiling, note the joist location on a strip of masking tape. Then use an electronic stud finder to detect the joists. Remember that the joists in most rooms run in only one direction, so expect that on some walls there may be no convenient framing in the ceiling. You may find that a joist runs within an inch or two of a parallel wall, and this can provide a spot to fasten your molding.

5 Use the sliding compound miter saw to make the miter cuts on baseboard stock for the ceiling molding. Orient the material on the saw table so that the molded edge faces out and the square edge is against the fence—this will keep any chip-out on the edge of the molding that will be hidden against the wall.

6 Whenever possible, screw the baseboard stock to the ceiling joists, but be sure to locate the screws in the area of the molding that will be covered by the casing.

7 Hold a piece of ceiling molding in place to mark the locations of the ceiling joists on the stock. Use a square to transfer the joist centers to the back edge of the molding, and then drill and countersink pilot holes for the screws.

8 In those locations where no ceiling joists are available for fastening the molding, you can install spiral anchors to accept the screws. Hold the molding in position, and drill through the pilot holes in the baseboard to mark the ceiling. Then screw the anchors into the drywall.

scarf joints in ceiling molding

IF YOUR ROOM has a wall that is longer than the available molding stock, you will need to create a joint in the ceiling molding. The preferred technique is to fashion a scarf joint for the least visible seam.

1 Cut an inside or outside miter on one end of the molding stock and an open bevel on the end to receive the scarf joint. Hold the molding in place on the ceiling to mark the locations of ceiling joists, and drill and countersink pilot holes for screws. If there are no ceiling joists where you need them, bore pilot holes and then hold the molding in place and drill through the holes to mark the locations on the ceiling. Install spiral anchors to accept the screws. Mount the piece of molding to the ceiling.

2 Measure the length of the piece required to cover the remaining part of the wall. Cut a closed bevel for the scarf joint and an inside or outside miter for the far end of the stock. Drill and countersink pilot holes for mounting the molding, and install anchors to the ceiling if necessary. Apply glue to the mating surfaces of the scarf joint, and screw the molding in place. Use brads to pin the joint together, and sand it lightly to smooth any irregularities in the transition between the two pieces.

9 Cut an inside miter on one end of a piece of baseboard stock, and then hold the molding in place against the layout line to mark the length of the outside miter on the edge of the piece.

10 For long pieces of molding, you may need to temporarily screw them to the ceiling to accurately mark the length of the miter joints. Of course, if you have a helper to hold the other end of the baseboard, you can simply hold it in place to mark the joint.

11 To provide support for the top edge of the casing, install backing strips, such as 1-by common pine. The thickness of the strips must match that of the baseboard molding that sits below it. Because the baseboard stock is $^{19}/_{32}$ in. thick and the pine strips are $^{3}/_{4}$ in. thick, you must rip them to the same thickness. Drill and countersink pilot holes for screws, and fasten the strips to the wall top plate directly below the ceiling molding.

12 Begin installing the baseboard frieze to the walls. Make a square cut on one of the pieces of stock, and butt that end to an inside corner wall to mark the back side of the outside miter joint directly on the molding. Use the sliding compound miter saw to carefully make the beveled cut for the joint. It is often best to cut the piece about $^{1}/_{8}$ in. long and then take small, incremental cuts until you reach the mark.

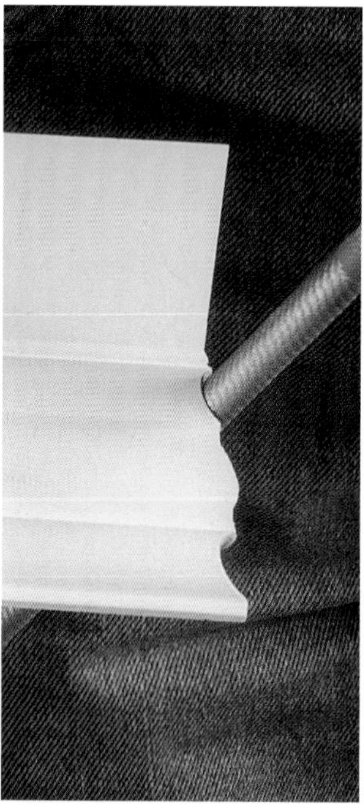

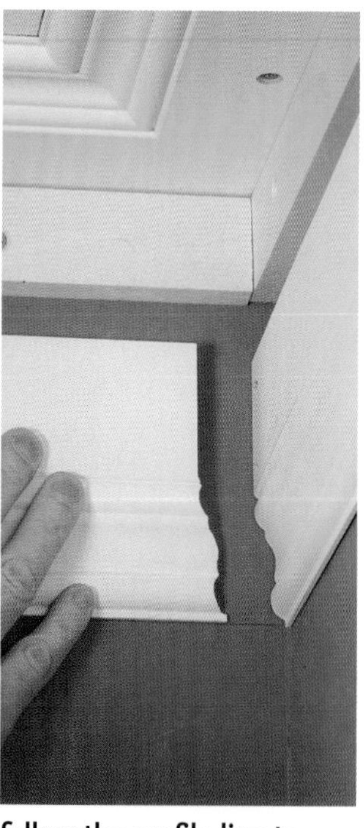

15 Use a coping saw to follow the profile line to create a coped joint. Finish trimming the joint with rasps and files (left). Test the fit of each coped joint, and note any areas that require further adjustment (right). Refine the profile with rasps and files until you are satisfied with the fit, and then install the molding.

16 Install the first piece of casing so that its top edge rests tightly against the ceiling molding. The first piece at an inside corner should butt tightly to both the frieze and spacer blocking. Cut coped and miter joints for inside and outside corners using the same techniques used for the frieze.

13 Once you are satisfied with the fit of an outside miter joint, install the molding for one side of the joint by nailing the inverted baseboard to the wall studs. Next, apply some glue to the mating surfaces of the miter joint, and nail the second piece to the wall framing. Finally, use brads to pin the joint together.

14 Set the bevel angle to 45 deg. and the miter angle to 0 deg. on the sliding compound miter saw to make the open bevel cut for a coped joint. If your saw only tilts to one side, you will need to change the orientation of the stock for joints on the opposite end of a piece of molding, placing the shaped edge against the saw fence instead of the square edge.

17 Here's a detail of a miter cut on one half of an outside corner joint. Apply glue to the mating surfaces of the joint before nailing the second piece to the wall. Use brads to pin the joint together.

18 Here is the finished three-piece MDF flat cornice with baseboard and casing profiles.

PINE CORNICE WITH PICTURE MOLDING, CHAIR RAIL, AND BASEBOARD

This three-piece molding assembly is relatively simple to install, yet it is quite substantial in appearance. Depending on the way you decide to finish it, it can be a subtle or very bold architectural detail. Even though its overall dimension is over 10 inches, it would look at home in a room with a modest ceiling height.

The moldings that make up this cornice are readily available at home centers or lumberyards, and you will most likely find them offered in clear and finger-jointed pine as well as red oak and possibly MDF.

To further increase your design options, this cornice can easily be varied by changing the spacing between the bottom edge of the inverted baseboard and picture rail. You can also finish the area between those two moldings in a variety of ways. In our example, we treated the wall surface as an extension of the frieze and painted it the same color as the molding. Alternatively, you can paint it the same color used for the rest of the wall, select a new complementary color, or apply wallpaper or fabric.

The picture-rail molding creates a strong horizontal line at the bottom of the cornice, but don't forget that it provides a functional option as well. You can purchase special hooks that engage the top edge of the molding for hanging art work.

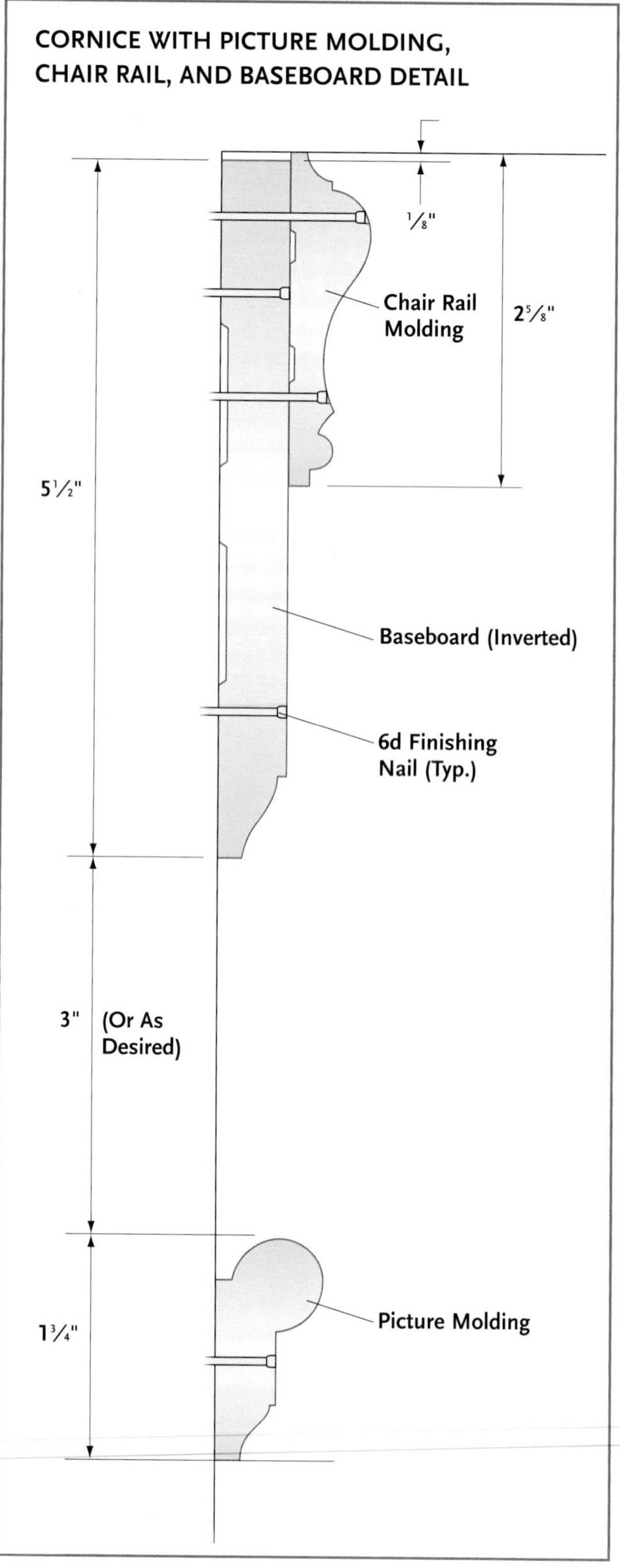

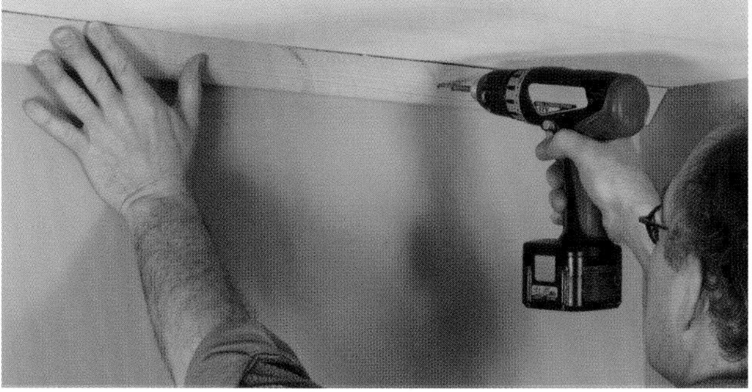

1 Using a $2^{5}/_{8}$ in. x $4^{1}/_{4}$ in. gauge, mark both wall and ceiling to indicate the edges of the cornice (top). Rip blocking from 2x4 stock to a bevel angle of 38 deg. Install the strips by screwing them to the top plate. (bottom). Leave space at inside corners for the first pieces of crown molding to extend up to the frieze.

2 Mark stud locations on the blocking strip to indicate the center of each (top). Next, cut the first piece of frieze to extend between two inside corners, and nail it in place (bottom). Whenever possible, plan the cuts on the frieze so that part of the dentil will intersect the coped corner joint rather than the space between the dentils.

3 Hold frieze stock upside down on the miter saw table. Locate the bevel cut so that it bisects one of the dentils on the molding and will therefore provide the best coverage for the adjacent profile. Use a small square block of wood as a guide to extend the line of cut from the dentil to the top edge of the molding.

4 One of the things learned by experience is pinpointing critical details. When coping this molding, stop the coped profile at the bottom edge at the point where the small bead flattens out (top). If you make a square cut at this point, the molding will butt cleanly to the adjacent piece (bottom).

5 If your room has outside corners, it is best to begin fitting the frieze there, so that the most prominent joints are balanced. Cut both pieces of frieze stock for each joint, so that the size of the exposed dentils at the corner is the same on either side of the joint.

6 Install the first piece of cove molding, letting its bottom edge rest on the dentil frieze. At an inside corner, let the cove butt tightly to the upper portion of the adjacent frieze molding.

9 Test the fit of an outside corner joint to be sure that it will close tightly, and then nail one of the pieces in place. Spread glue on the mating surfaces of the miter joint, and install the second piece of molding. Use brads to pin the miter together.

10 Cut the egg-and-dart insert to size, apply a small bead of glue, and slide it into the rabbet in the crown molding (top). Use brads to pin the carved insert to the crown molding (bottom).

7 Cut open miters to expose the profile for the coped inside corner joints, and then use a coping saw, rasps, and files to shape the joint. In those spots where the molding returns on a horizontal plane, you can cut the profile square rather than allowing a thin sliver of material to run under the adjacent profile.

8 Hold a piece of molding in place to mark the length for an outside corner joint. Make sure that the opposite end joint is tight, and then place a sharp pencil mark on the back bottom edge flush with the top portion of the frieze. Use the miter saw to carefully cut the piece to length, barely leaving the pencil line.

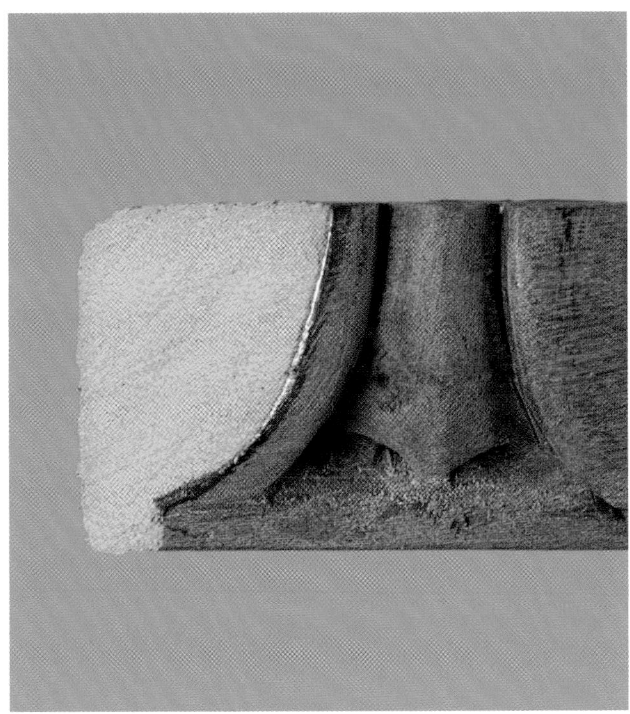

11 At inside corners, cut an open bevel to expose the profile for a coped joint. Whenever possible, locate the cut on the wide basket portion of the egg and dart so that the cope fully covers the adjacent molding.

12 Here is the completed cherry three-piece cornice with dentil frieze and egg-and-dart insert.

POPLAR CORNICE WITH LARGE COVE, FRIEZE, AND PANEL MOLDING

Here is a project that could be the crowning touch to a library, formal dining room, or elegant home office, and a perfect complement to a custom-paneled wall treatment. If you have a room with 9- or 10-foot ceilings and are looking to add a stylish and graceful cornice, this is a well-qualified candidate. All of the moldings are available as stock items in poplar from White River Hardwoods-Woodworks, Inc.

If you want to apply a stained finish to your cornice, it will be much simpler to apply the color to the molding before you begin the installation. For a very intense color, you will find that solvent or water-based dyes offer much better penetration, and deeper coloring, than oil-based products.

The installation of this cornice includes some areas that will challenge your carpentry skills. In particular, the cove molding will inevitably require some extra attention and fussing because its large scale makes the corner joints more difficult to fit; the shape and size of the profile give it a tendency to "cup" rather than staying perfectly flat on its back side. To accommodate this problem, you may need to use small shims between the molding and the miter saw table to support it while cutting. Other areas that require special attention are the corner joints of the highly detailed frieze. Because the pattern on the frieze does not include symmetrical figures, you will need to make slight adjustments in the cope profiles and decorative detailing to create tight and attractive joints.

Note: Although the cove molding in this project might appear to be symmetrical, it does have a top and bottom edge. If you study the drawing of the cornice, you will notice that the top edge of the molding is thinner than the bottom edge (1/2 inch versus 5/8 inch), which is particularly important because the panel molding has a 1/2-inch-deep rabbet that must fit over the top edge. To avoid confusion in both cutting and installation, take the time to clearly mark the edges of the molding before beginning the job.

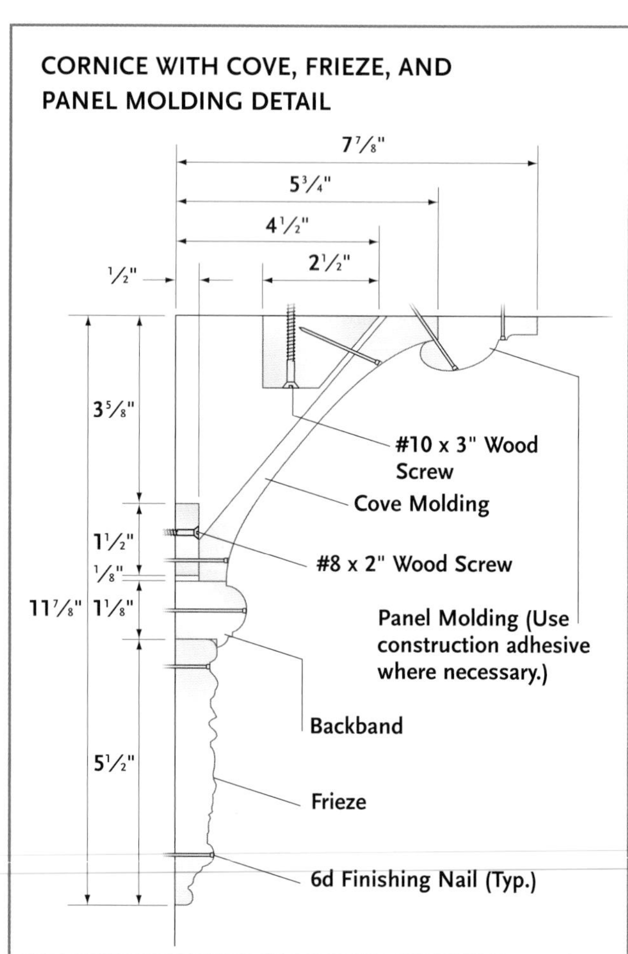

1 The entire cornice structure is supported by strips of nominal 2x2 lumber screwed to the wall studs. Mark the height of the top edge of the strips on the walls near each corner. Use a chalk line to snap lines connecting these marks. Find the centerline of each stud, and screw the strips to the wall.

2 The electrical feed for your lights can be located in many different ways. If you find that the cable enters at the height of your blocking strip, mark the location and bore a $^3/_4$-in.-diameter hole to allow it to pass through. Of course, you should always make sure that power to the electrical cables is disconnected before you begin work.

3 Rip the soffit boards from 1x6 lumber. Cut the first piece to length so that it butts tightly to the inside corners. Use a plate joiner to cut slots in the face of the board to form joints with the soffit on the adjacent walls. (See "Using Joining Plates at Soffit Joints," page 207.) Screw the first board to the blocking, spacing the screws 6 to 8 in. apart.

4 At an outside corner, the best technique for determining the length of the soffit boards is to mark them in place. Cut the boards to rough length, and temporarily screw the first board to the blocking strip. Hold the second board in place—tight to the wall—and use it as a guide to scribe the length of the first board.

installing xenon light strips

XENON LIGHTS ARE AN EXCELLENT CHOICE for cove lighting applications. Bulbs are available with an extremely long life, making them a good choice for areas that are hard to reach. Their lower operating temperatures in comparison to halogen bulbs make them a safe choice, as well.

The system used for our project is the Ambiance LX Lighting System from Sea Gull Lighting (www.SeaGullLighting.com). The basis of the system is a flexible cable that mounts in a plastic track. Individual lampholders snap onto the track at intervals as close as 2 inches. Lamps are available in a variety of intensities, and you can adjust the illumination to almost any situation. You can also install a dimmer to provide even greater control over the lighting. As a low-voltage system, a transformer is required, and a number of models are offered with different power ratings.

Always consult with an electrician or electrical supply house when planning your system to be sure that your design is safe, with adequate transformers for the number of lights you require—300 watts per run is the maximum recommended load for a 12V system.

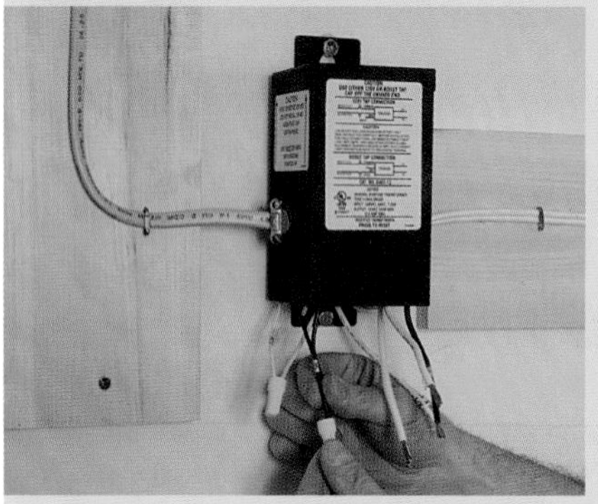

1 **Install transformers vertically in an area with good air circulation. A normal 120V supply line is connected to one set of leads and the low-voltage cable is connected to the second set of leads.**

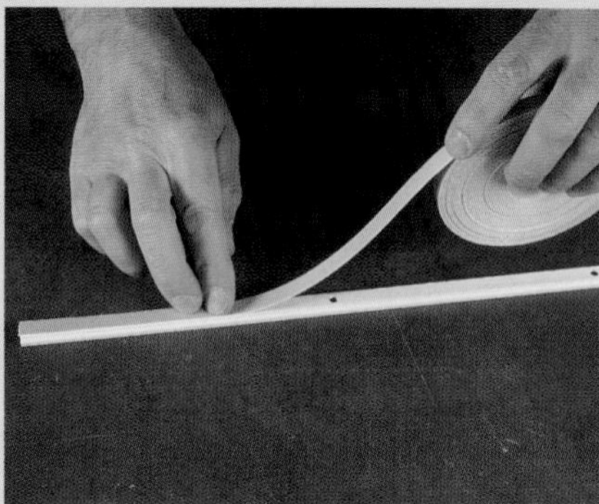

2 **The plastic track comes in 4-ft. sections and can be easily cut. You can screw the track to the soffit with small screws, but it is much simpler to use a double-sided adhesive tape that comes in the kit. Press the tape onto the bottom of the track, and then remove the paper backer and adhere the track firmly to the soffit.**

3 **The low-voltage cable is extremely soft and flexible; simply press it into the track. You can easily bend the cable around corners. Track covers are available for use on non-illuminated sections of the cable; as an alternative, standard electrical conduit can be used to protect the cable.**

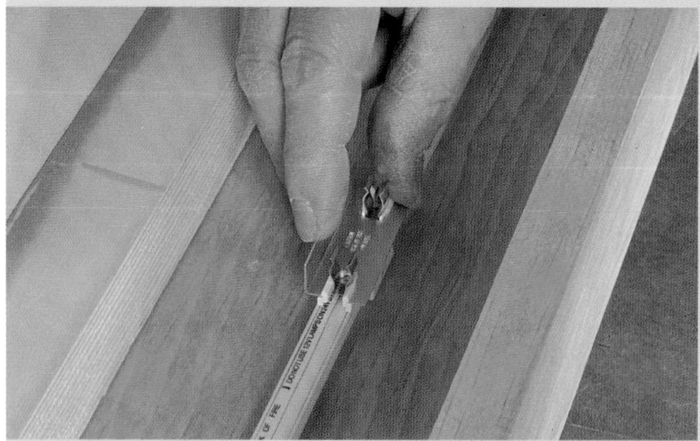

4 **Push down on the lampholders to snap them onto the track. Each holder has small prongs on the bottom that puncture the cable to make the electrical connection.**

5 **The lampholders accept festoon lamps that easily snap into clips at both ends. Lamps are available in both 5- and 10-watt ratings.**

5 Temporarily screw the second board in place at the outside corner; then clamp a straight piece of scrap lumber flush to the outside edge of the adjacent soffit board. Use this as a guide to mark the length of the soffit. Remove it and cut it to length.

6 Cut matching joining plate slots in the mating surfaces of the soffit boards at an outside corner. Screw the first board in place; then spread a light coating of glue in both slots and also on the joining plate. Assemble the joint, and screw the second soffit board to the blocking strip.

7 To further strengthen the joints between adjacent soffit boards, toenail 4d finishing nails to fasten the outer edges of the boards together. Use a nail set to drive the nails flush with the edge of the board.

8 Simple butt joints are fine at the inside corners of the 1x4 fascia boards. However, to keep the joints tight, bore pilot holes for screws in the first piece of fascia at a corner. Position the first piece of fascia so that it drops ¼ in. below the soffit, and then nail it to the soffit edge.

9 Install the second fascia board at an inside corner; then use a stubby screwdriver to drive the screws to fasten the corner joint. Because the pine boards are so soft, you do not need to drill pilot holes into the end grain.

10 Cut outside bevel joints on fascia stock for any outside corners in the room. Apply glue to the joint surfaces, and then nail the joint together.

13 As with any other molding, it is best to mark the length of the cove profile at an outside corner by holding it in place and directly scribing along the wall.

14 Nail the cove molding to both the soffit boards and wall studs. You can use either 4d finishing nails or $1\frac{1}{2}$-in. brads. Because the molding is quite small, it will easily conform to minor irregularities in the wall surface, covering any gaps between the soffit and the wall.

11 Begin installing the chair-rail molding by cutting square ends on the stock to butt against the fascia at an inside corner. Use 1-in.-long brads to fasten the molding to the fascia.

12 Cut coped joints in chair-rail stock at inside corners and bevel joints at outside corners. Because the molding is a flat profile and the material is soft, cutting the joints is not difficult.

15 Here is the finished cornice with indirect lighting.

PINE CORNICE WITH SOFFIT

A built-up cornice provides much more than a simple transition between the walls and ceiling in a room: It presents an elegant focal point that draws your attention and is suggestive of tradition and elegance. More than most other usual trim items, a complex cornice assembly can create a very particular sense of style.

This project combines common millwork elements into a substantial and stylish design. By adding a soffit, a flat horizontal element, to the assembly, the cornice is extended away from the walls, toward the center of the room. While the overall assembly has a relatively complex configuration, the individual elements are simple, and the installation process is not much more difficult than for a simple cornice design. By following a planned, methodical approach, even a novice do-it-yourself carpenter can execute this design.

All of the molding profiles and 1-by lumber are carried as stock items at any home center or lumberyard, in a variety of materials. If you use clear pine stock for the cornice, you have the option of applying a clear or stained finish. For a paint-grade finish, you could substitute either finger-jointed pine or MDF stock. If you plan to create the same cornice design in red oak, you will have no trouble finding the necessary elements in that species. Of course, materials in other hardwood species would need to be obtained through special order.

If you already have some experience in cornice construction, you can think about modifying the design to reflect your own taste. With so many possible combinations of stock moldings and standard trim lumber, you can always add a personal detail to a cornice design. Simple changes, such as varying the spacing of elements, extending or shortening a soffit or frieze, or changing a molding profile, can be very effective ways to customize your cornice. If you are planning to make changes to this or another design, consider assembling a small sample cornice—18 to 24 inches long—to make sure that you will be happy with all of the elements and proportions. As an alternative, you can draw a full-size cross section of the cornice to get an idea of the overall appearance.

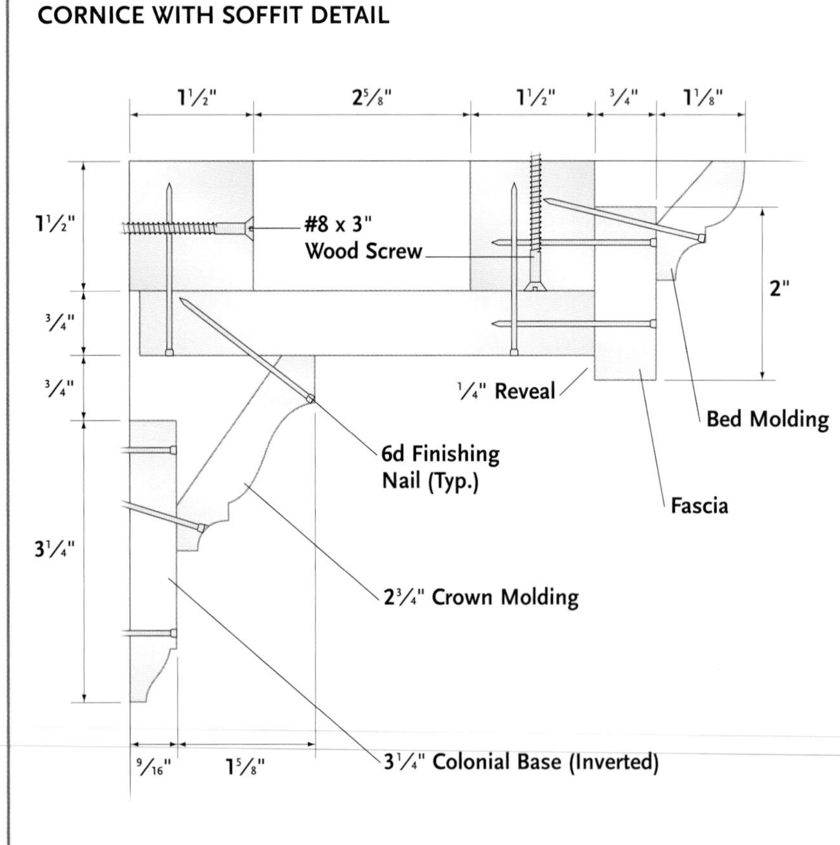

1 Careful layout is an important element for success of this installation. Place marks on the ceiling near each room corner to indicate the position of the outer edge of the soffit board. Connect those points. Rip blocking strips from 2x4 lumber to a dimension of 1½ x 1½ in., and attach them to the wall.

2 Mount blocking strips to the ceiling with their outer edges aligned with the previously marked chalk line. Where possible, drive screws into ceiling joists; where there are no joists, install hollow-wall anchors.

using joining plates at soffit joints

TO RESIST MINOR MOVEMENTS, you can provide a positive connection at these joints. Installing a joining plate between adjacent soffit members is a simple and quick way to ensure a tight and smooth joint.

A plate joiner is an extremely handy tool for those who wish to become involved in cabinetmaking or general woodworking. These tools can be found in a wide range of prices, with models appropriate for use by professionals and others suited for strictly amateur pursuits. If you see no need to add another tool to your collection, most rental centers offer these tools on a daily or hourly basis.

1 Cut 1x6 to length for the soffits. Mark the center of the board's width. Hold both the board and plate joiner tight to the flat tabletop while you cut the groove.

2 Cut a matching groove in the adjacent soffit board. After cutting both grooves, nail one of the soffit boards to the blocking strips; spread glue in the grooves.

3 Spread a light coating of glue on both sides of the joining plate. Connect the two boards, holding the second soffit board tightly in place while nailing.

3 Cut 1x6 stock to length, and nail it to the 2x2 strips to form the soffit. Keep the edge flush with the edge of the outer blocking strip. While simple butt joints are perfectly acceptable between adjacent soffit pieces, you can use joining plates to help ensure that the joints stay perfectly aligned.

4 Place marks on the walls near each corner and at 3- or 4-ft. intervals to indicate the bottom edge of the frieze. Begin at an inside corner. Cut the baseboard molding to length so that it butts tightly to the walls at both ends and is aligned with the previously established guide marks. Nail the molding to the wall studs.

7 Rip fascia boards from 1x6 lumber to a width of 2 in. Mount the fascia so that it extends below the soffit by ¼ in. Nail it to both the blocking strip and front edge of the soffit board. Use simple butt joints at inside corners.

8 Cut bevel joints on the fascia stock at all outside corners.

5 Cut coped joints at all inside corners, proceeding around the room installing the frieze molding. If your room has one or more outside corners, it is usually best to install those pieces last; that way you can usually avoid having pieces that require coped joints on both ends.

6 Cut a short piece of crown molding to use as a gauge to mark every 3 or 4 ft. along every wall. Without these points of reference, it is possible to twist the molding, resulting in problems when fitting the corner joints. Use the coping saw and rasps to shape the joints. Attach the crown molding to the frieze and the soffit.

9 Install the bed molding to bridge the space between the fascia and the ceiling. Use the traditional techniques of coped joints at inside corners and miter joints at outside corners. Because the molding is quite small, it is only necessary to nail it to the fascia, so you don't need to worry about locating the ceiling joists.

10 Here is the finished five-piece pine cornice.

PINE 5-PIECE COMPOUND CORNICE

This compound cornice design is an assembly of simple and widely available parts. And, while it extends more than 7 inches down the wall and 5 inches along the ceiling, it hugs those surfaces quite closely and is not particularly imposing; as a result you can use it in a room with modest ceiling height. This is strictly a paint-grade assembly, mixing moldings of various materials, so it makes the most economical use of the different profiles. The casing and base cap moldings are finger-jointed pine, the crown molding is MDF, and the small soffit is 1x4 clear pine; all materials are stock items at home centers.

While the individual elements of this cornice are not complex, a successful installation will require considerable care and attention to detail. You will find that all of the normal joinery techniques for moldings are incorporated into the design—inside and outside miters, and coped joints on both flat and sprung moldings. The 1x4 soffit serves double duty, as both a design element and a nailing backer for the top edge of the crown molding; but you will need to install a simple, flat blocking strip to provide support and catch the nails for the bottom edge of the molding.

When working with the MDF crown molding, you should be aware that the material is quite soft and it can be damaged easily. So take extra care when cutting the corner joints and also when nailing it. The finished surface has a tendency to pucker around the heads of gun nails. This can be avoided if you hold the nail gun perpendicular to the face of the molding.

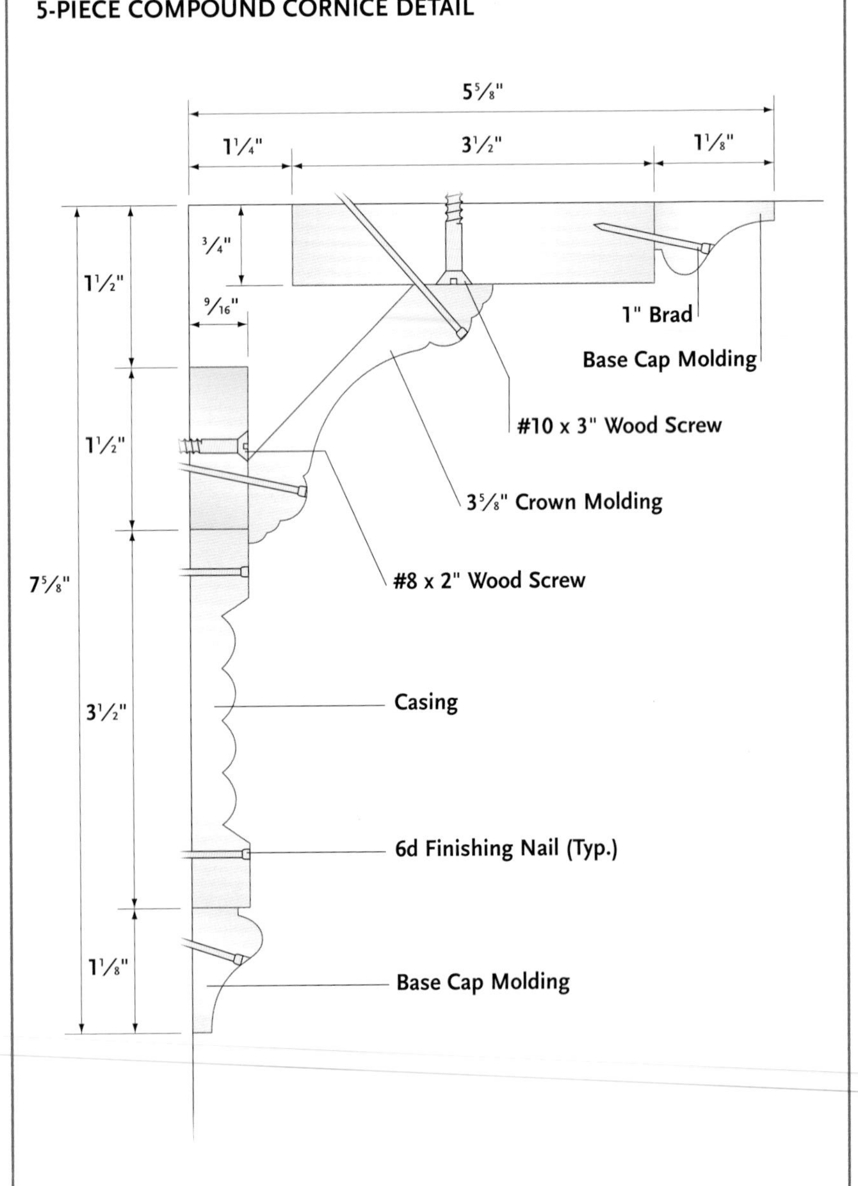

Skill 2: Subtracting From 1, 2, and 3

Directions: For each story, draw a picture and write a number sentence.

Example:
Brooke had 3 cat books.
She gave 2 to her friend.
Now, she has 1 book.

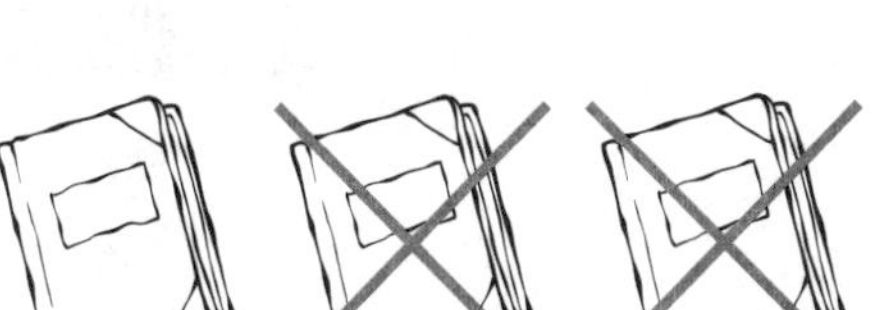

3 − 2 = 1 books

Tyler had 2 truck books.
He lost 1. Now, he has 1 book.

______ = ____ books

Lee had 2 joke books.
She gave 2 to her brother.
Now, she has 0 books.

______ = ____ books

Dan had 3 insect books.
His dog chewed up 2.
Now, he has 1 book.

______ = ____ books

MATH

Skill 3: Adding to 4 and 5

Directions: Add.

2 + 3 = ___5___

$$\begin{array}{r} 2 \\ +\ 3 \\ \hline 5 \end{array}$$

1 + 3 = ______

$$\begin{array}{r} 1 \\ +\ 3 \\ \hline \end{array}$$

3 + 2 = ______

$$\begin{array}{r} 3 \\ +\ 2 \\ \hline \end{array}$$

3 + 1 = ______

$$\begin{array}{r} 3 \\ +\ 1 \\ \hline \end{array}$$

2 + 2 = ______

$$\begin{array}{r} 2 \\ +\ 2 \\ \hline \end{array}$$

0 + 4 = ______

$$\begin{array}{r} 0 \\ +\ 4 \\ \hline \end{array}$$

4 + 0 = ______

$$\begin{array}{r} 4 \\ +\ 0 \\ \hline \end{array}$$

5 + 0 = ______

$$\begin{array}{r} 5 \\ +\ 0 \\ \hline \end{array}$$

4 + 1 = ______

$$\begin{array}{r} 4 \\ +\ 1 \\ \hline \end{array}$$

0 + 5 = ______

$$\begin{array}{r} 0 \\ +\ 5 \\ \hline \end{array}$$

1 + 4 = ______

$$\begin{array}{r} 1 \\ +\ 4 \\ \hline \end{array}$$

MATH

Skill 3: Adding to 4 and 5

Directions: For each story, draw a picture. Write the answer on the line.

Alvin has 2 aunts.
He also has 3 uncles.
How many aunts and uncles does Alvin have in all?

_____ aunts and uncles

Ben has 2 grandmas.
He also has 2 grandpas.
How many grandparents does Ben have in all?

_____ grandparents

Lily has 3 boy cousins.
She also has 2 girl cousins.
How many cousins does Lily have in all?

_____ cousins

Owen has 2 brothers.
He also has 2 sisters.
How many brothers and sisters does Owen have in all?

_____ brothers and sisters

MATH

Skill 4: Adding to 6

Directions: Add.

4 + 2 = ___6___ | 4 + 2 = 6

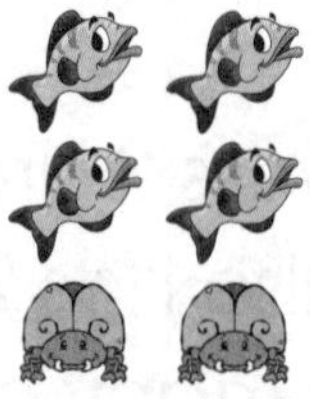

6 + 0 = ______ | 6 + 0

2 + 4 = ______ | 2 + 4

0 + 6 = ______ | 0 + 6

5 + 1 = ______ | 5 + 1

3 + 3 = ______ | 3 + 3

1 + 5 = ______ | 1 + 5

Directions: Draw a picture to show each number sentence.

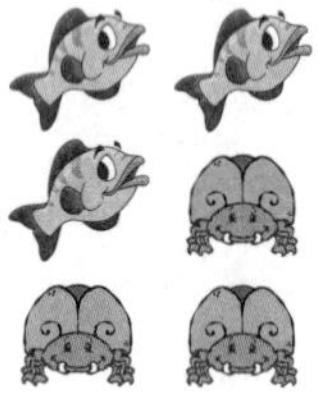

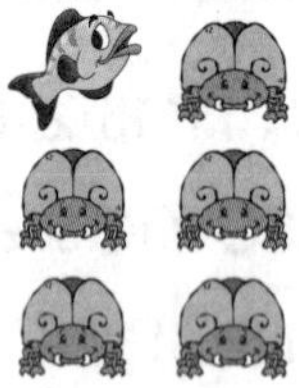

2 + 4 = ______

1 + 5 = ______

Skill 4: Adding to 6

Directions: For each story, draw a picture. Write the answer on the line.

Alicia ate 3 chocolate chip cookies and 3 peanut butter cookies. How many cookies did Alicia eat in all?

_____ cookies

Gavin bought 2 packs of strawberry gum and 4 packs of apple gum. How many packs of gum does Gavin have in all?

_____ packs of gum

In the pond, 5 turtles and 1 duck are swimming. How many animals are swimming in the pond in all?

_____ animals

Jill has 4 pink flowers and 2 red flowers in a vase. How many flowers does Jill have in the vase in all?

_____ flowers

MATH

Skill 5: Subtracting From 4 and 5

Directions: Subtract.

5 – 2 = ________

$$\begin{array}{r} 5 \\ -\ 2 \\ \hline \end{array}$$

4 – 2 = ________

$$\begin{array}{r} 4 \\ -\ 2 \\ \hline \end{array}$$

4 – 4 = ________

$$\begin{array}{r} 4 \\ -\ 4 \\ \hline \end{array}$$

5 – 0 = ________

$$\begin{array}{r} 5 \\ -\ 0 \\ \hline \end{array}$$

5 – 1 = ________

$$\begin{array}{r} 5 \\ -\ 1 \\ \hline \end{array}$$

4 – 1 = ________

$$\begin{array}{r} 4 \\ -\ 1 \\ \hline \end{array}$$

Skill 5: Subtracting From 4 and 5

Directions: For each story, draw a picture and write a number sentence.

Jayla had 5 flies.
Then, 1 flew away.
How many flies were left?

______________ = _____ flies

Sally had 5 butterflies.
Then, 4 fluttered away.
How many butterflies were left?

______________ = _____ butterfly

Greg had 4 bees.
Then, 3 went back to the hive. How many bees were left?

______________ = _____ bees

Penny had 4 caterpillars.
Then, 2 crawled away.
How many caterpillars were left?

______________ = _____ caterpillars

MATH

Skill 6: Subtracting From 6

Directions: Subtract.

6 − 4 = __________

$$\begin{array}{r} 6 \\ -\ 4 \\ \hline \end{array}$$

6 − 0 = __________

$$\begin{array}{r} 6 \\ -\ 0 \\ \hline \end{array}$$

6 − 1 = __________

$$\begin{array}{r} 6 \\ -\ 1 \\ \hline \end{array}$$

6 − 2 = __________

$$\begin{array}{r} 6 \\ -\ 2 \\ \hline \end{array}$$

6 − 3 = __________

$$\begin{array}{r} 6 \\ -\ 3 \\ \hline \end{array}$$

6 − 5 = __________

$$\begin{array}{r} 6 \\ -\ 5 \\ \hline \end{array}$$

Skill 6: Subtracting From 6

Directions: For each number sentence, write a "taking from" story.

Example:

6 − 4 = 2 I had 6 computer games. I gave my friend 2 games. Now, I have 4 computer games.

6 − 5 = 1 ______________________________

6 − 3 = 3 ______________________________

6 − 0 = 6 ______________________________

MATH

Skill 7: Fact Families 0 Through 6

A **fact family** is a group of related addition and subtraction facts made from the same numbers.

Directions: Add or subtract.

$$\begin{array}{r} 2 \\ +\,3 \\ \hline \end{array} \quad \begin{array}{r} 3 \\ +\,2 \\ \hline \end{array} \quad \begin{array}{r} 5 \\ -\,2 \\ \hline \end{array} \quad \begin{array}{r} 5 \\ -\,3 \\ \hline \end{array}$$

$$\begin{array}{r} 5 \\ +\,1 \\ \hline \end{array} \quad \begin{array}{r} 1 \\ +\,5 \\ \hline \end{array} \quad \begin{array}{r} 6 \\ -\,5 \\ \hline \end{array} \quad \begin{array}{r} 6 \\ -\,1 \\ \hline \end{array}$$

3 + 1 = ______

1 + 3 = ______

4 − 3 = ______

4 − 1 = ______

3 + 3 = ______

6 − 3 = ______

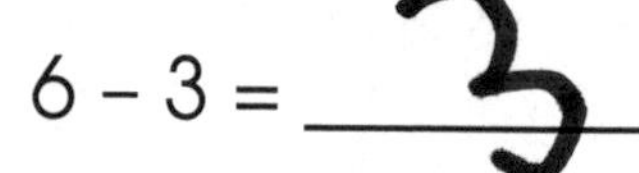

MATH

Skill 7: Fact Families 0 Through 6

Directions: Add or subtract.

$\begin{array}{r} 1 \\ +\ 2 \\ \hline \end{array}$ $\begin{array}{r} 2 \\ +\ 1 \\ \hline \end{array}$ $\begin{array}{r} 3 \\ -\ 1 \\ \hline \end{array}$ $\begin{array}{r} 3 \\ -\ 2 \\ \hline \end{array}$

$\begin{array}{r} 4 \\ +\ 0 \\ \hline \end{array}$ $\begin{array}{r} 0 \\ +\ 4 \\ \hline \end{array}$ $\begin{array}{r} 4 \\ -\ 4 \\ \hline \end{array}$ $\begin{array}{r} 4 \\ -\ 0 \\ \hline \end{array}$

$\begin{array}{r} 2 \\ +\ 2 \\ \hline \end{array}$ $\begin{array}{r} 4 \\ -\ 2 \\ \hline \end{array}$

$\begin{array}{r} 4 \\ +\ 1 \\ \hline \end{array}$ $\begin{array}{r} 1 \\ +\ 4 \\ \hline \end{array}$ $\begin{array}{r} 5 \\ -\ 4 \\ \hline \end{array}$ $\begin{array}{r} 5 \\ -\ 1 \\ \hline \end{array}$

MATH

Skill

8: Adding to 7 and 8

Directions: Add.

5 + 2 = ______

5
+ 2

6 + 2 = ______

6
+ 2

2 + 5 = ______

2
+ 5

2 + 6 = ______

2
+ 6

1 + 7 = ______

1
+ 7

7 + 0 = ______

7
+ 0

7 + 1 = ______

7
+ 1

0 + 7 = ______

0
+ 7

MATH

Skill 8: Adding to 7 and 8

Directions: For each story, draw a picture and write a number sentence.

Example:

Brad had 3 balloons.
His mom got him 4 more.
Now, he has 7 balloons.

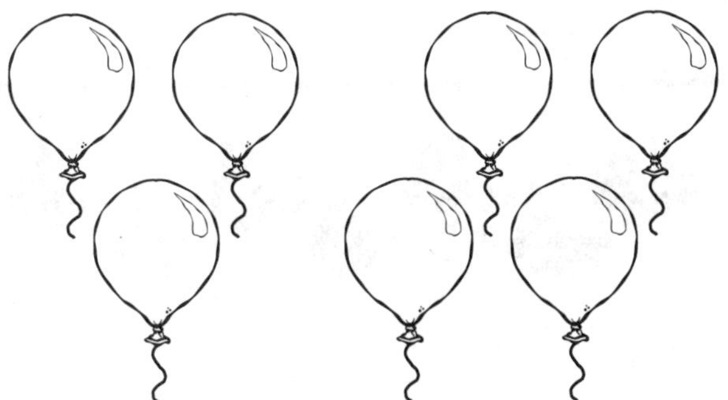

3 + 4 = 7 balloons

Tia had 4 balloons.
She blew up 4 more.
Now, she has 8 balloons.

__________ = _____ balloons

Zeb had 3 balloons.
His sister gave him 5 more.
Now, he has 8 balloons.

__________ = _____ balloons

Rose had 1 balloon.
Her dad gave her 6 more.
Now, she has 7 balloons.

__________ = _____ balloons

Skill 9: Subtracting From 7 and 8

Directions: Subtract.

7 – 3 = ________ $\begin{array}{r} 7 \\ -\ 3 \\ \hline \end{array}$

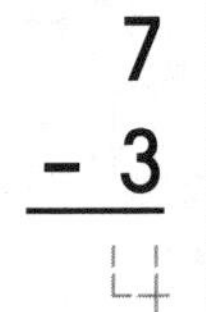

8 – 1 = ________ $\begin{array}{r} 8 \\ -\ 1 \\ \hline \end{array}$

8 – 5 = ________ $\begin{array}{r} 8 \\ -\ 5 \\ \hline \end{array}$

7 – 0 = ________ $\begin{array}{r} 7 \\ -\ 0 \\ \hline \end{array}$

7 – 6 = ________ $\begin{array}{r} 7 \\ -\ 6 \\ \hline \end{array}$

8 – 4 = ________ $\begin{array}{r} 8 \\ -\ 4 \\ \hline \end{array}$

8 – 2 = ________ $\begin{array}{r} 8 \\ -\ 2 \\ \hline \end{array}$

7 – 7 = ________ $\begin{array}{r} 7 \\ -\ 7 \\ \hline \end{array}$

Skill 9: Subtracting From 7 and 8

Directions: For each story, draw a picture and write a number sentence.

Jenna had 7 books.
She gave 2 away.
How many books were left?

_____________ = _____ books

Andy had 8 stuffed bears.
He gave 4 to his sister.
How many stuffed bears were left?

_____________ = _____ stuffed bears

Jack had 8 hats.
He lost 3 hats.
How many hats were left?

_____________ = _____ hats

Pedro had 7 plates.
He broke 4.
How many plates were left?

_____________ = _____ plates

Skill 10: Adding to 9 and 10

Directions: Add.

3 + 6 = 9

$$\begin{array}{r} 3 \\ +\ 6 \\ \hline 9 \end{array}$$

9 + 0 = ______

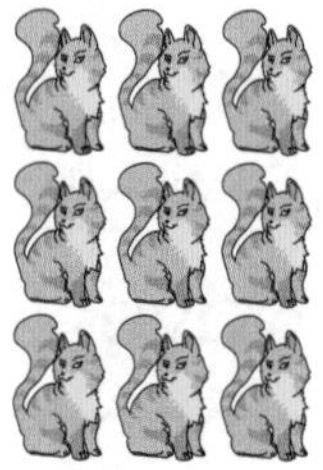

$$\begin{array}{r} 9 \\ +\ 0 \\ \hline \end{array}$$

6 + 3 = ______

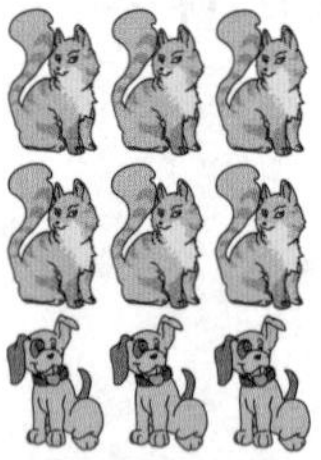

$$\begin{array}{r} 6 \\ +\ 3 \\ \hline \end{array}$$

0 + 9 = ______

$$\begin{array}{r} 0 \\ +\ 9 \\ \hline \end{array}$$

1 + 9 = ______

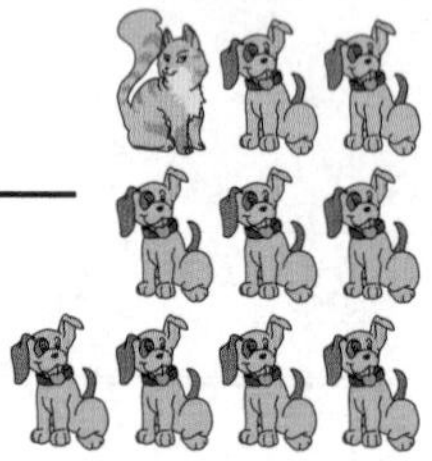

$$\begin{array}{r} 1 \\ +\ 9 \\ \hline \end{array}$$

3 + 7 = ______

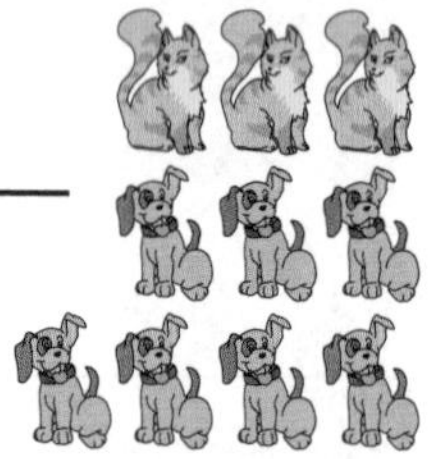

$$\begin{array}{r} 3 \\ +\ 7 \\ \hline \end{array}$$

9 + 1 = ______

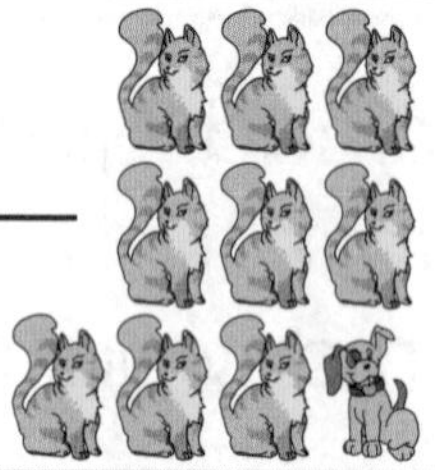

$$\begin{array}{r} 9 \\ +\ 1 \\ \hline \end{array}$$

7 + 3 = ______

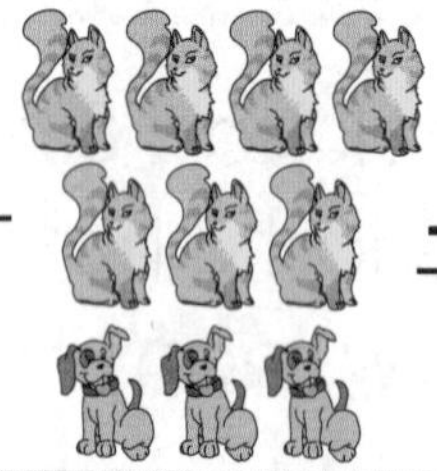

$$\begin{array}{r} 7 \\ +\ 3 \\ \hline \end{array}$$

5 + 4 = ______

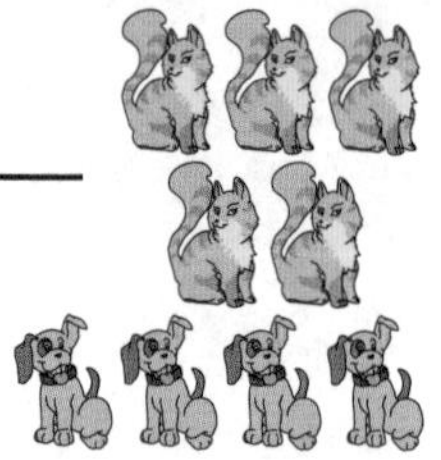

$$\begin{array}{r} 5 \\ +\ 4 \\ \hline \end{array}$$

7 + 2 = ______

$$\begin{array}{r} 7 \\ +\ 2 \\ \hline \end{array}$$

4 + 5 = ______

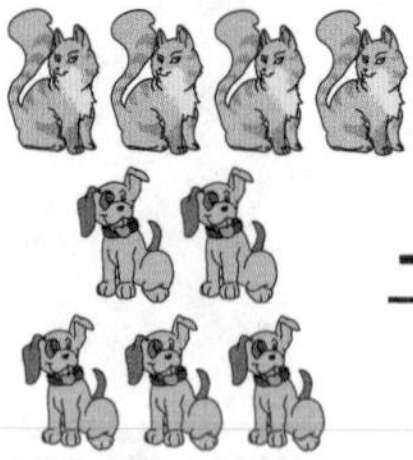

$$\begin{array}{r} 4 \\ +\ 5 \\ \hline \end{array}$$

2 + 7 = ______

$$\begin{array}{r} 2 \\ +\ 7 \\ \hline \end{array}$$

Skill 10: Adding to 9 and 10

Directions: For each number sentence, write an "adding to" story.

Example:

5 + 5 = 10 I had 5 purple markers. My friend gave me 5 more. Now, I have 10 purple markers.

4 + 5 = 9 ______

7 + 3 = 10 ______

5 + 4 = 9 ______

MATH

Skill 11: Subtracting From 9 and 10

Directions: Subtract.

9 – 7 = 2

$$\begin{array}{r} 9 \\ -\ 7 \\ \hline 2 \end{array}$$

10 – 3 = ________

$$\begin{array}{r} 10 \\ -\ 3 \\ \hline \end{array}$$

10 – 5 = ________

$$\begin{array}{r} 10 \\ -\ 5 \\ \hline \end{array}$$

9 – 1 = ________

$$\begin{array}{r} 9 \\ -\ 1 \\ \hline \end{array}$$

9 – 2 = ________

$$\begin{array}{r} 9 \\ -\ 2 \\ \hline \end{array}$$

10 – 4 = ________

$$\begin{array}{r} 10 \\ -\ 4 \\ \hline \end{array}$$

Skill 11: Subtracting From 9 and 10

Directions: Subtract.

10 − 6 = 4

$$\begin{array}{r} 10 \\ -\ 6 \\ \hline 4 \end{array}$$

9 − 5 = ______

$$\begin{array}{r} 9 \\ -\ 5 \\ \hline \end{array}$$

9 − 3 = ______

$$\begin{array}{r} 9 \\ -\ 3 \\ \hline \end{array}$$

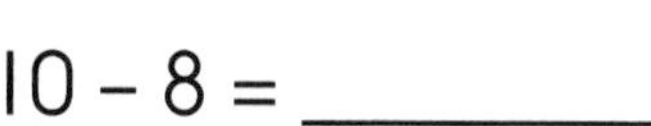

10 − 8 = ______

$$\begin{array}{r} 10 \\ -\ 8 \\ \hline \end{array}$$

10 − 1 = ______

$$\begin{array}{r} 10 \\ -\ 1 \\ \hline \end{array}$$

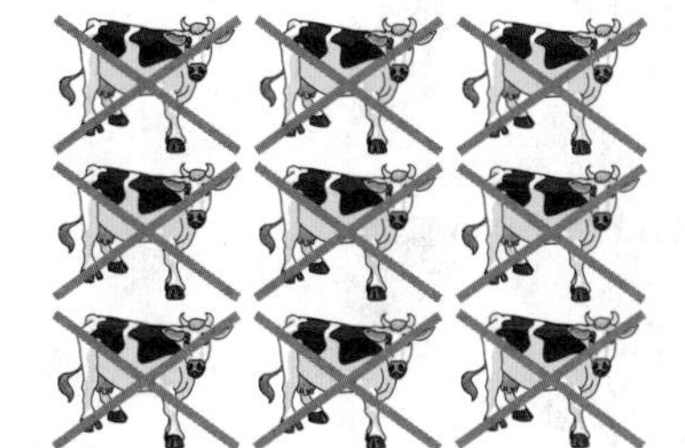

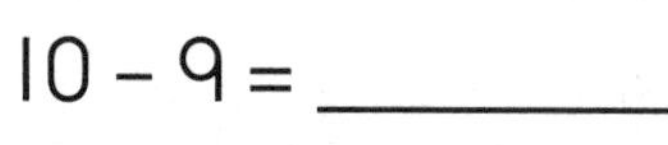

10 − 9 = ______

$$\begin{array}{r} 10 \\ -\ 9 \\ \hline \end{array}$$

MATH

Skill 12: Fact Families 7 Through 10

A **fact family** is a group of related addition and subtraction facts made from the same numbers.

Directions: Add or subtract.

4	5	9	9
+ 5	+ 4	− 4	− 5
9	9	5	4

3	7	10	10
+ 7	+ 3	− 3	− 7

5 + 2 = ________

2 + 5 = ________

7 − 5 = ________

7 − 2 = ________

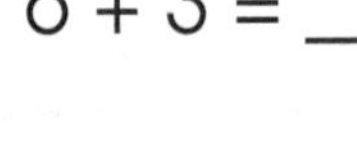

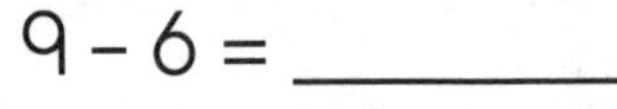

6 + 3 = ________

3 + 6 = ________

9 − 6 = ________

9 − 3 = ________

MATH

Skill 12: Fact Families 7 Through 10

Directions: Add or subtract.

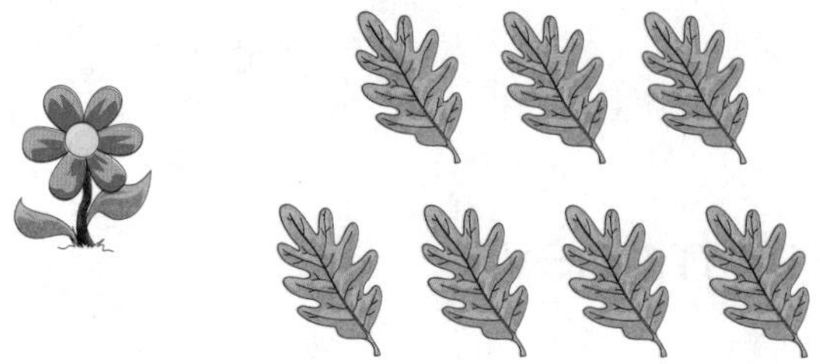

1	7	8	8
+ 7	+ 1	- 1	- 7

5	10
+ 5	- 5

4	3	7	7
+ 3	+ 4	- 4	- 3

2	6	8	8
+ 6	+ 2	- 2	- 6

MATH

Skill 13: Adding and Subtracting With Money

I penny	I nickel	I dime

1¢	5¢	10¢

Directions: Add and write how much money.

1+1+5 ___7___ ¢

___8___ ¢

___30___ ¢

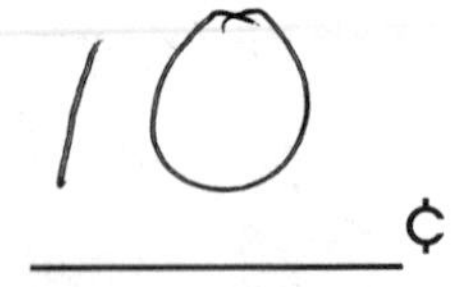

_______ ¢

_______ ¢

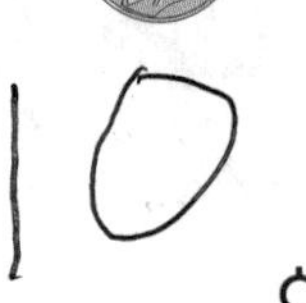

_______ ¢

_______ ¢

_______ ¢

Skill 13: Adding and Subtracting With Money

Directions: Solve each problem.

Maria has 10¢.

She buys for 3¢.

How much money does she have left? ___7___¢

$$\begin{array}{r} 10 \\ -\ 3 \\ \hline 7 \end{array}$$

Sonia has 3¢.

She finds 5¢.

How much money does she have? ________¢

Ines buys  for 6¢.

She buys  for 4¢.

How much money did she spend? ________¢

Victor has 7¢.

He buys for 6¢.

How much money does he have left? ________¢

Elaine has 10¢.

She gives 4¢ to Maxine.

How much money does Elaine have left? ________¢

Skill 14: More- and Less-Than Facts Through 10

Directions: Add to find more than. Subtract to find less than.

How many is 2 more than 7 ? 9

2 + 7 = 9

What is 1 less than 9 ? ________

There are 2 less than 10 .

How many are there? ________

What is 1 more than 8 ? ________

MATH

Skill 14: More- and Less-Than Facts Through 10

Directions: Add to find more than. Subtract to find less than.

There is 1 more than 7 .

How many are there? ________

How many is 1 more than 9 ? ________

How many is 1 less than 10 ? ________

What is 2 less than 8 ? ________

There is 1 less than 8 .

How many are there? ________

MATH

Skill 15: Using Addition for Subtraction

Directions: Think addition for subtraction. Solve each problem.

8 − 4 = ___4___ 4 + ________ = 8

7 − 3 = ________ 3 + ________ = 7

5 − 1 = ________ 1 + ________ = 5

9 − 4 = ________ 4 + ________ = 9

7 − 2 = ________ 2 + ________ = 7

MATH

Skill 15: Using Addition for Subtraction

Directions: Think addition for subtraction. Solve each problem.

8 − 2  = ________ 2  + ________ = 8

8  − 5  = ________ 5  + ________ = 8

7  − 4  = ________ 4  + ________ = 7

9  − 7  = ________ 7  + ________ = 9

10  − 3  = ________ 3  + ________ = 10

MATH

Skill 16: Doubles and Near-Doubles

Directions: Add to find the sum.

$$\begin{array}{r} 2 \\ +\ 2 \\ \hline 4 \end{array}$$

3 + 3 = 6 + 1 = 7

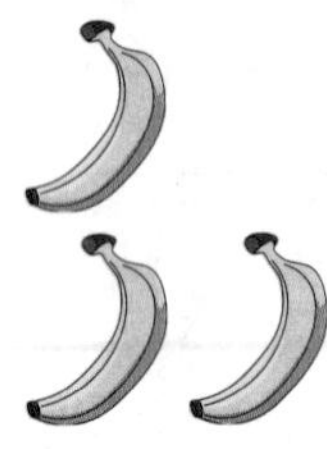

1 + 1 = ______ + 1 = ______

$$\begin{array}{r} 5 \\ +\ 5 \\ \hline \end{array}$$

$$\begin{array}{r} 3 \\ +\ 3 \\ \hline \end{array}$$

4 + 4 = ______ + 1 = ______

MATH

Skill 16: Doubles and Near-Doubles

Directions: Add to find the sum.

$$\begin{array}{r} 4 \\ +\ 4 \\ \hline \end{array}$$

$$\begin{array}{r} 1 \\ +\ 1 \\ \hline \end{array}$$

2 + 2 = _______ + 1 = _______

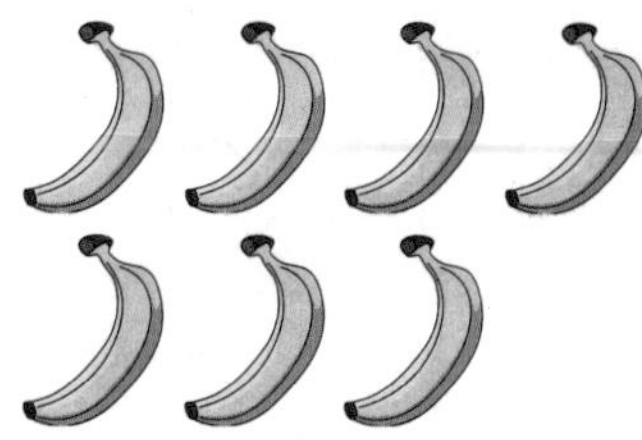

3 + 3 = _______ + 1 = _______

$$\begin{array}{r} 5 \\ +\ 5 \\ \hline \end{array}$$

5 + 5 = _______ + 1 = _______

Skill 17: Counting and Writing 10 Through 29

Directions: Complete.

__1__ tens __0__ ones = __10__

 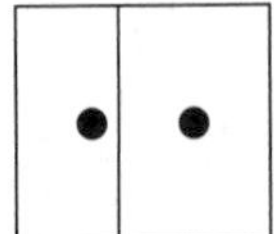

_____ tens _____ ones = _________

_____ tens _____ ones = _________

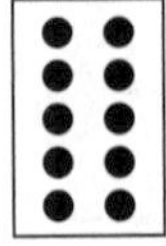 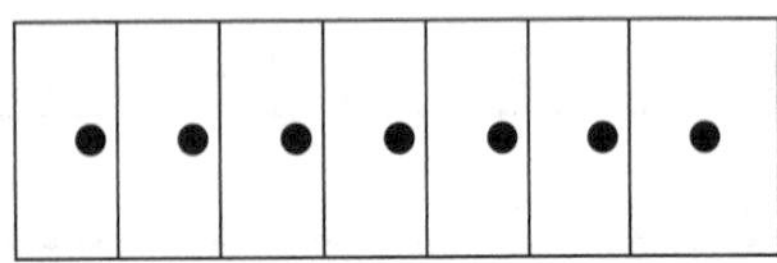

_____ tens _____ ones = _________

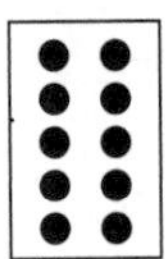 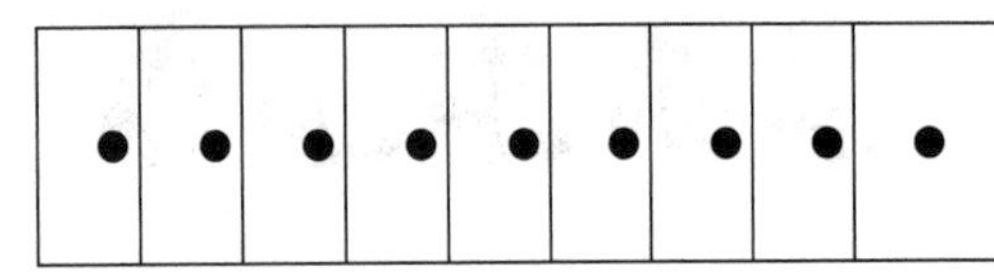

_____ tens _____ ones = _________

MATH

Skill 17: Counting and Writing 10 Through 29

Directions: Complete.

2 tens 0 ones = 20

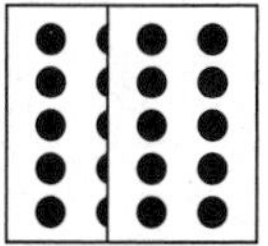 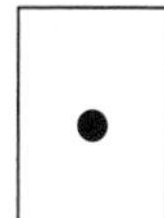

_____ tens _____ ones = _________

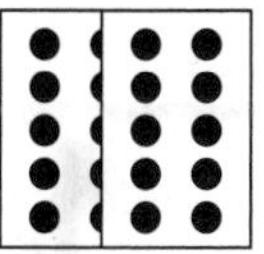 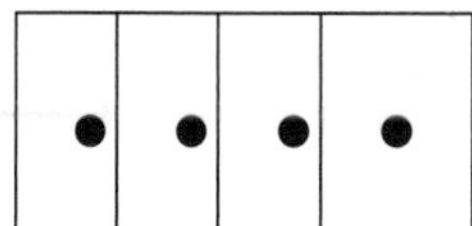

_____ tens _____ ones = _________

 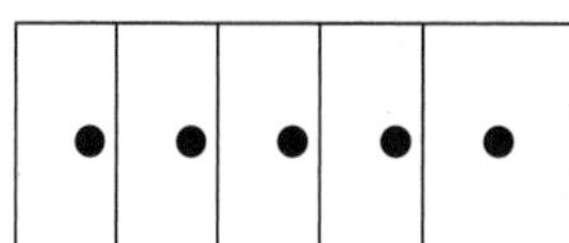

_____ tens _____ ones = _________

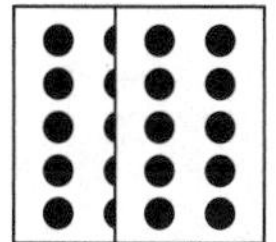 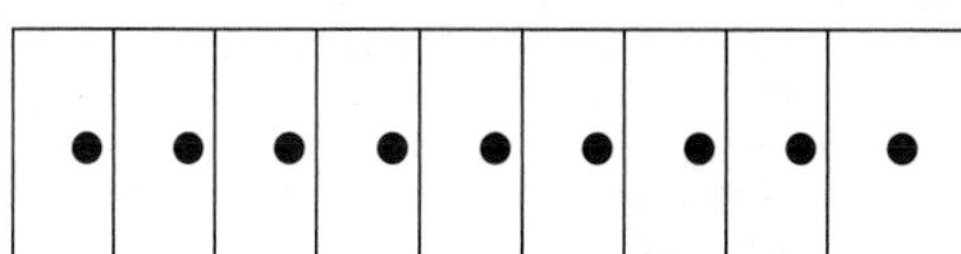

____ tens ____ ones = ________

MATH

Skill 18: Counting and Writing 30 Through 49

Directions: Complete.

__3__ tens __4__ ones = __34__

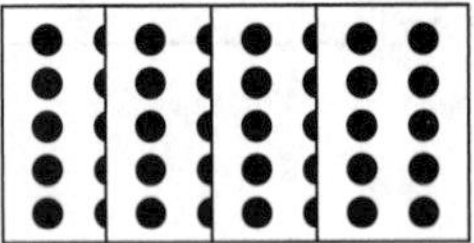

_____ tens _____ ones = ________

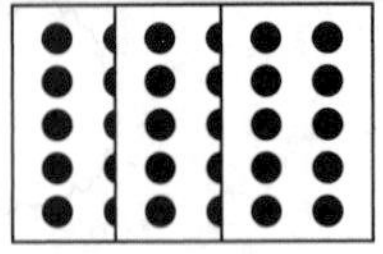

_____ tens _____ ones = ________

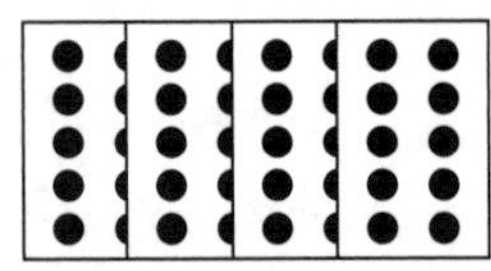

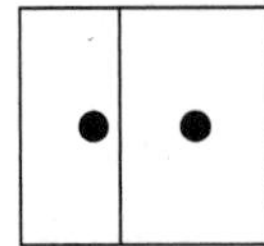

_____ tens _____ ones = ________

MATH

Skill 23: Comparing Numbers

Compare 2-digit numbers.

43 (>) 36 Compare tens. 4 is greater than 3. 43 is greater than 36.

74 (<) 77 If tens are the same, compare ones. 4 is less than 7. 74 is less than 77.

Directions: Compare 2-digit numbers. Use > (greater than), < (less than), or = (equal to).

16 ◯ 22 81 ◯ 43 86 ◯ 88

12 ◯ 20 45 ◯ 45 15 ◯ 26

51 ◯ 56 62 ◯ 41 92 ◯ 92

70 ◯ 70 24 ◯ 25 21 ◯ 17

71 ◯ 61 40 ◯ 30 48 ◯ 89

MATH

Skill

22: Counting Forward to and Backward From 120

Directions: Count backward. Write the missing numbers.

79, 78, _____, 76, _____, 74, _____, 72, _____, 70, _____, 68

84, _____, 82, 81, _____, 79, 78, 77, _____, _____, _____, 73

24, 22, _____, 18, 16, _____, 12, _____, 8, 6, _____, 2

120, _____, 110, 105, _____, 95, 90, _____, _____, 75, 70, 65

75, 70, 65, _____, 55, _____, 45, 40, 35, _____, 25, _____

_____, _____, 90, _____, 70, 60, _____, _____, 30, _____

MATH

Skill 25: Subtracting From 11 and 12

Directions: Subtract.

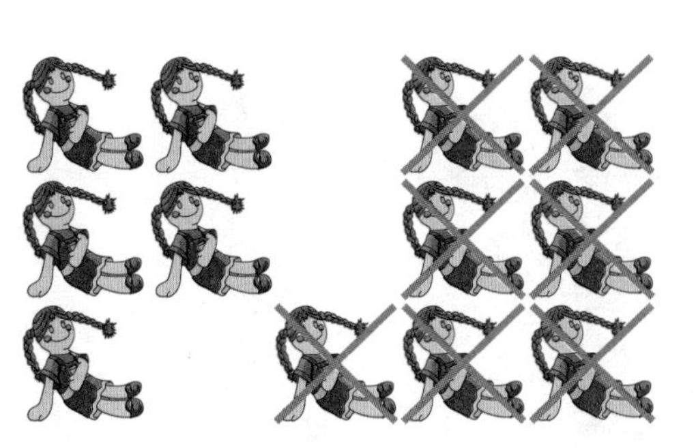

12
− 7
5

12
− 5

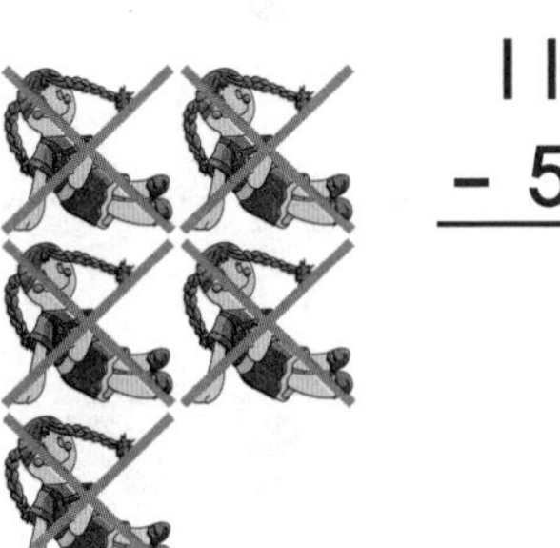

11
− 5

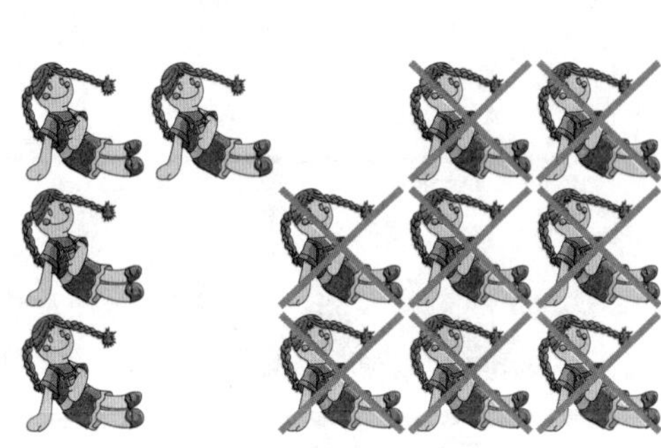

12
− 8

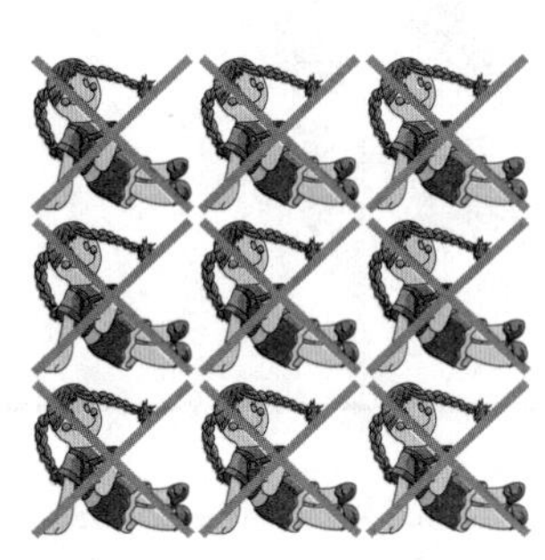

12
− 9

11
− 7

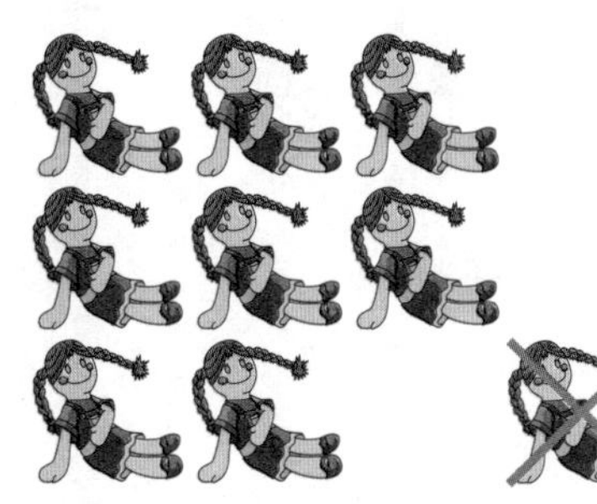

12
− 4

11
− 2

Skill 26: Adding to 13 and 14

Directions: Add.

6
+ 7
13

9
+ 5

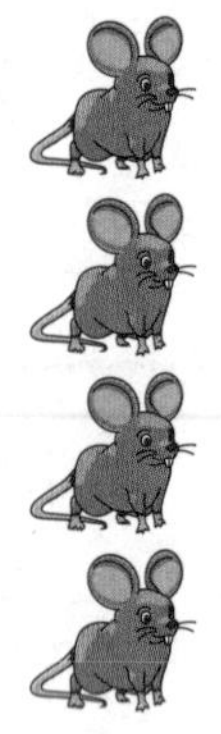

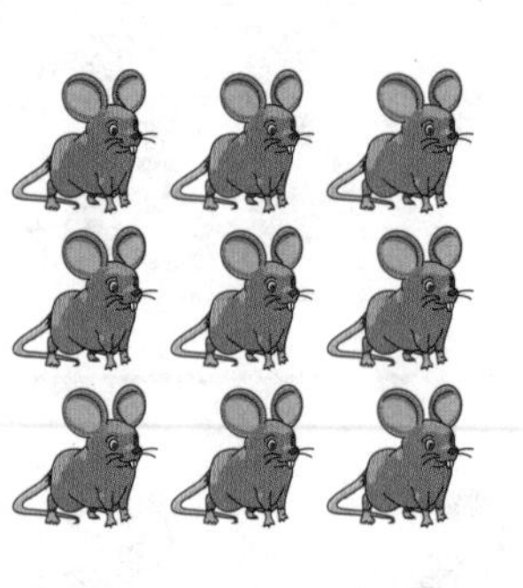

4
+ 9

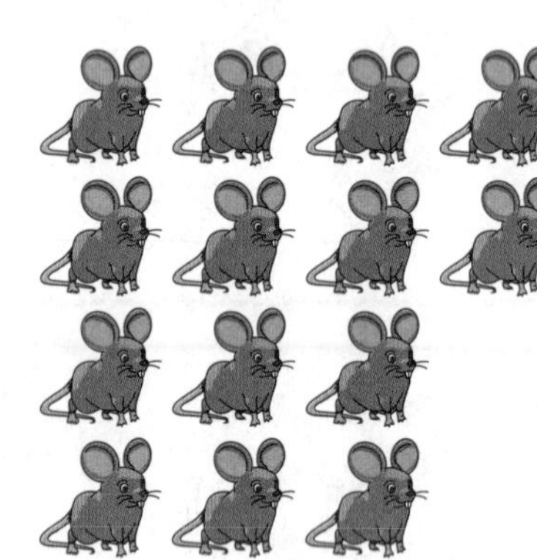

14
+ 0

5
+ 8

8
+ 5

MATH

Skill 26: Adding to 13 and 14

Directions: Add.

$$\begin{array}{r} 5 \\ +\ 9 \\ \hline 14 \end{array}$$

$$\begin{array}{r} 7 \\ +\ 6 \\ \hline \end{array}$$

$$\begin{array}{r} 6 \\ +\ 8 \\ \hline \end{array}$$

$$\begin{array}{r} 8 \\ +\ 6 \\ \hline \end{array}$$

$$\begin{array}{r} 7 \\ +\ 7 \\ \hline \end{array}$$

$$\begin{array}{r} 9 \\ +\ 4 \\ \hline \end{array}$$

MATH

Skill 27: Subtracting From 13 and 14

Directions: Subtract.

$$\begin{array}{r} 13 \\ -\ 9 \\ \hline 4 \end{array}$$

$$\begin{array}{r} 14 \\ -\ 8 \\ \hline \end{array}$$

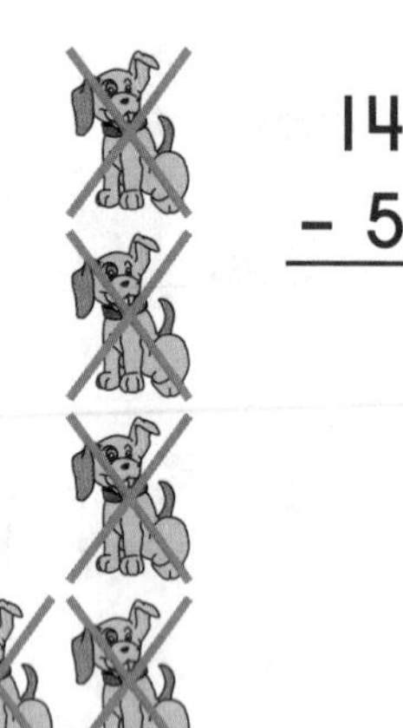

$$\begin{array}{r} 14 \\ -\ 5 \\ \hline \end{array}$$

$$\begin{array}{r} 13 \\ -\ 0 \\ \hline \end{array}$$

$$\begin{array}{r} 13 \\ -\ 8 \\ \hline \end{array}$$

$$\begin{array}{r} 14 \\ -\ 0 \\ \hline \end{array}$$

Skill 27: Subtracting From 13 and 14

Directions: Subtract.

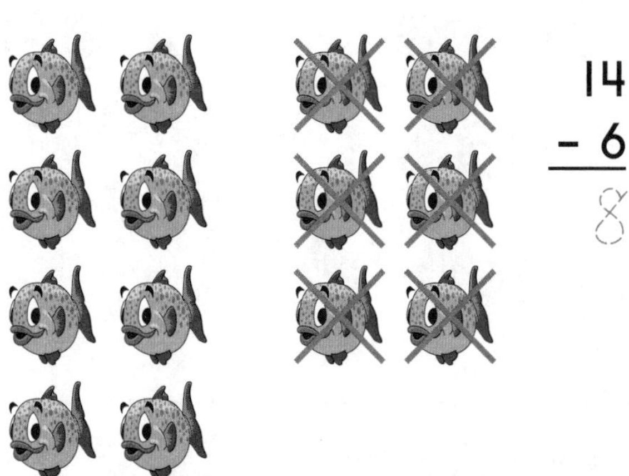

$$\begin{array}{r} 14 \\ -\ 6 \\ \hline 8 \end{array}$$

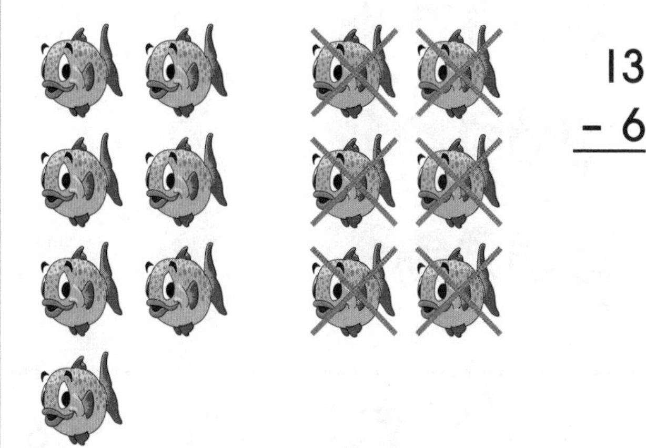

$$\begin{array}{r} 13 \\ -\ 6 \\ \hline \end{array}$$

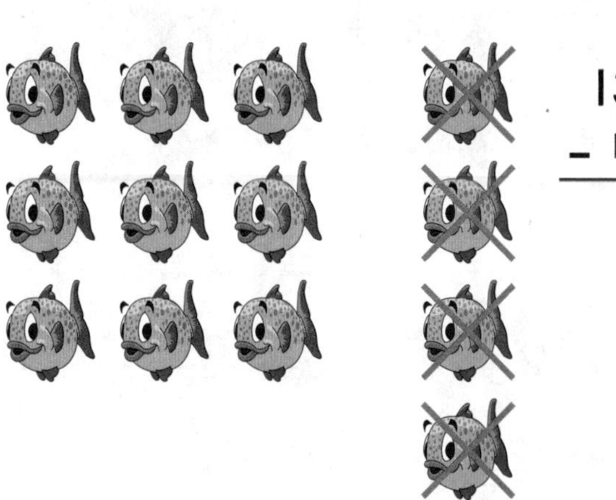

$$\begin{array}{r} 13 \\ -\ 4 \\ \hline \end{array}$$

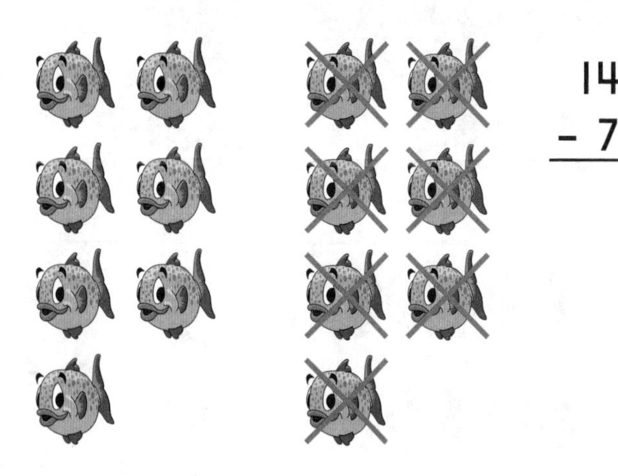

$$\begin{array}{r} 14 \\ -\ 7 \\ \hline \end{array}$$

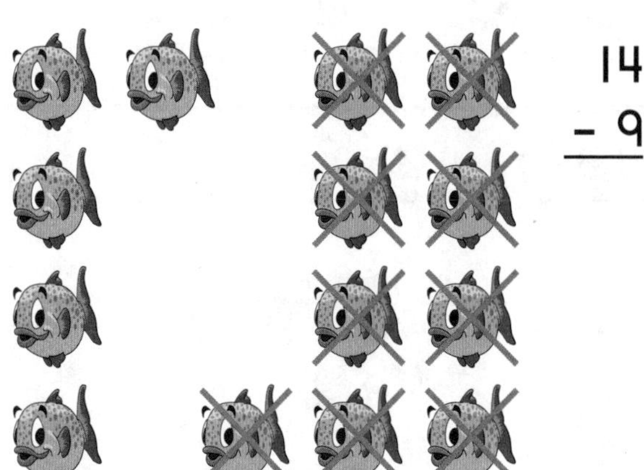

$$\begin{array}{r} 14 \\ -\ 9 \\ \hline \end{array}$$

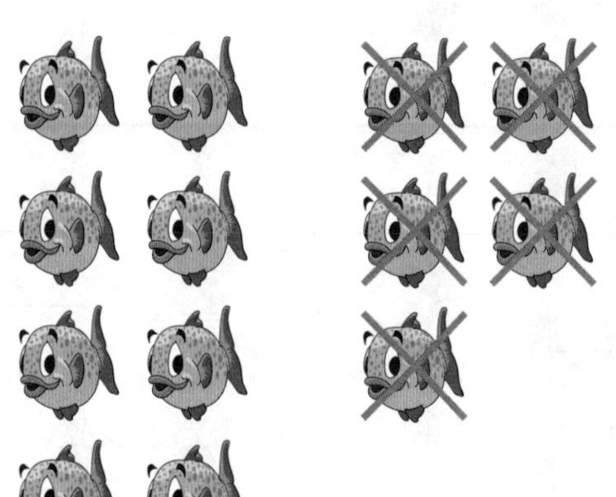

$$\begin{array}{r} 13 \\ -\ 5 \\ \hline \end{array}$$

Skill 28: Adding to and Subtracting From 15 and 16

Directions: Add or subtract.

15
+ 3
18

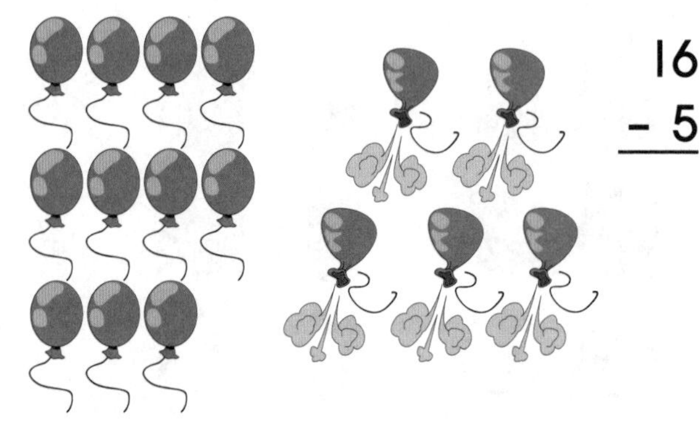

16
− 5

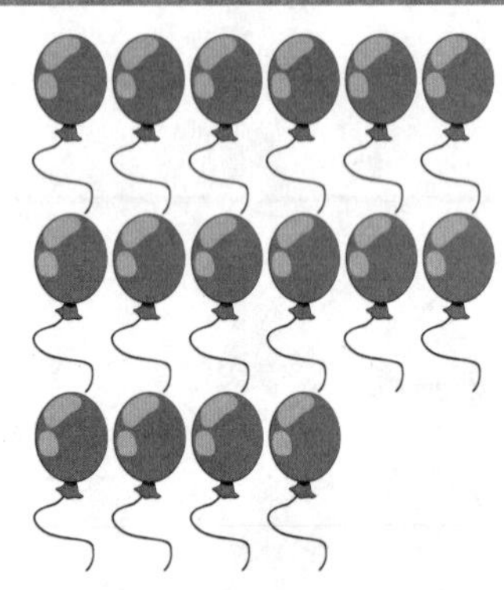

16
+ 7

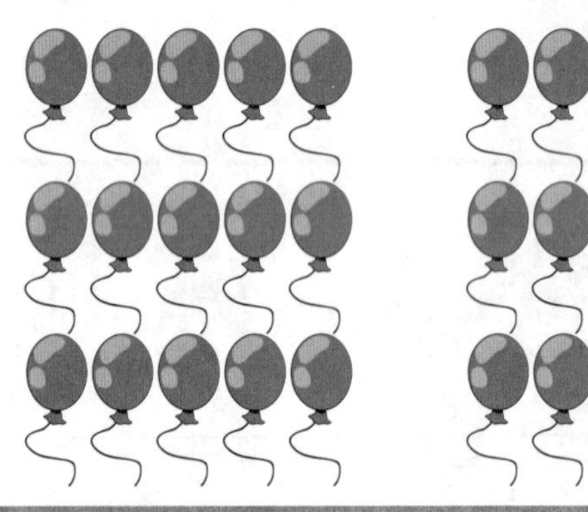

15
+ 9

15
+ 2

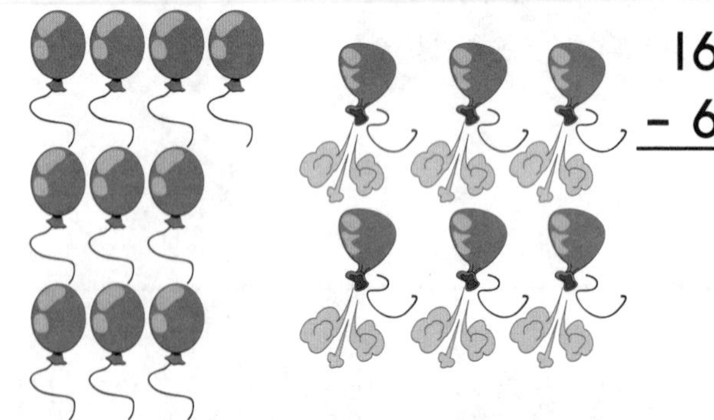

16
− 6

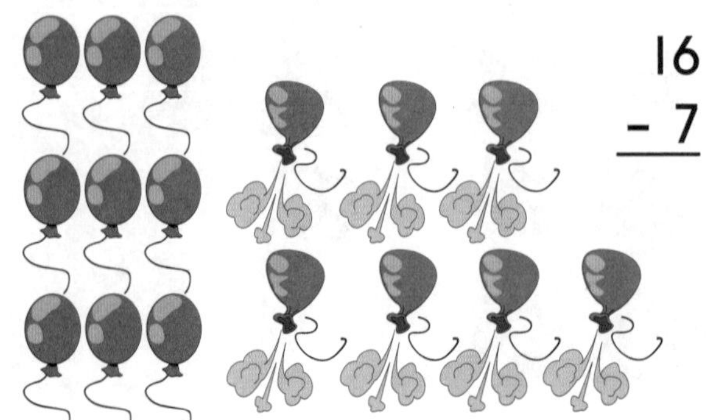

16
− 7

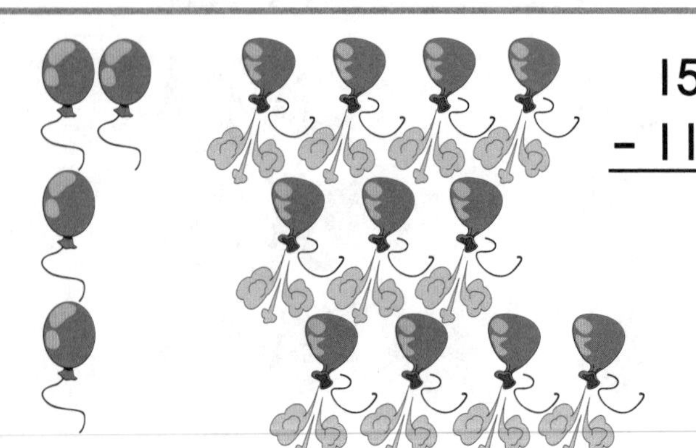

15
− 11

MATH

Skill 28: Adding to and Subtracting From 15 and 16

Directions: Add or subtract.

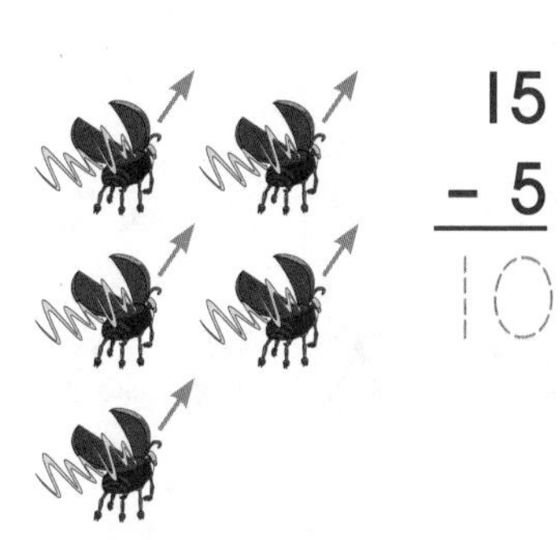

15
− 5
10

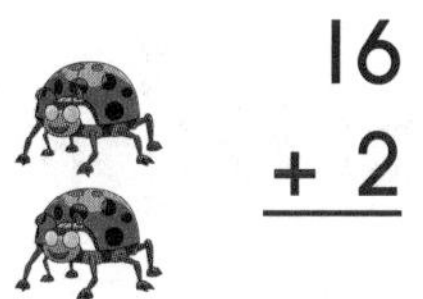

16
+ 2

16
− 10

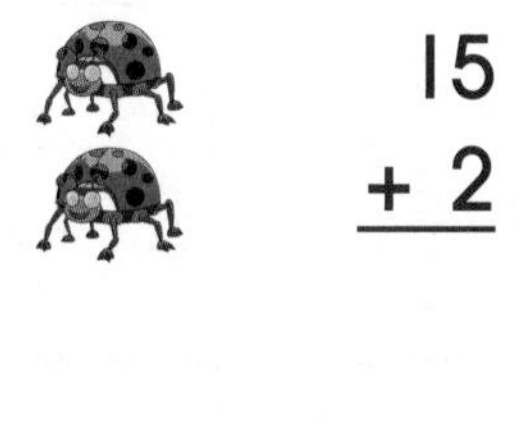

15
+ 2

15
− 3

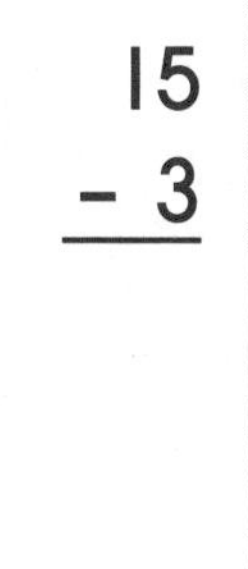

16
− 9

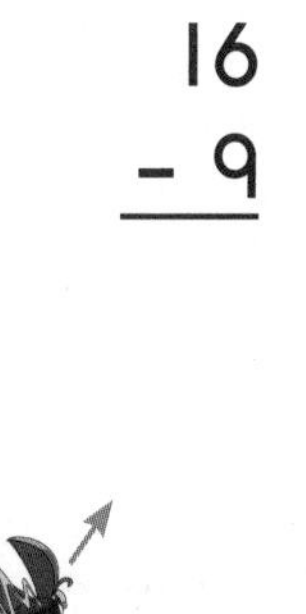
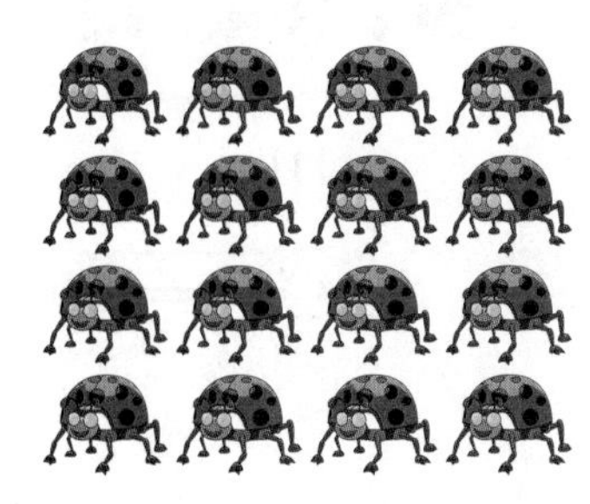
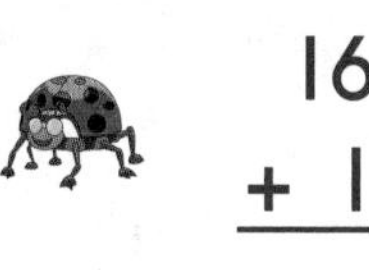

16
+ 1

15
+ 4

MATH

Skill 29: Fact Families 11 Through 15

A **fact family** is a group of related addition and subtraction facts made from the same numbers.

Directions: Add or subtract.

12 + 1	1 + 12	13 – 1	13 – 12

15 + 0 = ________ 15 – 15 = ________

0 + 15 = ________ 15 – 0 = ________

11 + 3	3 + 11	14 – 3	14 – 11

MATH

Skill 23: Comparing Numbers

Directions: Write the number in each box that answers the riddle.

I am less than 10.
I am greater than 5.
I am not equal to 8.

What number am I? ______

12

17

I am less than 15.
I am greater than 10.
I am not equal to 12.

What number am I? ______

I am less than 6.
I am greater than 3.
I am not equal to 4.

What number am I? ______

I am less than 20.
I am greater than 13.
I am not equal to 15.

What number am I? ______

Skill 24: Adding to 11 and 12

Directions: Add.

$$\begin{array}{r} 7 \\ +\ 4 \\ \hline \end{array}$$

$$\begin{array}{r} 3 \\ +\ 9 \\ \hline \end{array}$$

$$\begin{array}{r} 4 \\ +\ 8 \\ \hline \end{array}$$

$$\begin{array}{r} 9 \\ +\ 2 \\ \hline \end{array}$$

$$\begin{array}{r} 4 \\ +\ 7 \\ \hline \end{array}$$

$$\begin{array}{r} 6 \\ +\ 6 \\ \hline \end{array}$$

$$\begin{array}{r} 5 \\ +\ 6 \\ \hline \end{array}$$

$$\begin{array}{r} 2 \\ +\ 9 \\ \hline \end{array}$$

MATH

Skill 24: Adding to 11 and 12

Directions: Add.

9 + 3 = 12	3 + 9 =
6 + 5 =	5 + 7 =
7 + 5 =	3 + 8 =
4 + 8 =	2 + 9 =

MATH

Skill 25: Subtracting From 11 and 12

Directions: Subtract.

$$\begin{array}{r} 11 \\ -\ 8 \\ \hline 3 \end{array}$$

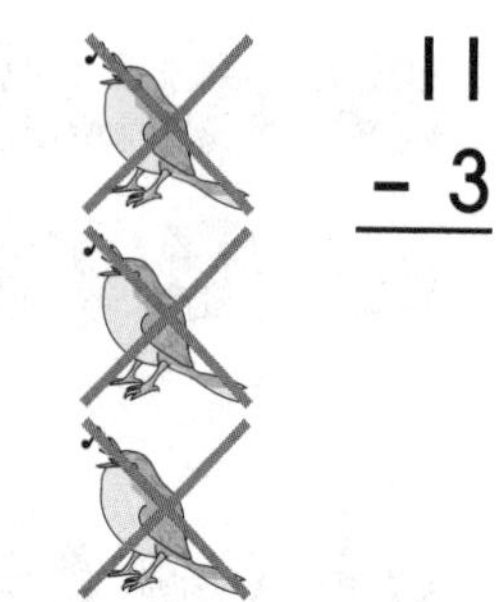

$$\begin{array}{r} 11 \\ -\ 3 \\ \hline \end{array}$$

$$\begin{array}{r} 12 \\ -\ 6 \\ \hline \end{array}$$

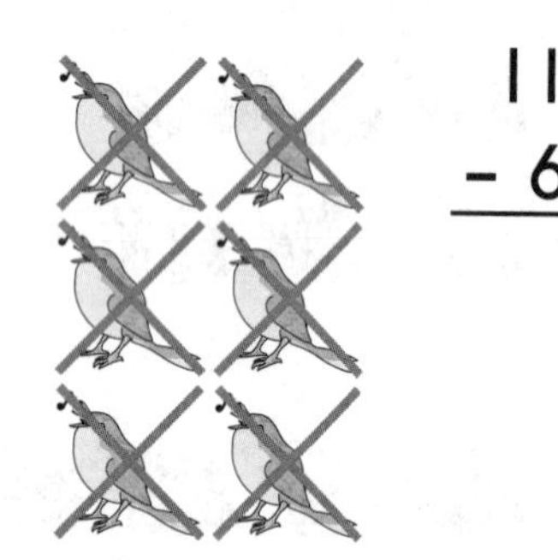

$$\begin{array}{r} 11 \\ -\ 6 \\ \hline \end{array}$$

$$\begin{array}{r} 11 \\ -\ 4 \\ \hline \end{array}$$

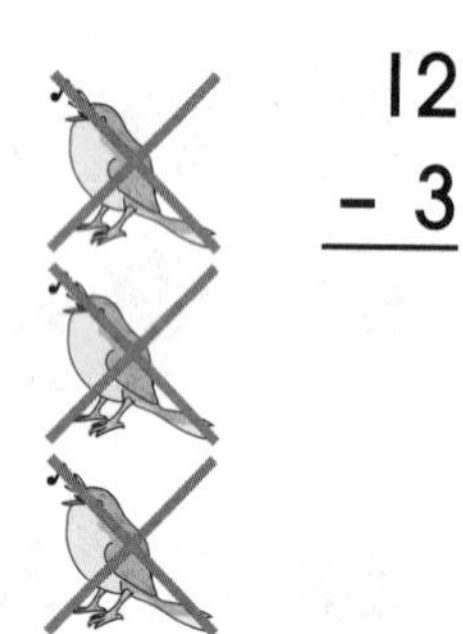

$$\begin{array}{r} 12 \\ -\ 3 \\ \hline \end{array}$$

$$\begin{array}{r} 11 \\ -\ 2 \\ \hline \end{array}$$

$$\begin{array}{r} 11 \\ -\ 9 \\ \hline \end{array}$$

Skill 29: Fact Families 11 Through 15

Directions: Add or subtract.

3 + 12 = ________ 15 – 3 = ________

12 + 3 = ________ 15 – 12 = ________

13 + 5 = ________ 18 – 13 = ________

5 + 13 = ________ 18 – 5 = ________

7 + 5 = ________ 12 – 7 = ________

5 + 7 = ________ 12 – 5 = ________

MATH

Skill 30: Fact Families 16 Through 20

Directions: Add or subtract.

18	1	19	19
+ 1	+ 18	− 1	− 18

---

2 + 16 = ________ 16 + 2 = ________

18 − 2 = ________ 18 − 16 = ________

14	3	17	17
+ 3	+ 14	− 3	− 14

MATH

Skill 30: Fact Families 16 Through 20

Directions: Add or subtract.

16 + 4 = ________   4 + 16 = ________

20 − 16 = ________   20 − 4 = ________

18	2	20	20
+ 2	+ 18	− 2	− 18

3 + 15 = ________   15 + 3 = ________

18 − 3 = ________   18 − 15 = ________

MATH

Skill 31: More- and Less-Than Facts 11 Through 20

Directions: Add to find more than. Subtract to find less than.

How many is 3 more than 11 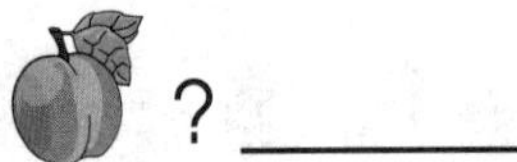 ? ________

What is 4 less than 14 ? ________

There are 5 less than 15  .

How many  are there? ________

What is 4 more than 16  ? ________

What is 6 less than 17  ? ________

There are 4 more than 13  .

How many  are there? ________

Skill 31: More- and Less-Than Facts 11 Through 20

Directions: Add to find more than. Subtract to find less than.

How many is 2 less than 19 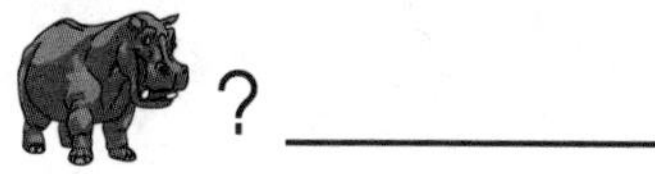 ? ________

What is 5 more than 12  ? ________

There are 8 less than 20 .

How many are there? ________

What is 2 less than 17  ? ________

How many is 1 less than 19  ? ________

There are 4 less than 20  .

How many  are there? ________

MATH

Skill **32: Adding 2-Digit and 1-Digit Numbers**

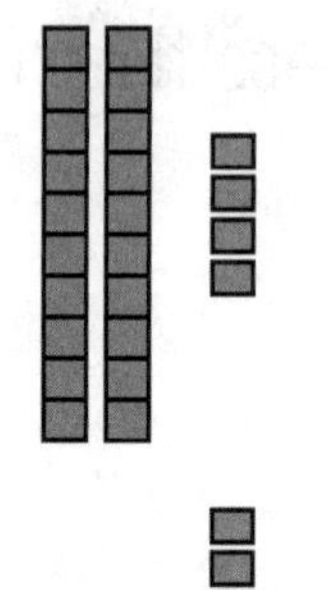

	First add ones.	Then, add tens.
24 + 4	24 + 4 = 8	24 + 4, sum = 28

Add the ones.	Put the ones in the ones place. Put the ten in the tens place.	Add the tens.
38 + 4 = ? ; 8 + 4 = 12	1 over 38 + 4 = 2	1 over 38 + 4, sum = 42

12 = 1 ten and 2 ones

1
19
6
25

Directions: Add.

1 over 22 + 6 = 28	1 over 27 + 5 = 32	1 19 + 6 = 5	1 29 + 3 = 32
38 + 8	15 + 2	20 + 6	87 + 2
53 + 6	63 + 5	47 + 2	41 + 4

MATH

Skill 39: Ordering Objects

Directions: Number the objects as follows: 1– long, 2 – medium, 3 – short.

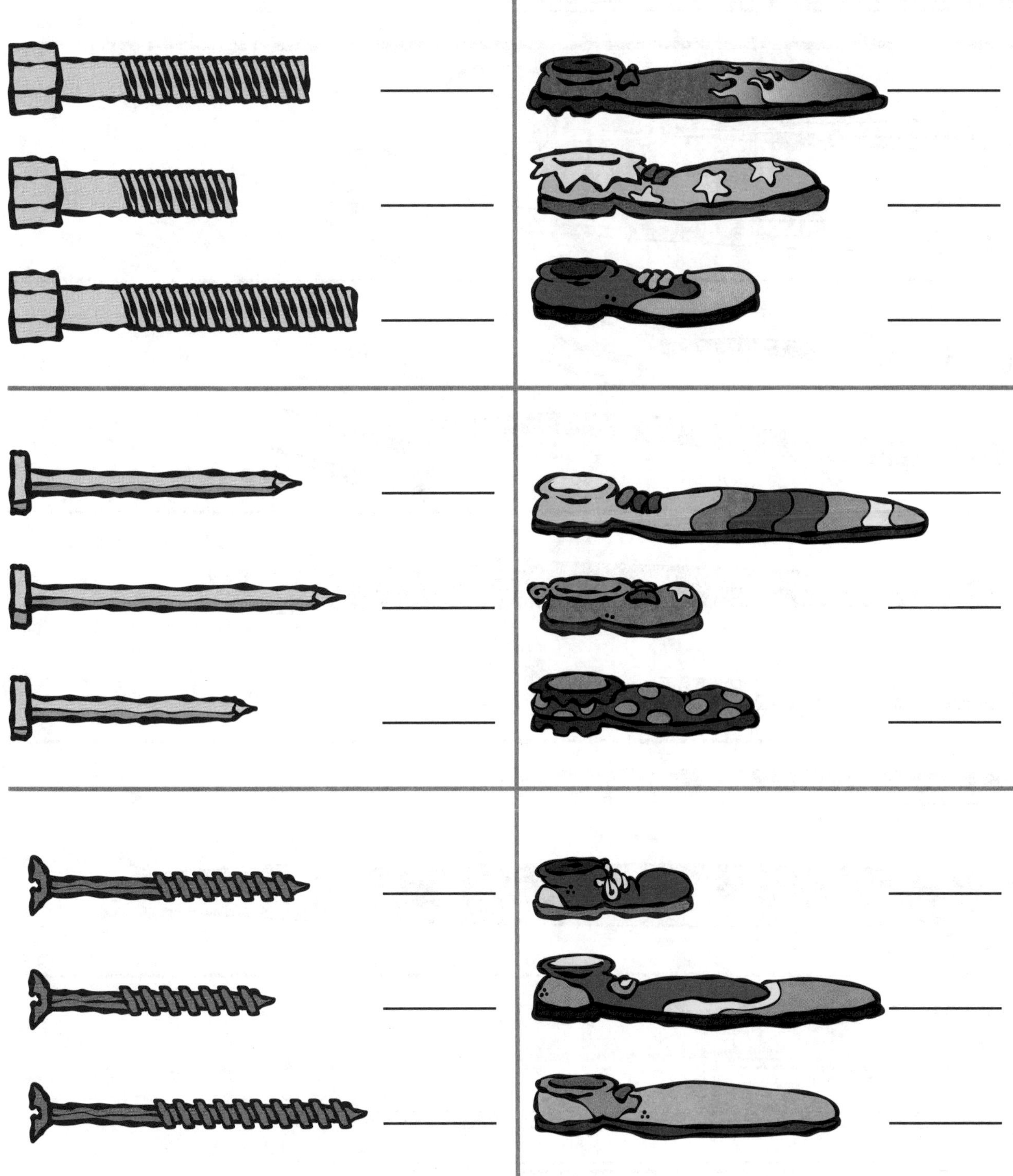

Skill 40: Comparing Lengths of Objects

Directions: Circle the object that is longer than the pencil in each row.

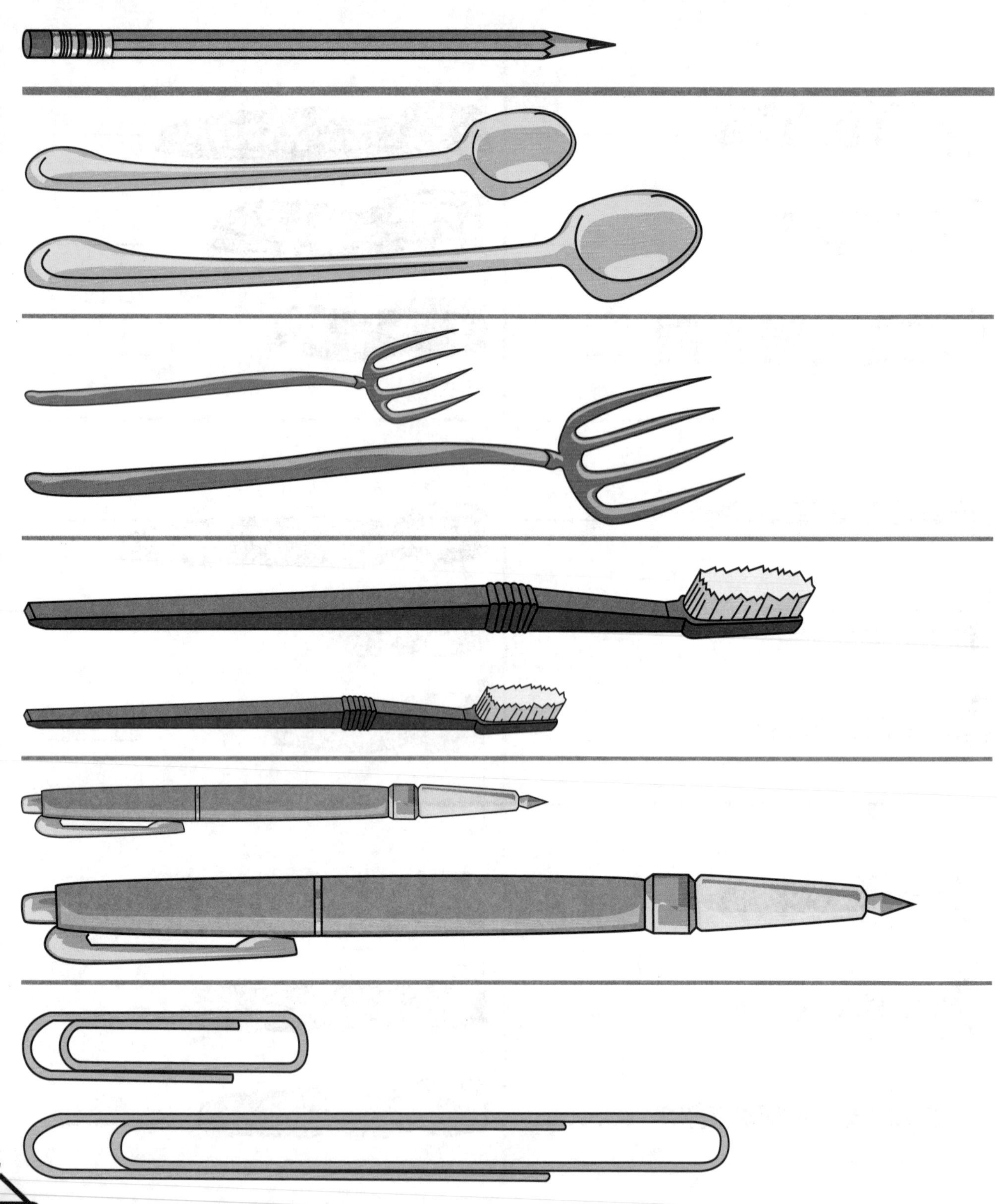

Skill 40: Comparing Lengths of Objects

Directions: Circle the object that is shorter than the pen in each row.

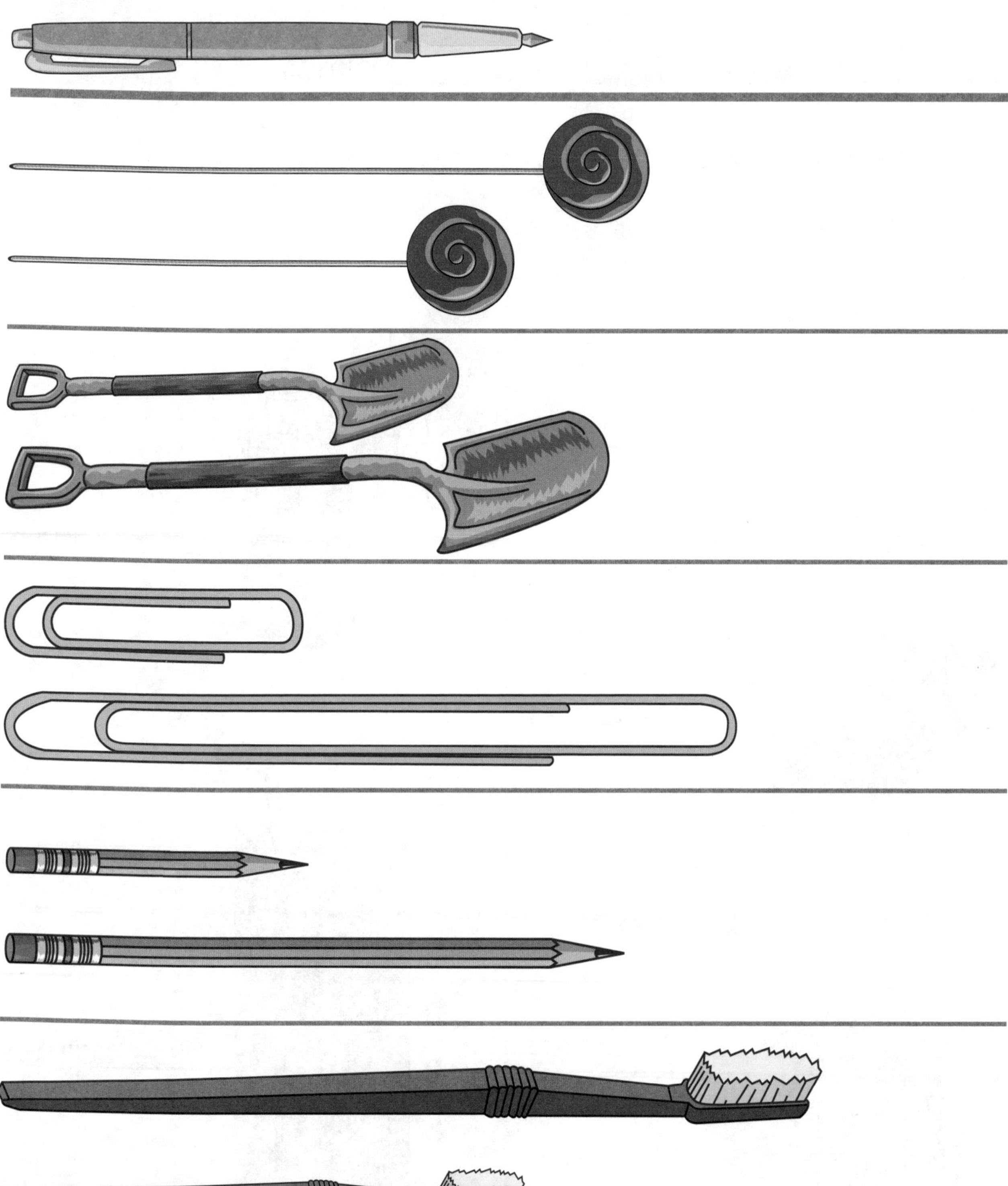

MATH

Skill 41: Measuring Length and Height

Use dimes to measure.

___7___ dimes

Directions: Use dimes to measure each object.

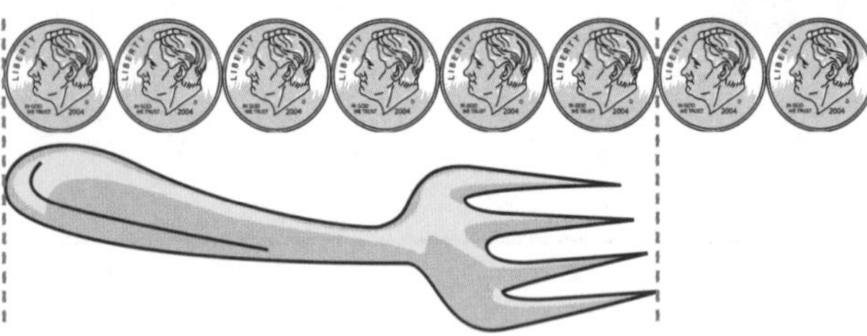

_______ dimes

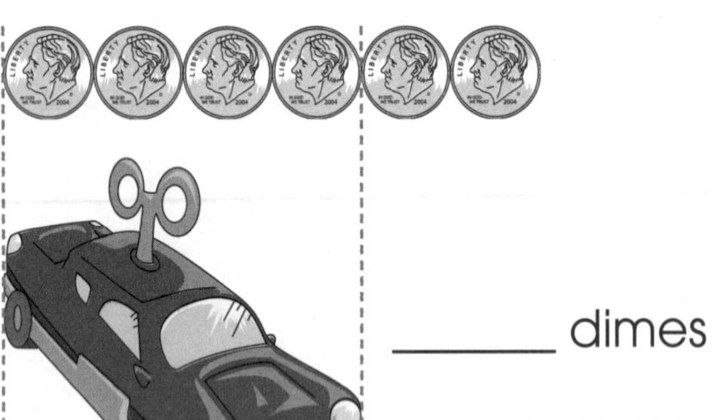

_______ dimes

_______ dimes

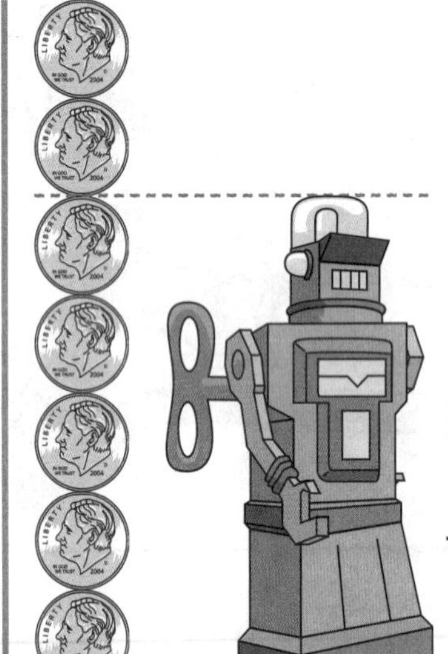

_______ dimes

_______ dimes

MATH

Skill 41: Measuring Length and Height

Directions: Use dimes to measure each object.

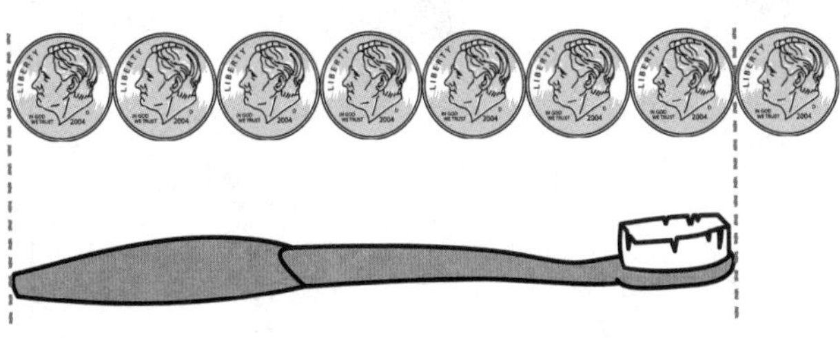

_______ dimes

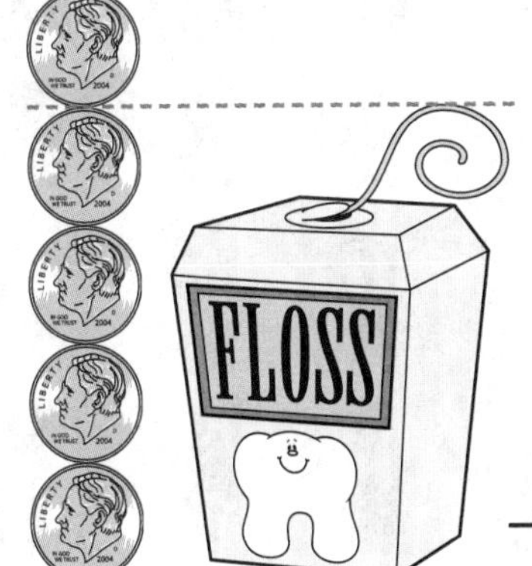

_______ dimes

_______ dimes

_______ dimes

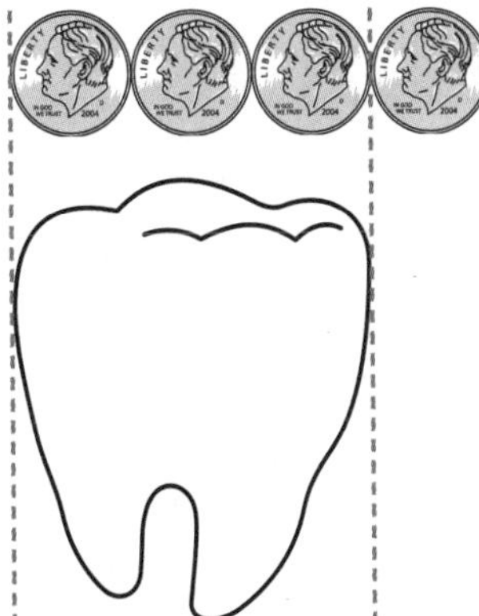

_______ dimes

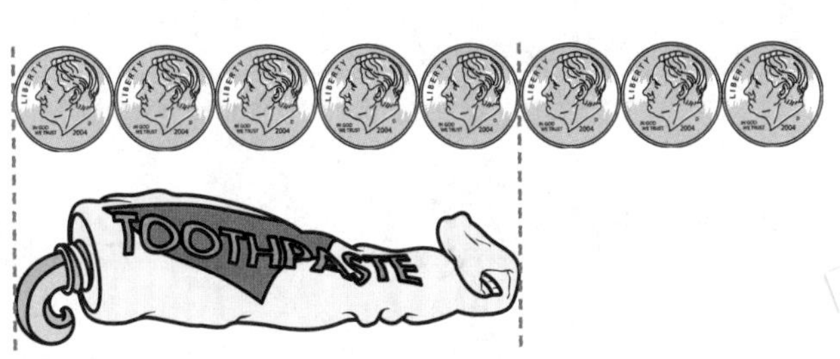

_______ dimes

Skill 42: More or Fewer

Directions: Look at the picture graph.

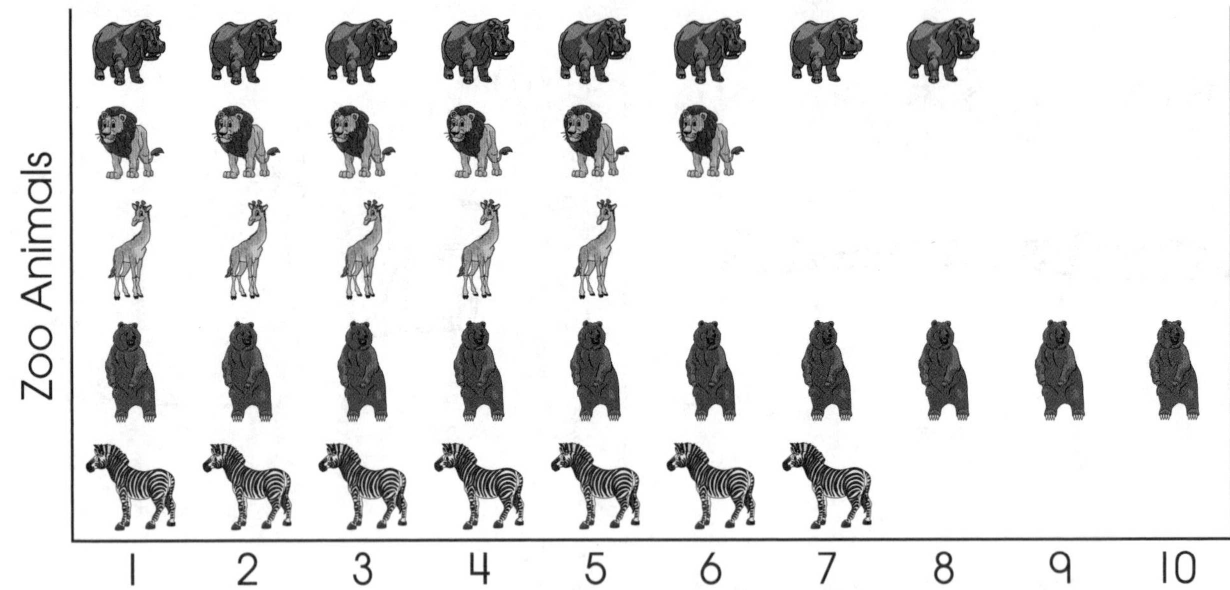

Circle the one that has more.  

Circle the one that has fewer.  

How many ? ________

How many ? ________

How many ? ________

How many ? ________

How many ? ________

Skill 42: More or Fewer

Directions: Look at the picture graph.

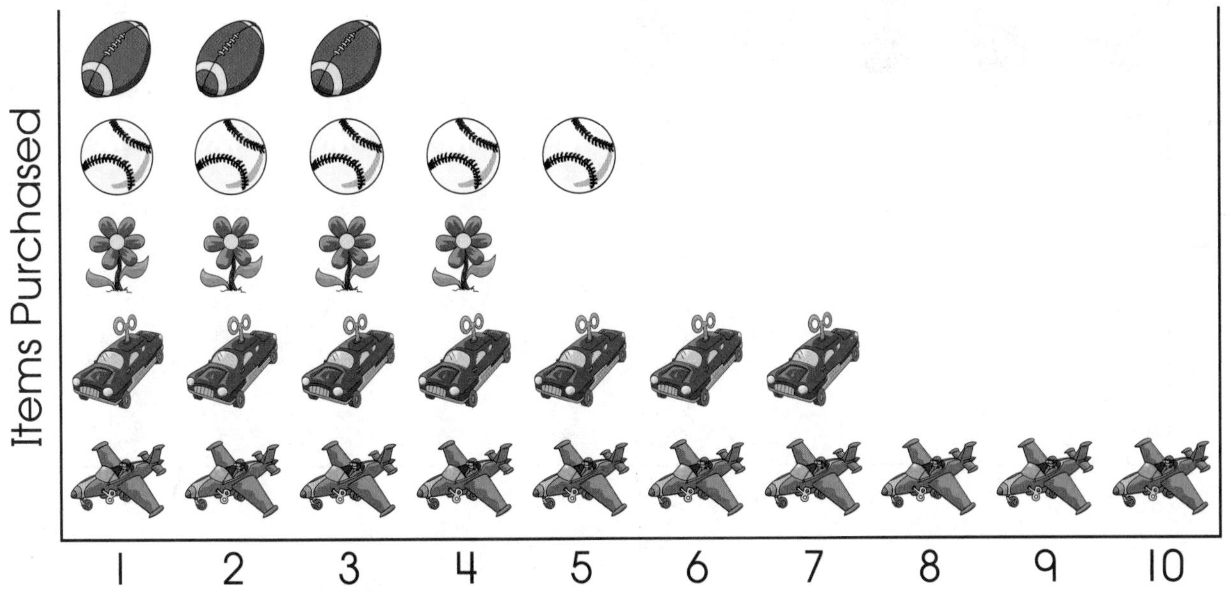

Circle the one that has more.  

Circle the one that has fewer.  

How many ? ________

How many ? ________

How many ? ________

How many ? ________

How many ? ________

Skill 43: More Than, Less Than, and Equal To

Directions: Look at the picture graph.

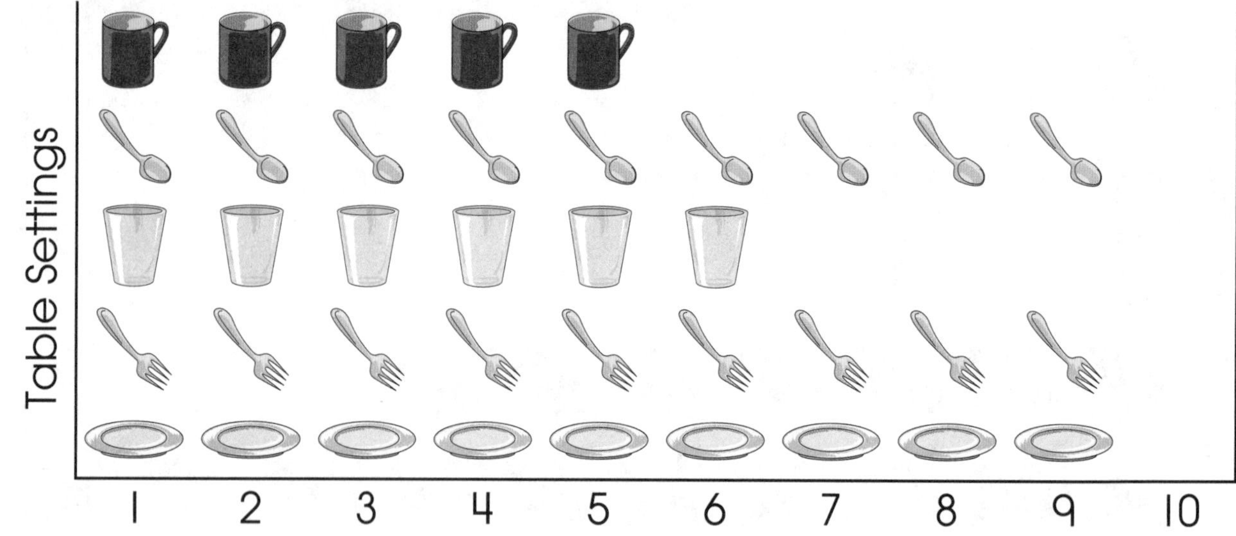

Circle the object that is greater than . 

Circle the object that is less than  

Circle the object that is equal to  

Directions: Fill in the ________ with *greater than, less than,* or *equal to*.

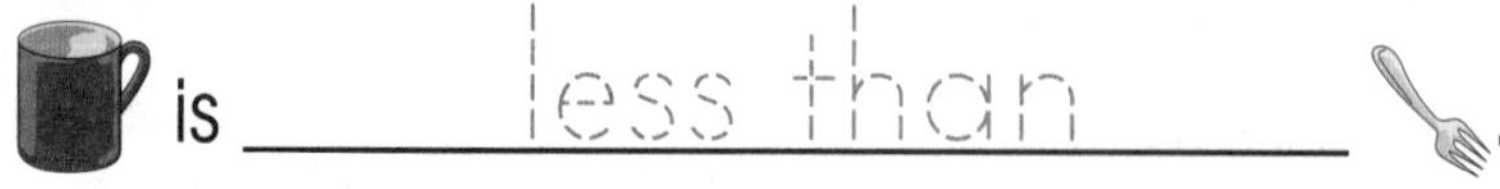

Skill 43: More Than, Less Than, and Equal To

Directions: Look at the picture graph.

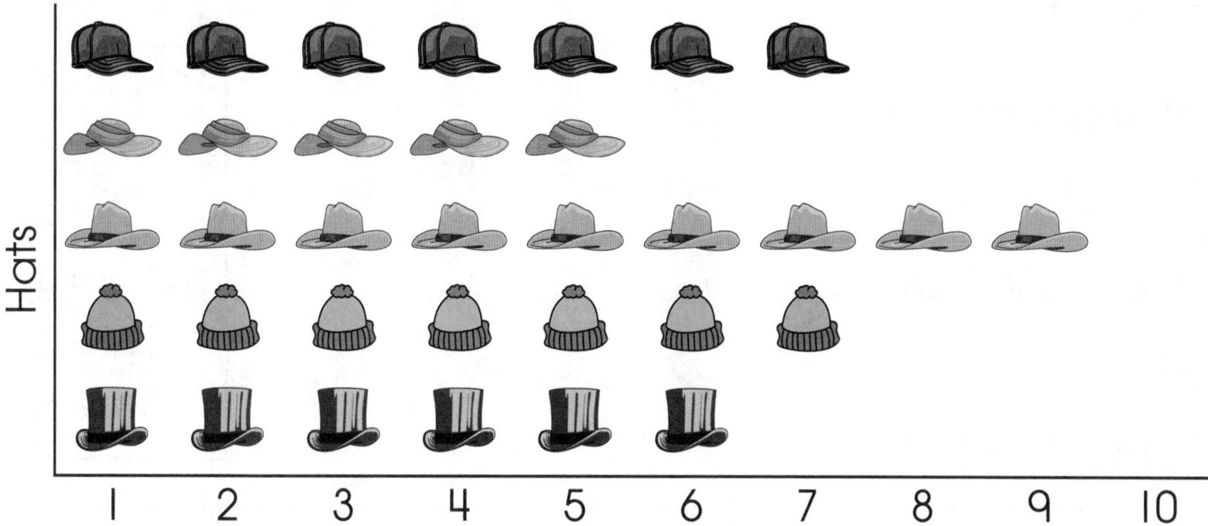

Circle the object that is greater than . 

Circle the object that is less than . 

Circle the object that is equal to . 

Directions: Fill in the ________ with *greater than, less than,* or *equal to*.

 is ______________________________ .

 is ______________________________ .

  is ______________________________ .

 is ______________________________ .

Skill 44: Collecting Data

Directions: Make a food chart for one day. Show what you ate. Use tally marks.

Bread and Grains 

Vegetables 

Meat and Dairy 

Fruits 

Other Foods

Tally Marks
| = 1
|| = 2
||| = 3
|||| = 4
~~||||~~ = 5

Breakfast	
Lunch	
Dinner	
Snacks	

What food did you eat the most? ____________________

At which meal did you eat the most? ____________________

How many of each did you eat?

Fruits ________ Bread and Grains ________

Vegetables ________ Other Foods ________

Meat and Dairy ________

What is your favorite food? ____________________

MATH

Skill 44: Collecting Data

Directions: Ask 20 people if they have a pet. Use tally marks to show what kind.

					Other	None

Directions: Write the number.

How many people have 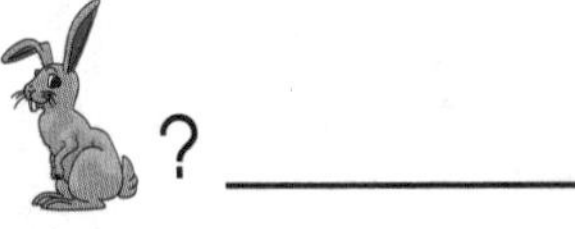 ? ________

How many people have  ? ________

How many people have 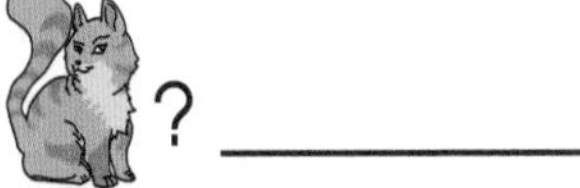 ? ________

How many people have 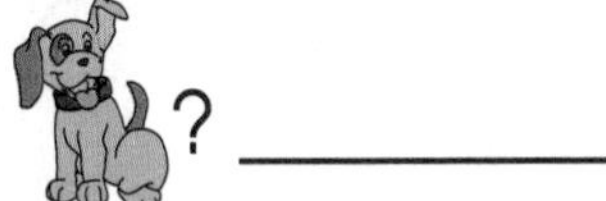 ? ________

How many people have  ? ________

How many people have a pet that is not pictured? ________

How many people have no pets? ________

Which pet is the favorite? ________________

Which pet is the least favorite? ________________

Skill 45: Identifying and Drawing Shapes

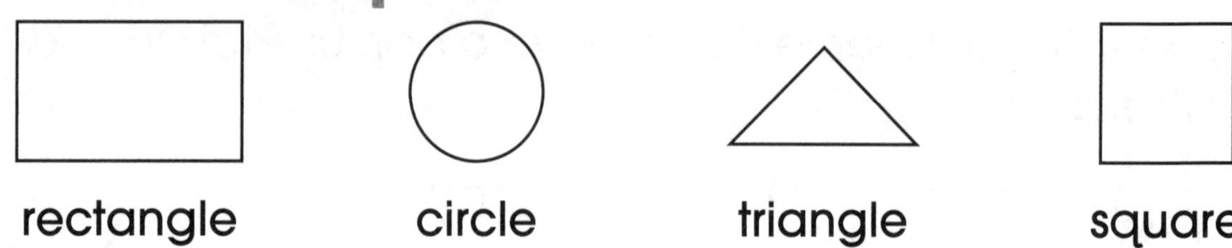

rectangle circle triangle square

Directions: Color all the circles red. Color all the rectangles blue. Color all the squares green. Color all the triangles yellow.

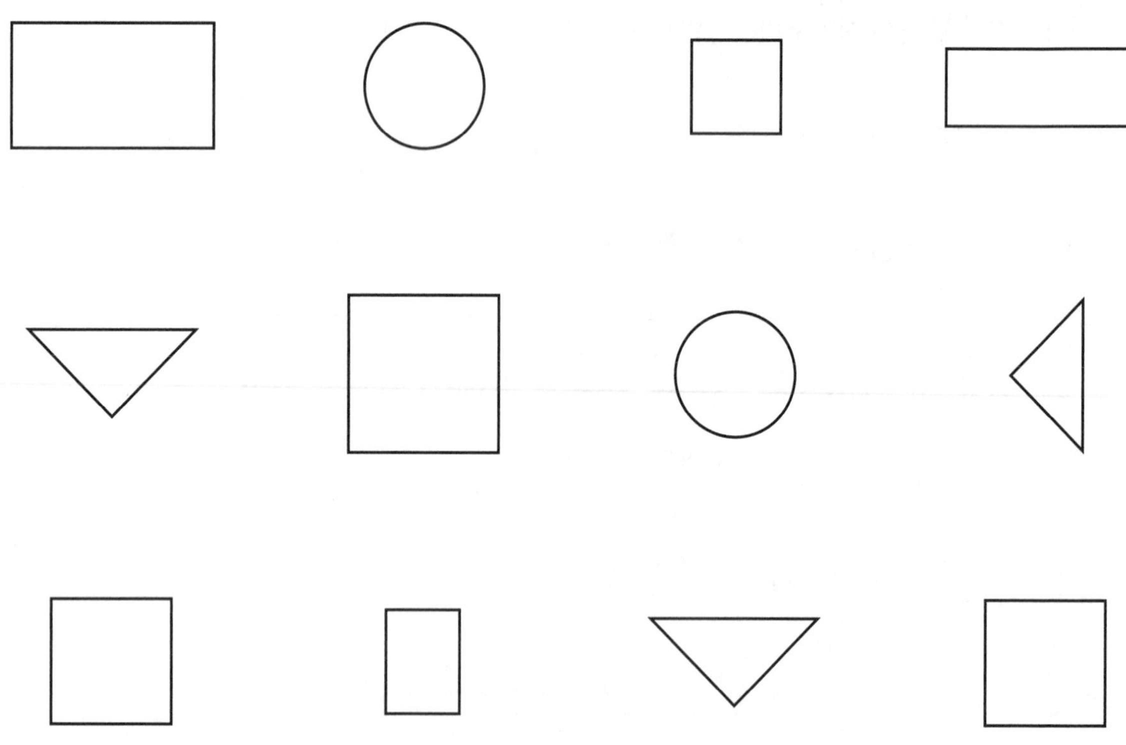

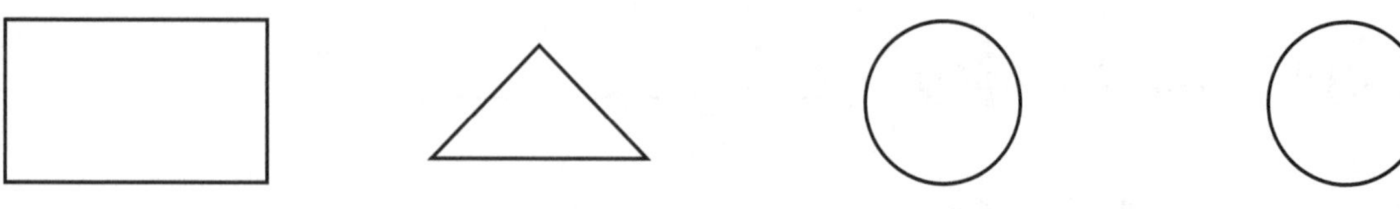

MATH

Skill 45: Identifying and Drawing Shapes

Directions: Draw the shape.

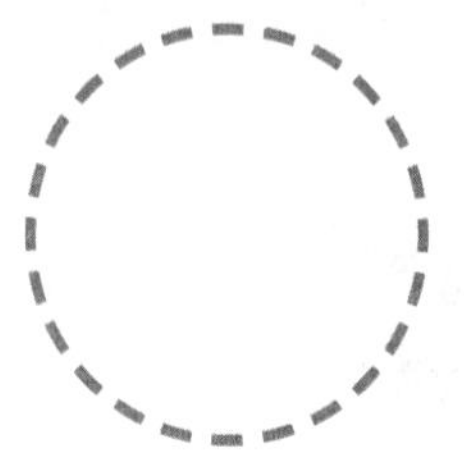

Circle
It is a closed curve.

Rectangle
It has 4 sides.

Square
It has 4 sides.
The sides are the same length.

Triangle
It has 3 sides.

Directions: Draw something that is a rectangle.

MATH

Skill 46: Finding Shapes

Directions: Write the name of each shape. Then, draw the shape.

triangle

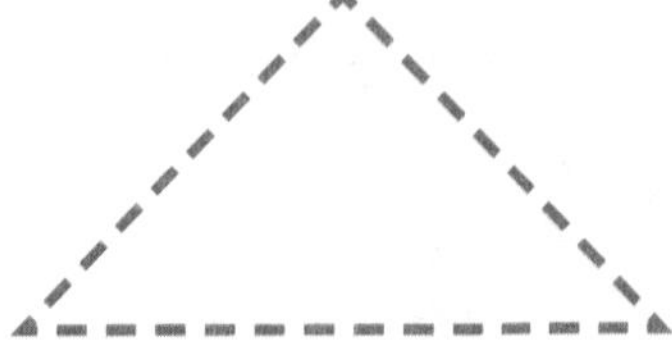

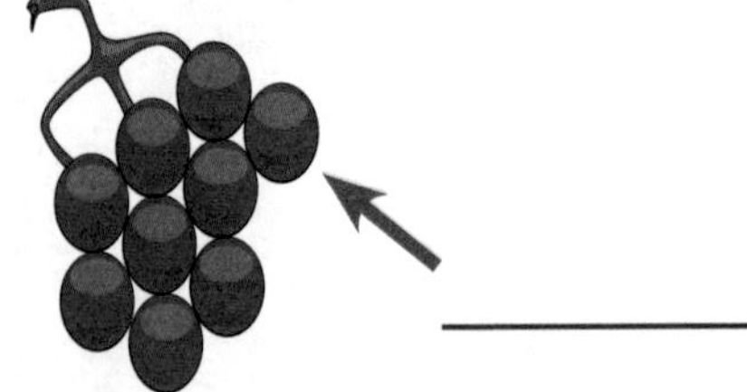

MATH

Skill 46: Finding Shapes

Directions: Look at the picture of a log cabin.

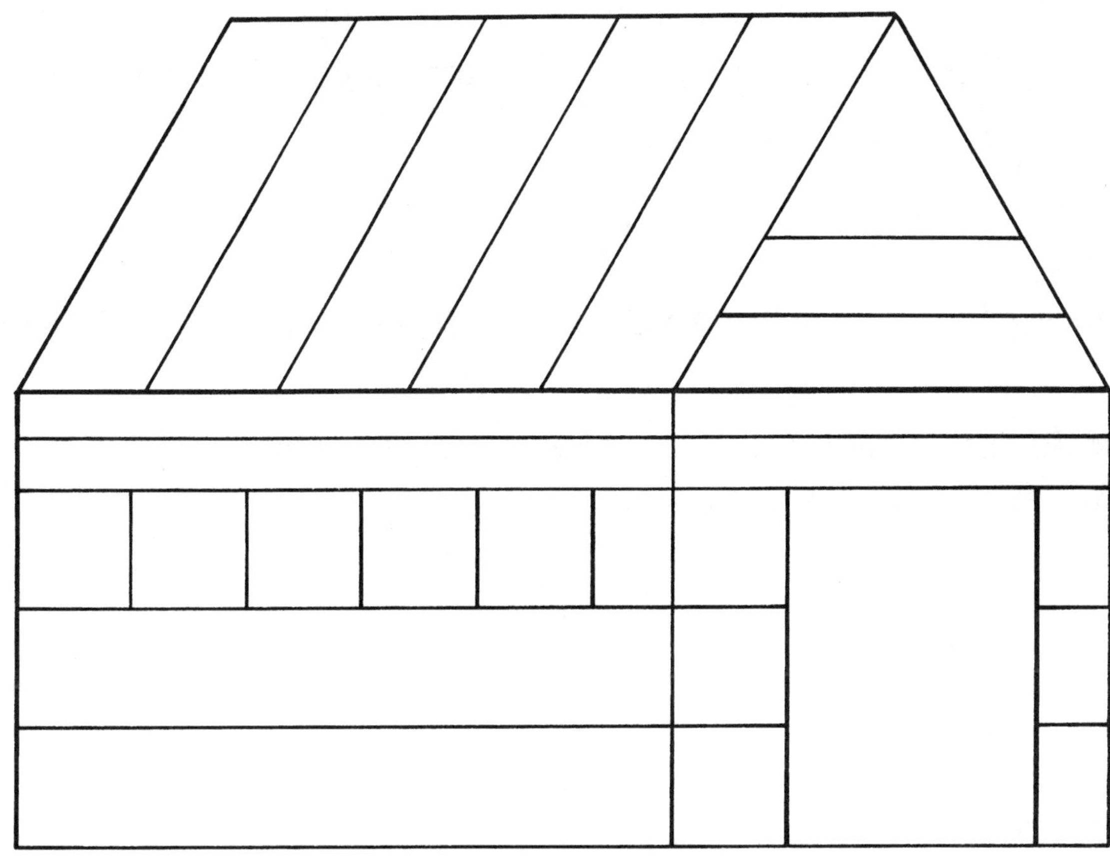

Color all the triangles purple.

Color all the rectangles orange.

Color all the squares blue.

Color the rest of the cabin brown.

How many corners does each shape have?

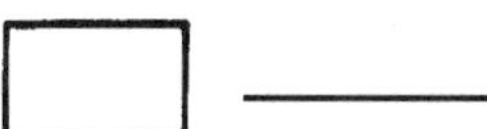

Skill 47: 2-D Shapes

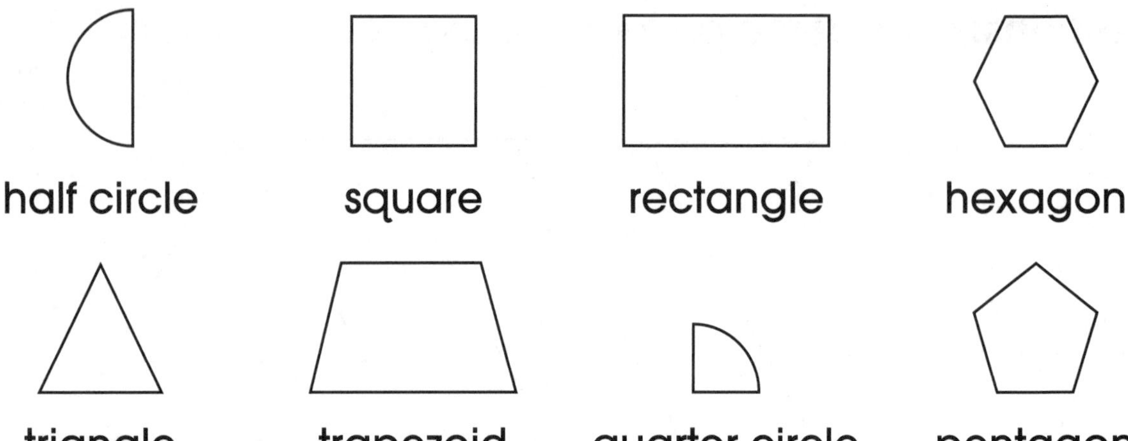

Directions: Draw the shape you have when you put the following shapes together.

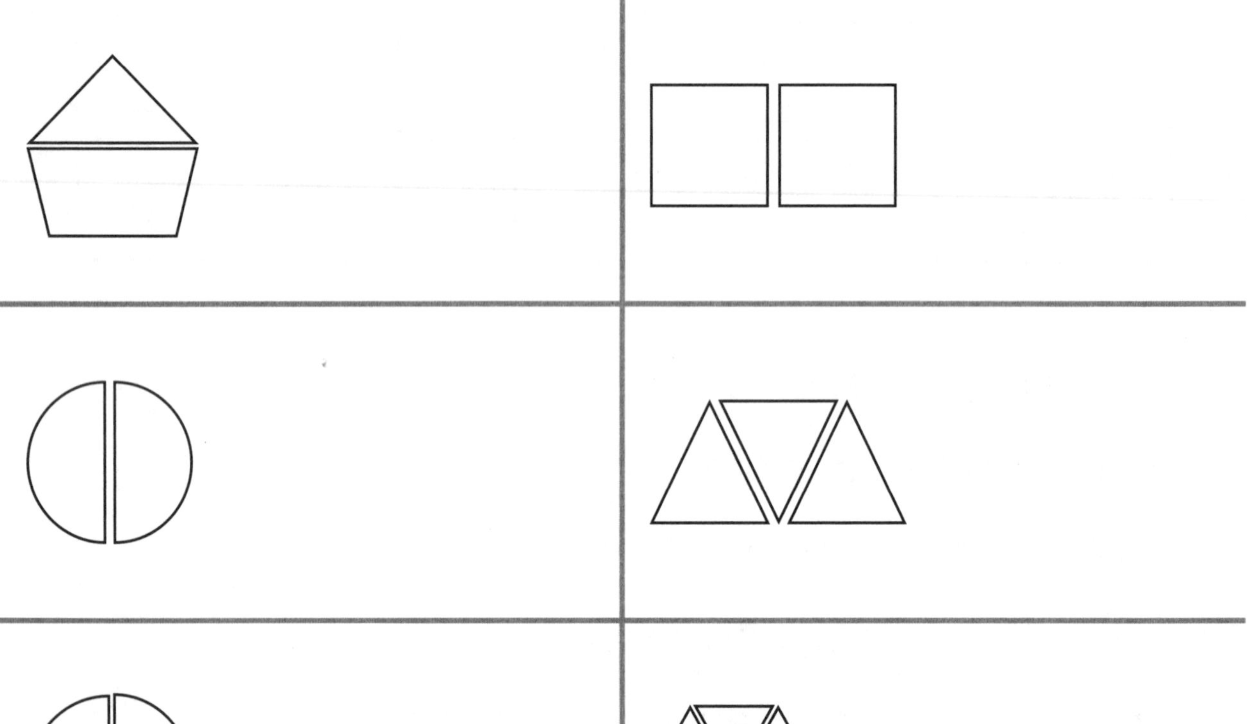

Skill 47: 2-D Shapes

Directions: Jan made cookies with her new cookie cutters. Count how many sides each cookie has. Then, answer the questions below.

_____ sides  _____ sides _____ sides

H	S	T	P
hexagon cookie	square cookie	triangle cookie	pentagon cookie

Which cookie has the fewest sides? ____________________

Which cookie has the most sides? ____________________

Write the cookie letters in order of the number of sides the shapes have.

_______ _______ _______ _______

fewest sides most sides

How many more sides does **H** have than **S**? _______

How many fewer sides does **T** have than **P**? _______

Skill 48: 3-D Shapes

cone

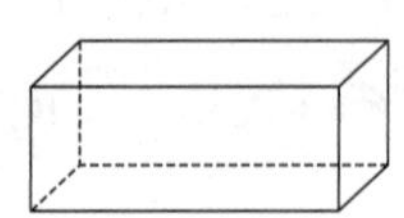

rectangular prism

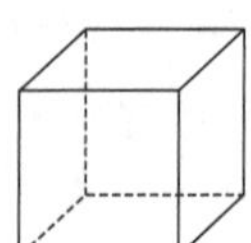

cube

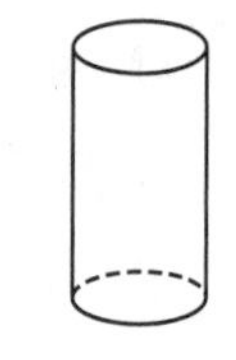

cylinder

The flat side of a solid shape is called a face.

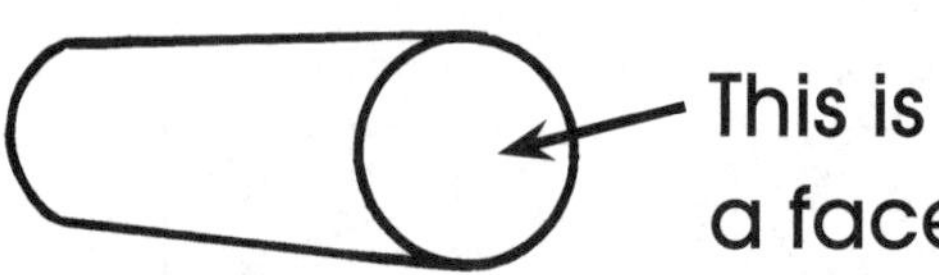

This is a face.

Directions: Draw the shape you have when you put the following shapes together.

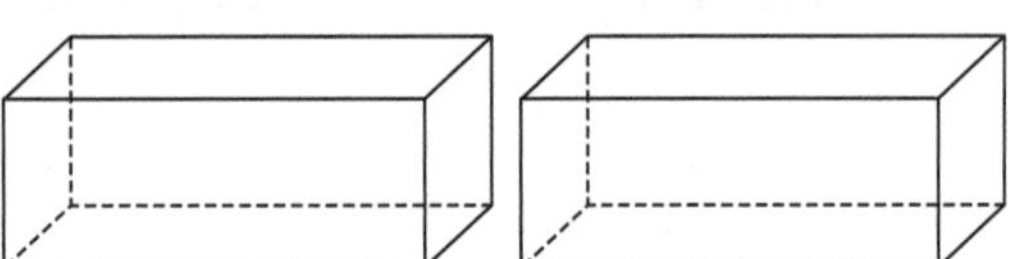

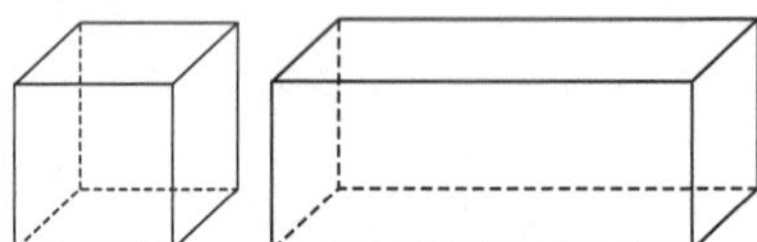

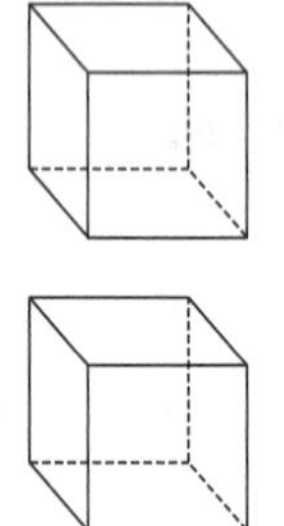

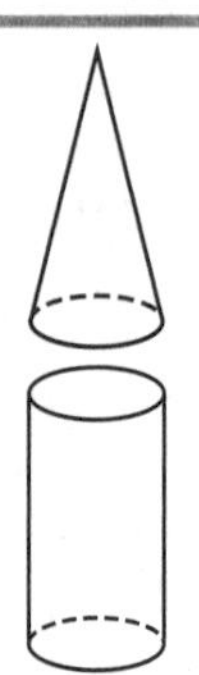

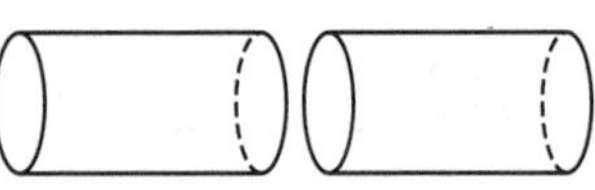

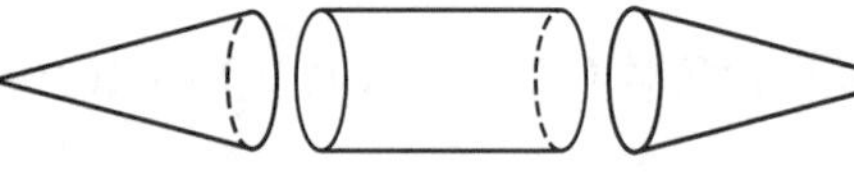

MATH

Skill 48: 3-D Shapes

Directions: Complete the table. Then, in the drawing, color the cube red, the rectangular prism blue, the cone green, and the cylinder yellow.

Spatial Shape	Number of Faces
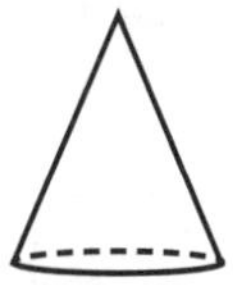	
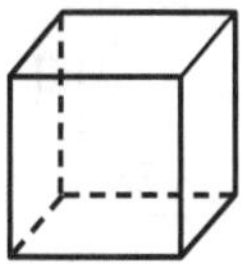	
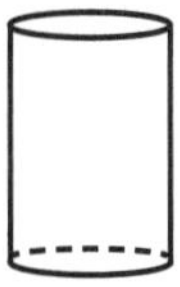	
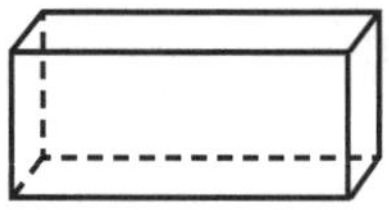	
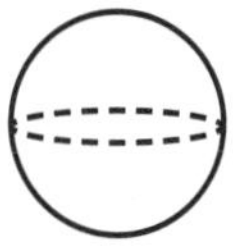	

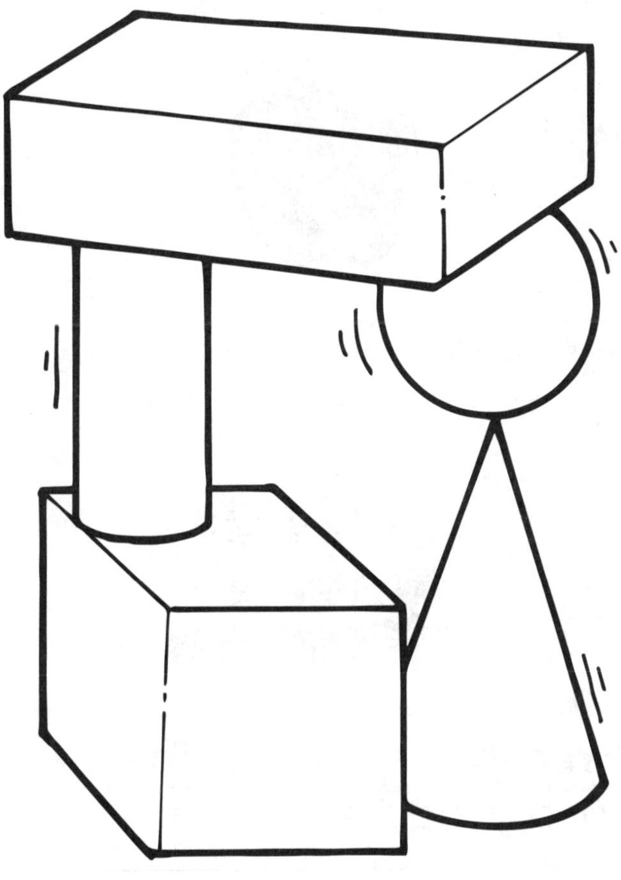

Skill 49: Partitioning Shapes

A shape can be divided into equal pieces. It can be divided into two equal pieces, three equal pieces, or four equal pieces.

Directions: Draw lines to show how you and a friend can equally share each item.

Directions: Draw lines to show how you and 2 friends can equally share each item.

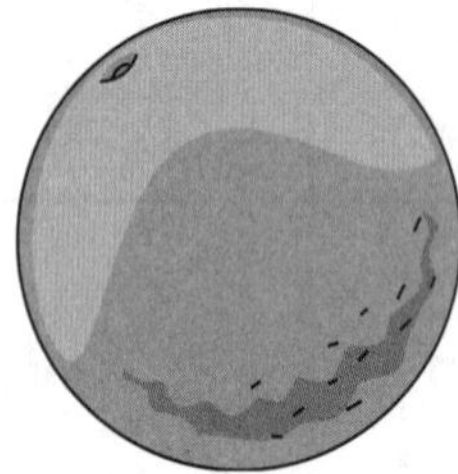

Directions: Draw lines to show how you and 3 friends can equally share each item.

50 LANGUAGE ARTS SKILLS

Skill 51: Common Nouns

A **noun** names a person, place, or thing.

Examples:	Person	Place	Thing
	mom	school	bench
	dentist	office	moon

Directions: Write each noun in the correct column.

girl	park	city
aunt	letter	ball

Person	Place	Thing
girl	park	ball
aunt	city	letter

Directions: Circle the two nouns in each sentence.

1. The cloud is shaped like a rabbit.
2. The letter is from my friend.

Skill 51: Common Nouns

Directions: Write each noun in the correct column.

kite	boy	shell
beach	town	chief

Person	**Place**	**Thing**

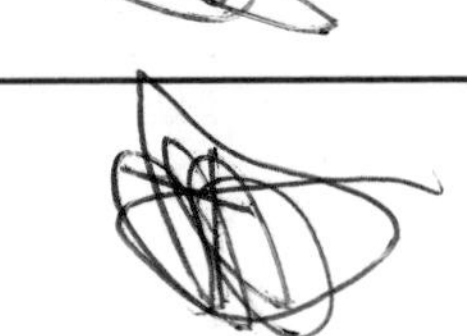

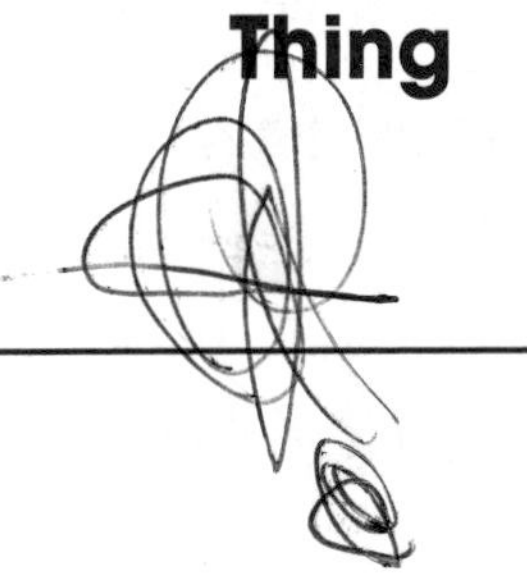

Directions: Circle the two nouns in each sentence.

1. She put the glass in the kitchen.
2. The kite sailed with the breeze.
3. My aunt owns a store.
4. The girl read a book.
5. My sister finished her homework.

LANGUAGE ARTS

Skill 52: Proper Nouns

A **proper noun** names a specific person, place, or thing. Proper nouns begin with a capital letter.

Directions: Use capital letters to write the name of each person or pet correctly.

1. cindy lewis ______________________
2. ms. cohen ______________________
3. dan li ______________________
4. ellen garza ______________________
5. fifi ______________________
6. julie ______________________
7. spot ______________________
8. angelo ______________________

Skill 52: Proper Nouns

Directions: Use capital letters to write the name of each place correctly.

1. the corner store ____________________
2. miller park ____________________
3. jameston airport ____________________
4. mexico ____________________
5. first stop shop ____________________
6. los angeles, california ____________________
7. woodland school ____________________
8. paris, france ____________________

Skill 53: Verbs

Verbs are action words. They tell what happens in a sentence.

Examples: Mia **reads** the book
Tomas **drives** the car.

Directions: Underline the verb in each sentence.

1. Imani and Kate jump rope.
2. José swims.
3. Blanche catches the ball.
4. Zach helps his friend.
5. Mom bakes a cake.
6. Jake plants a tree.
7. Kira trips on the rope.
8. Maria watches the parade.

LANGUAGE ARTS

Skill 53: Verbs

Directions: Circle the verb in each sentence.

1. My dog runs fast.
2. Erin thinks about the question.
3. He goes to class.
4. We paint pictures.
5. They climb to the top.
6. Jim plays his guitar.
7. Henry builds snowmen.
8. Hailey and I go to camp.

Directions: Write a sentence about your class using a verb.

____

____

Skill 54: Pronouns

A pronoun is a word that can take the place of a noun.

Examples: Drew draws a picture. **He** paints a picture.
Omar and I like to dance. **We** like to dance.

The words **I**, **me**, **you**, **he**, **she**, **him**, **her**, **it**, **we**, **us**, **they**, and **them** are pronouns.

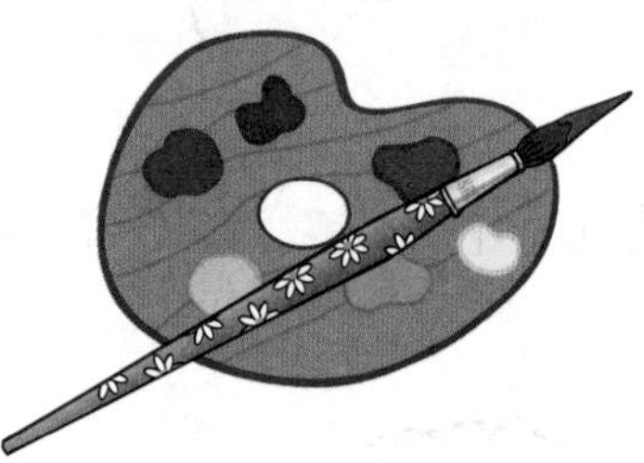

Directions: Draw a line to match each word or words on the left with a pronoun on the right.

Emma	he
the pen	they
Andy	it
Mom and Dad	she

Directions: Write one sentence using a noun. Then, rewrite it using a pronoun.

____

____

Skill 54: Pronouns

Directions: Write a pronoun in place of the underlined words.

1. <u>The computer</u> was a gift.

   ______________ was a gift.

2. <u>The Johnsons</u> moved.

   ______________ moved.

3. <u>My dad</u> likes to cook.

   ______________ likes to cook.

4. Marla wants to surprise <u>Javier</u>.

   Marla wants to surprise ______________.

5. The shirt is for <u>Tim</u>.

   The shirt is for ______________.

6. <u>Chris and I</u> are going camping.

   ______________ are going camping.

Skill 55: Adjectives

An **adjective** is a word that describes a noun. It tells more about a noun. Adjectives can answer the question **What kind?**

Examples: the **green** frog the **soft** pillow

Directions: Circle the adjective in each sentence. Make a line under the noun it tells about.

Example: Winter is usually cold.

1. Jada picked the pink roses.
2. Lex looked up at the tall sunflower.
3. The sunshine feels warm.
4. The kitten is cute.
5. A tiny bee buzzed around the garden.
6. What a hot day!

LANGUAGE ARTS

Skill 55: Adjectives

Directions: Write the best adjective to complete each group of words.

famous	shiny	cool
smooth	narrow	golden

1. the _______________ sun
2. a _______________ rock
3. a _______________ penny
4. the _______________ breeze
5. a _______________ path
6. a _______________ person

Directions: Circle the adjective that describes the weather today.

1. Today, the weather is (warm/cool).
2. The sky is (blue/gray).
3. It is (wet/dry).
4. It is a (beautiful/cloudy) day!

Skill 56: Articles

A, **an**, and **the** are called **articles**. They help nouns.

A is used before a noun that begins with a consonant.

Example: **a** beetle

An is used before a noun that begins with a vowel.

Example: **an** ant

The is used before a noun that names a particular person, place, or thing.

Example: **the** bear

Directions: Write **a** or **an** for each noun.

1. ______ forest
2. ______ plant
3. ______ arrow
4. ______ triangle
5. ______ idea
6. ______ newspaper

Directions: Write **a**, **an**, or **the** to finish each sentence.

1. Miriam walked to ______ pond.
2. They saw ______ lizard.
3. They saw a fish swimming in ______ water.
4. Todd ate ______ apple.

Skill 56: Articles

Directions: Write **a** or **an** for each noun.

1. ______ owl
2. ______ dish
3. ______ brother
4. ______ oven
5. ______ sale
6. ______ actor

Directions: Write a sentence with **a**.

____

____

Directions: Write a sentence with **an**.

____

____

Directions: Write a sentence with **the**.

____

____

Skill 57: Prepositions

A **preposition** can show location (where) or time (when). Prepositions link nouns to other words in the sentence. Some common prepositions are **to**, **from**, **in**, **on**, **behind**, **at**, **below**, **near**, **by**, **above**, **into**, **off**, and **with**.

Example: The book is **below** the shelf.

Directions: Find and circle the prepositions.

1. Jan put her shoes on her feet.
2. It was hot in the room.
3. Water dripped from the faucet.
4. A tree fell near Tom's tent.
5. The cave was filled with bats!
6. At 6:00, the cave tour was done.

Skill 57: Prepositions

Directions: Use the words in the box to complete each item below.

beside	above	in	behind	under

1. Where is the girl?

_______________ the covers

2. Where is the bear?

_______________ the boy

3. Where is the fox?

_______________ a box

4. Where is the dog house?

_______________ the dog

5. Where is the cat?

_______________ the dog

LANGUAGE ARTS

Skill 58: Sentences

A **sentence** is a group of words that tells a complete idea.

Example: Sentence — We traveled around the United States.

Not a sentence — Around the United States.

Directions: Read each set of words below. Rewrite them as a sentence. Make sure to start with a capital letter and end with a period.

1. our classroom has a snake

   ____

2. the cat is white with black spots

   ____

3. his name is Chet

   ____

4. the dog likes to ride in the car

   ____

Directions: Write two sentences about your favorite animal.

____

____

____

Skill 58: Sentences

Directions: Write **S** if the words below make a sentence. Write **NS** if they do not make a sentence.

1. _____ We went to Texas.
2. _____ Colorado is a beautiful state.
3. _____ Tall mountains and cool air.
4. _____ I would like to live there.
5. _____ We also saw California.
6. _____ The beautiful ocean.

Directions: Write words of your own to complete each sentence.

1. This summer, ____

   ____.

2. One day, ____

   ____.

LANGUAGE ARTS

Skill 59: Statements

A **statement** is a telling sentence. It starts with a capital letter. It ends with a period (.).

Example: Statement — I bought bread at the bakery.
Not a Statement — How will you carry it home?

Directions: Rewrite the sentences. Each should begin with a capital letter and end with a period.

1. carla has a telescope

   ____

2. carla looks for stars

   ____

3. dad showed her Mars

   ____

4. she can find the Big Dipper

   ____

5. the moon is easy to find

   ____

Skill 59: Statements

Directions: Write **S** for each sentence that is statement. Write **NS** for each sentence that is not a statement.

1. _____ The baker is Ms. Smith.

2. _____ She bakes bread and cookies.

3. _____ Does anyone help her?

4. _____ A boy named Sam helps her.

5. _____ How much does it cost?

6. _____ The bread smells good.

Directions: Write each statement with a capital letter and a period.

1. the ocean is deep

____

2. some mammals live in the ocean

____

Skill 60: Questions

A **question** is an asking sentence. A question starts with a capital letter. It ends with a question mark.

Examples: What did you have for lunch?
Where is my bike?

Directions: Complete each question with a question mark.

1. Who is the U.S. president____
2. Where were you born____
3. Where do you live____
4. What movie do you want to see____
5. What is your favorite animal____
6. What time is it ____
7. Where are my shoes____
8. Is it raining____

Skill 60: Questions

Directions: Write **Q** for each sentence that asks a question. Write **NQ** for each sentence that does not ask a question.

1. _____ Do you like to draw?
2. _____ I like to use a pencil.
3. _____ Will you show me how to draw?
4. _____ I want to draw a horse.
5. _____ Is drawing easy for you?
6. _____ Which pencil is yours?

Directions: Write each question with a capital letter and a question mark.

1. does John like to paint

____

2. which color is his favorite

____

LANGUAGE ARTS

Skill 61: Exclamations

An **exclamation** is a sentence that shows excitement. It can also show surprise or strong feeling. It starts with a capital letter. It ends with an exclamation point.

Examples: I am happy for you! That is great news!

Directions: Read each pair of sentences. One sentence in each pair is a statement. The other sentence is an exclamation. Add the correct end marks.

1. I won the race____

   Today is Saturday____

2. Jack is my brother____

   Jack found ten dollars____

3. I have two sisters____

   Wait for me____

4. The dog got out____

   I lost the book____

Skill 61: Exclamations

Directions: Write **E** for each sentence that is an exclamation. Write **NE** for each sentence that is not an exclamation.

1. _____ You are doing a great job!
2. _____ That is a nice shirt.
3. _____ There is a mouse!
4. _____ Is the wind blowing?
5. _____ Boo!

Directions: Write each exclamation with a capital letter and an exclamation mark.

1. ouch

____

2. what an amazing sunset

____

3. this is the best soup ever

____

LANGUAGE ARTS

Skill 62: Combining Sentences

Sometimes, two sentences can be made into one. Both sentences must tell about the same thing.

Example: Dolphins live in the ocean. Sharks live in the ocean.

Use the word **and** to join the parts of the sentence.

Example: Dolphins **and** sharks live in the ocean.

Directions: Read the sentences. Fill in the missing words.

1. Todd went to the pool. Pedro went to the pool.

   Todd ____________ Pedro went to the pool.

2. The snow is cold. The snow is pretty.

   The snow is cold ____________ pretty.

3. Coats are fun to wear. Mittens are fun to wear.

   Coats and mittens are ____________ to wear.

4. Li played three games. Dad played three games.

   ____________ and Dad played three games.

Skill 62: Combining Sentences

Directions: Read the letter. Three pairs of sentences can be joined. Underline each pair.

Dear Katie,

Guess what? We went to the ocean. I had fun. Nate had fun. We rode many waves. Tammy stayed home. Jess stayed home. They are too little for the ocean.

My towel was lost. My hat was lost. Don't worry, I was lucky. Nate found them. I left them on the beach. It was a fun day. I love the ocean.

Hope to see you soon!

Your friend,

Heather

Skill 63: Capitalizing the First Word in a Sentence

A sentence always begins with a capital letter. This shows that a new sentence is starting.

Examples: Where is your bike? Aden has two cats.

Directions: Look for the words that should be capitalized. Circle the letters that should be capitalized.

I drew a forest. I showed my mom my drawing. she loved it. I told her how I drew it. then, I showed it to my dad. he asked if I could draw something for him. I drew a picture of a panda. pandas are my favorite animal. dad loved my drawing!

Directions: Write two sentences about your favorite place. Be sure to begin each sentence with a capital letter.

____

____

____

____

Skill 63: Capitalizing the First Word in a Sentence

Directions: Rewrite each sentence. Be sure to begin each sentence with a capital letter.

1. it is time to wake up.

   ____

2. put on your clothes.

   ____

3. breakfast is ready.

   ____

4. can you be ready in five minutes?

   ____

5. remember your homework.

   ____

6. the bus leaves soon.

   ____

LANGUAGE ARTS

Skill 64: Capitalizing the Pronoun I

The pronoun **I** is always capitalized. It can start a sentence. It can be in the middle of a sentence.

Examples: I like apples. I will wear boots.
Min and I want to swim.

Directions: Circle each letter that needs to be capitalized.

1. Andrew and i went camping.
2. i have Friday off.
3. i am reading a book called Saving the Ocean.
4. i would like to visit Boulder, Colorado.
5. Can i go to Grace's house?
6. James and i will be in the talent show.
7. i am glad that my friends will be there.
8. i sent a card to grandma.
9. i told him what happened.

Skill 64: Capitalizing the Pronoun I

Directions: Read each sentence below. Write the word **I** in the box. Fill in the other blank with a word that completes the sentence.

1. ☐ like the color ____________________.

2. ____________________ and ☐ play soccer.

3. ☐ like to draw ____________________.

4. ☐ have a new ____________________.

5. My ____________________ and ☐ like to watch movies together.

6. Each weekend, ☐ go ____________________.

Skill 65: Capitalizing Names

Names begin with a capital letter. A person's name starts with a capital letter. A pet's name starts with a capital letter, too.

Examples: My aunt's name is Joyce.
I have a cat named Lola.

Directions: Name each child and pet. Choose a set of names from the box. Write them next to the picture. Make sure you start each name with a capital letter.

sara and salem dan and bubbles	tom and chirpy chris and spot	stella and star

____________ and ____________

____________ and ____________

____________ and ____________

____________ and ____________

____________ and ____________

Skill 65: Capitalizing Names

Directions: The names below do not start with a capital letter. Find each letter that should be a capital letter. Make three lines below it (≡). Then, write the capital letter above it.

1. luke, jason, and leo are all sam's brothers.

2. paco named the puppies bella and sassy.

3. jack saw his friend anita at the store.

4. tanya got to feed penny and samson at the farm.

Directions: Write a sentence about two of your friends. Use their names in the sentence.

____

____

Skill 66: Capitalizing Place Names

Place names begin with a capital letter.

Examples: Miami, Florida   Jackson Library
Mars   Germany

Directions: Circle each letter that should be capitalized.

Example: We are going to maine this fall.

1. Do you think there is life on venus?

2. Ann is moving to san diego, california.

3. It snowed two feet in minnesota!

4. Jon goes to sundance elementary.

5. Make a left turn on hudson street.

6. Lex swims at minden lake.

Skill 66: Capitalizing Place Names

Directions: Answer each question. Make sure to start each place name with a capital letter.

1. What country do you live in?

____

2. What state are you from?

____

3. What is a place you would like to visit?

____

4. What is the name of your school?

____

5. What is the name of your favorite place?

____

LANGUAGE ARTS

Skill 67: Capitalizing Days and Months

The **days of the week** start with a capital letter.

Examples: Monday, Tuesday, Wednesday, Thursday, Friday, Saturday, Sunday

The **months of the year** start with a capital letter, too.

Examples: January, April, December

Directions: Read each clue. Write the day of the week that matches it. Use the list above.

1. The word **sun** is in my name. ________________

2. I am the first weekday.
   My name starts with **m**. ________________

3. I am the first day of the
   weekend. ________________

4. My name starts with **t**. I come
   near the end of the week. ________________

5. I come in the middle of the week
   and my name starts with **w**. ________________

6. I am the last weekday
   before the weekend. ________________

7. My name starts with **t**. I come
   near the start of the week. ________________

Skill 67: Capitalizing Days and Months

Directions: Fill in the month in each sentence. Make sure to use a capital letter.

1. (january) Nancy's birthday is in ____________________.
2. (august) Pedro likes to swim in ____________________.
3. (december) Jake builds a snowman in ________________.
4. (march) Mina met Rachel in ____________________.
5. (october) ____________________ is my favorite month.
6. (september) School starts in ____________________.

When is your birthday? ____________________

In what month is your favorite holiday? ____________________

LANGUAGE ARTS

Skill 68: Capitalizing Book and Movie Titles

The first word and all important words in book and movie titles should begin with a **capital letter**.

Examples: The Magic School Bus

Dictionary of Animals

Directions: Circle each letter that needs to be capitalized.

1. the little red engine
2. lily goes to rome
3. playing the guitar
4. guide to dinosaurs
5. learn to make a kite
6. bingo chases sticks
7. where the sidewalk ends
8. star wars
9. a bug's life
10. charlotte's web

Skill 68: Capitalizing Book and Movie Titles

Directions: Circle each letter that needs to be capitalized.

1. toy story
2. green eggs and ham
3. frozen
4. ivy and bean

Directions: Answer each question with a book or movie title.

1. What is your favorite book?

____

2. What is your favorite movie?

____

3. What book are you reading now?

____

4. What was the last movie you saw?

____

LANGUAGE ARTS

Skill 69: Periods

A period is an end mark. It comes at the end of a sentence.

Examples: Laura is my sister⊙ My name is Luis⊙

Directions: Each sentence below is missing a period. Add it and circle it.

Example: Turn on the lights⊙

1. There are not many eagles left in the wild
2. Goats live in the mountains
3. Giant pandas are found in China
4. The lettuce is fresh
5. The clock has stopped
6. Tina is taking an art class
7. The sky is dark
8. I really liked that

Skill 69: Periods

Directions: Rewrite each sentence. Make sure it starts with a capital letter and ends with a period.

1. the shoes are too big

____

2. the kitchen is painted yellow

____

3. i will be home late

____

4. i cannot carry this box much longer

____

5. the parrot repeated what Lucy said

____

6. we need an umbrella right now

____

Skill 70: Question Marks

A **question mark** comes at the end of a question. It shows where the question ends.

Examples: Can you play cards? Have you seen Max?

Directions: Rewrite each question. Make sure it starts with a capital letter and ends with a question mark.

1. will you be at the party

____

2. have you packed yet

____

3. what do you want for dinner

____

4. what color is your new bike

____

5. how far away is it

____

Skill 70: Question Marks

Directions: Rewrite each question. Make sure it starts with a capital letter and ends with a question mark.

1. when does school start

   ____

2. what is your favorite day of the week

   ____

3. where do your cousins live

   ____

4. when is the play

   ____

5. when is your birthday

   ____

6. what town or city do you live in

   ____

7. what is today's date

   ____

8. where would you like to visit

   ____

Skill 71: Exclamation Points

An **exclamation point** comes at the end of an exclamation. An exclamation is a sentence that shows excitement. It can also show surprise.

Examples: I can't believe it! We won!

Directions: Read each pair of sentences. Add a period after each statement. Add an exclamation point after each exclamation.

1. Watch out for that branch____

   Mom will pick up the branches____

2. Don't forget your coat____

   Sonia has a blue coat____

3. Today is Thursday____

   It snowed six inches today____

4. Jaya did not step in the puddle____

   I dropped my bag in the puddle____

71: Exclamation Points

Directions: Write an exclamation about each picture. Begin with a capital letter. End with an exclamation point.

Skill 72: Commas With Dates

A **comma** is a punctuation mark. In a date, it goes between the day and the year.

Examples: December 20, 1973   October 31, 2006

If a comma is missing, use this mark (^,) to add it.

Example: November 3^, 2014

Directions: Commas are missing from the dates below. Use this mark (^,) to add them.

1. Grandma and Grandpa got married on April 2 1960.
2. Uncle Brian was born on March 5 1979.
3. Cory moved to Florida on February 23 2009.
4. I met Jada on July 11 2008.
5. Riley's birthday is January 13 2004.

Directions: When were you born? Write the date.

____

Directions: Ask a friend when he or she was born. Write the date.

____

LANGUAGE ARTS

Skill 72: Commas With Dates

Directions: Rewrite each date. Use commas where they are needed.

1. February 9 2015 ____________________

2. November 22 2016 ____________________

3. October 4 1999 ____________________

4. January 5 1984 ____________________

5. September 12 1965 ____________________

6. July 31 1944 ____________________

7. April 29 1814 ____________________

Skill 73: Commas With Cities and States

A **comma** is used between the name of a city and state.

Examples: Columbus, Ohio   Philadelphia, Pennsylvania

Directions: Add a comma between each city and state. Use this mark (^) to add each comma.

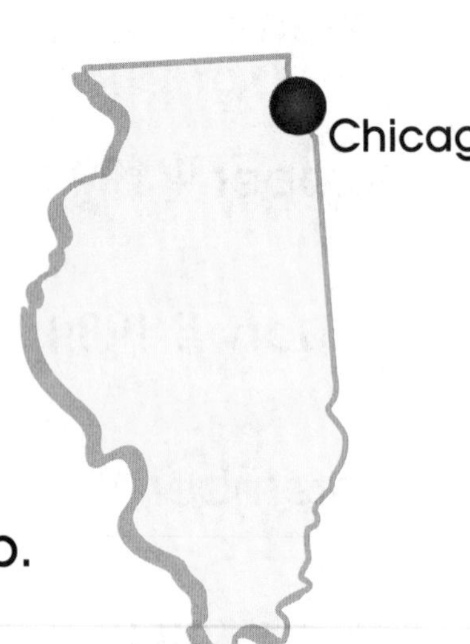

1. Have you been to Chicago Illinois?

2. You might know Dallas Texas.

3. Point to Anchorage Alaska on the map.

4. Would you like to go to Tucson Arizona?

5. How about Seattle Washington?

6. Have you heard of San Jose California?

7. What is it like in St. Louis Missouri?

Skill 73: Commas With Cities and States

Directions: Finish each sentence with a city and state from the box. Use commas where they are needed.

Lima Ohio	Reno Nevada	Austin Texas
Macon Georgia	Portland Maine	Miami Florida

1. Jordan's uncle lives in ______________________________.

2. In March, Liz will go to ______________________________.

3. Ashley is moving to ______________________________.

4. Stefanie has lived in ______________________________ for 9 years.

5. Angela found ______________________________ on the map.

6. It will take Cassie three days to drive to

______________________________.

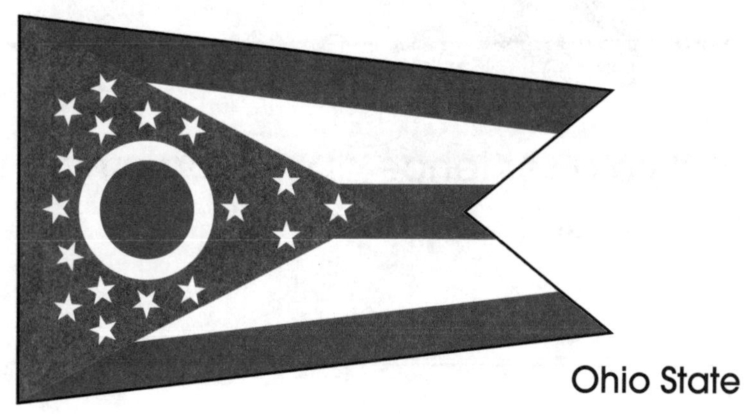

Ohio State Flag

LANGUAGE ARTS

Skill 74: Apostrophes With Possessives

An apostrophe plus **s** (**'s**) shows that someone owns something.

Examples: Adam**'s** car   Keisha**'s** book

Directions: Add **'s** to each blank below. Draw a line under the item each person owns.

1. Mr. Dante_____ truck
2. Diego_____ pencil
3. Eli_____ painting
4. Matt_____ kite
5. Kat_____ rabbit
6. Caleb_____ leaf

Directions: Write a sentence about something a friend owns. Use **'s** to show what he or she owns.

____

Skill 74: Apostrophes With Possessives

Directions: Read each pair of sentences. Make a check mark (✓) next to the one that is correct.

1. _____ John's scarf

   _____ Johns scarf

2. _____ Amys snake'

   _____ Amy's snake

3. _____ Amad's boots

   _____ Amads boots

4. _____ Noels cookie

   _____ Noel's cookie

5. _____ Kims bird

   _____ Kim's bird

LANGUAGE ARTS

Skill 75: Subject-Verb Agreement

When a sentence is about one person or thing, add **s** to the verb.

Example: The leaf blow**s** away.

When a sentence is about more than one person or thing, do not add **s**.

Example: The cats sleep all day.

Directions: Draw a line to match each sentence to the correct ending.

1. The bell	ring at 3:00. rings at 3:00.
2. The oranges	fall on the ground. falls on the ground.
3. Ms. Swan	drops the pencils. drop the pencils.
4. Jacob	runs after school. run after school.
5. The boys	paints in the art room. paint in the art room.

Skill 75: Subject-Verb Agreement

Directions: Circle the word that completes each sentence.

1. Simon (puts, put) on his space suit.
2. He (slip, slips) on the boots.
3. He (drop, drops) the gloves on the floor.
4. Simon and his dog (travel, travels) to outer space.
5. They (sees, see) Earth from far above.
6. They (looks, look) for Mars.
7. Simon's mom (calls, call) him home for dinner.

Skill 76: Irregular Verbs: Am, Is, Are

The words **am**, **is**, and **are** are all verbs.

Use **am** with the word **I**.

Examples: I **am** hot. I **am** sad.

Use **is** with one person or thing.

Examples: The car **is** blue. Sam **is** at the farm.

Use **are** with more than one person or thing.

Examples: The papers **are** on my desk. The girls **are** outside.

Directions: Each sentence below has the wrong verb. Rewrite it with the correct verb. Choose from **is**, **am**, or **are**.

1. I is glad to help my friend.

   ____

2. The farmer am ready to feed the chickens.

   ____

3. The ducks is by the pond.

   ____

4. The dog are black and white.

   ____

Skill 76: Irregular Verbs: Am, Is, Are

Directions: Complete each sentence with the correct word from the box. Write it on the line.

1. is are — The balloon ____________ in the sky.

2. am are — I ____________ sure I took the trash out.

3. are is — Peter and Jose ____________ in the kitchen.

4. am is — The horse ____________ next to the pond.

5. is are — The ducks ____________ with their babies.

6. is are — The pony ____________ eight months old.

LANGUAGE ARTS

Skill 77: Past-Tense Verbs: Was, Were

The words **was** and **were** tell about something that happened in the past.

Use **was** with one person or thing.

Examples: The stove **was** broken
Sanjay **was** ready for lunch.

Use **were** with more than one person or thing.

Examples: Drew and Liza **were** at the store.
The towels **were** in the closet.

Directions: Read each sentence. Check to see if the verbs **was** and **were** are correct. If you find a mistake, cross it out. Write the correct word above it.

Example: The koala ~~were~~ **was** in the tree.

1. The dance were at 6:00.

2. The kids was excited to go.

3. The balloons were red, yellow, and green.

4. The band were very loud.

5. Amit and Maggy was the first to dance.

Skill 77: Past-Tense Verbs: Was, Were

Directions: Write **was** or **were** to complete each sentence.

1. My window ____________ open all night.
2. I ____________ surprised on my birthday this year.
3. You ____________ running to the library.
4. Eli ____________ at the play last night.
5. Mom and Dad ____________ sitting in the front row.
6. You ____________ the winner!
7. They ____________ able to see the ocean.
8. Jorge ____________ trying to catch a fly.
9. The evening light ____________ soft.
10. The clothes ____________ on sale.

Skill 78: Past Tense: Add d or ed

Verbs in the **past tense** tell about things that already happened. Add **ed** to most verbs to tell about the past.

Examples: Hilo knock**ed** on the wall. It start**ed** to snow.

If a verb ends in **e**, just add **d**.

Examples: race → race**d** live → live**d**

Directions: Circle the past tense verb in each sentence.

1. The game started at 4:00.
2. A ball landed right next to my mom!
3. Dad picked it up.
4. The fans cheered.
5. The game ended with a score of 5 to 8.

Directions: Write a sentence about something that happened last year. Use a verb that ends with **ed**.

____

____

LANGUAGE ARTS

Skill 78: Past Tense: Add d or ed

Directions: Write the past tense of each verb.

1. mow ____________________
2. climb ____________________
3. bake ____________________
4. open ____________________
5. push ____________________
6. fill ____________________
7. boil ____________________
8. type ____________________
9. talk ____________________
10. jump ____________________

Skill 79: Verbs: Has and Have

Some **verbs** do not show action. They tell about something that exists now or that existed in the past. **Has** and **have** are examples of these types of verbs.

Use **has** to tell about one person, place, or thing.

Example: She **has** blue eyes.

Use **have** with **you** and **I** and with more than one person, place, or thing.

Example: Dan and Sue **have** black hair.

Directions: Write **has** or **have** to complete each sentence.

1. Sharon's apartment ______________ lots of windows.
2. I ______________ a dog and two cats.
3. You ______________ beautiful eyes.
4. Jackie ______________ many books.
5. Some houses ______________ fences.
6. He ______________ two sisters.
7. The cats ______________ many toys.
8. Kelly and Mac ______________ a red wagon.

Skill 79: Verbs: Has and Have

Directions: Write **has** or **have** to complete each sentence.

1. We ____________ fun plans for this summer.

2. The school ____________ Friday off.

3. My dad ____________ three fishing poles.

4. The girl ____________ a hat.

5. Lia and I ____________ tomatoes on our sandwiches.

6. The doghouses ____________ new roofs.

7. His sister ____________ dance shoes.

8. The zoo ____________ many animals.

Directions: Write a sentence with the word **has**.

____

Directions: Write a sentence with the word **have**.

____

Skill 80: Contractions With Not

A **contraction** is made when two words are put together. It is a shorter way to say something. An apostrophe (') takes the place of the missing letters.

Examples: Here are some contractions with **not**.

is not = isn't	are not = aren't
was not = wasn't	were not = weren't
does not = doesn't	did not = didn't
have not = haven't	can not = can't

Directions: Read each sentence below. On the line, write a contraction for the underlined words.

1. I <u>can not</u> wait to go swimming. ________________
2. I <u>have not</u> ever gone before. ________________
3. Mom said it <u>is not</u> hard to learn. ________________
4. It <u>was not</u> hard to hold my breath underwater. ___________
5. There <u>were not</u> too many people at the pool. ___________
6. We <u>are not</u> going to be home by bedtime! ___________

Skill 80: Contractions With Not

Directions: Write the contraction for each group of words

1. is not = ________________
2. does not = ________________
3. would not = ________________
4. have not = ________________
5. can not = ________________

Directions: Write a contraction to complete each sentence.

1. We ________________ seen the movie.
   (have not)
2. Ryan ________________ able to visit Aunt Anne.
   (was not)
3. He said he ________________ be there at 2:00 p.m.
   (can not)

Directions: Write a sentence using each contraction.

1. isn't: ____

   ____
2. didn't: ____

   ____

LANGUAGE ARTS

Skill 81: Plural Nouns With s

Plural means **more than one**. To make most nouns plural, just add **s**.

Examples: one hand → two hands one plane → four planes
one tent → six tents one hen → twelve hens

Directions: Add an **s** to each noun to make it plural.

1. Did you see the bee_____ fly back to their hive?

2. Draw that spider with your pencil_____.

3. Sanj found four ladybug_____.

4. Watch out for tick_____ when you camp!

5. Our dog_____ get fleas every spring.

6. Jose saw four slug_____ in the park.

7. Six caterpillar_____ crawled up the leaf.

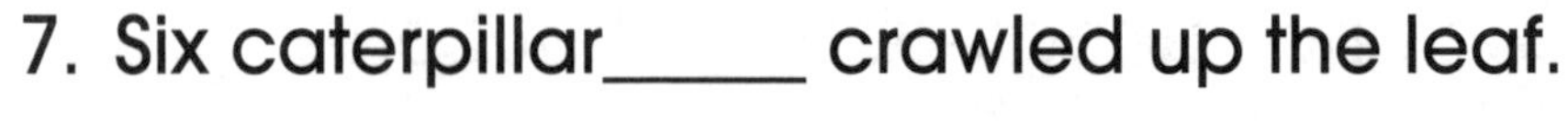

Skill 81: Plural Nouns With s

Directions: Write each noun in the correct column.

peanut	toes	crickets	guitar	swing
band	shirts	letters	keys	pond

Singular	**Plural**
____________	____________
____________	____________
____________	____________
____________	____________
____________	____________

Directions: Circle the correct word to finish each sentence.

1. Andrea fed each elephant one (peanut/peanuts).
2. There were three (guitar/guitars) at the store.
3. All of the (swing/swings) in the park were full.
4. Mark likes to swim in a (pond/ponds) in the summer.

LANGUAGE ARTS

Skill 82: Irregular Plural Nouns

For some words, do not add **s** to make the plural. Instead, the whole word changes.

Examples:

One	More Than One
woman	women
mouse	mice
goose	geese
child	children
tooth	teeth
man	men
foot	feet

Other words do not change at all. Use the same word for one and more than one.

Examples: one moose → eight moose   one deer → five deer
one sheep → three sheep   one fish → ten fish

Directions: Look at each picture. Circle the word that names the picture.

children child	feet foot
woman women	deers deer
moose mooses	gooses geese

Skill 82: Irregular Plural Nouns

Directions: Look at each number and picture below. Fill in the missing word on the line.

mouse	sheep	mice	deer
men	fish	teeth	geese

6 ____________________

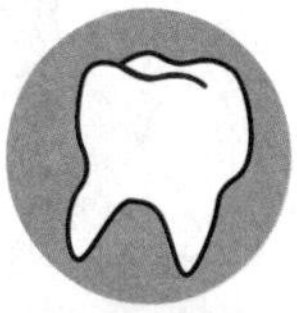

5 ____________________

14 ____________________

50 ____________________

1 ____________________

6 ____________________

4 ____________________

9 ____________________

Skill 83: Prefixes and Suffixes

A **prefix** is added to the beginning of a root word. A **suffix** is added to the end of a root word. They change the meaning of the words.

The prefix **un** means **not** or **opposite of**.

The prefix **re** means **again**.

The suffix **er** means **one who**.

The suffix **ed** means that something happened **in the past**.

Directions: On the line, write a word with a prefix to match each meaning.

1. not sure= ____________________

2. read again= ____________________

3. not able= ____________________

4. told again= ____________________

5. copy again= ____________________

6. fill again= ____________________

Skill 83: Prefixes and Suffixes

Directions: Each **bold** word is missing a suffix. Add the suffix **er** or **ed**. Use the meaning of the sentence to decide which one to add.

1. Lin **tuck**_____ her doll into bed.
2. Kendra **smile**_____ at the baby.
3. Alyssa wants to be a **paint**_____ one day.
4. Grandpa handed a check to the **bank**_____.

Directions: Write the words under the correct headings.

unhurt	reuse	unfair
liked	farmer	singer

Words With Prefixes	**Words With Suffixes**
____________________	____________________
____________________	____________________
____________________	____________________

LANGUAGE ARTS

Skill 84: Pronouns I and Me

You use the words **I** and **me** to talk about yourself.

Examples: **I** made pizza. Sandy gave **me** a coat.

When you talk about yourself and another person, put them first.

Examples: **Darren and I** ride bikes.
Alex made lunch for **Mom and me**.

Directions: Circle **I** or **me** for each sentence.

1. (I, me) like to run.
2. Mr. Grange gave (I, me) homework.
3. (I, me) take an art class on Mondays.
4. Mom asked (I, me) to play the piano for Uncle Logan.
5. Uncle Logan told (I, me) that I play very well.
6. (I, me) want to play in a recital this winter.

Skill 84: Pronouns I and Me

Directions: Read the story. Write **I** or **me** in each blank to complete the sentences.

______ play the guitar. My cousin gave ______ one. It was his. ______ have a painting of him playing it. He told ______ to practice whenever ______ can.

My friend Ben and ______ take lessons. I started when ______ was six. He and ______ like to play guitar together. He told ______ he wants to play the piano, too. My cousin says he can teach Ben and ______.

Skill 85: Comparative Adjectives

Some adjectives are used to compare. Add **er** to an adjective to compare two things. Add **est** to compare three or more things.

Example: Liam's dog is small.
Jake's dog is small**er**.
Bella's dog is small**est**.

Directions: Read the sentences. Choose the correct adjective from the box. Write it on the line.

1. louder loudest — My alarm clock is ______________ than yours.
2. softer softest — Lola's pillow is ______________ than mine.
3. oldest older — Lynn is the ______________ of all her cousins.
4. slower slowest — Kiku's turtle is ______________ than Eric's turtle.
5. shorter shortest — Leslie has the ______________ hair of all.

Directions: Write two sentences. Compare two things in each sentence using adjectives.

____

____

Skill 85: Comparative Adjectives

Directions: Write the missing form of each word.

	Compares Two Things	Compares More Than Two Things
1.	longer	________
2.	________	tallest
3.	warmer	________
4.	________	shortest
5.	________	fastest
6.	________	highest
7.	sharper	________
8.	cooler	________
9.	________	oldest
10.	younger	________

Skill 86: Synonyms

Synonyms are words that mean the same or almost the same thing.

Examples: sick, ill   angry, mad

Directions: Read each word. Find its synonym in the box. Write it on the matching mitten.

small	sleepy	glad
fast	shout	large

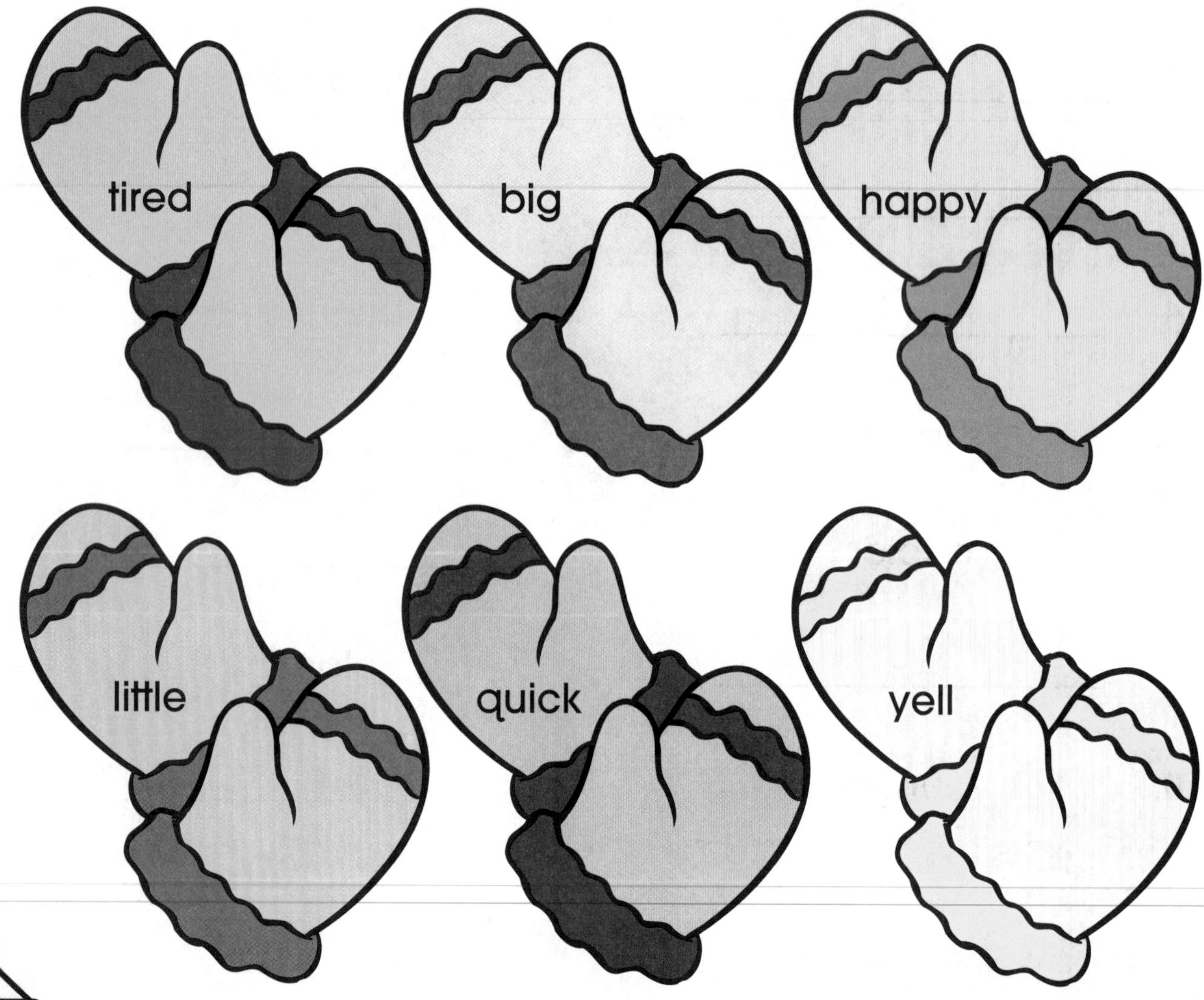

Skill

86: Synonyms

Directions: Read each sentence. Find a synonym in the box for the underlined word. Write the synonym on the line.

start	laughs	simple
ship	small	neat

1. Luke has a <u>little</u> bird. ____________________
2. Your desk is very <u>tidy</u>. ____________________
3. This test is <u>easy</u>. ____________________
4. It's time to <u>begin</u> our lesson. ____________________
5. Devi <u>giggles</u> at my jokes. ____________________
6. The <u>boat</u> is red and yellow. ____________________

Skill 87: Antonyms

Antonyms are words that are opposites.

Examples: hot, cold
quiet, loud
tall, short

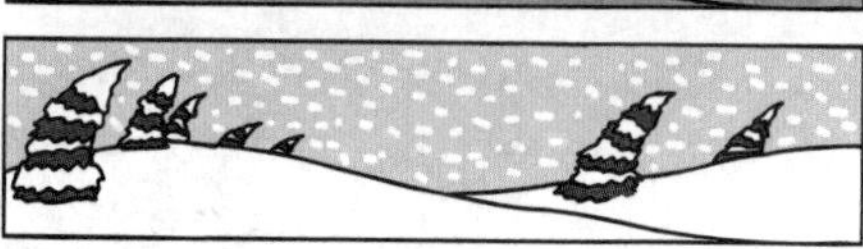

Directions: Fill in each blank with a word from the box.

sad	front	go
night	down	full

1. The opposite of **empty**  is ____________________.

2. The opposite of **day**  is ____________________.

3. The opposite of **stop** 

is ____________________.

4. The opposite of **up**  is ____________________.

5. The opposite of **happy**  is ____________________.

6. The opposite of **back**  is ____________________.

Skill 87: Antonyms

Directions: Draw a line to match each word to its antonym.

begin	early
late	tiny
close	stop
win	down
huge	open
up	lose

Directions: Draw a picture of two things that are opposites.

Skill 88: Homophones

Homophones are words that sound the same. But they have different spellings and different meanings.

Examples:

won = past tense of **win**	The Spartans **won** the game!
one = the number **1**	**One** lizard ran away.
to = toward	Throw it **to** me.
two = the number **2**	Rosa has **two** cats.
too = also or very	Jason will come, **too**.
right = the opposite of left	Raise your **right** arm.
write = to put words on paper	Can you **write** your name?

Directions: Underline the correct word to complete each sentence.

1. Mary can (write, right) down the recipes.
2. Joan bakes (too, two) pans of brownies.
3. Pedro bakes (won, one) pie.
4. Naomi (won, one) first place in the baking contest!
5. The chocolate chips are on the shelf on your (write, right).

Skill 88: Homophones

Directions: Draw a line through each incorrect homophone. Write the correct word above it.

1. Claire will bring the muffins two camp.

2. Set up too tables for the bake sale.

3. Right down the names of all the cookies.

4. Only won brownie is left!

Directions: Write a sentence using the word **write**.

____

____

Directions: Write a sentence using the word **two**.

____

____

Skill 89: Multiple-Meaning Words

Some words are spelled the same but have different meanings.

Example: It is **cold** outside. **cold** = chilly
Lane caught a **cold** last week. **cold** = an illness

Directions: Read each sentence. Think about how the word in **bold** is used. Draw a line to the picture that shows it.

1. The **bat** flew out of our cabin.

2. Sanjay swung the **bat**.

3. **Watch** the stars in the sky.

4. Madison can tell time on her new **watch**.

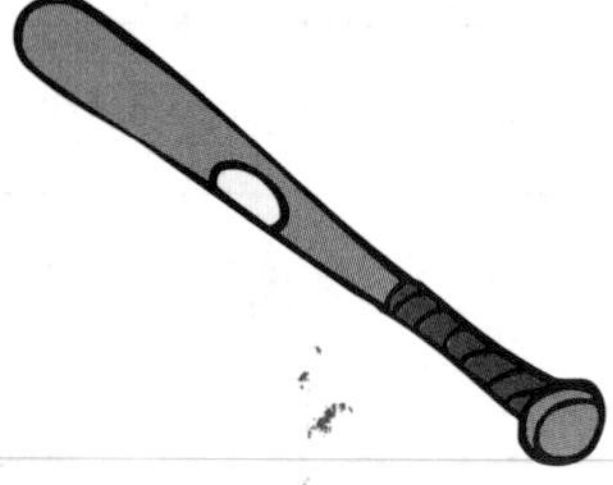

Skill

89: Multiple-Meaning Words

Directions: Read each pair of sentences. Look at the meaning of the first word in **bold**. Then, write the word's other meaning.

1. We **saw** balloons in the sky.

   saw: watched or looked at

   Use the **saw** to cut the log.

   saw: ______________________________

2. **Park** the car in front of the school.

   park: to drive a car into a space

   There is a new slide at the **park**.

   park: ______________________________

3. Did you hear the phone **ring**?

   ring: the sound a phone makes

   Claudia tried on Grandma's wedding **ring**.

   ring: ______________________________

LANGUAGE ARTS

Skill 90: Beginning Sounds

Directions: Say each picture name out loud. Listen to the beginning sound. Then, write the beginning letter.

1. ______

2. ______

3. ______

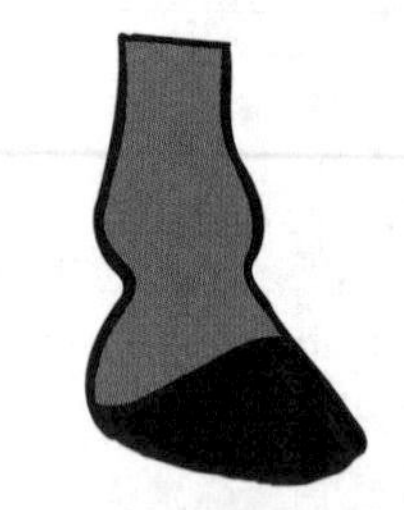

4. ______

5. ______

6. ______

7. ______

8. ______

9. ______

Skill 90: Beginning Sounds

Directions: Say each picture name out loud. Listen to the beginning sound. Then, write the beginning letter.

1. ________ 2. ________ 3. ________

4. ________ 5. ________ 6. ________

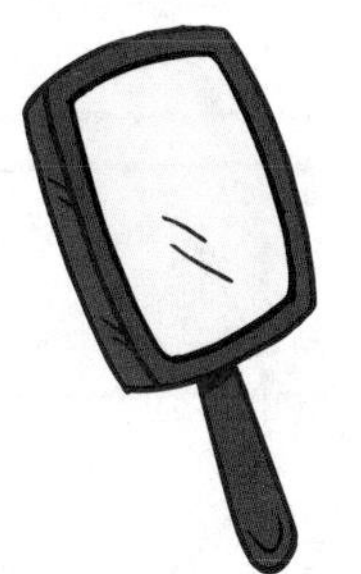

7. ________ 8. ________ 9. ________

LANGUAGE ARTS

LANGUAGE ARTS

Skill 91: Consonant Sounds

Every word has a **beginning sound**. It is the first sound the word makes. The consonant letters **b**, **d**, **f**, **h**, **j**, **k**, **l**, **m**, **n**, **p**, **q**, **r**, **t**, **v**, and **z** each make one sound.

Directions: Circle the letter that makes the beginning sound of each picture.

Skill 91: Consonant Sounds

Directions: Say the name of each picture. Write the letter that makes the beginning sound.

1. ________

2. ________

3. ________

4. ________

5. ________

6. ________

7. ________

8. ________

9. ________

Skill 92: Consonant Blends

A **consonant blend** is when two or more consonants are blended together. Each sound may be heard in the blend.

Directions: Write the first two letters of each word. These are blends.

1. ________

2. ________

3. ________

4. ________

5. ________

6. ________

Skill 92: Consonant Blends

Directions: Write the first two letters of each word. These are blends.

1. ________

2. ________

3. ________

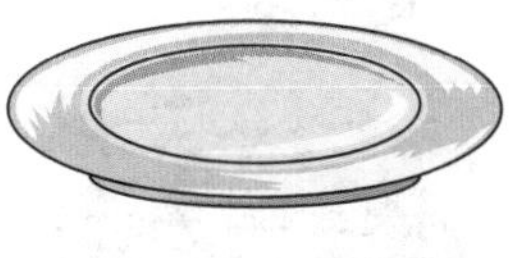

4. ________

5. ________

6. ________

Skill 93: Digraphs

In a consonant digraph, two consonants stand together to represent a single sound. The common digraphs are **sh**, **ch**, **th**, and **wh**.

Directions: Say the name of each picture. Write the digraph.

1. ________

2. ________

3. ________

4. ________

5. ________

6. ________

LANGUAGE ARTS

Skill 93: Digraphs

Directions: Say the name of each picture. Write the digraph.

1. ________

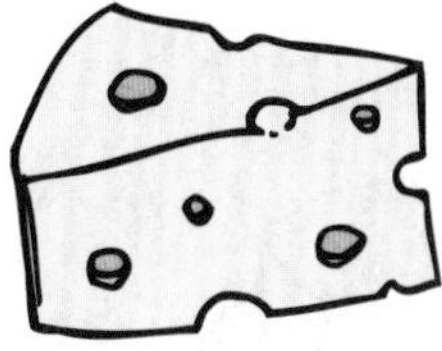

2. ________

3. ________

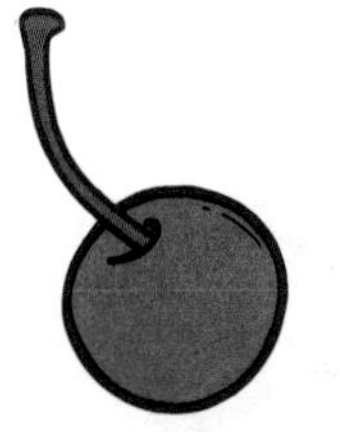

4. ________

5. ________

6. ________

LANGUAGE ARTS

Skill

94: Vowel Sounds

Directions: Name each picture. Then, write the vowel sound on the line. Vowels are the letters **a**, **e**, **i**, **o**, and **u**.

1. ________

2. ________

3. ________

4. ________

5. ________

6. ________

7. ________

8. ________

9. ________

LANGUAGE ARTS

Skill 94: Vowel Sounds

Directions: Name each picture. Then, write the vowel sound on the line. Vowels are the letters **a**, **e**, **i**, **o**, and **u**.

1. ________

2. ________

3. ________

4. ________

5. ________

6. ________

7. ________

8. ________

9. ________

Skill 95: Short and Long Aa

Short **a** is the sound you hear in **ant**.

Long **a** is the sound you hear in **hay**.

Long vowel sounds say their own names.

Directions: Say each word aloud. Write **short** or **long** next to the word to tell if it contains a short or a long **a** sound.

1. ate ________________

2. at ________________

3. ape ________________

4. act ________________

5. ant ________________

6. age ________________

7. rake ________________

8. way

Skill 18: Counting and Writing 30 Through 49

Directions: Complete.

4 tens 4 ones = 44

3 tens 6 ones = ________

3 tens 9 ones = ________

4 tens 1 ones = ________

4 tens 5 ones = ________

3 tens 7 ones = ________

3 tens 8 ones = ________

4 tens 0 ones = ________

3 tens 3 ones = ________

4 tens 6 ones = ________

MATH

Skill 19: Counting and Writing 50 Through 69

Directions: Complete.

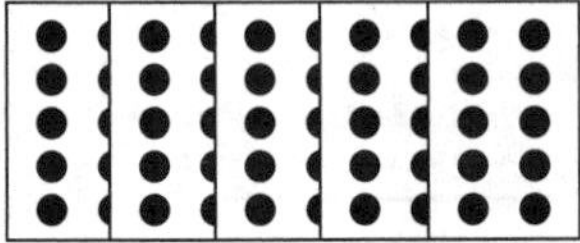

_____ tens _____ ones = _________

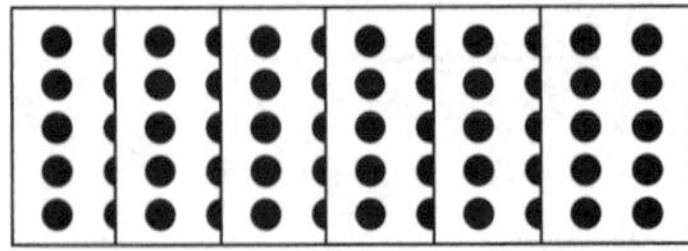

_____ tens _____ ones = _________

 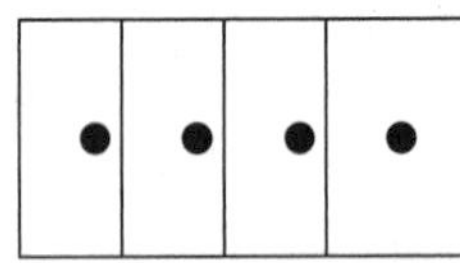

_____ tens _____ ones = _________

 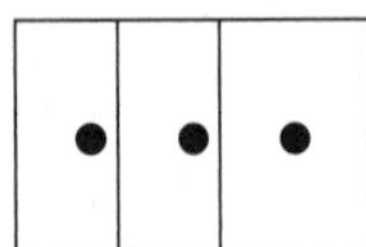

_____ tens _____ ones = _________

Skill 19: Counting and Writing 50 Through 69

Directions: Complete.

6 tens 4 ones = 64

6 tens 9 ones = ________

5 tens 2 ones = ________

6 tens 0 ones = ________

6 tens 7 ones = ________

5 tens 3 ones = ________

5 tens 5 ones = ________

6 tens 6 ones = ________

5 tens 7 ones = ________

5 tens 8 ones = ________

MATH

Skill **20: Counting and Writing 70 Through 99**

Directions: Complete.

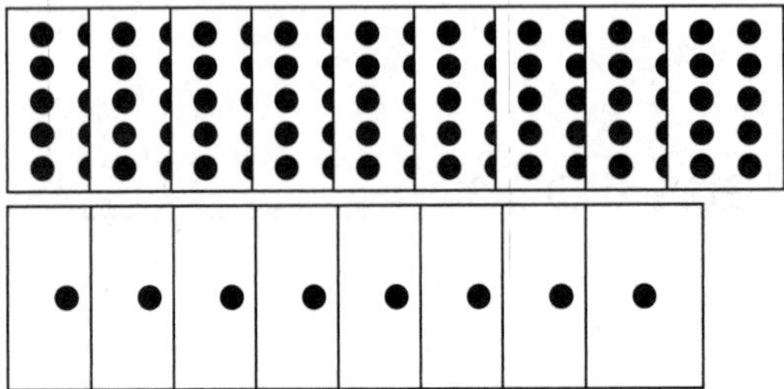

9 tens 8 ones = 98

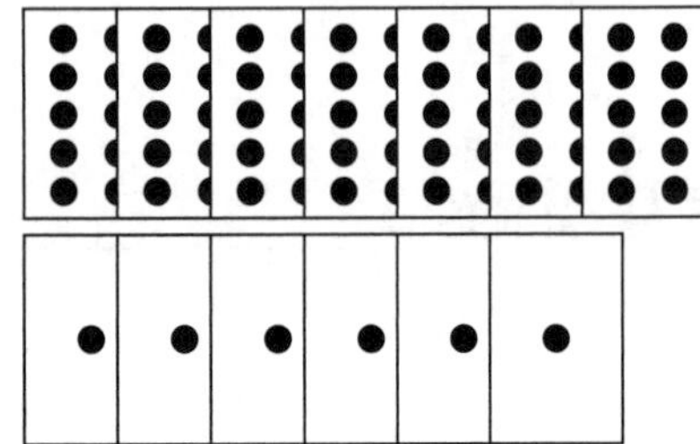

7 tens 6 ones = 76

8 tens 3 ones = 83

7 tens 1 ones = ________

8 tens 0 ones = ________

7 tens 5 ones = ________

MATH

Skill 20: Counting and Writing 70 Through 99

Directions: Complete.

9 tens 1 ones = ________

9 tens 4 ones = ________

7 tens 0 ones = ________

7 tens 9 ones = ________

8 tens 2 ones = ________

9 tens 9 ones = ________

8 tens 7 ones = ________

8 tens 6 ones = ________

9 tens 2 ones = ________

8 tens 8 ones = ________

MATH

Skill 21: Counting to 120

Directions: Count forward. Write the missing numbers.

1		3				7			10
11			14		16		18		
	22			25			28		30
	32			35		37			40
		43		45				49	
51				55		57			60
61			64		66		68		
		73					78		
81				85					90
			94		96		98		
		103							
	112			115		117		119	

MATH

Skill 21: Counting to 120

Directions: Write the number that comes one before.

	5			89
	23			117

Directions: Write the number that comes between.

11		13	35		37
62		64	98		100

Directions: Write the number that comes one after.

79		92	
50		114	
41		103	

MATH

MATH

Skill 22: Counting Forward to and Backward From 120

Directions: Count forward. Write the missing numbers.

36, 37, 38, 39, 40, 41, 42, 43, 44, 45, 46

92, _____, _____, 95, _____, _____, 98, _____, _____, 101, _____, 103

_____, 67, _____, 69, 70, 71, _____, 73, 74, _____, 76, 77

100, 101, _____, 103, _____, 105, 106, _____, 108, 109, _____, 111

_____, 10, 15, _____, 25, _____, 35, 40, _____, 50, 55, _____

_____, 20, _____, _____, 50, 60, 70, 80, _____, _____, _____, _____

Skill 95: Short and Long Aa

Directions: Say each word aloud. Write **short** or **long** next to the word to tell if it contains a short or a long **a** sound.

1. ray 

2. able 

3. rat 

4. rack 

5. rate 

6. Andy 

7. Alex ____________________

8. Abe ____________________

9. ask ____________________

10. take ____________________

Skill 96: Short and Long Ee

Short **e** is the sound you hear in **elephant**.

Long **e** is the sound you hear in **me**.

Directions: Say each word aloud. Write **short** or **long** next to the word to tell if it contains a short or a long **e** sound.

1. pen __________________

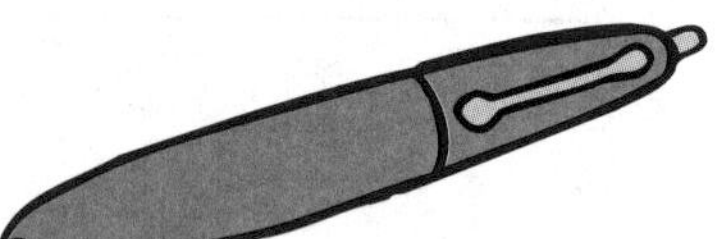

2. pencil __________________

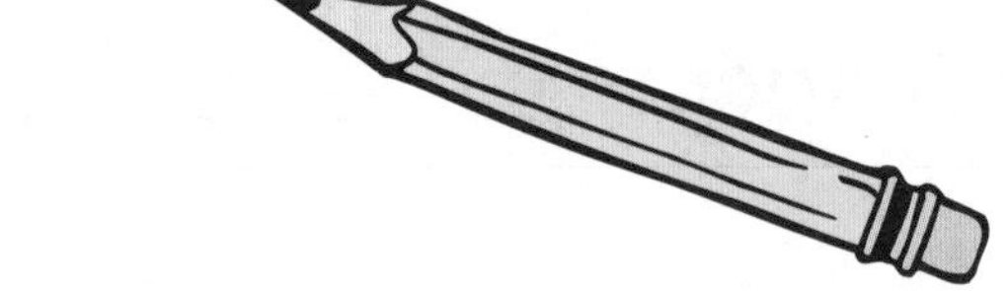

3. plea __________________
4. pea __________________

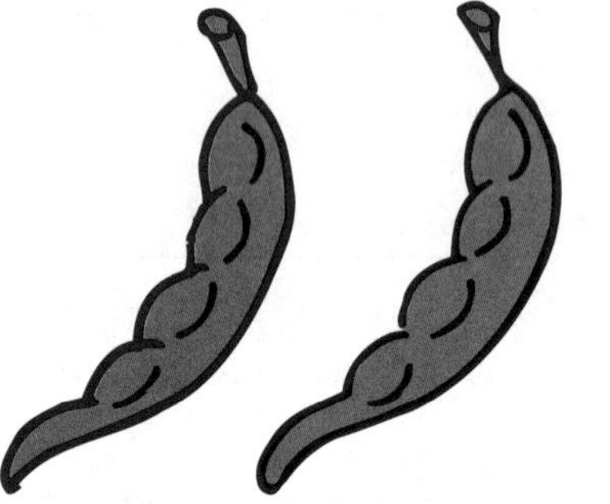

5. glee __________________
6. green __________________

7. tea __________________
8. rest __________________

Skill 96: Short and Long Ee

Directions: Say each word aloud. Write short or long next to the word to tell if it contains a short or a long **e** sound.

1. ten ____________________

2. teen ____________________

3. hen ____________________

4. fence ____________________

5. bee ____________________

6. be ____________________

7. bend ____________________

8. Ben ____________________

9. flea ____________________

10. free ____________________

LANGUAGE ARTS

Skill 97: Short and Long Ii

Short **i** is the sound you hear in **igloo**.

Long **i** is the sound you hear in **pie**.

Directions: Say each word aloud. Write **short** or **long** next to the word to tell if it contains a short or a long **i** sound.

1. pie ____________________
2. pin ____________________
3. pine ____________________
4. pink ____________________
5. pit ____________________
6. tin ____________________
7. time ____________________
8. mine ____________________

LANGUAGE ARTS

Skill 97: Short and Long Ii

Directions: Say each word aloud. Write **short** or **long** next to the word to tell if it contains a short or a long **i** sound.

1. tiny ____________________

2. tick ____________________

3. Tim ____________________

4. die ____________________

5. dim ____________________

6. diet ____________________

7. dine ____________________

8. dinner ____________________

9. fine ____________________

10. grin ____________________

Skill 98: Short and Long Oo

Short **o** is the sound you hear in **word**.

Long **o** is the sound you hear in **no**.

Directions: Say each word aloud. Write **short** or **long** next to the word to tell if it contains a short or a long **o** sound.

1. pot ____________________

2. spot ____________________

3. snow ____________________

4. not ____________________

5. oat ____________________

6. on ____________________

7. box ____________________

8. go ____________________

Skill 98: Short and Long Oo

Directions: Say each word aloud. Write **short** or **long** next to the word to tell if it contains a short or a long **o** sound.

1. mop 

2. rope 

3. Oliver 

4. show 

5. shop 

6. store ______________________

7. stop ______________________

8. slope ______________________

9. flow ______________________

10. row ______________________

Skill 99: Short and Long Uu

Short **u** is the sound you hear in **under**.

Long **u** is the sound you hear in **cute**.

Directions: Say each word aloud. Write **short** or **long** next to the word to tell if it contains a short or a long **u** sound.

1. under ____________________

2. cube ____________________

3. umbrella ____________________

4. cut ____________________

5. cute ____________________

6. butter ____________________

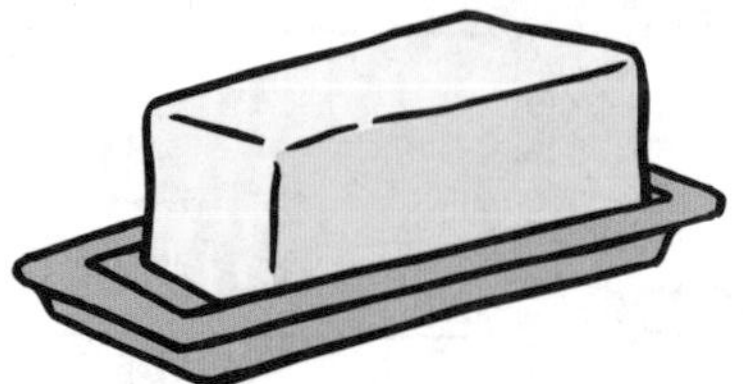

7. yummy ____________________

8. bus ____________________

Skill 99: Short and Long Uu

Directions: Say each word aloud. Write **short** or **long** next to the word to tell if it contains a short or a long **u** sound.

1. mule 

2. club ______________________

3. duck ______________________

4. dune ______________________

5. tuck ______________________

6. tune ______________________

7. run ______________________

8. funny ______________________

9. suit ______________________

10. truck ______________________

Skill 100: Rhyming Words

Words that sound alike are called **rhyming words**. The beginning sounds of the words are usually different.

Directions: Write the rhyming word from the Word Bank below each picture.

boy	shop	brown
two	tent	can
kiss	day	three

Skill 100: Rhyming Words

Directions: Read each list of words. Circle the words that rhyme with the first word.

1. jig	jug	fig	pig	jog	big
2. sap	sip	map	tap	stop	trap
3. vine	fine	tree	line	pine	vet
4. ball	bell	wall	tall	bowl	hall
5. hot	tot	cold	warm	cot	not
6. pail	pill	nail	sail	pile	tail
7. old	young	fold	cold	age	sold

LANGUAGE ARTS

Answer Key

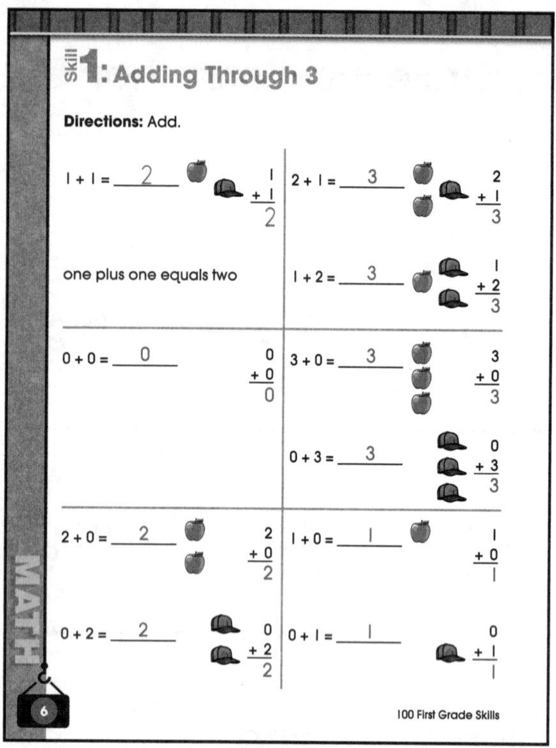

Skill 1: Adding Through 3

Directions: Add.

1 + 1 = 2   1 + 1 = 2

one plus one equals two

2 + 1 = 3   2 + 1 = 3

1 + 2 = 3   1 + 2 = 3

0 + 0 = 0   0 + 0 = 0

3 + 0 = 3   3 + 0 = 3

0 + 3 = 3   0 + 3 = 3

2 + 0 = 2   2 + 0 = 2

1 + 0 = 1   1 + 0 = 1

0 + 2 = 2   0 + 2 = 2

0 + 1 = 1   0 + 1 = 1

MATH

6   100 First Grade Skills

Page 6

Skill 1: Adding Through 3

Directions: Count the dots on each domino. Solve each problem.

1 + 2 = 3

2 + 1 = 3

0 + 3 = 3

1 + 1 = 2

0 + 2 = 2

3 + 0 = 3

100 First Grade Skills   7

MATH

Page 7

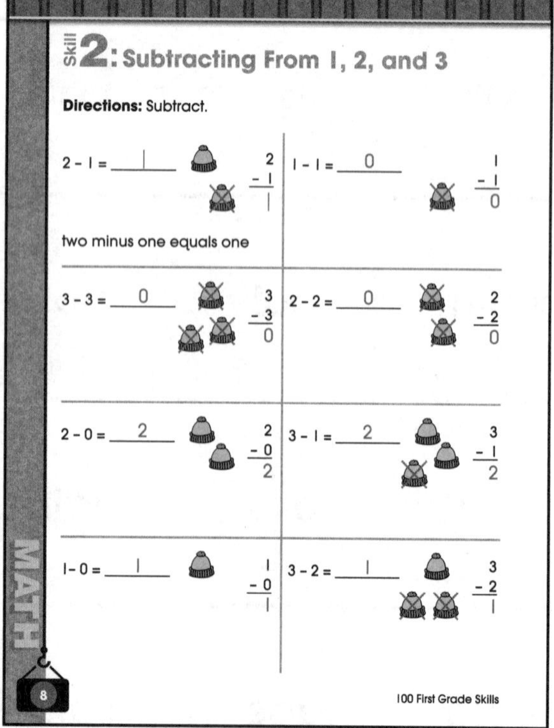

Skill 2: Subtracting From 1, 2, and 3

Directions: Subtract.

2 - 1 = 1   2 - 1 = 1

two minus one equals one

1 - 1 = 0   1 - 1 = 0

3 - 3 = 0   3 - 3 = 0

2 - 2 = 0   2 - 2 = 0

2 - 0 = 2   2 - 0 = 2

3 - 1 = 2   3 - 1 = 2

1 - 0 = 1   1 - 0 = 1

3 - 2 = 1   3 - 2 = 1

MATH

8   100 First Grade Skills

Page 8

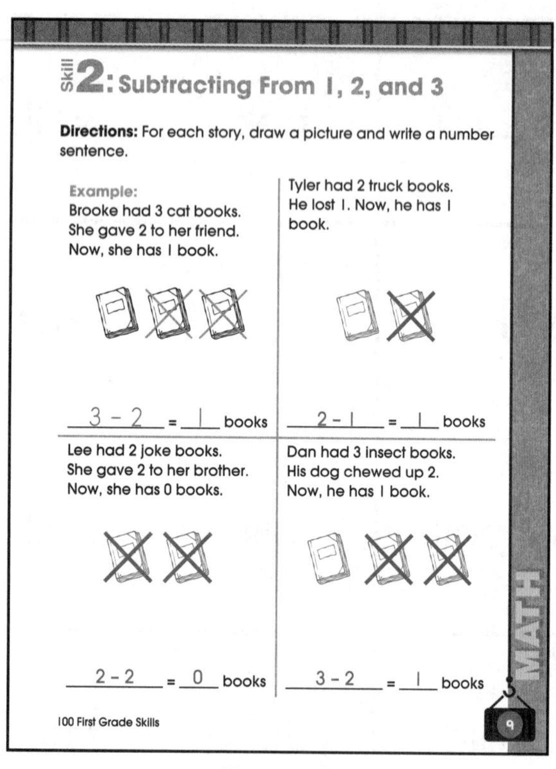

Skill 2: Subtracting From 1, 2, and 3

Directions: For each story, draw a picture and write a number sentence.

Example:
Brooke had 3 cat books. She gave 2 to her friend. Now, she has 1 book.

3 - 2 = 1 books

Tyler had 2 truck books. He lost 1. Now, he has 1 book.

2 - 1 = 1 books

Lee had 2 joke books. She gave 2 to her brother. Now, she has 0 books.

2 - 2 = 0 books

Dan had 3 insect books. His dog chewed up 2. Now, he has 1 book.

3 - 2 = 1 books

MATH

100 First Grade Skills   9

Page 9

Answer Key

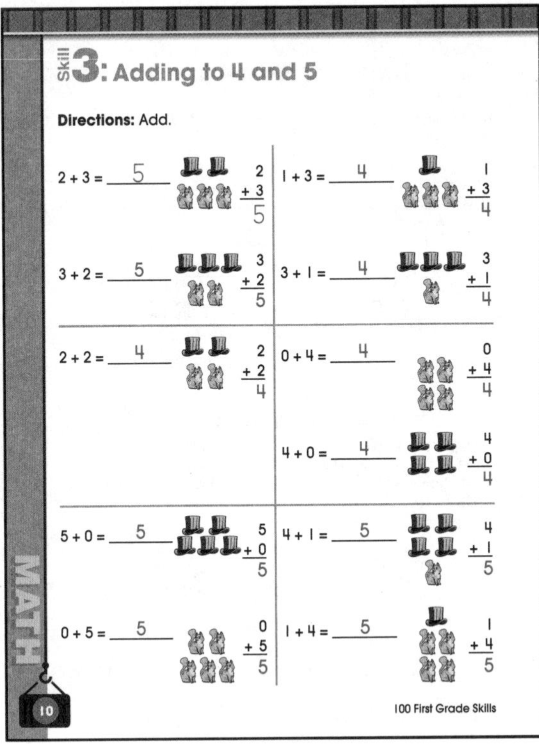

Skill 3: Adding to 4 and 5

Directions: Add.

2 + 3 = 5 | 2 + 3 = 5
1 + 3 = 4 | 1 + 3 = 4
3 + 2 = 5 | 3 + 2 = 5
3 + 1 = 4 | 3 + 1 = 4
2 + 2 = 4 | 2 + 2 = 4
0 + 4 = 4 | 0 + 4 = 4
4 + 0 = 4 | 4 + 0 = 4
5 + 0 = 5 | 5 + 0 = 5
4 + 1 = 5 | 4 + 1 = 5
0 + 5 = 5 | 0 + 5 = 5
1 + 4 = 5 | 1 + 4 = 5

MATH

10 100 First Grade Skills

Page 10

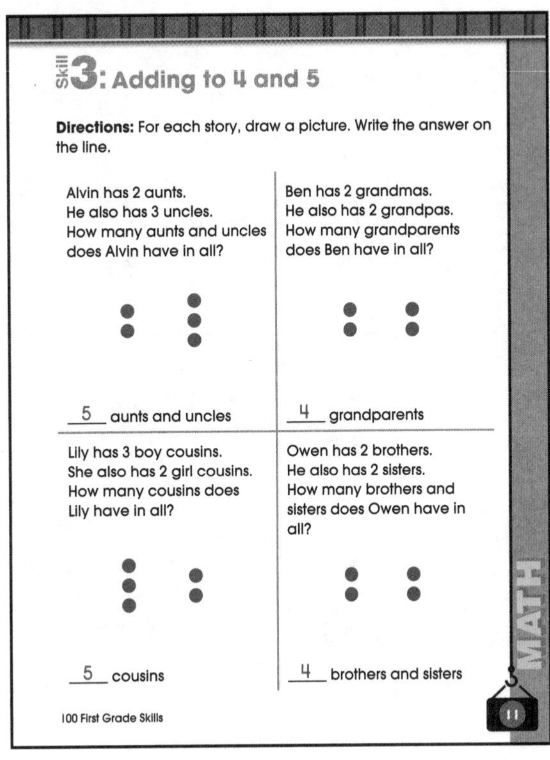

Skill 3: Adding to 4 and 5

Directions: For each story, draw a picture. Write the answer on the line.

Alvin has 2 aunts. He also has 3 uncles. How many aunts and uncles does Alvin have in all?

5 aunts and uncles

Ben has 2 grandmas. He also has 2 grandpas. How many grandparents does Ben have in all?

4 grandparents

Lily has 3 boy cousins. She also has 2 girl cousins. How many cousins does Lily have in all?

5 cousins

Owen has 2 brothers. He also has 2 sisters. How many brothers and sisters does Owen have in all?

4 brothers and sisters

MATH

100 First Grade Skills 11

Page 11

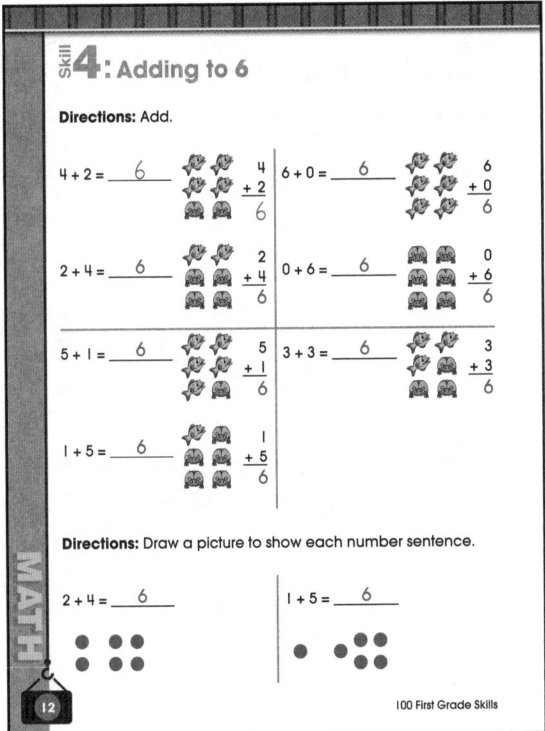

Skill 4: Adding to 6

Directions: Add.

4 + 2 = 6 | 4 + 2 = 6
6 + 0 = 6 | 6 + 0 = 6
2 + 4 = 6 | 2 + 4 = 6
0 + 6 = 6 | 0 + 6 = 6
5 + 1 = 6 | 5 + 1 = 6
3 + 3 = 6 | 3 + 3 = 6
1 + 5 = 6 | 1 + 5 = 6

Directions: Draw a picture to show each number sentence.

2 + 4 = 6

1 + 5 = 6

MATH

12 100 First Grade Skills

Page 12

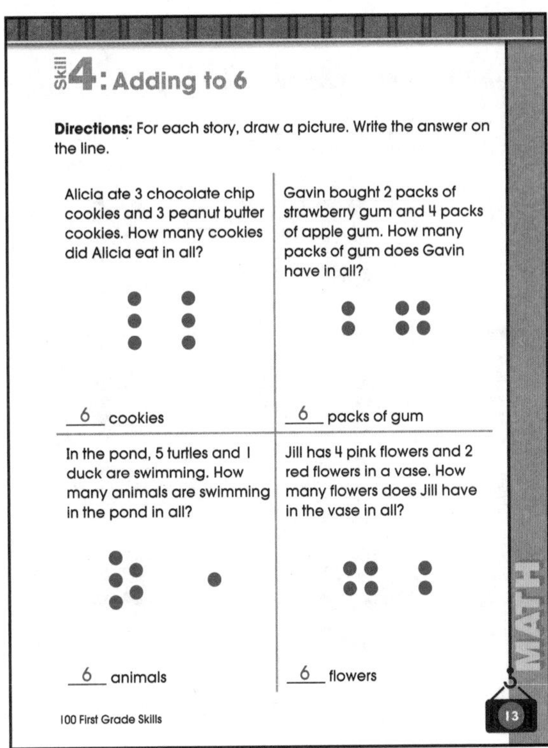

Skill 4: Adding to 6

Directions: For each story, draw a picture. Write the answer on the line.

Alicia ate 3 chocolate chip cookies and 3 peanut butter cookies. How many cookies did Alicia eat in all?

6 cookies

Gavin bought 2 packs of strawberry gum and 4 packs of apple gum. How many packs of gum does Gavin have in all?

6 packs of gum

In the pond, 5 turtles and 1 duck are swimming. How many animals are swimming in the pond in all?

6 animals

Jill has 4 pink flowers and 2 red flowers in a vase. How many flowers does Jill have in the vase in all?

6 flowers

MATH

100 First Grade Skills 13

Page 13

Answer Key

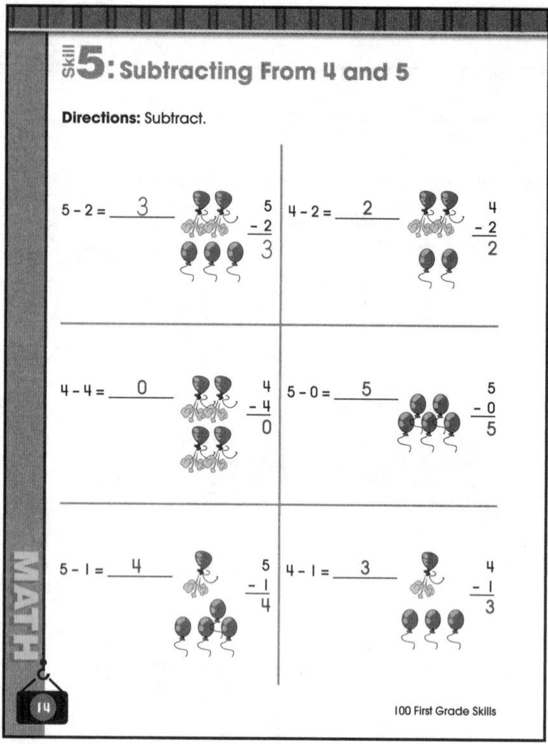

Page 14

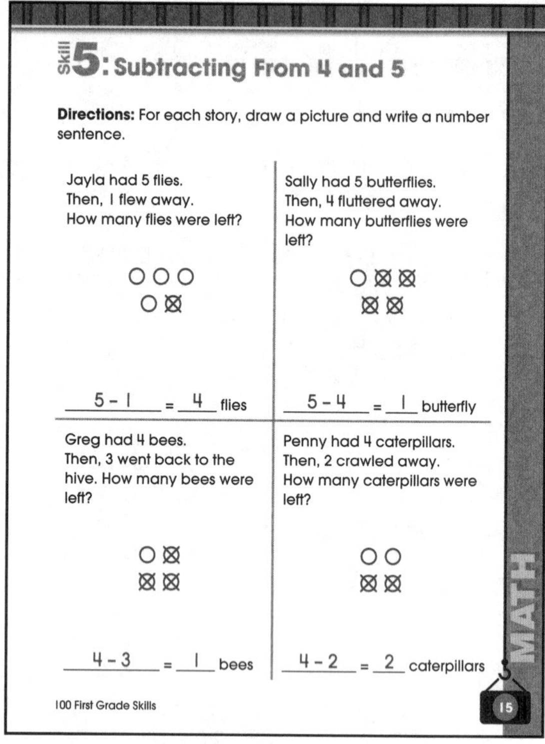

Page 15

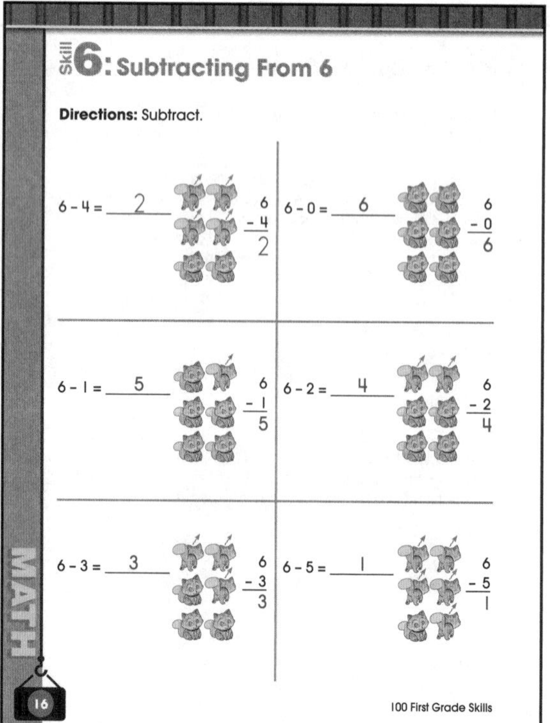

Page 16

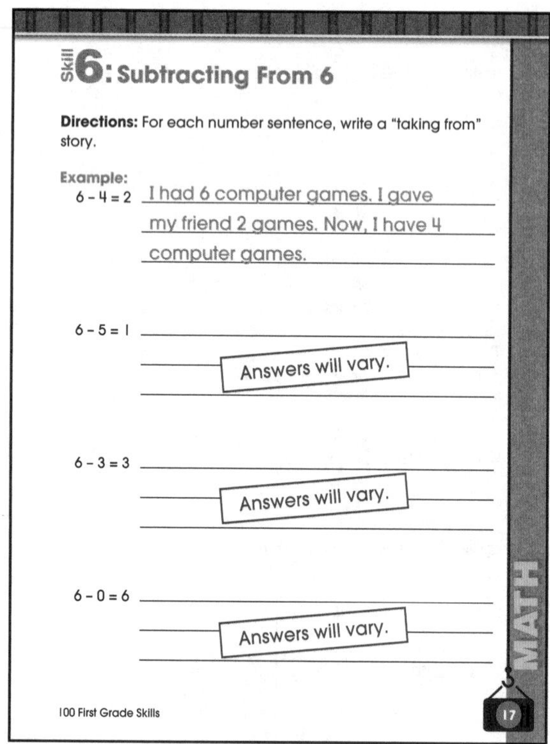

Page 17

Answer Key

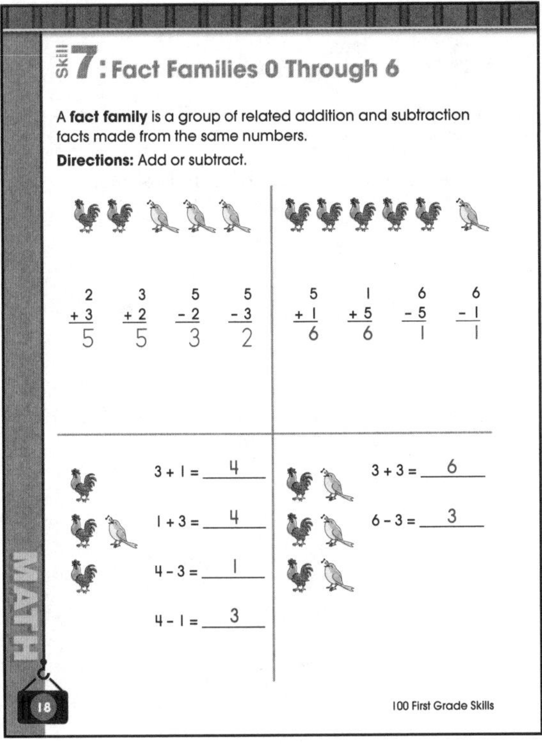

Skill **7**: Fact Families 0 Through 6

A **fact family** is a group of related addition and subtraction facts made from the same numbers.

Directions: Add or subtract.

2 + 3 = 5 3 + 2 = 5 5 − 2 = 3 5 − 3 = 2

5 + 1 = 6 1 + 5 = 6 6 − 5 = 1 6 − 1 = 1

3 + 1 = 4
1 + 3 = 4
4 − 3 = 1
4 − 1 = 3

3 + 3 = 6
6 − 3 = 3

18 100 First Grade Skills

Page 18

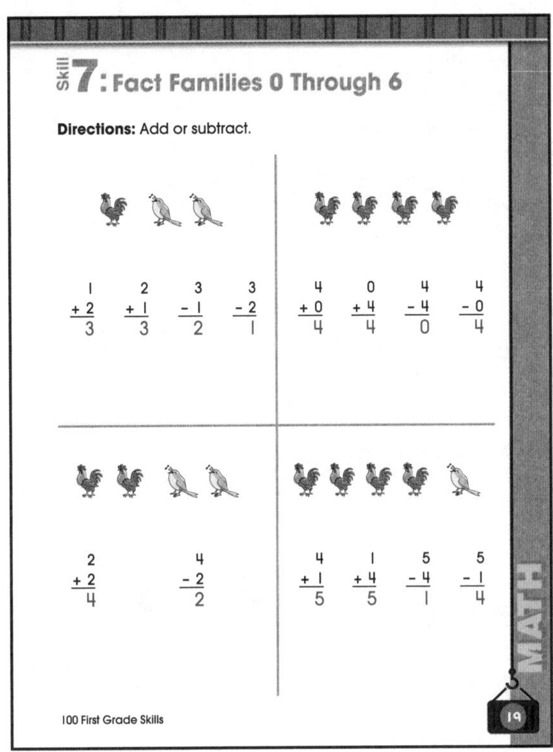

Skill **7**: Fact Families 0 Through 6

Directions: Add or subtract.

1 + 2 = 3 2 + 1 = 3 3 − 1 = 2 3 − 2 = 1

4 + 0 = 4 0 + 4 = 4 4 − 4 = 0 4 − 0 = 4

2 + 2 = 4 4 − 2 = 2

4 + 1 = 5 1 + 4 = 5 5 − 4 = 1 5 − 1 = 4

100 First Grade Skills 19

Page 19

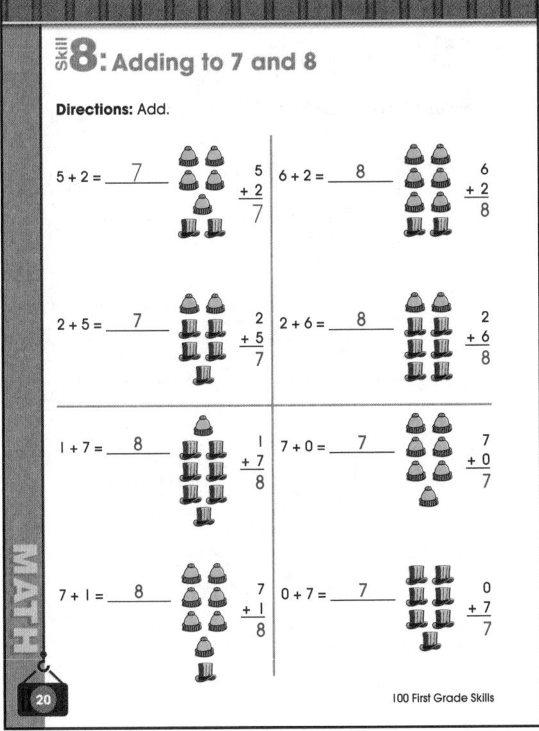

Skill **8**: Adding to 7 and 8

Directions: Add.

5 + 2 = 7 (5 + 2 = 7)

6 + 2 = 8 (6 + 2 = 8)

2 + 5 = 7 (2 + 5 = 7)

2 + 6 = 8 (2 + 6 = 8)

1 + 7 = 8 (1 + 7 = 8)

7 + 0 = 7 (7 + 0 = 7)

7 + 1 = 8 (7 + 1 = 8)

0 + 7 = 7 (0 + 7 = 7)

20 100 First Grade Skills

Page 20

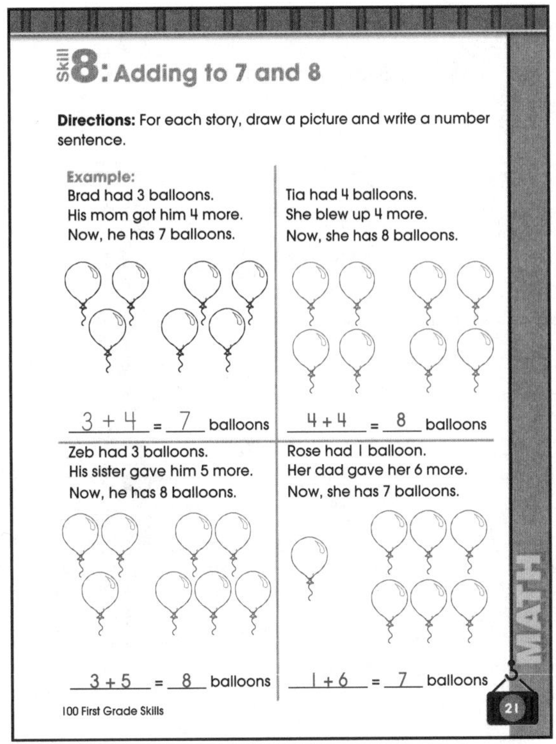

Skill **8**: Adding to 7 and 8

Directions: For each story, draw a picture and write a number sentence.

Example:
Brad had 3 balloons.
His mom got him 4 more.
Now, he has 7 balloons.

3 + 4 = 7 balloons

Tia had 4 balloons.
She blew up 4 more.
Now, she has 8 balloons.

4 + 4 = 8 balloons

Zeb had 3 balloons.
His sister gave him 5 more.
Now, he has 8 balloons.

3 + 5 = 8 balloons

Rose had 1 balloon.
Her dad gave her 6 more.
Now, she has 7 balloons.

1 + 6 = 7 balloons

100 First Grade Skills 21

Page 21

Answer Key

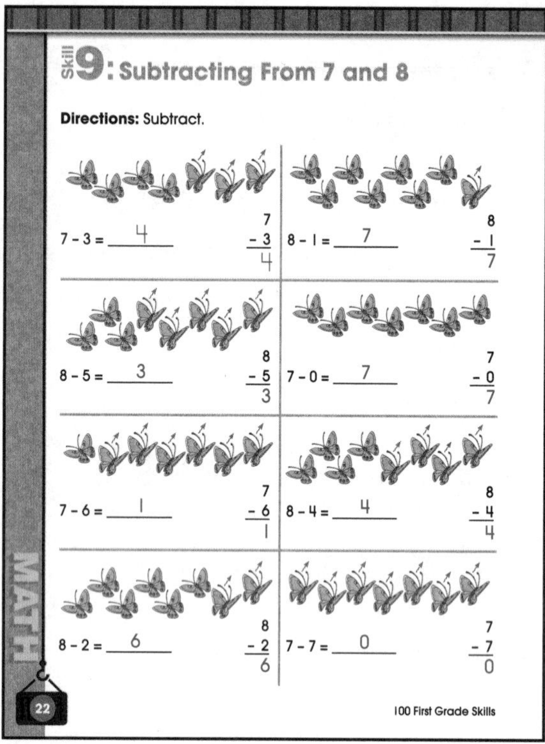

Skill 9: Subtracting From 7 and 8

Directions: Subtract.

7 - 3 = 4 | 7 - 3 = 4
8 - 1 = 7 | 8 - 1 = 7
8 - 5 = 3 | 8 - 5 = 3
7 - 0 = 7 | 7 - 0 = 7
7 - 6 = 1 | 7 - 6 = 1
8 - 4 = 4 | 8 - 4 = 4
8 - 2 = 6 | 8 - 2 = 6
7 - 7 = 0 | 7 - 7 = 0

22 100 First Grade Skills

Page 22

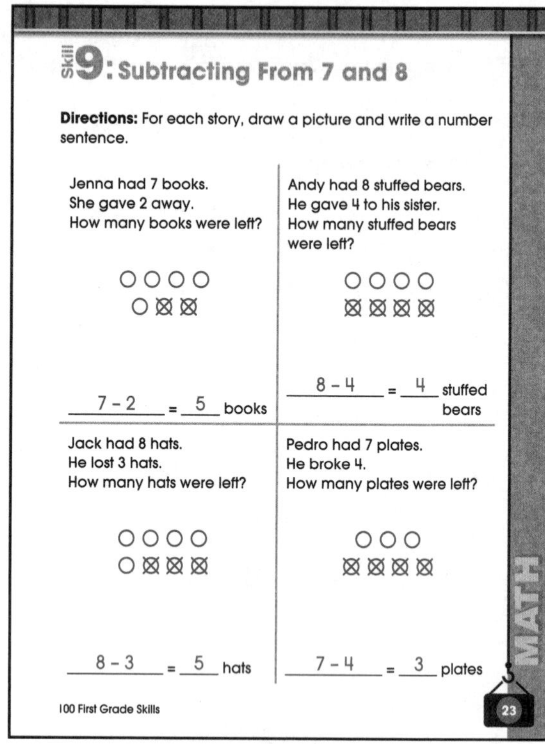

Skill 9: Subtracting From 7 and 8

Directions: For each story, draw a picture and write a number sentence.

Jenna had 7 books. She gave 2 away. How many books were left?

7 - 2 = 5 books

Andy had 8 stuffed bears. He gave 4 to his sister. How many stuffed bears were left?

8 - 4 = 4 stuffed bears

Jack had 8 hats. He lost 3 hats. How many hats were left?

8 - 3 = 5 hats

Pedro had 7 plates. He broke 4. How many plates were left?

7 - 4 = 3 plates

100 First Grade Skills 23

Page 23

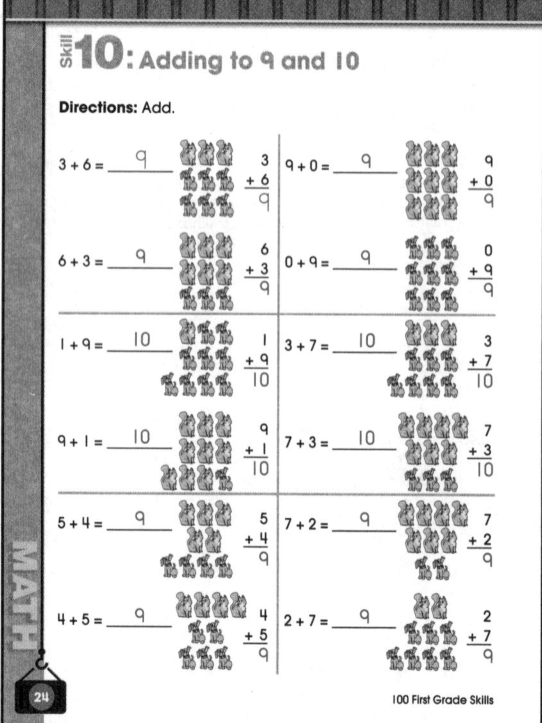

Skill 10: Adding to 9 and 10

Directions: Add.

3 + 6 = 9 | 3 + 6 = 9
9 + 0 = 9 | 9 + 0 = 9
6 + 3 = 9 | 6 + 3 = 9
0 + 9 = 9 | 0 + 9 = 9
1 + 9 = 10 | 1 + 9 = 10
3 + 7 = 10 | 3 + 7 = 10
9 + 1 = 10 | 9 + 1 = 10
7 + 3 = 10 | 7 + 3 = 10
5 + 4 = 9 | 5 + 4 = 9
7 + 2 = 9 | 7 + 2 = 9
4 + 5 = 9 | 4 + 5 = 9
2 + 7 = 9 | 2 + 7 = 9

24 100 First Grade Skills

Page 24

Skill 10: Adding to 9 and 10

Directions: For each number sentence, write an "adding to" story.

Example:
5 + 5 = 10 I had 5 purple markers. My friend gave me 5 more. Now, I have 10 purple markers.

4 + 5 = 9 Answers will vary.

7 + 3 = 10 Answers will vary.

5 + 4 = 9 Answers will vary.

100 First Grade Skills 25

MATH

Page 25

Answer Key

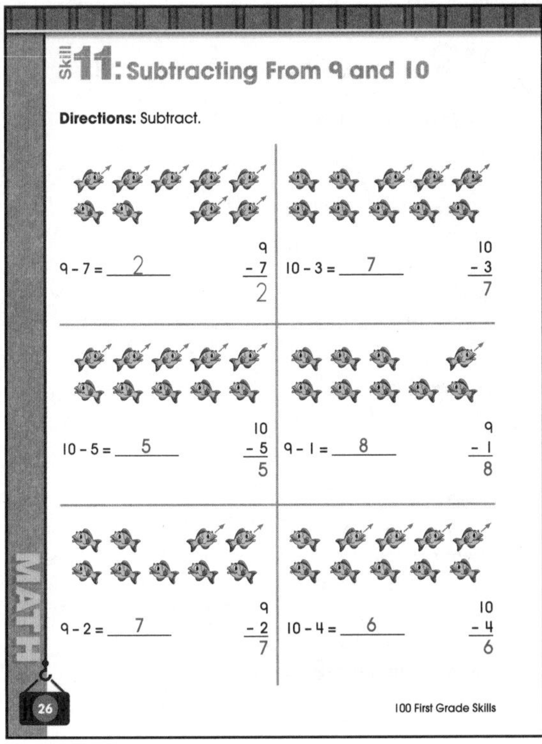

Skill 11: Subtracting From 9 and 10

Directions: Subtract.

9 − 7 = 2 | 9 − 7 = 2

10 − 3 = 7 | 10 − 3 = 7

10 − 5 = 5 | 10 − 5 = 5

9 − 1 = 8 | 9 − 1 = 8

9 − 2 = 7 | 9 − 2 = 7

10 − 4 = 6 | 10 − 4 = 6

MATH

26 100 First Grade Skills

Page 26

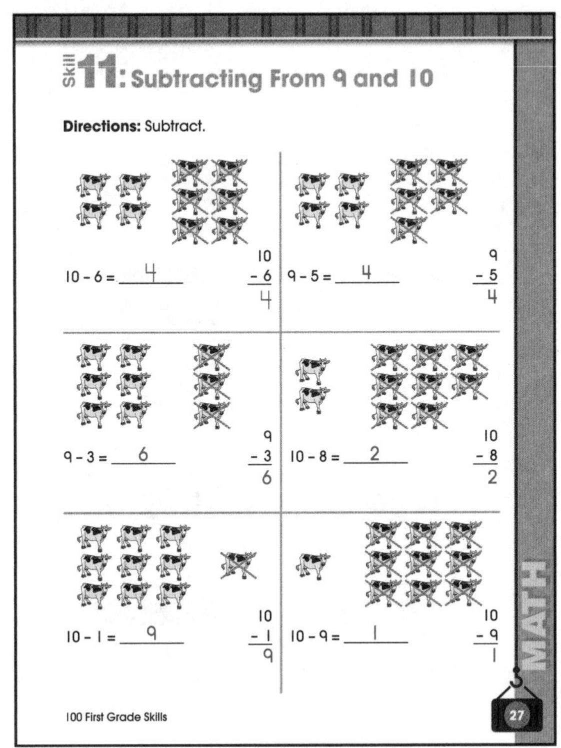

Skill 11: Subtracting From 9 and 10

Directions: Subtract.

10 − 6 = 4 | 10 − 6 = 4

9 − 5 = 4 | 9 − 5 = 4

9 − 3 = 6 | 9 − 3 = 6

10 − 8 = 2 | 10 − 8 = 2

10 − 1 = 9 | 10 − 1 = 9

10 − 9 = 1 | 10 − 9 = 1

MATH

100 First Grade Skills 27

Page 27

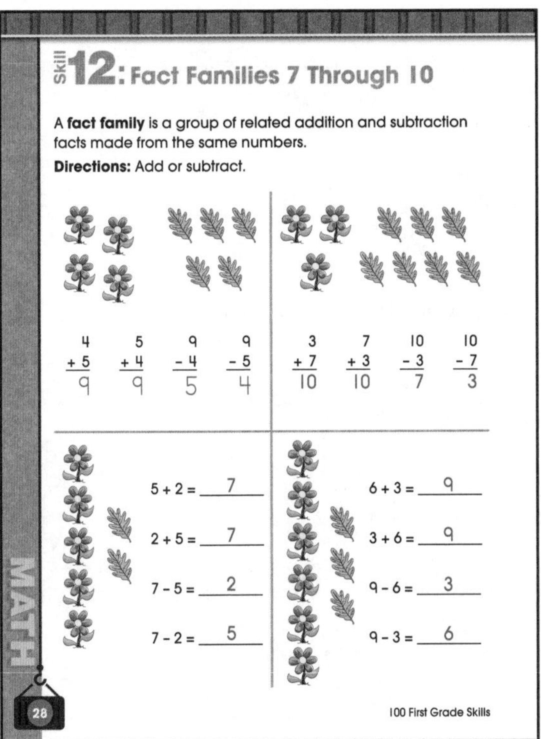

Skill 12: Fact Families 7 Through 10

A **fact family** is a group of related addition and subtraction facts made from the same numbers.

Directions: Add or subtract.

4 + 5 = 9 | 5 + 4 = 9 | 9 − 4 = 5 | 9 − 5 = 4

3 + 7 = 10 | 7 + 3 = 10 | 10 − 3 = 7 | 10 − 7 = 3

5 + 2 = 7
2 + 5 = 7
7 − 5 = 2
7 − 2 = 5

6 + 3 = 9
3 + 6 = 9
9 − 6 = 3
9 − 3 = 6

MATH

28 100 First Grade Skills

Page 28

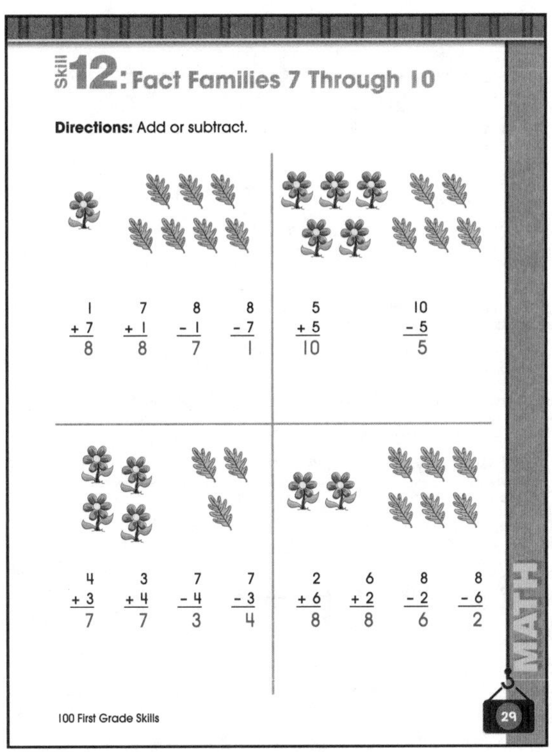

Skill 12: Fact Families 7 Through 10

Directions: Add or subtract.

1 + 7 = 8 | 7 + 1 = 8 | 8 − 1 = 7 | 8 − 7 = 1

5 + 5 = 10 | 10 − 5 = 5

4 + 3 = 7 | 3 + 4 = 7 | 7 − 4 = 3 | 7 − 3 = 4

2 + 6 = 8 | 6 + 2 = 8 | 8 − 2 = 6 | 8 − 6 = 2

MATH

100 First Grade Skills 29

Page 29

Answer Key

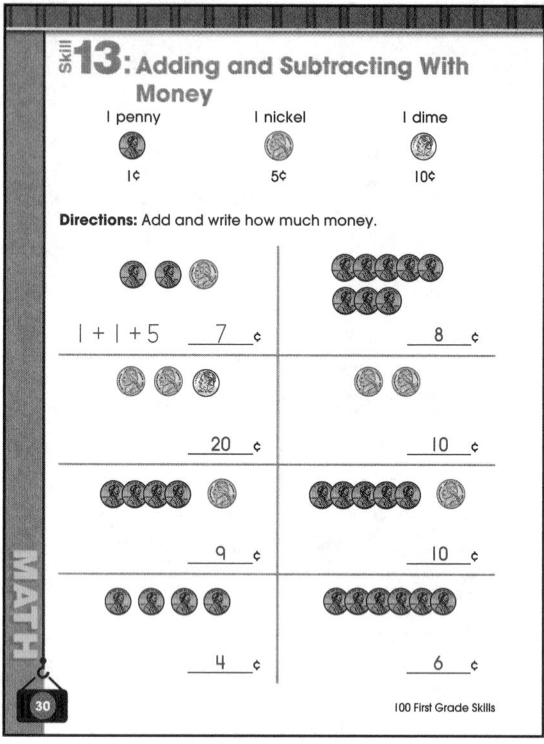

Skill **13: Adding and Subtracting With Money**

1 penny — 1¢ | 1 nickel — 5¢ | 1 dime — 10¢

Directions: Add and write how much money.

1 + 1 + 5   7 ¢

8 ¢

20 ¢

10 ¢

9 ¢

10 ¢

4 ¢

6 ¢

30   100 First Grade Skills

Page 30

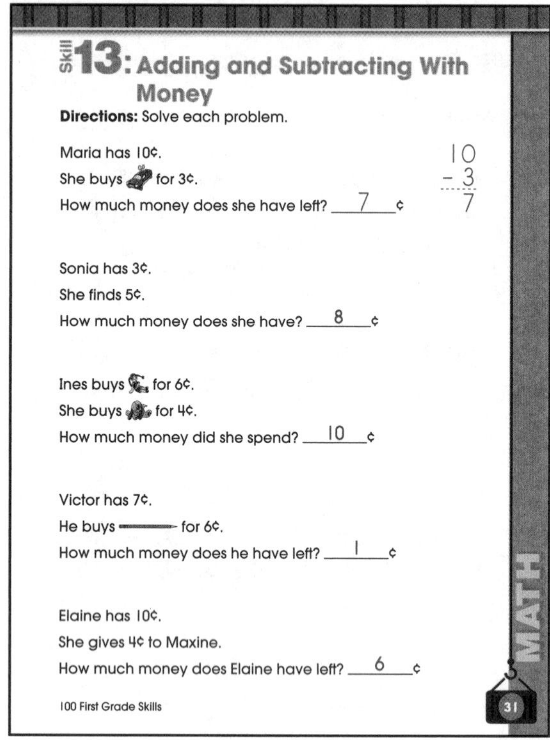

Skill **13: Adding and Subtracting With Money**

Directions: Solve each problem.

Maria has 10¢.
She buys for 3¢.
How much money does she have left? 7 ¢

$10 - 3 = 7$

Sonia has 3¢.
She finds 5¢.
How much money does she have? 8 ¢

Ines buys for 6¢.
She buys for 4¢.
How much money did she spend? 10 ¢

Victor has 7¢.
He buys for 6¢.
How much money does he have left? 1 ¢

Elaine has 10¢.
She gives 4¢ to Maxine.
How much money does Elaine have left? 6 ¢

100 First Grade Skills   31

Page 31

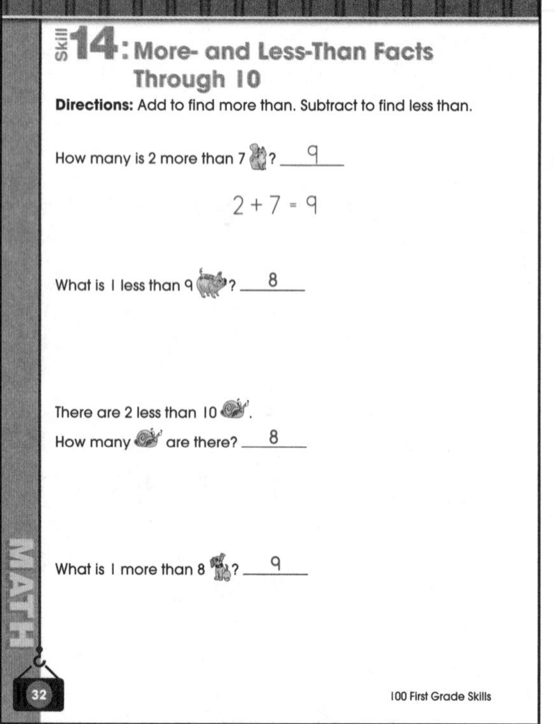

Skill **14: More- and Less-Than Facts Through 10**

Directions: Add to find more than. Subtract to find less than.

How many is 2 more than 7? 9

2 + 7 = 9

What is 1 less than 9? 8

There are 2 less than 10.
How many are there? 8

What is 1 more than 8? 9

32   100 First Grade Skills

Page 32

Skill **14: More- and Less-Than Facts Through 10**

Directions: Add to find more than. Subtract to find less than.

There is 1 more than 7.
How many are there? 8

How many is 1 more than 9? 10

How many is 1 less than 10? 9

What is 2 less than 8? 6

There is 1 less than 8.
How many are there? 7

100 First Grade Skills   33

Page 33

Answer Key

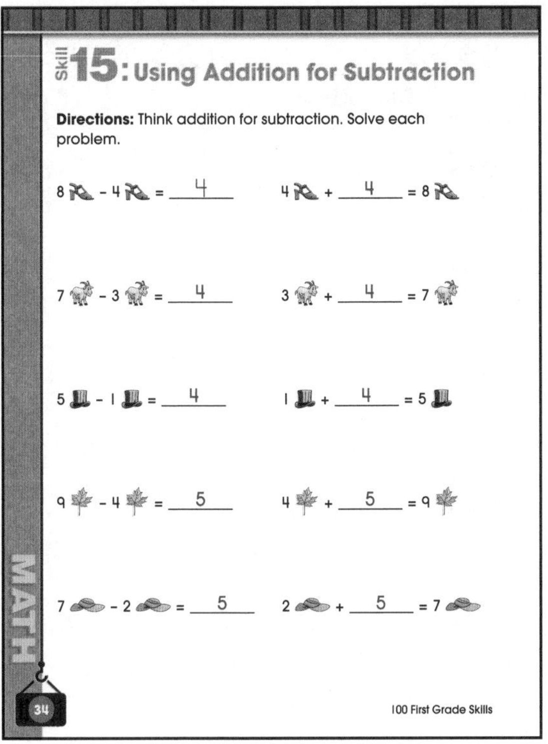

Skill 15: Using Addition for Subtraction

Directions: Think addition for subtraction. Solve each problem.

8 - 4 = 4 4 + 4 = 8

7 - 3 = 4 3 + 4 = 7

5 - 1 = 4 1 + 4 = 5

9 - 4 = 5 4 + 5 = 9

7 - 2 = 5 2 + 5 = 7

MATH

34 100 First Grade Skills

Page 34

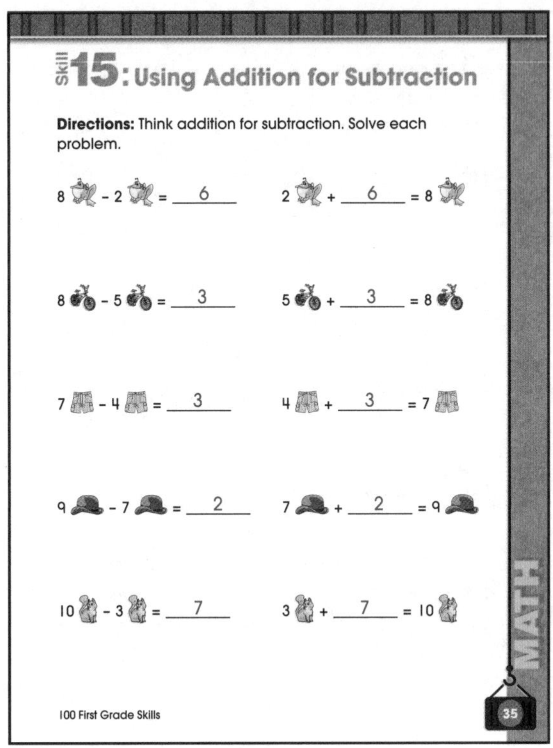

Skill 15: Using Addition for Subtraction

Directions: Think addition for subtraction. Solve each problem.

8 - 2 = 6 2 + 6 = 8

8 - 5 = 3 5 + 3 = 8

7 - 4 = 3 4 + 3 = 7

9 - 7 = 2 7 + 2 = 9

10 - 3 = 7 3 + 7 = 10

MATH

100 First Grade Skills 35

Page 35

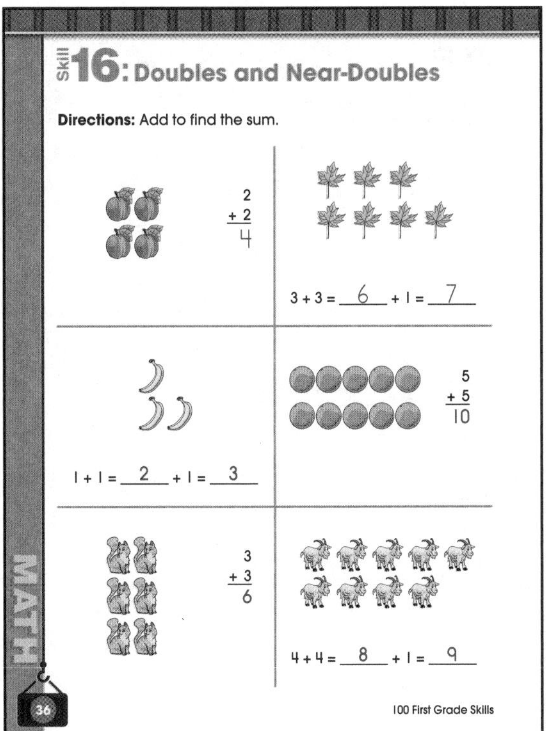

Skill 16: Doubles and Near-Doubles

Directions: Add to find the sum.

2 + 2 = 4

3 + 3 = 6 + 1 = 7

1 + 1 = 2 + 1 = 3

5 + 5 = 10

3 + 3 = 6

4 + 4 = 8 + 1 = 9

MATH

36 100 First Grade Skills

Page 36

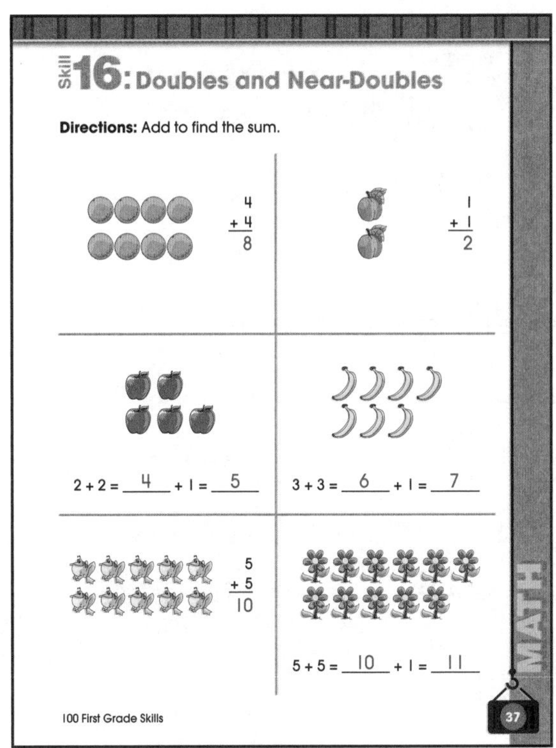

Skill 16: Doubles and Near-Doubles

Directions: Add to find the sum.

4 + 4 = 8

1 + 1 = 2

2 + 2 = 4 + 1 = 5

3 + 3 = 6 + 1 = 7

5 + 5 = 10

5 + 5 = 10 + 1 = 11

MATH

100 First Grade Skills 37

Page 37

Answer Key

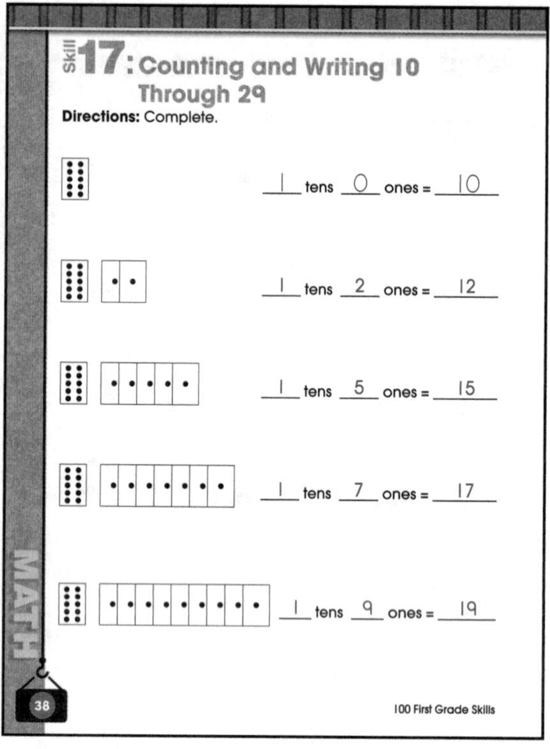

Skill 17: Counting and Writing 10 Through 29

Directions: Complete.

1 tens 0 ones = 10

1 tens 2 ones = 12

1 tens 5 ones = 15

1 tens 7 ones = 17

1 tens 9 ones = 19

MATH

38

100 First Grade Skills

Page 38

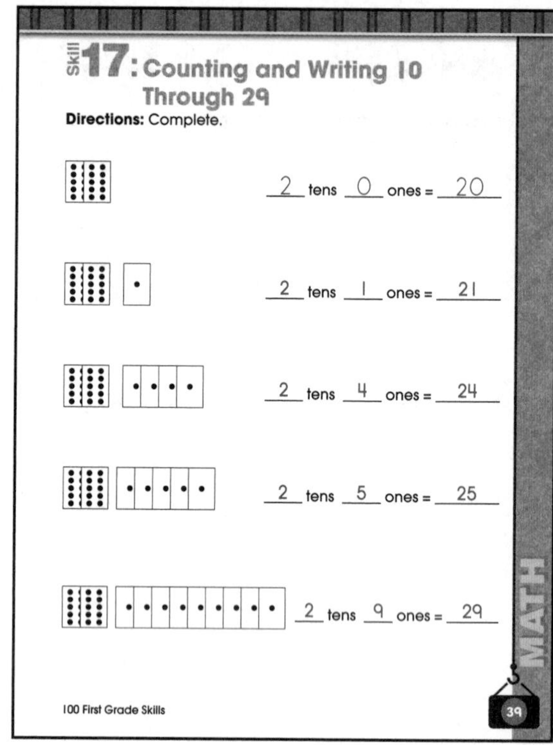

Skill 17: Counting and Writing 10 Through 29

Directions: Complete.

2 tens 0 ones = 20

2 tens 1 ones = 21

2 tens 4 ones = 24

2 tens 5 ones = 25

2 tens 9 ones = 29

MATH

100 First Grade Skills

39

Page 39

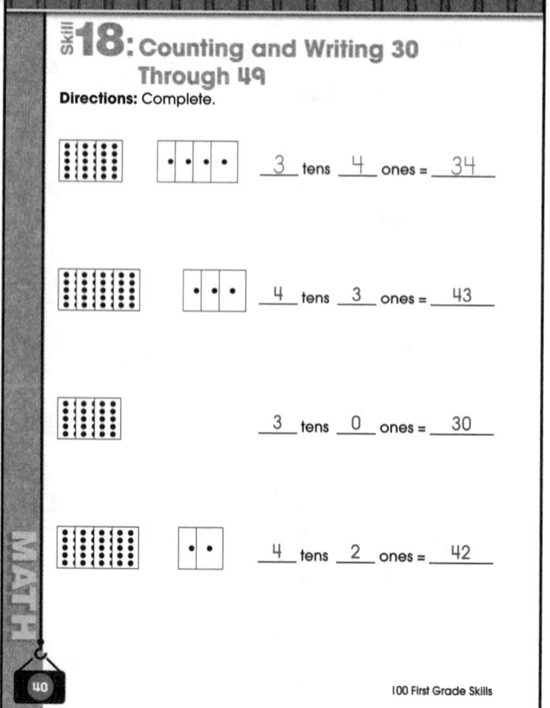

Skill 18: Counting and Writing 30 Through 49

Directions: Complete.

3 tens 4 ones = 34

4 tens 3 ones = 43

3 tens 0 ones = 30

4 tens 2 ones = 42

MATH

40

100 First Grade Skills

Page 40

Skill 18: Counting and Writing 30 Through 49

Directions: Complete.

4 tens 4 ones = 44

3 tens 9 ones = 39

4 tens 5 ones = 45

3 tens 8 ones = 38

3 tens 3 ones = 33

3 tens 6 ones = 36

4 tens 1 ones = 41

3 tens 7 ones = 37

4 tens 0 ones = 40

4 tens 6 ones = 46

MATH

100 First Grade Skills

41

Page 41

Answer Key

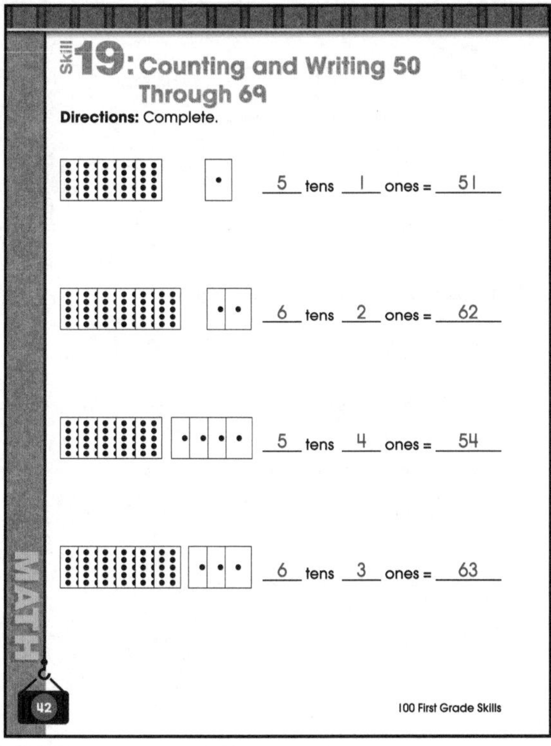

Skill **19: Counting and Writing 50 Through 69**

Directions: Complete.

5 tens 1 ones = 51

6 tens 2 ones = 62

5 tens 4 ones = 54

6 tens 3 ones = 63

MATH

42 100 First Grade Skills

Page 42

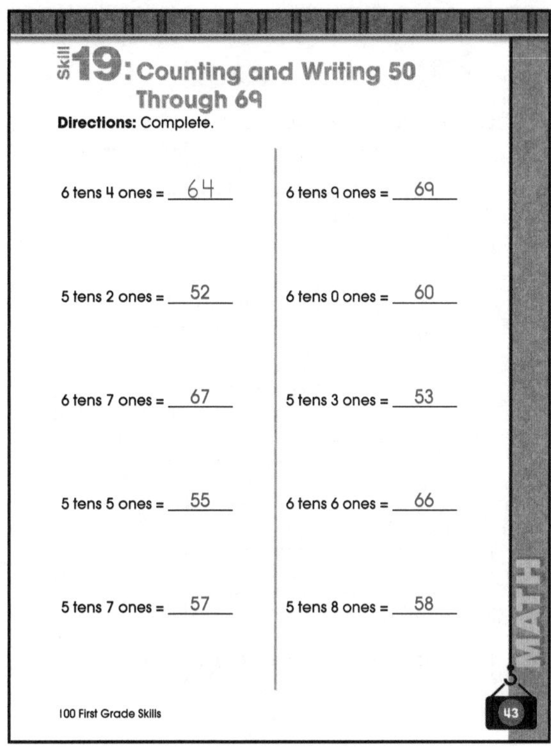

Skill **19: Counting and Writing 50 Through 69**

Directions: Complete.

6 tens 4 ones = 64

5 tens 2 ones = 52

6 tens 7 ones = 67

5 tens 5 ones = 55

5 tens 7 ones = 57

6 tens 9 ones = 69

6 tens 0 ones = 60

5 tens 3 ones = 53

6 tens 6 ones = 66

5 tens 8 ones = 58

MATH

100 First Grade Skills 43

Page 43

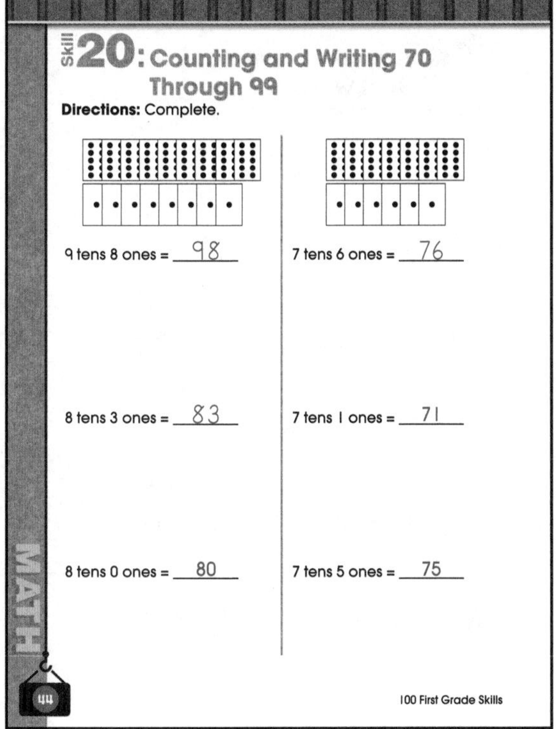

Skill **20: Counting and Writing 70 Through 99**

Directions: Complete.

9 tens 8 ones = 98

8 tens 3 ones = 83

8 tens 0 ones = 80

7 tens 6 ones = 76

7 tens 1 ones = 71

7 tens 5 ones = 75

MATH

44 100 First Grade Skills

Page 44

Skill **20: Counting and Writing 70 Through 99**

Directions: Complete.

9 tens 1 ones = 91

9 tens 4 ones = 94

7 tens 0 ones = 70

7 tens 9 ones = 79

8 tens 2 ones = 82

9 tens 9 ones = 99

8 tens 7 ones = 87

8 tens 6 ones = 86

9 tens 2 ones = 92

8 tens 8 ones = 88

MATH

100 First Grade Skills 45

Page 45

Answer Key

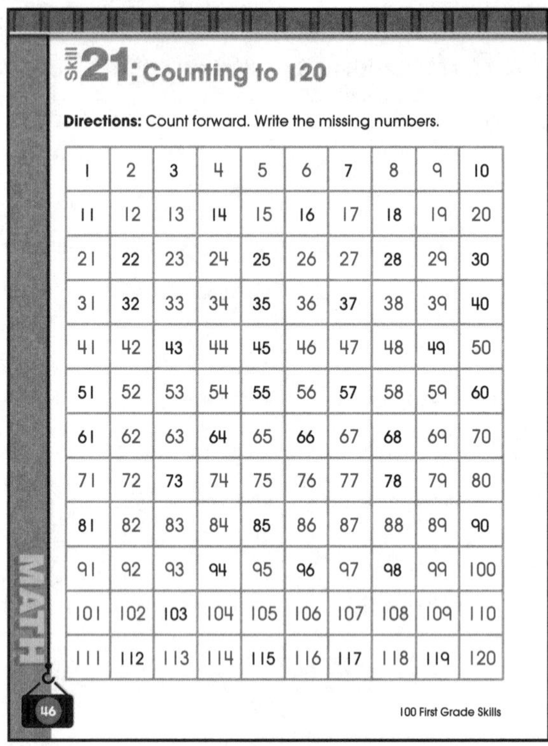

Skill 21: Counting to 120

Directions: Count forward. Write the missing numbers.

1	2	3	4	5	6	7	8	9	10
11	12	13	14	15	16	17	18	19	20
21	22	23	24	25	26	27	28	29	30
31	32	33	34	35	36	37	38	39	40
41	42	43	44	45	46	47	48	49	50
51	52	53	54	55	56	57	58	59	60
61	62	63	64	65	66	67	68	69	70
71	72	73	74	75	76	77	78	79	80
81	82	83	84	85	86	87	88	89	90
91	92	93	94	95	96	97	98	99	100
101	102	103	104	105	106	107	108	109	110
111	112	113	114	115	116	117	118	119	120

MATH

46 100 First Grade Skills

Page 46

Skill 21: Counting to 120

Directions: Write the number that comes one before.

4 5 | 88 89

22 23 | 116 117

Directions: Write the number that comes between.

11 12 13 | 35 36 37

62 63 64 | 98 99 100

Directions: Write the number that comes one after.

79 80 | 92 93

50 51 | 114 115

41 42 | 103 104

100 First Grade Skills 47

MATH

Page 47

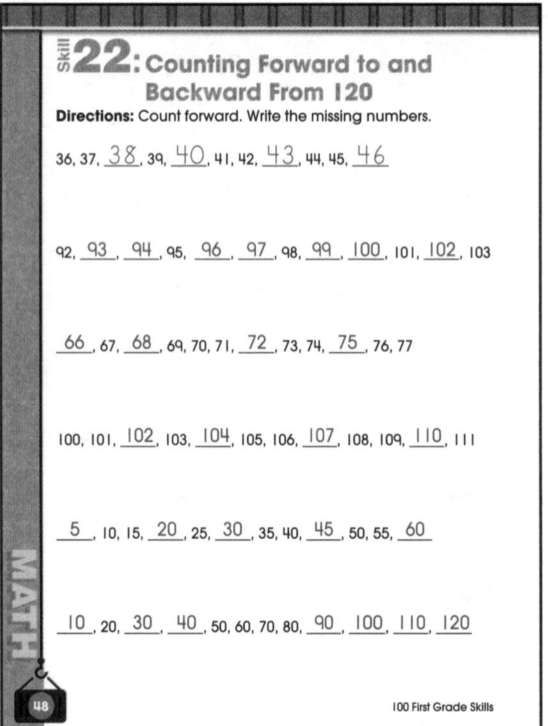

Skill 22: Counting Forward to and Backward From 120

Directions: Count forward. Write the missing numbers.

36, 37, 38, 39, 40, 41, 42, 43, 44, 45, 46

92, 93, 94, 95, 96, 97, 98, 99, 100, 101, 102, 103

66, 67, 68, 69, 70, 71, 72, 73, 74, 75, 76, 77

100, 101, 102, 103, 104, 105, 106, 107, 108, 109, 110, 111

5, 10, 15, 20, 25, 30, 35, 40, 45, 50, 55, 60

10, 20, 30, 40, 50, 60, 70, 80, 90, 100, 110, 120

MATH

48 100 First Grade Skills

Page 48

Skill 22: Counting Forward to and Backward From 120

Directions: Count backward. Write the missing numbers.

79, 78, 77, 76, 75, 74, 73, 72, 71, 70, 69, 68

84, 83, 82, 81, 80, 79, 78, 77, 76, 75, 74, 73

24, 22, 20, 18, 16, 14, 12, 10, 8, 6, 4, 2

120, 115, 110, 105, 100, 95, 90, 85, 80, 75, 70, 65

75, 70, 65, 60, 55, 50, 45, 40, 35, 30, 25, 20

110, 100, 90, 80, 70, 60, 50, 40, 30, 20

100 First Grade Skills 49

MATH

Page 49

Answer Key

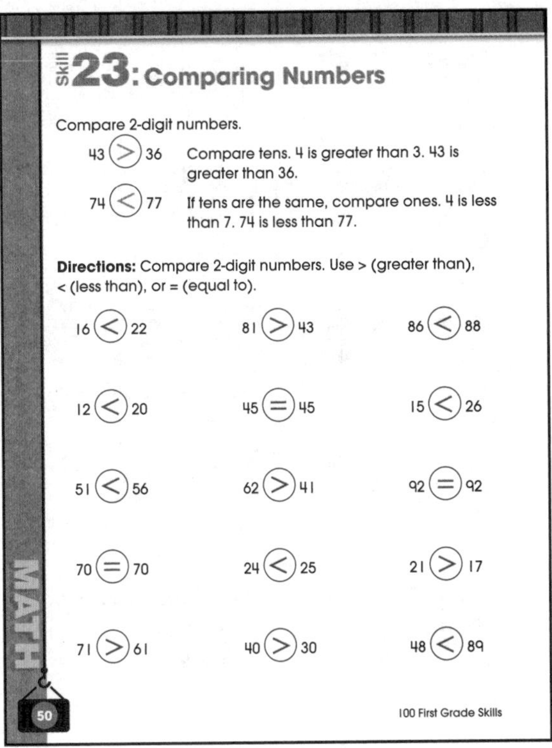

Skill **23: Comparing Numbers**

Compare 2-digit numbers.

43 (>) 36 Compare tens. 4 is greater than 3. 43 is greater than 36.

74 (<) 77 If tens are the same, compare ones. 4 is less than 7. 74 is less than 77.

Directions: Compare 2-digit numbers. Use > (greater than), < (less than), or = (equal to).

16 (<) 22	81 (>) 43	86 (<) 88
12 (<) 20	45 (=) 45	15 (<) 26
51 (<) 56	62 (>) 41	92 (=) 92
70 (=) 70	24 (<) 25	21 (>) 17
71 (>) 61	40 (>) 30	48 (<) 89

MATH

50 100 First Grade Skills

Page 50

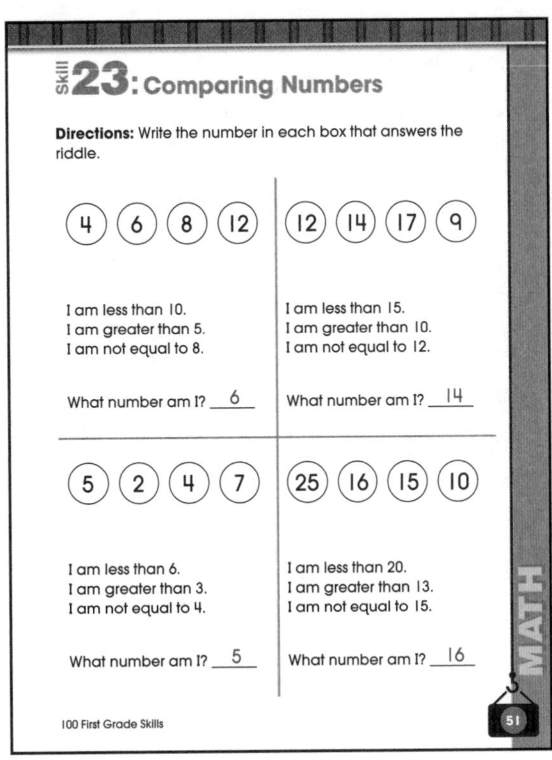

Skill **23: Comparing Numbers**

Directions: Write the number in each box that answers the riddle.

(4) (6) (8) (12)

I am less than 10.
I am greater than 5.
I am not equal to 8.

What number am I? 6

(12) (14) (17) (9)

I am less than 15.
I am greater than 10.
I am not equal to 12.

What number am I? 14

(5) (2) (4) (7)

I am less than 6.
I am greater than 3.
I am not equal to 4.

What number am I? 5

(25) (16) (15) (10)

I am less than 20.
I am greater than 13.
I am not equal to 15.

What number am I? 16

100 First Grade Skills MATH 51

Page 51

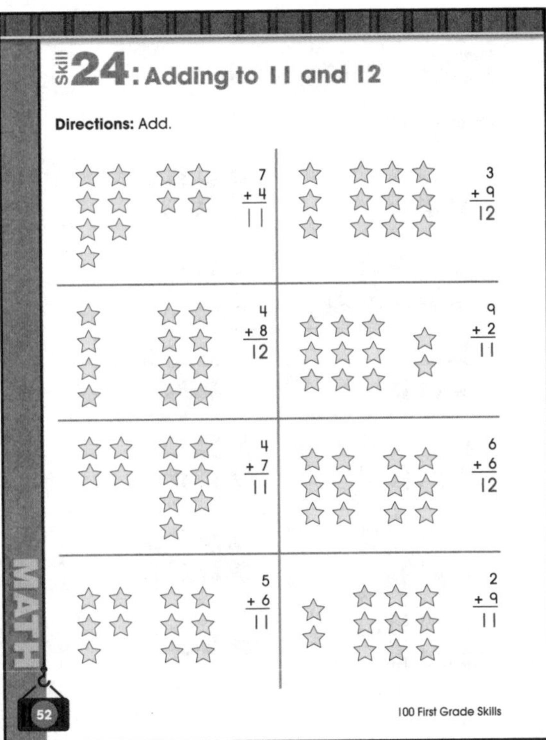

Skill **24: Adding to 11 and 12**

Directions: Add.

7 + 4 = 11	3 + 9 = 12
4 + 8 = 12	9 + 2 = 11
4 + 7 = 11	6 + 6 = 12
5 + 6 = 11	2 + 9 = 11

MATH

52 100 First Grade Skills

Page 52

Skill **24: Adding to 11 and 12**

Directions: Add.

9 + 3 = 12	3 + 9 = 12
6 + 5 = 11	5 + 7 = 12
7 + 5 = 12	3 + 8 = 11
4 + 8 = 12	2 + 9 = 11

100 First Grade Skills MATH 53

Page 53

Answer Key

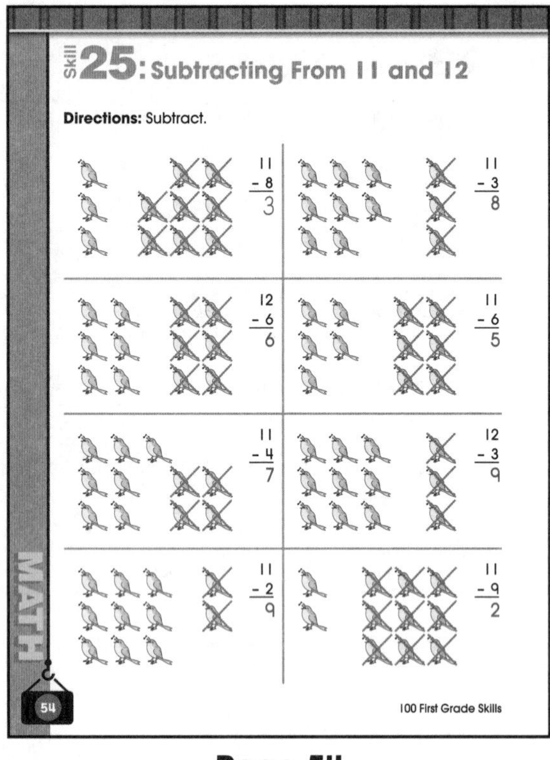

Page 54

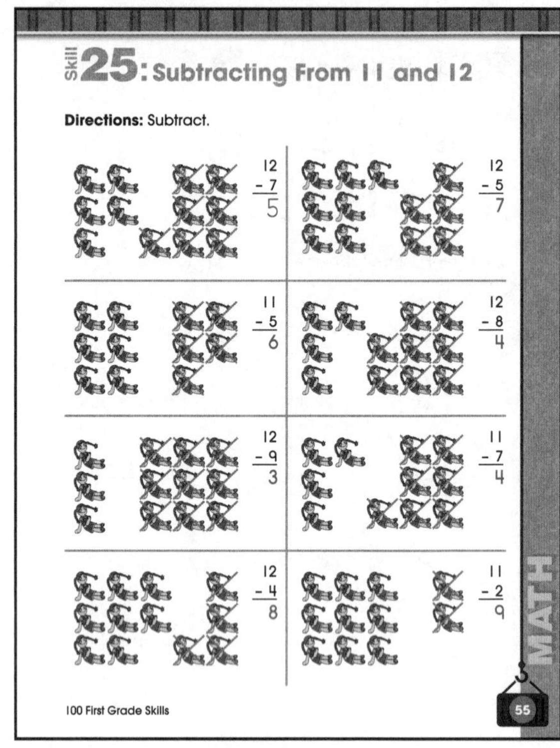

Page 55

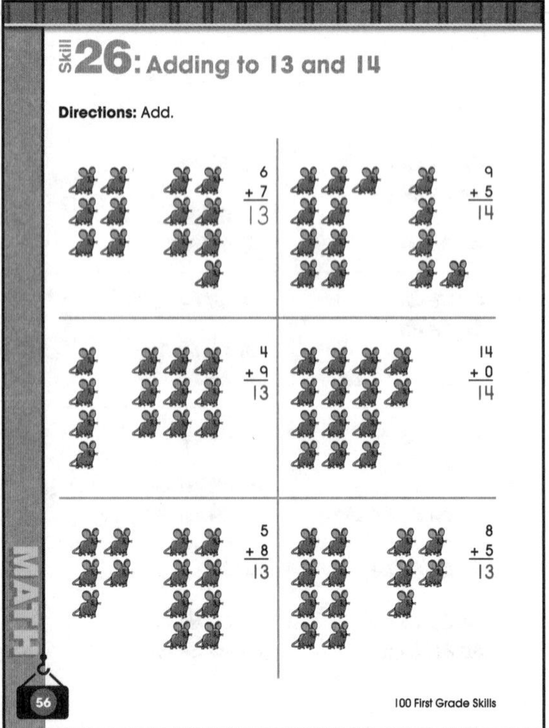

Page 56

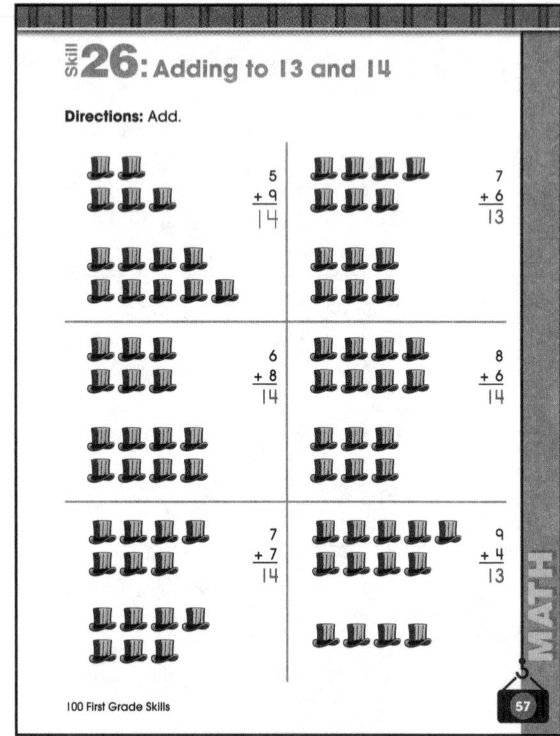

Page 57

Answer Key

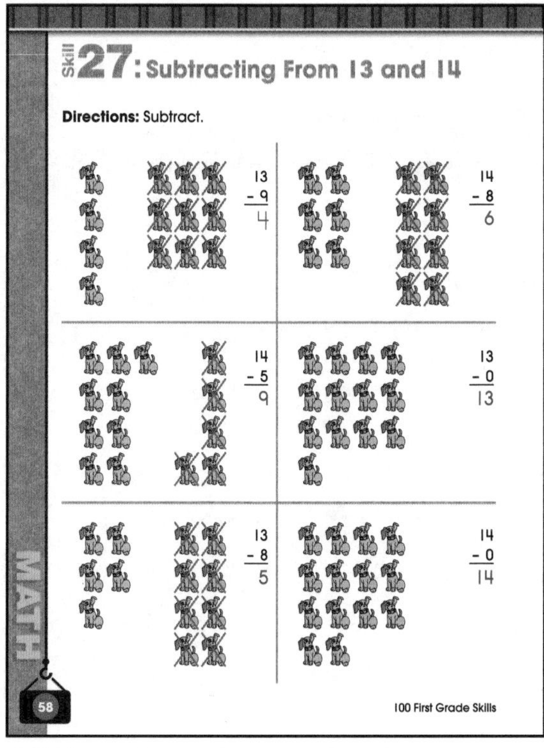

Skill **27**: Subtracting From 13 and 14

Directions: Subtract.

13 − 9 = 4

14 − 8 = 6

14 − 5 = 9

13 − 0 = 13

13 − 8 = 5

14 − 0 = 14

MATH

58 100 First Grade Skills

Page 58

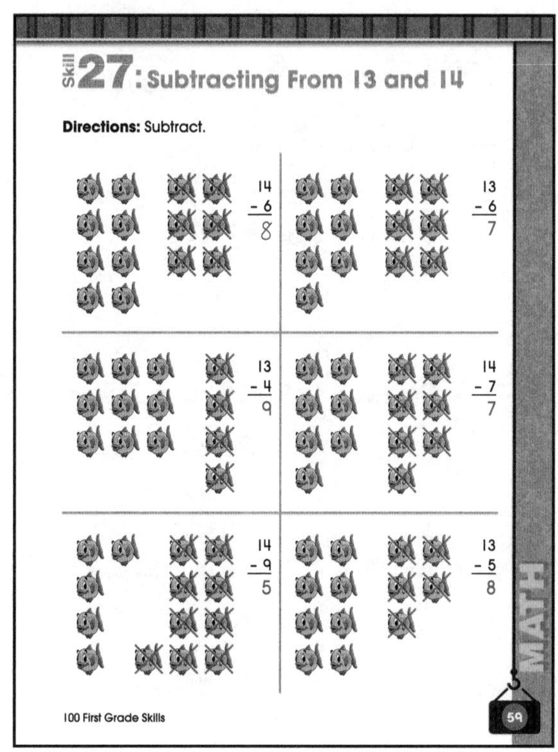

Skill **27**: Subtracting From 13 and 14

Directions: Subtract.

14 − 6 = 8

13 − 6 = 7

13 − 4 = 9

14 − 7 = 7

14 − 9 = 5

13 − 5 = 8

100 First Grade Skills 59

MATH

Page 59

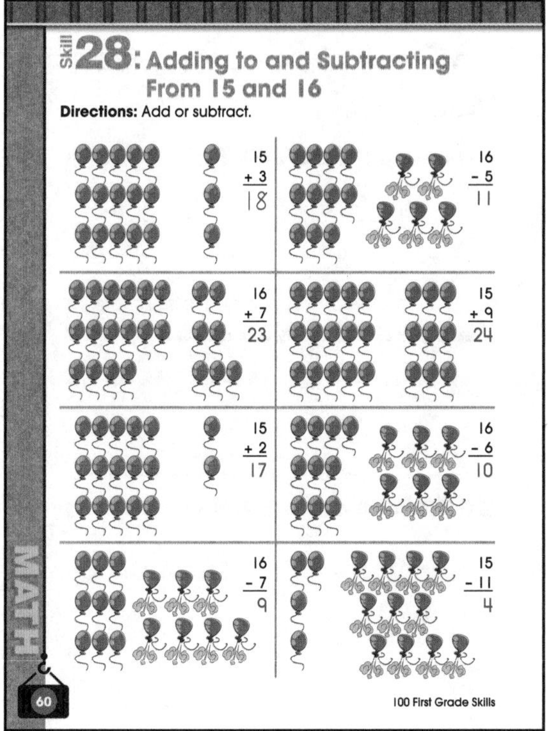

Skill **28**: Adding to and Subtracting From 15 and 16

Directions: Add or subtract.

15 + 3 = 18

16 − 5 = 11

16 + 7 = 23

15 + 9 = 24

15 + 2 = 17

16 − 6 = 10

16 − 7 = 9

15 − 11 = 4

MATH

60 100 First Grade Skills

Page 60

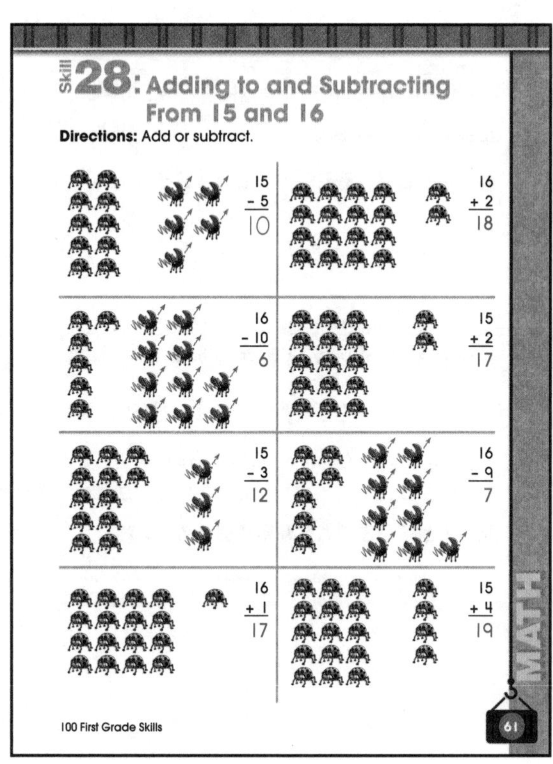

Skill **28**: Adding to and Subtracting From 15 and 16

Directions: Add or subtract.

15 − 5 = 10

16 + 2 = 18

16 − 10 = 6

15 + 2 = 17

15 − 3 = 12

16 − 9 = 7

16 + 1 = 17

15 + 4 = 19

100 First Grade Skills 61

MATH

Page 61

Answer Key

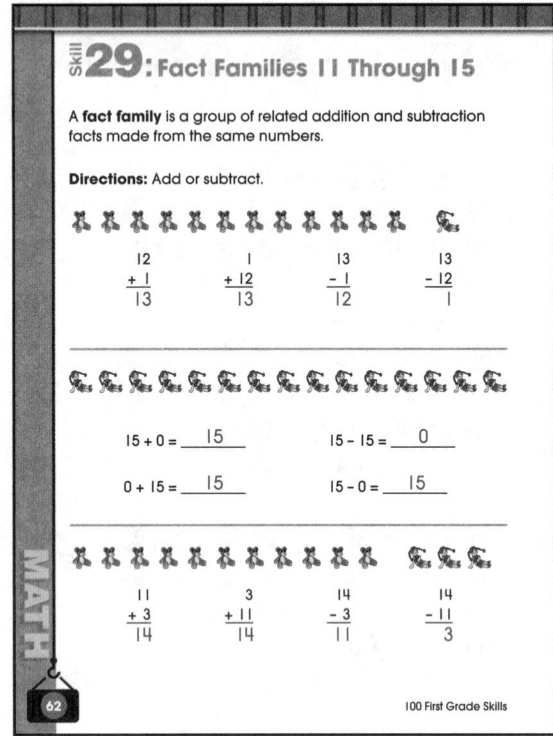
Skill 29: Fact Families 11 Through 15

A **fact family** is a group of related addition and subtraction facts made from the same numbers.

Directions: Add or subtract.

12 + 1 = 13; 1 + 12 = 13; 13 − 1 = 12; 13 − 12 = 1

15 + 0 = 15; 15 − 15 = 0; 0 + 15 = 15; 15 − 0 = 15

11 + 3 = 14; 3 + 11 = 14; 14 − 3 = 11; 14 − 11 = 3

Page 62

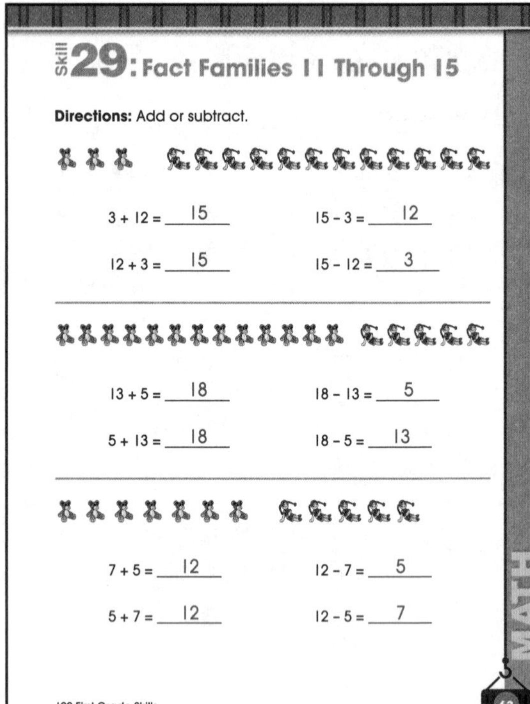
Skill 29: Fact Families 11 Through 15

Directions: Add or subtract.

3 + 12 = 15; 15 − 3 = 12; 12 + 3 = 15; 15 − 12 = 3

13 + 5 = 18; 18 − 13 = 5; 5 + 13 = 18; 18 − 5 = 13

7 + 5 = 12; 12 − 7 = 5; 5 + 7 = 12; 12 − 5 = 7

Page 63

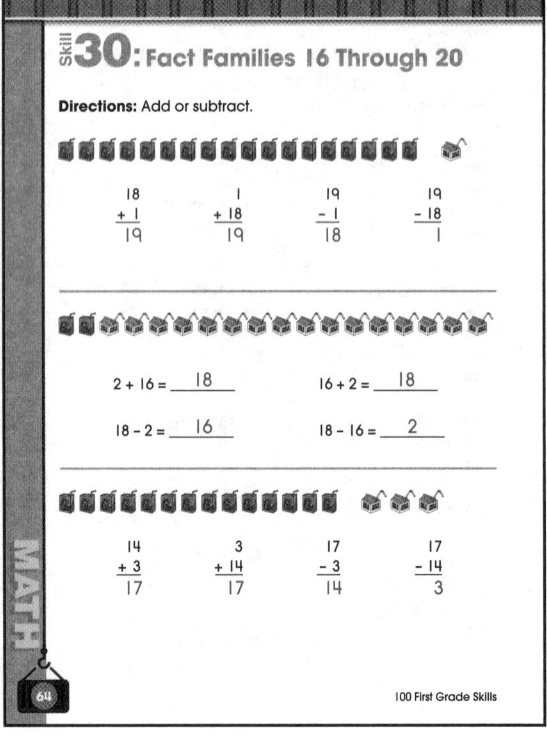
Skill 30: Fact Families 16 Through 20

Directions: Add or subtract.

18 + 1 = 19; 1 + 18 = 19; 19 − 1 = 18; 19 − 18 = 1

2 + 16 = 18; 16 + 2 = 18; 18 − 2 = 16; 18 − 16 = 2

14 + 3 = 17; 3 + 14 = 17; 17 − 3 = 14; 17 − 14 = 3

Page 64

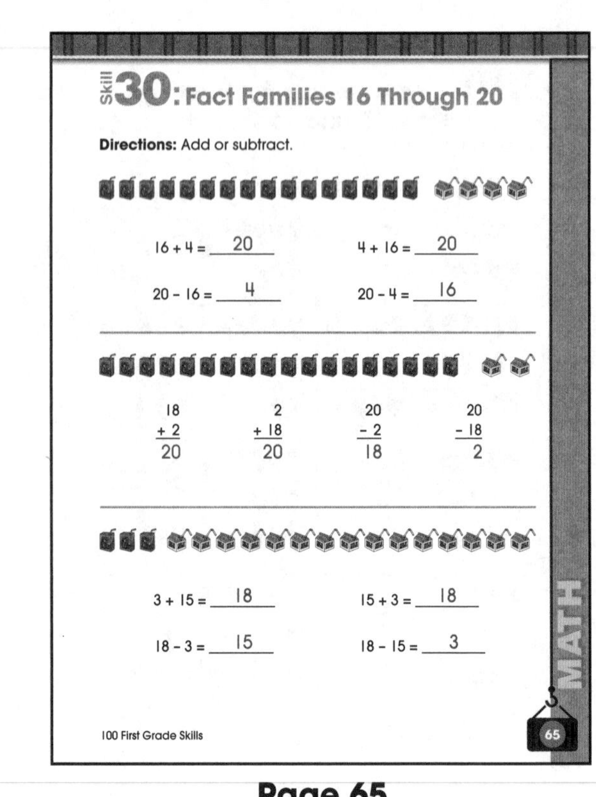
Skill 30: Fact Families 16 Through 20

Directions: Add or subtract.

16 + 4 = 20; 4 + 16 = 20; 20 − 16 = 4; 20 − 4 = 16

18 + 2 = 20; 2 + 18 = 20; 20 − 2 = 18; 20 − 18 = 2

3 + 15 = 18; 15 + 3 = 18; 18 − 3 = 15; 18 − 15 = 3

Page 65

Answer Key

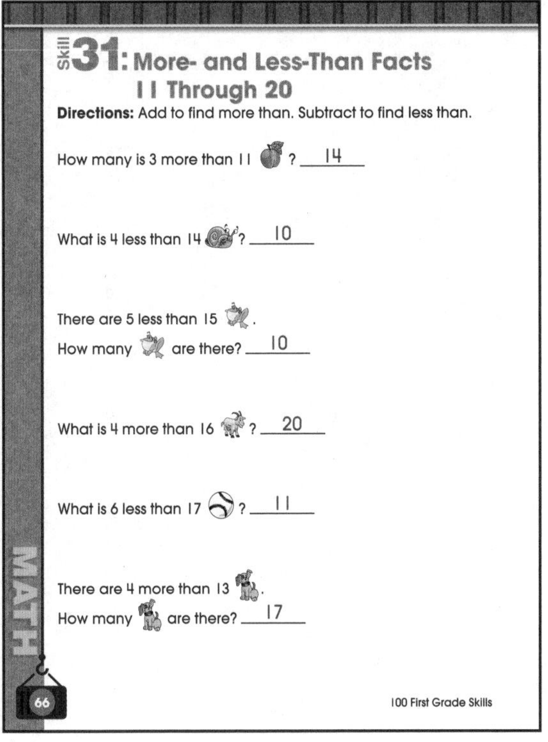

Skill **31: More- and Less-Than Facts 11 Through 20**

Directions: Add to find more than. Subtract to find less than.

How many is 3 more than 11 ? 14

What is 4 less than 14 ? 10

There are 5 less than 15 . How many are there? 10

What is 4 more than 16 ? 20

What is 6 less than 17 ? 11

There are 4 more than 13 . How many are there? 17

MATH 66 100 First Grade Skills

Page 66

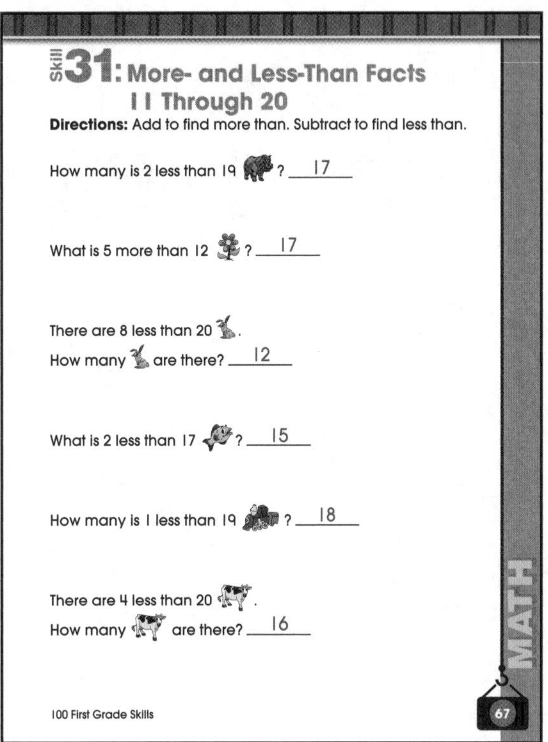

Skill **31: More- and Less-Than Facts 11 Through 20**

Directions: Add to find more than. Subtract to find less than.

How many is 2 less than 19 ? 17

What is 5 more than 12 ? 17

There are 8 less than 20 . How many are there? 12

What is 2 less than 17 ? 15

How many is 1 less than 19 ? 18

There are 4 less than 20 . How many are there? 16

100 First Grade Skills MATH 67

Page 67

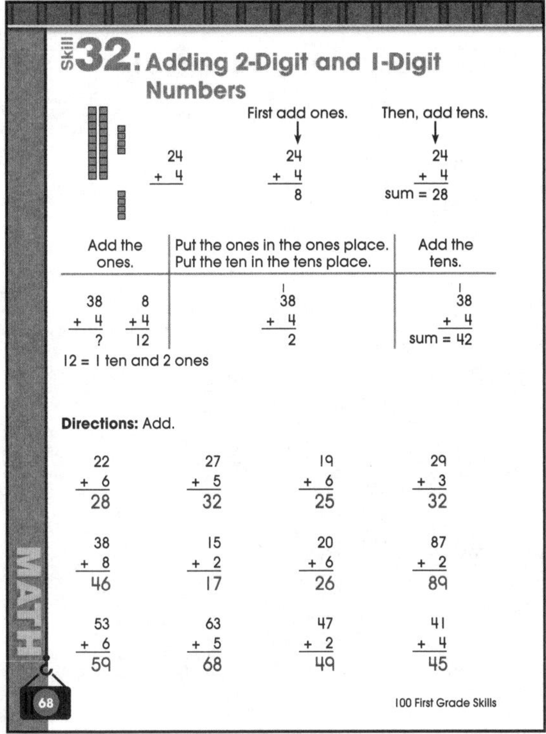

Skill **32: Adding 2-Digit and 1-Digit Numbers**

	First add ones.	Then, add tens.
24 + 4	24 + 4 = 8	24 + 4, sum = 28

Add the ones.	Put the ones in the ones place. Put the ten in the tens place.	Add the tens.
38 + 4 = ? 8 + 4 = 12	38 + 4 = 2	38 + 4, sum = 42

12 = 1 ten and 2 ones

Directions: Add.

22 + 6 = 28	27 + 5 = 32	19 + 6 = 25	29 + 3 = 32
38 + 8 = 46	15 + 2 = 17	20 + 6 = 26	87 + 2 = 89
53 + 6 = 59	63 + 5 = 68	47 + 2 = 49	41 + 4 = 45

MATH 68 100 First Grade Skills

Page 68

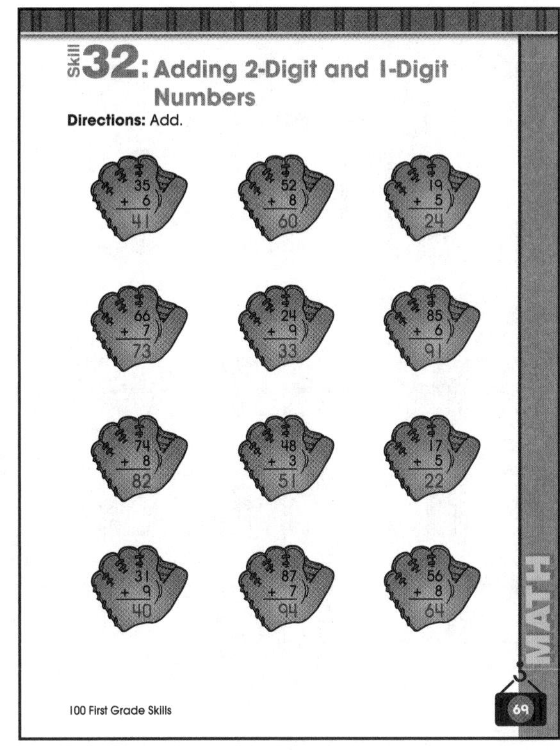

Skill **32: Adding 2-Digit and 1-Digit Numbers**

Directions: Add.

35 + 6 = 41	52 + 8 = 60	19 + 5 = 24
66 + 7 = 73	24 + 9 = 33	85 + 6 = 91
74 + 8 = 82	48 + 3 = 51	17 + 5 = 22
31 + 9 = 40	87 + 7 = 94	56 + 8 = 64

100 First Grade Skills MATH 69

Page 69

Answer Key

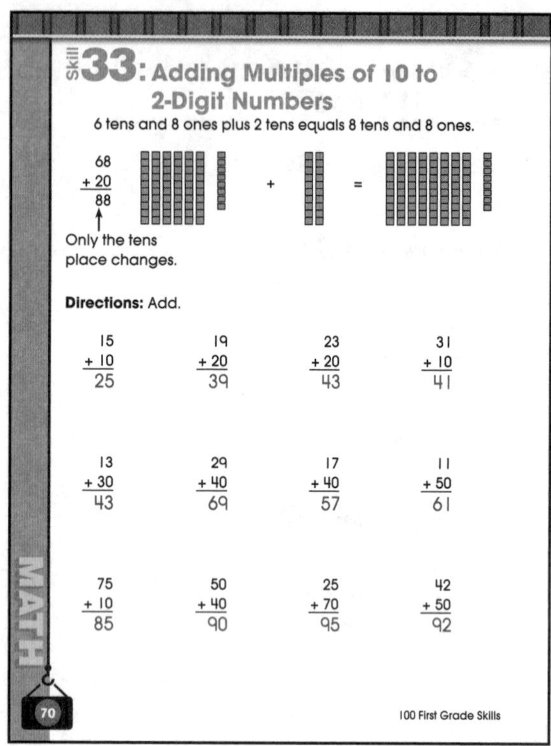

Skill **33**: Adding Multiples of 10 to 2-Digit Numbers

6 tens and 8 ones plus 2 tens equals 8 tens and 8 ones.

68 + 20 = 88

Only the tens place changes.

Directions: Add.

15 + 10 = 25	19 + 20 = 39	23 + 20 = 43	31 + 10 = 41
13 + 30 = 43	29 + 40 = 69	17 + 40 = 57	11 + 50 = 61
75 + 10 = 85	50 + 40 = 90	25 + 70 = 95	42 + 50 = 92

MATH

70

100 First Grade Skills

Page 70

Skill **33**: Adding Multiples of 10 to 2-Digit Numbers

Directions: Add.

43 + 20 = 63	16 + 30 = 46	71 + 10 = 81	24 + 60 = 84
85 + 10 = 95	39 + 40 = 79	15 + 80 = 95	46 + 50 = 96
57 + 10 = 67	63 + 30 = 93	24 + 70 = 94	73 + 10 = 83
15 + 70 = 85	59 + 20 = 79	25 + 70 = 95	17 + 40 = 57

MATH

100 First Grade Skills

71

Page 71

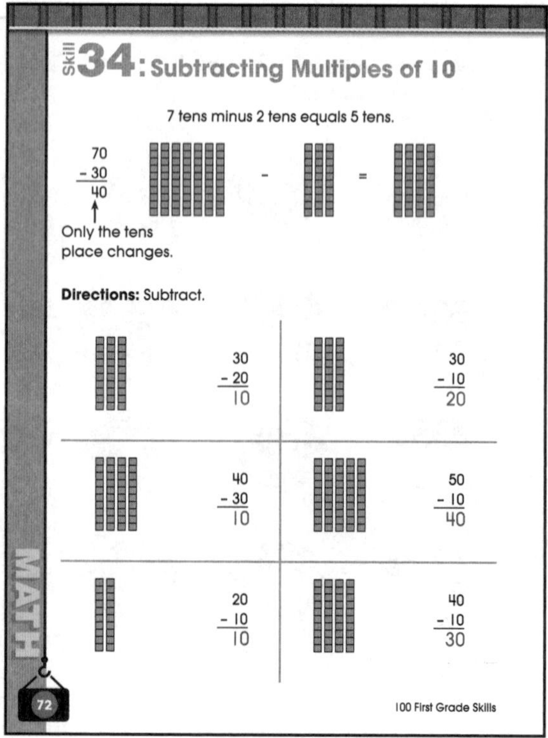

Skill **34**: Subtracting Multiples of 10

7 tens minus 2 tens equals 5 tens.

70 - 30 = 40

Only the tens place changes.

Directions: Subtract.

30 - 20 = 10	30 - 10 = 20
40 - 30 = 10	50 - 10 = 40
20 - 10 = 10	40 - 10 = 30

MATH

72

100 First Grade Skills

Page 72

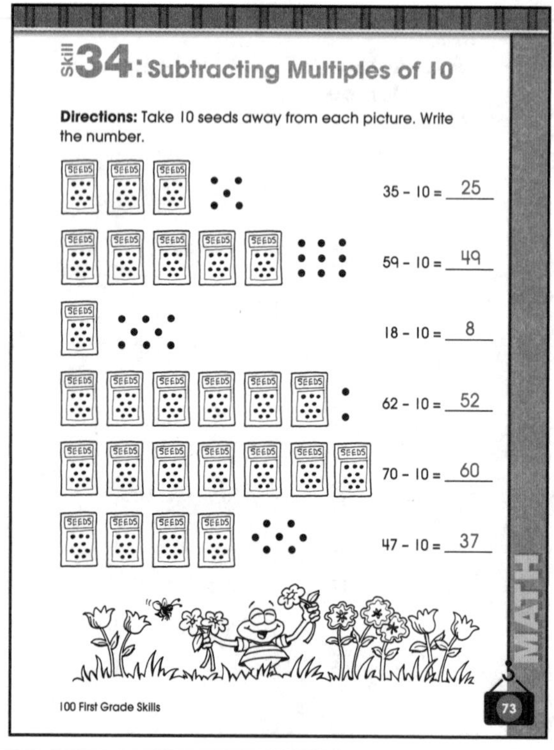

Skill **34**: Subtracting Multiples of 10

Directions: Take 10 seeds away from each picture. Write the number.

35 - 10 = 25

59 - 10 = 49

18 - 10 = 8

62 - 10 = 52

70 - 10 = 60

47 - 10 = 37

MATH

100 First Grade Skills

73

Page 73

Answer Key

Skill 35: Addition and Subtraction Through 100

Directions: Add.

9	58	16	27
+ 8	+ 7	+ 9	+ 8
17	65	25	35
18	78	29	67
+ 9	+ 6	+ 5	+ 9
27	84	34	76
9	28	37	66
+ 7	+ 5	+ 7	+ 7
16	33	44	73
87	49	8	79
+ 6	+ 9	+ 8	+ 6
93	58	16	85
46	96	39	46
+ 8	+ 4	+ 8	+ 9
54	100	47	55

MATH

74 100 First Grade Skills

Page 74

Skill 35: Addition and Subtraction Through 100

Directions: Subtract.

20	90	80	40
- 10	- 80	- 70	- 20
10	10	10	20
60	80	70	50
- 20	- 60	- 60	- 10
40	20	10	40
40	20	90	90
- 10	- 20	- 40	- 60
50	0	50	30
60	30	40	70
- 60	- 20	- 20	- 10
0	10	20	60
80	60	90	70
- 20	- 50	- 90	- 50
60	10	0	20

MATH

100 First Grade Skills 75

Page 75

Skill 36: Adding Three Numbers

		Add the ones.	Add the tens.
11	□□□□□□□□□□ □	11	11
4	□□□□	4	4
+ 3	□□□	+ 3	+ 3
		8	sum = 18

Directions: Add.

11	10	8	15
3	5	2	3
+ 5	+ 3	+ 1	+ 2
19	18	11	20
2	4	12	2
4	3	4	3
+ 1	+ 2	+ 1	+ 3
7	9	17	8
5	13	15	11
4	2	1	6
+ 1	+ 1	+ 1	+ 2
10	16	17	19

MATH

76 100 First Grade Skills

Page 76

Skill 36: Adding Three Numbers

Directions: Add.

3	3	7	6
5	8	1	4
+ 4	+ 6	+ 5	+ 1
12	17	13	11
9	4	2	3
2	5	1	3
+ 3	+ 4	+ 6	+ 5
14	13	9	11

David ate 1 banana, 8 grapes, and 9 blueberries for breakfast. How many pieces of fruit did he eat in all?

1 + 8 + 9 = 18 pieces of fruit

Myra drew 5 rabbits, 5 chicks, and 3 sheep in her picture. How many animals did she draw in all?

5 + 5 + 3 = 13 animals

MATH

100 First Grade Skills 77

Page 77

Answer Key

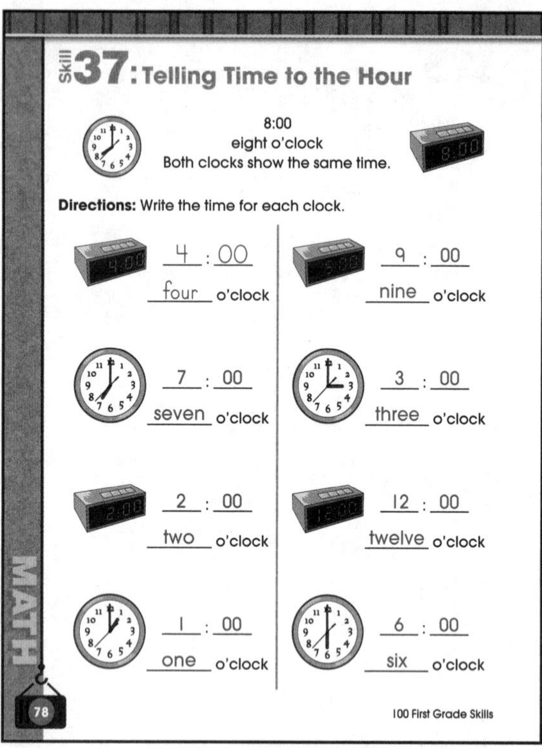

Skill **37: Telling Time to the Hour**

8:00
eight o'clock
Both clocks show the same time.

Directions: Write the time for each clock.

4 : 00 four o'clock
9 : 00 nine o'clock
7 : 00 seven o'clock
3 : 00 three o'clock
2 : 00 two o'clock
12 : 00 twelve o'clock
1 : 00 one o'clock
6 : 00 six o'clock

MATH

78 100 First Grade Skills

Page 78

Skill **37: Telling Time to the Hour**

Directions: What time is it on the first clock? Draw the hands to show this time on the second clock.

Directions: What time is it on the first clock? Write this time on the second clock.

6:00
8:00
7:00
11:00

MATH

100 First Grade Skills 79

Page 79

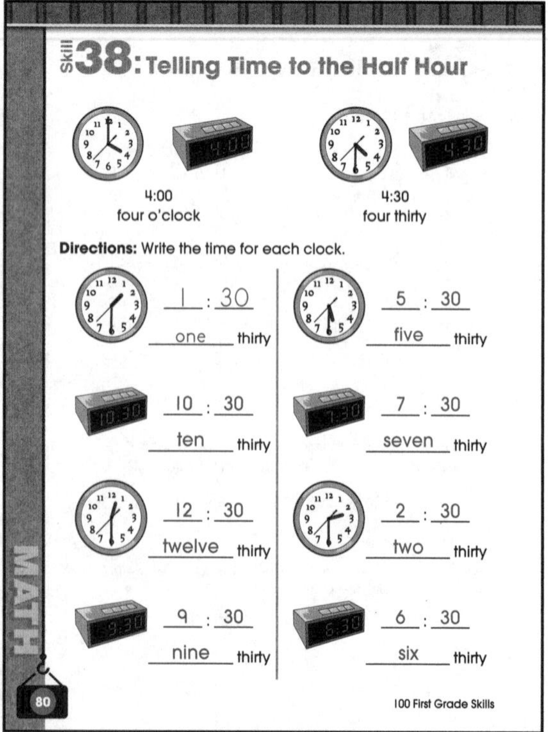

Skill **38: Telling Time to the Half Hour**

4:00
four o'clock

4:30
four thirty

Directions: Write the time for each clock.

1 : 30 one thirty
5 : 30 five thirty
10 : 30 ten thirty
7 : 30 seven thirty
12 : 30 twelve thirty
2 : 30 two thirty
9 : 30 nine thirty
6 : 30 six thirty

MATH

80 100 First Grade Skills

Page 80

Skill **38: Telling Time to the Half Hour**

Directions: What time is it on the first clock? Draw the hands to show this time on the second clock.

Directions: What time is it on the first clock? Write this time on the second clock.

4:30
8:30
11:30
3:30

MATH

100 First Grade Skills 81

Page 81

Answer Key

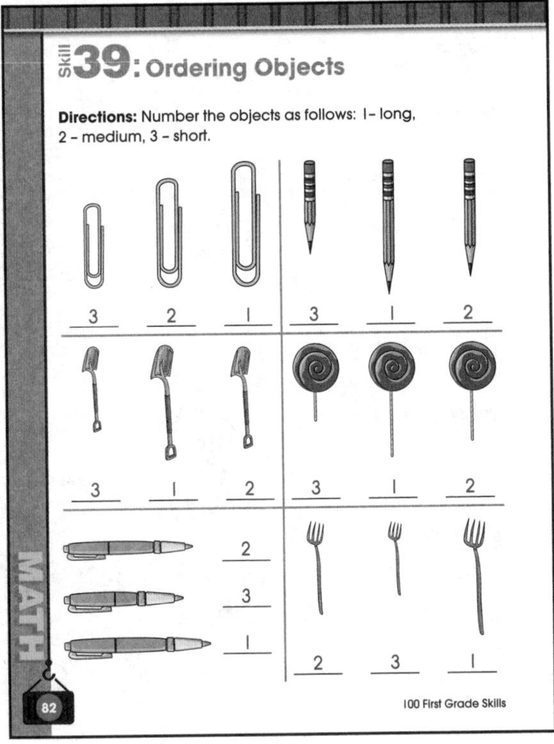

Page 82

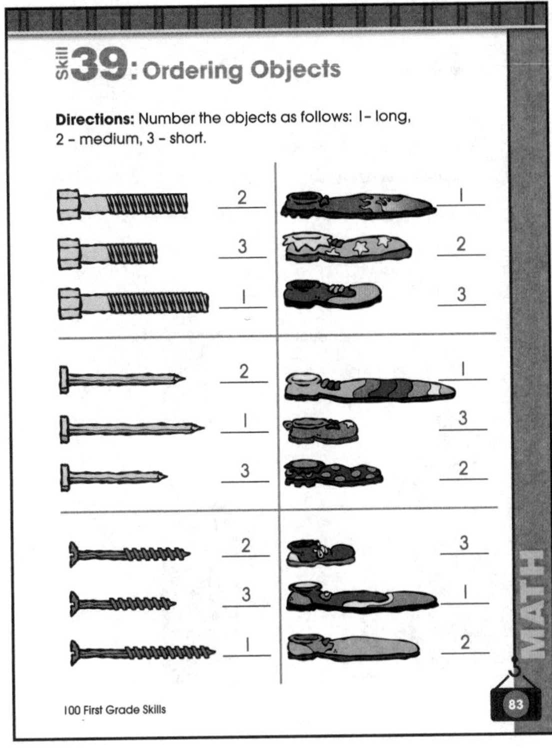

Page 83

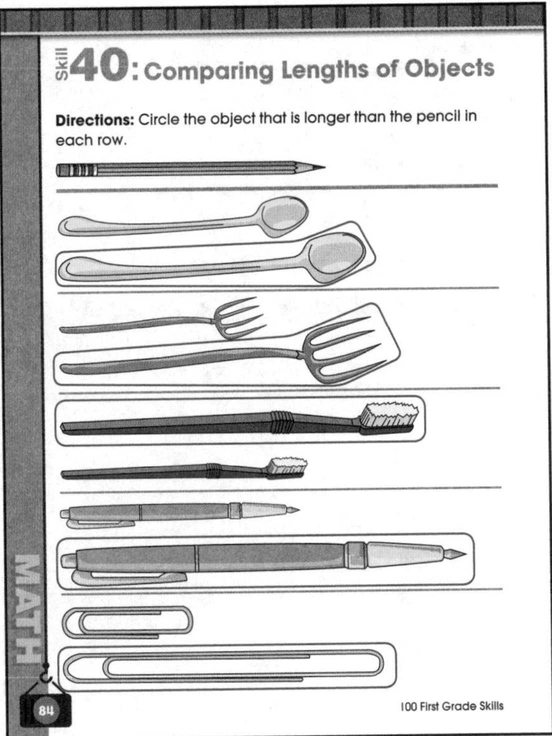

Page 84

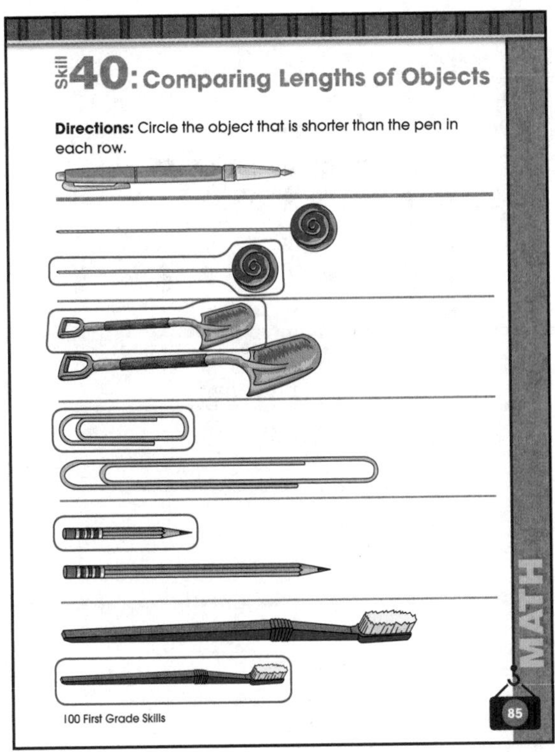

Page 85

Answer Key

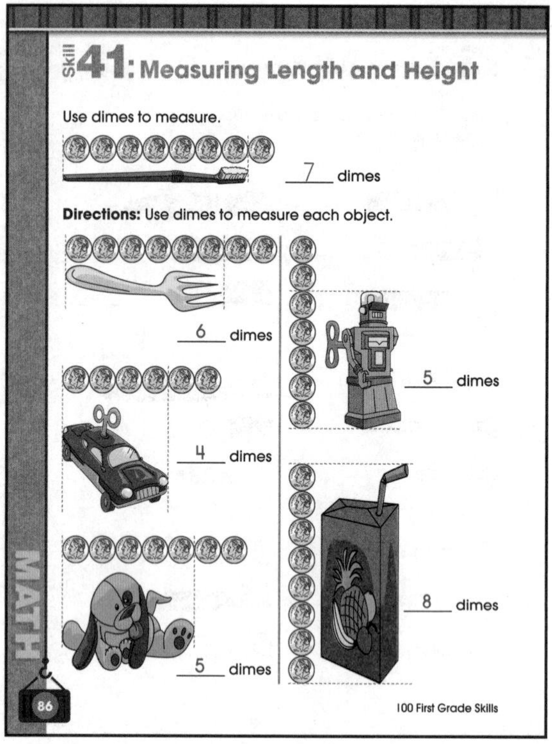

Skill **41: Measuring Length and Height**

Use dimes to measure.

7 dimes

Directions: Use dimes to measure each object.

6 dimes

5 dimes

4 dimes

8 dimes

5 dimes

MATH

86

100 First Grade Skills

Page 86

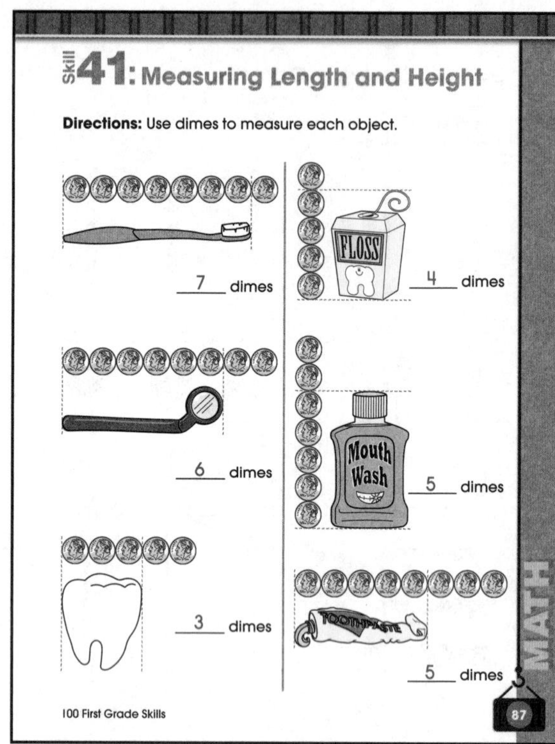

Skill **41: Measuring Length and Height**

Directions: Use dimes to measure each object.

7 dimes

4 dimes

6 dimes

5 dimes

3 dimes

5 dimes

MATH

100 First Grade Skills

87

Page 87

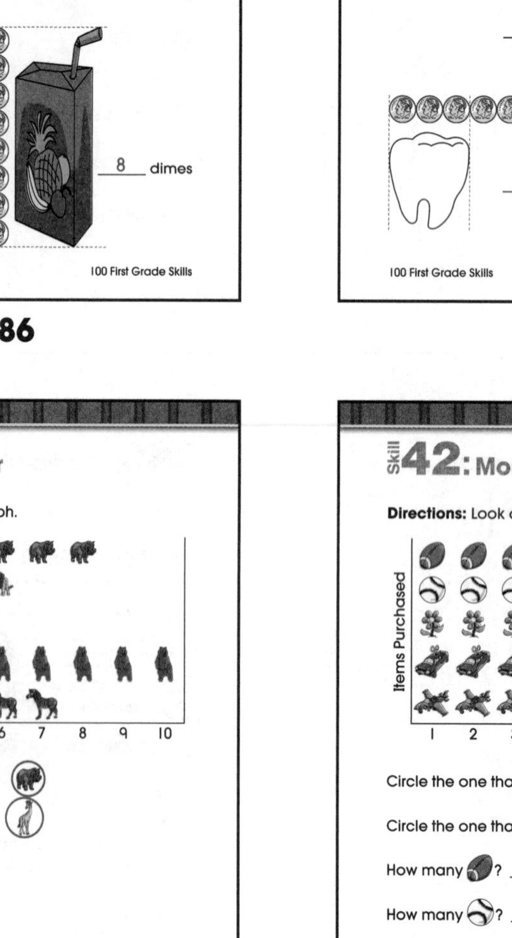

Skill **42: More or Fewer**

Directions: Look at the picture graph.

Circle the one that has more.

Circle the one that has fewer.

How many ? 6

How many ? 8

How many ? 5

How many ? 7

How many ? 10

MATH

88

100 First Grade Skills

Page 88

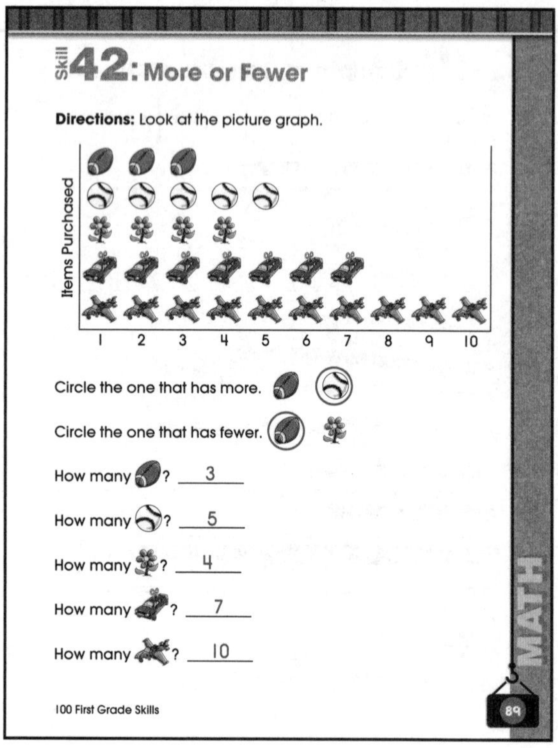

Skill **42: More or Fewer**

Directions: Look at the picture graph.

Circle the one that has more.

Circle the one that has fewer.

How many ? 3

How many ? 5

How many ? 4

How many ? 7

How many ? 10

MATH

100 First Grade Skills

89

Page 89

Answer Key

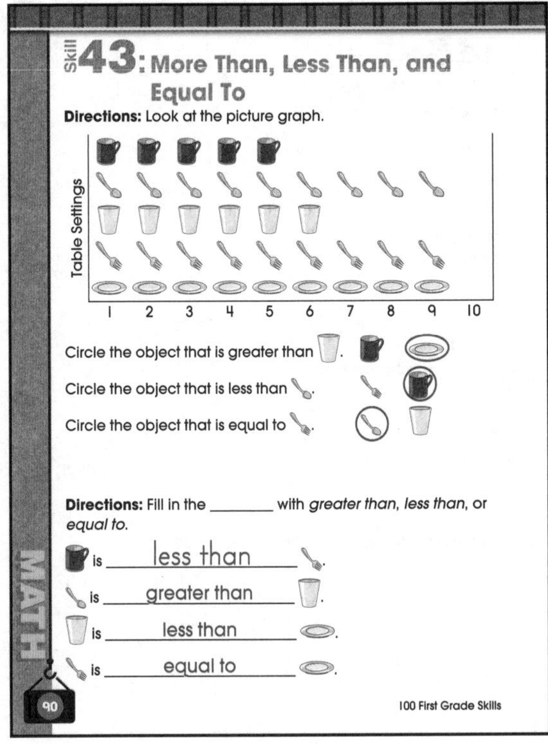
Skill 43: More Than, Less Than, and Equal To

Directions: Look at the picture graph.

Circle the object that is greater than [cup].

Circle the object that is less than [spoon].

Circle the object that is equal to [spoon].

Directions: Fill in the ______ with *greater than*, *less than*, or *equal to*.

[mug] is less than [spoon].

[spoon] is greater than [cup].

[cup] is less than [plate].

[spoon] is equal to [plate].

MATH

90 100 First Grade Skills

Page 90

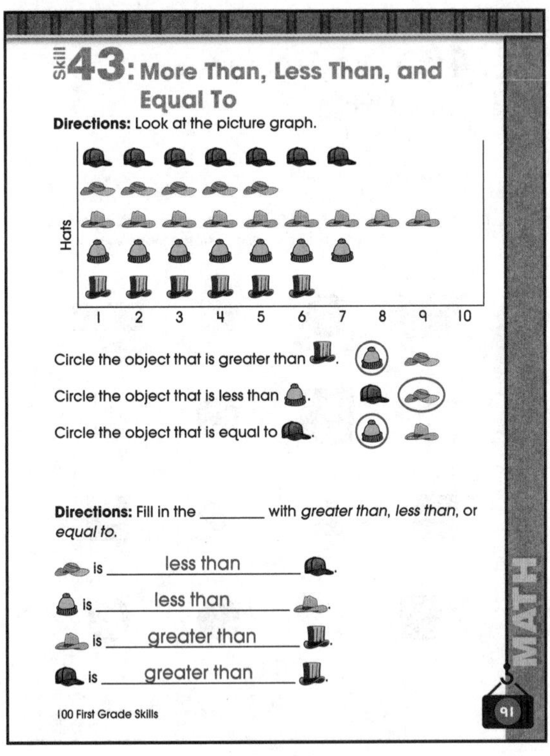
Skill 43: More Than, Less Than, and Equal To

Directions: Look at the picture graph.

Circle the object that is greater than [top hat].

Circle the object that is less than [knit hat].

Circle the object that is equal to [cap].

Directions: Fill in the ______ with *greater than*, *less than*, or *equal to*.

[sun hat] is less than [cap].

[knit hat] is less than [cowboy hat].

[cowboy hat] is greater than [top hat].

[cap] is greater than [top hat].

MATH

100 First Grade Skills 91

Page 91

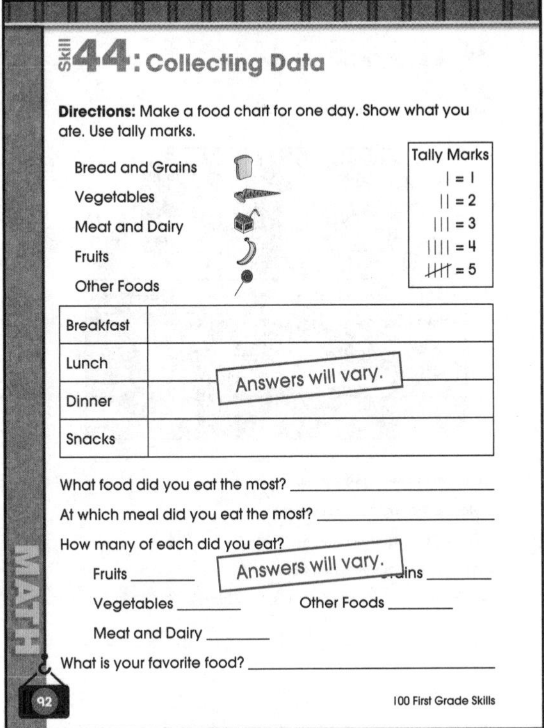
Skill 44: Collecting Data

Directions: Make a food chart for one day. Show what you ate. Use tally marks.

Bread and Grains

Vegetables

Meat and Dairy

Fruits

Other Foods

Tally Marks
| = 1
|| = 2
||| = 3
|||| = 4
~~||||~~ = 5

Breakfast	
Lunch	Answers will vary.
Dinner	
Snacks	

What food did you eat the most? ______

At which meal did you eat the most? ______

How many of each did you eat?

Fruits ______ Answers will vary. Grains ______

Vegetables ______ Other Foods ______

Meat and Dairy ______

What is your favorite food? ______

MATH

92 100 First Grade Skills

Page 92

Skill 44: Collecting Data

Directions: Ask 20 people if they have a pet. Use tally marks to show what kind.

[cat]	[dog]	[bird]	[fish]	[rabbit]	Other	None
	Answers will vary.					

Directions: Write the number.

How many people have [rabbit]? ______

How many people have [bird]? ______

How many people have [cat]? ______ Answers will vary.

How many people have [dog]? ______

How many people have [fish]? ______

How many people have a pet that is not pictured? ______

How many people have no pets? ______

Which pet is the favorite? ______

Which pet is the least favorite? ______

MATH

100 First Grade Skills 93

Page 93

Answer Key

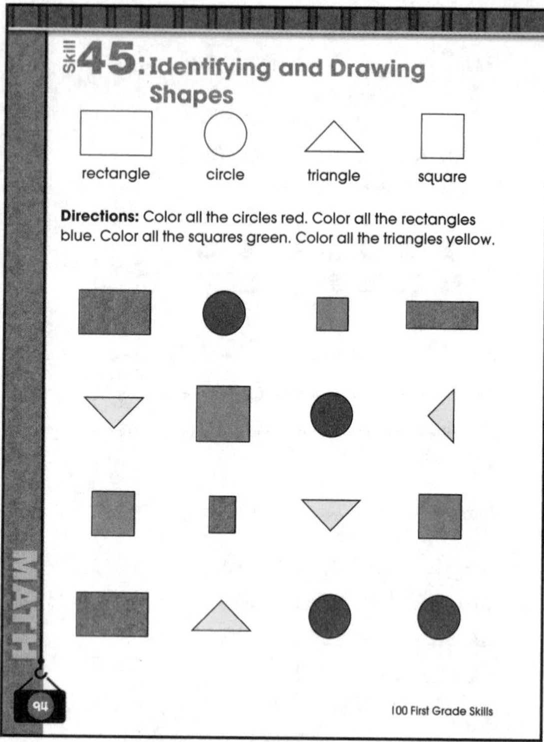

Page 94

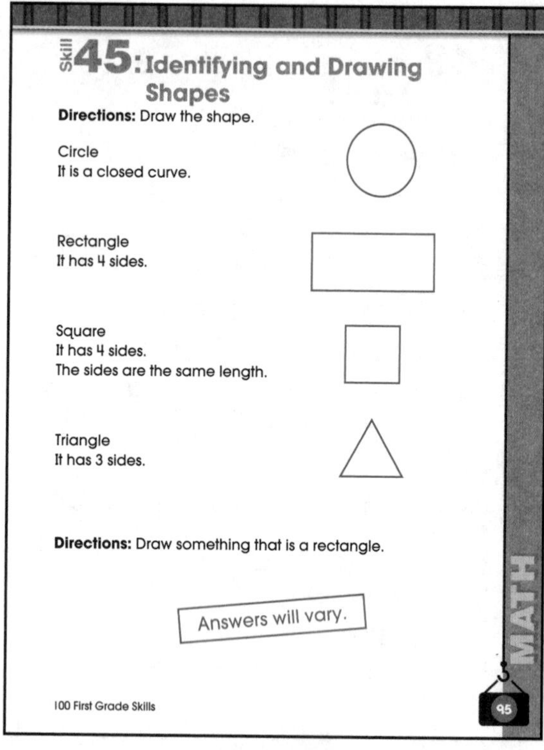

Page 95

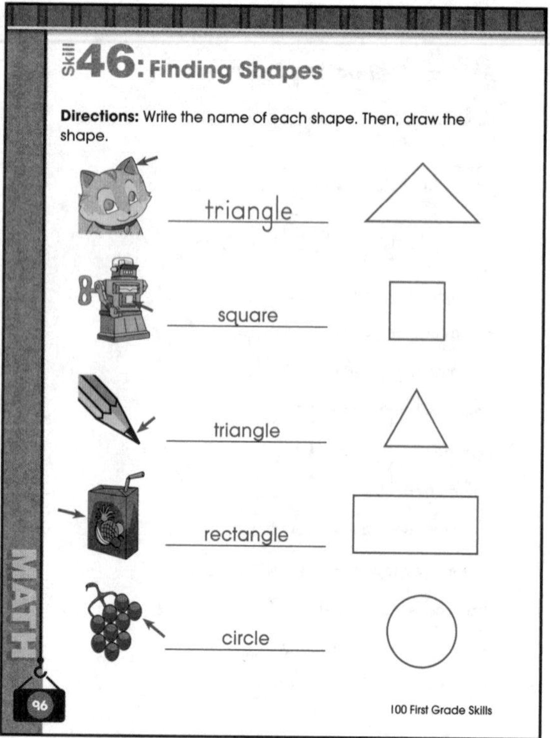

Page 96

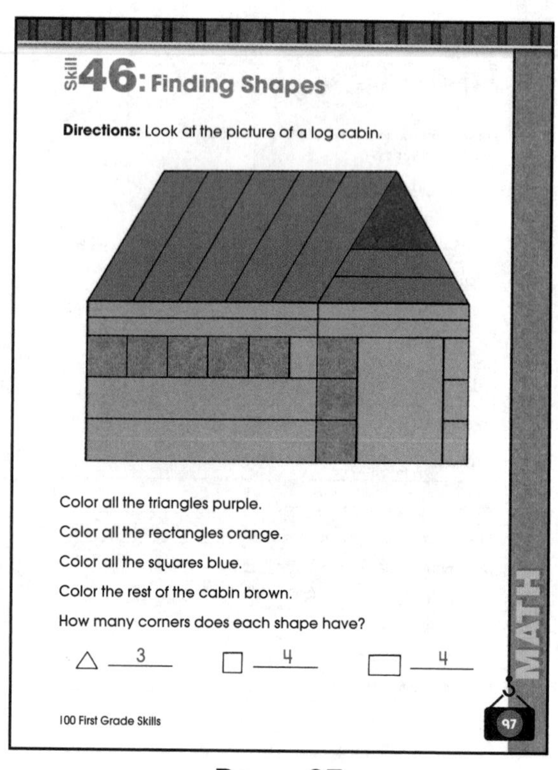

Page 97

Answer Key

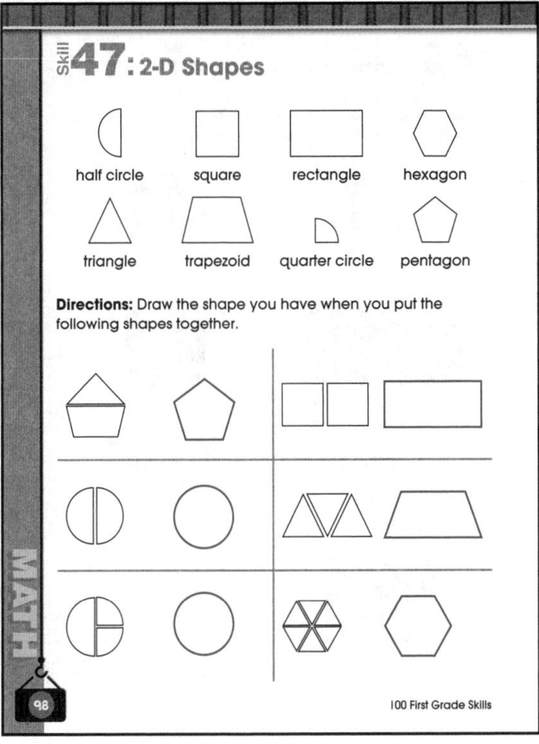

Skill **47: 2-D Shapes**

half circle | square | rectangle | hexagon

triangle | trapezoid | quarter circle | pentagon

Directions: Draw the shape you have when you put the following shapes together.

98

100 First Grade Skills

Page 98

Skill **47: 2-D Shapes**

Directions: Jan made cookies with her new cookie cutters. Count how many sides each cookie has. Then, answer the questions below.

6 sides | 4 sides | 3 sides | 5 sides

H hexagon cookie | S square cookie | T triangle cookie | P pentagon cookie

Which cookie has the fewest sides? triangle

Which cookie has the most sides? hexagon

Write the cookie letters in order of the number of sides the shapes have.

T (fewest sides) S P H (most sides)

How many more sides does **H** have than **S**? 2

How many fewer sides does **T** have than **P**? 2

100 First Grade Skills

99

Page 99

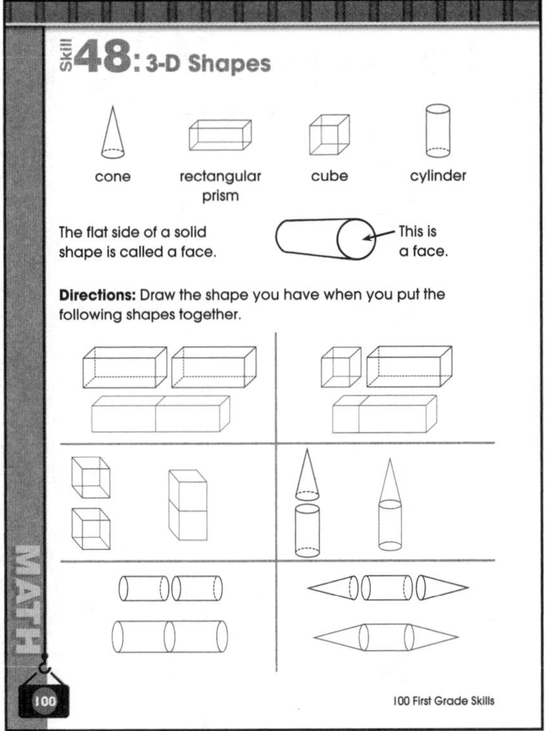

Skill **48: 3-D Shapes**

cone | rectangular prism | cube | cylinder

The flat side of a solid shape is called a face.

This is a face.

Directions: Draw the shape you have when you put the following shapes together.

100

100 First Grade Skills

Page 100

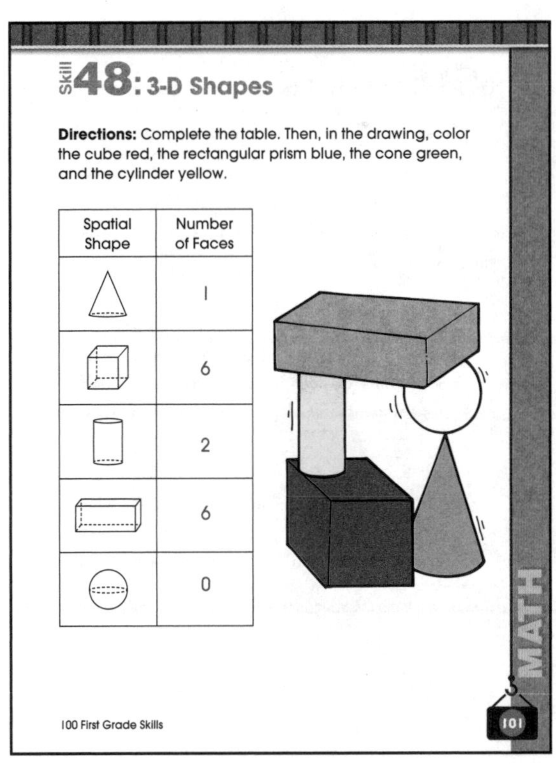

Skill **48: 3-D Shapes**

Directions: Complete the table. Then, in the drawing, color the cube red, the rectangular prism blue, the cone green, and the cylinder yellow.

Spatial Shape	Number of Faces
(cone)	1
(cube)	6
(cylinder)	2
(rectangular prism)	6
(sphere)	0

100 First Grade Skills

101

Page 101

Answer Key

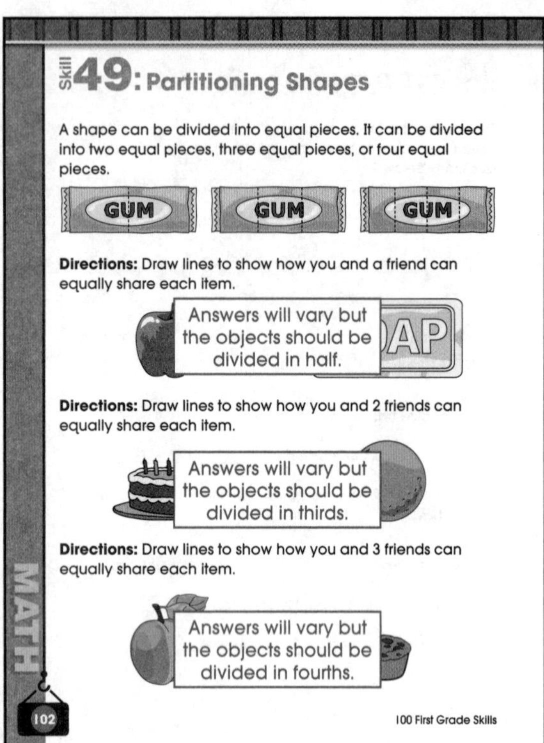

Skill **49: Partitioning Shapes**

A shape can be divided into equal pieces. It can be divided into two equal pieces, three equal pieces, or four equal pieces.

GUM GUM GUM

Directions: Draw lines to show how you and a friend can equally share each item.

Answers will vary but the objects should be divided in half.

Directions: Draw lines to show how you and 2 friends can equally share each item.

Answers will vary but the objects should be divided in thirds.

Directions: Draw lines to show how you and 3 friends can equally share each item.

Answers will vary but the objects should be divided in fourths.

MATH

102 100 First Grade Skills

Page 102

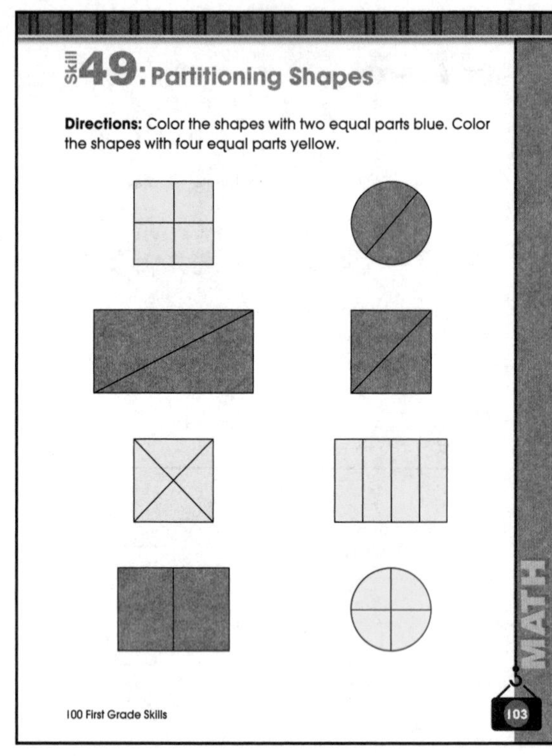

Skill **49: Partitioning Shapes**

Directions: Color the shapes with two equal parts blue. Color the shapes with four equal parts yellow.

MATH

100 First Grade Skills 103

Page 103

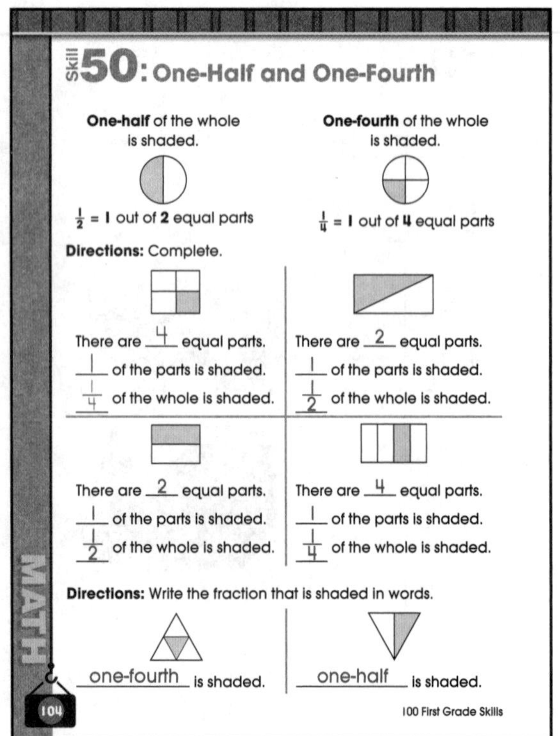

Skill **50: One-Half and One-Fourth**

One-half of the whole is shaded. $\frac{1}{2}$ = **1** out of **2** equal parts

One-fourth of the whole is shaded. $\frac{1}{4}$ = **1** out of **4** equal parts

Directions: Complete.

There are 4 equal parts. 1 of the parts is shaded. $\frac{1}{4}$ of the whole is shaded.

There are 2 equal parts. 1 of the parts is shaded. $\frac{1}{2}$ of the whole is shaded.

There are 2 equal parts. 1 of the parts is shaded. $\frac{1}{2}$ of the whole is shaded.

There are 4 equal parts. 1 of the parts is shaded. $\frac{1}{4}$ of the whole is shaded.

Directions: Write the fraction that is shaded in words.

one-fourth is shaded.

one-half is shaded.

MATH

104 100 First Grade Skills

Page 104

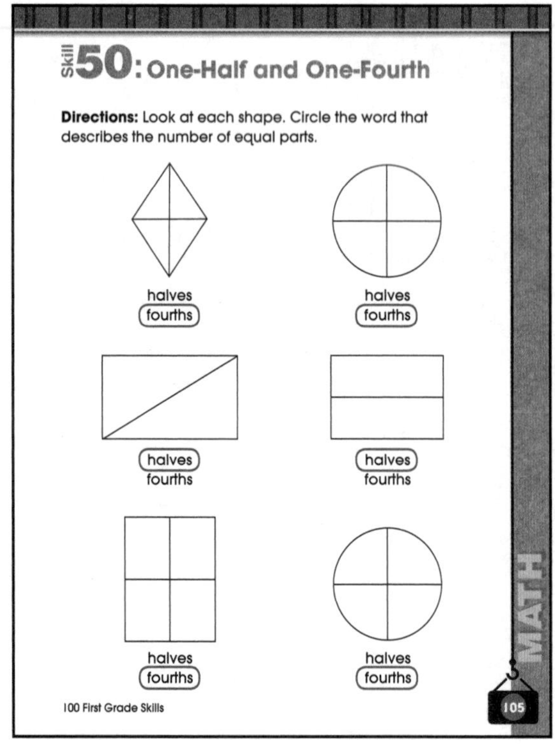

Skill **50: One-Half and One-Fourth**

Directions: Look at each shape. Circle the word that describes the number of equal parts.

halves (fourths) | halves (fourths)

(halves) fourths | (halves) fourths

halves (fourths) | halves (fourths)

MATH

100 First Grade Skills 105

Page 105

Answer Key

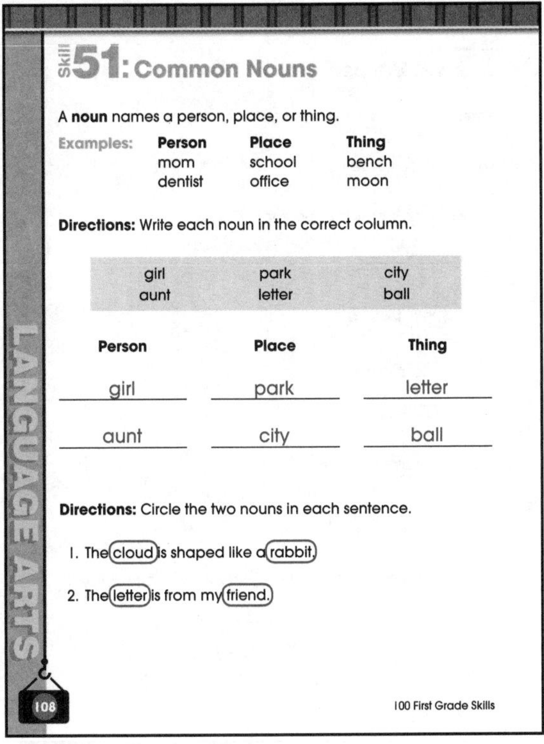

Skill 51: Common Nouns

A **noun** names a person, place, or thing.

Examples:

Person	Place	Thing
mom	school	bench
dentist	office	moon

Directions: Write each noun in the correct column.

girl, park, city, aunt, letter, ball

Person	Place	Thing
girl	park	letter
aunt	city	ball

Directions: Circle the two nouns in each sentence.

1. The (cloud) is shaped like a (rabbit).
2. The (letter) is from my (friend).

LANGUAGE ARTS

108 100 First Grade Skills

Page 108

Skill 51: Common Nouns

Directions: Write each noun in the correct column.

kite, boy, shell, beach, town, chief

Person	Place	Thing
boy	beach	kite
chief	town	shell

Directions: Circle the two nouns in each sentence.

1. She put the (glass) in the (kitchen).
2. The (kite) sailed with the (breeze).
3. My (aunt) owns a (store).
4. The (girl) read a (book).
5. My (sister) finished her (homework).

LANGUAGE ARTS

100 First Grade Skills 109

Page 109

Skill 52: Proper Nouns

A **proper noun** names a specific person, place, or thing. Proper nouns begin with a capital letter.

Directions: Use capital letters to write the name of each person or pet correctly.

1. cindy lewis — Cindy Lewis
2. ms. cohen — Ms. Cohen
3. dan li — Dan Li
4. ellen garza — Ellen Garza
5. fifi — Fifi
6. julie — Julie
7. spot — Spot
8. angelo — Angelo

LANGUAGE ARTS

110 100 First Grade Skills

Page 110

Skill 52: Proper Nouns

Directions: Use capital letters to write the name of each place correctly.

1. the corner store — The Corner Store
2. miller park — Miller Park
3. jameston airport — Jameston Airport
4. mexico — Mexico
5. first stop shop — First Stop Shop
6. los angeles, california — Los Angeles, California
7. woodland school — Woodland School
8. paris, france — Paris, France

LANGUAGE ARTS

100 First Grade Skills 111

Page 111

Answer Key

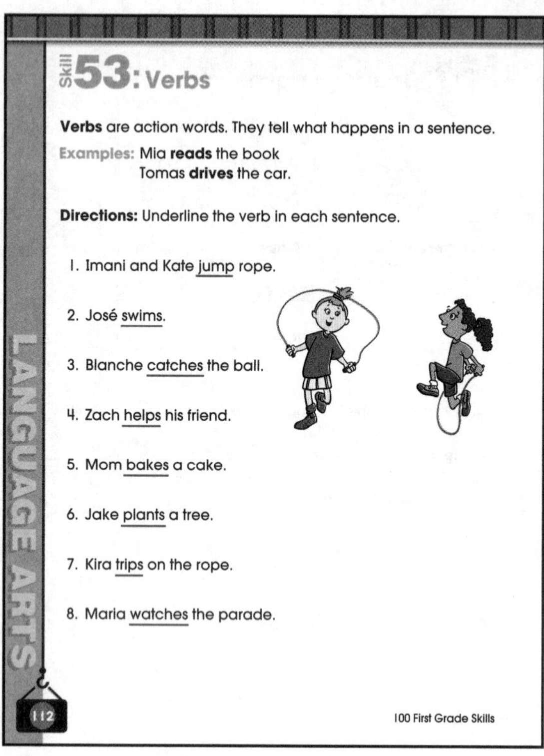

Skill **53: Verbs**

Verbs are action words. They tell what happens in a sentence.

Examples: Mia **reads** the book
Tomas **drives** the car.

Directions: Underline the verb in each sentence.

1. Imani and Kate jump rope.
2. José swims.
3. Blanche catches the ball.
4. Zach helps his friend.
5. Mom bakes a cake.
6. Jake plants a tree.
7. Kira trips on the rope.
8. Maria watches the parade.

LANGUAGE ARTS

112 100 First Grade Skills

Page 112

Skill **53: Verbs**

Directions: Circle the verb in each sentence.

1. My dog (runs) fast.
2. Erin (thinks) about the question.
3. He (goes) to class.
4. We (paint) pictures.
5. They (climb) to the top.
6. Jim (plays) his guitar.
7. Henry (builds) snowmen.
8. Hailey and I (go) to camp.

Directions: Write a sentence about your class using a verb.

Answers will vary.

100 First Grade Skills 113

LANGUAGE ARTS

Page 113

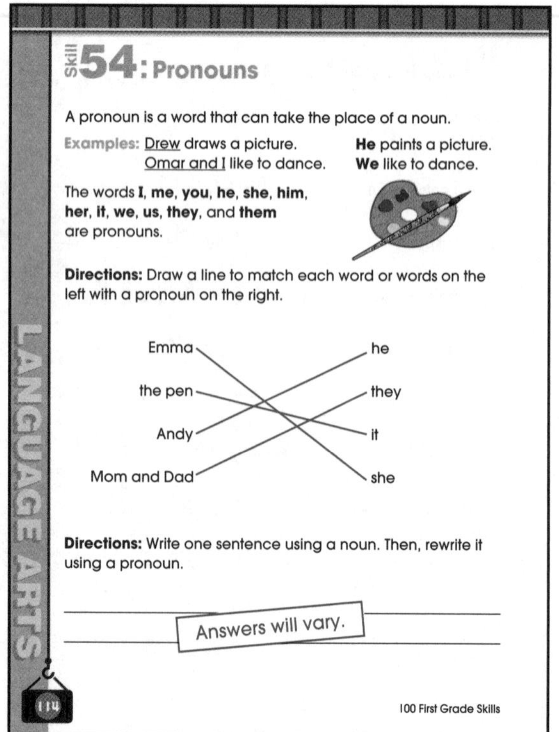

Skill **54: Pronouns**

A pronoun is a word that can take the place of a noun.

Examples: Drew draws a picture. **He** paints a picture.
Omar and I like to dance. **We** like to dance.

The words **I**, **me**, **you**, **he**, **she**, **him**, **her**, **it**, **we**, **us**, **they**, and **them** are pronouns.

Directions: Draw a line to match each word or words on the left with a pronoun on the right.

Emma — she
the pen — it
Andy — he
Mom and Dad — they

Directions: Write one sentence using a noun. Then, rewrite it using a pronoun.

Answers will vary.

LANGUAGE ARTS

114 100 First Grade Skills

Page 114

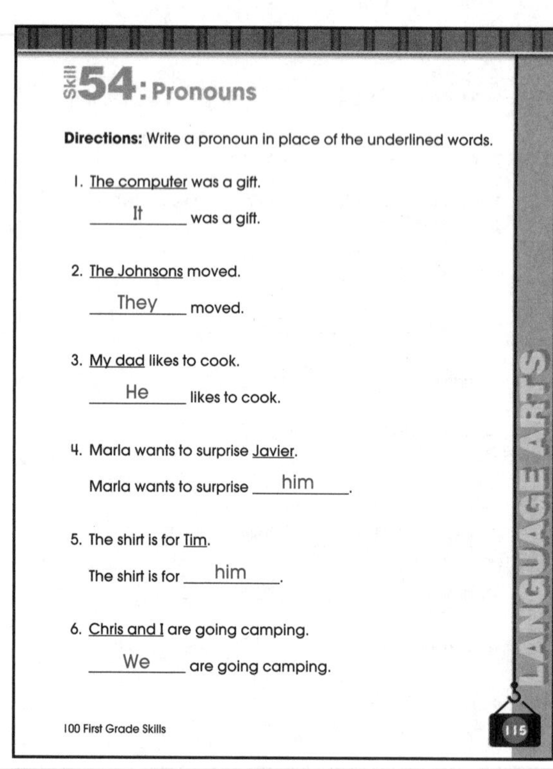

Skill **54: Pronouns**

Directions: Write a pronoun in place of the underlined words.

1. The computer was a gift.
   It was a gift.
2. The Johnsons moved.
   They moved.
3. My dad likes to cook.
   He likes to cook.
4. Marla wants to surprise Javier.
   Marla wants to surprise him.
5. The shirt is for Tim.
   The shirt is for him.
6. Chris and I are going camping.
   We are going camping.

100 First Grade Skills 115

LANGUAGE ARTS

Page 115

Answer Key

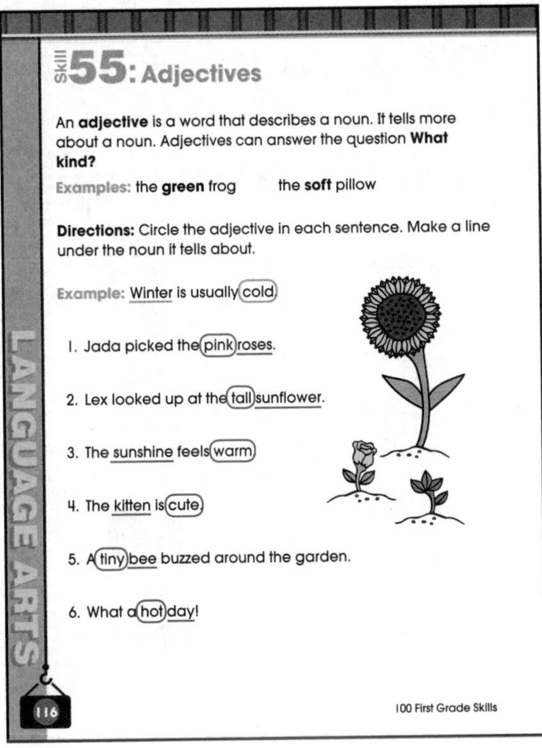

Skill 55: Adjectives

An **adjective** is a word that describes a noun. It tells more about a noun. Adjectives can answer the question **What kind?**

Examples: the **green** frog the **soft** pillow

Directions: Circle the adjective in each sentence. Make a line under the noun it tells about.

Example: Winter is usually (cold).

1. Jada picked the (pink) roses.
2. Lex looked up at the (tall) sunflower.
3. The sunshine feels (warm).
4. The kitten is (cute).
5. A (tiny) bee buzzed around the garden.
6. What a (hot) day!

LANGUAGE ARTS

116 100 First Grade Skills

Page 116

Skill 55: Adjectives

Directions: Write the best adjective to complete each group of words.

famous	shiny	cool
smooth	narrow	golden

1. the golden sun
2. a smooth rock
3. a shiny penny
4. the cool breeze
5. a narrow path
6. a famous person

Directions: Circle the adjective that describes the weather today.

1. Today, the weather is (warm/cool).
2. The sky is (blue/gray).
3. It is (wet/dry).
4. It is a (beautiful/cloudy) day!

Answers will vary.

LANGUAGE ARTS

100 First Grade Skills 117

Page 117

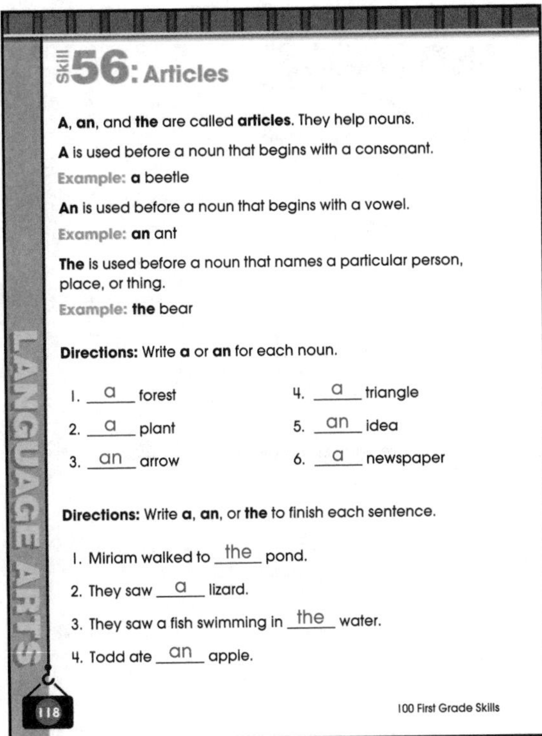

Skill 56: Articles

A, **an**, and **the** are called **articles**. They help nouns.

A is used before a noun that begins with a consonant.

Example: **a** beetle

An is used before a noun that begins with a vowel.

Example: **an** ant

The is used before a noun that names a particular person, place, or thing.

Example: **the** bear

Directions: Write **a** or **an** for each noun.

1. a forest
2. a plant
3. an arrow
4. a triangle
5. an idea
6. a newspaper

Directions: Write **a**, **an**, or **the** to finish each sentence.

1. Miriam walked to the pond.
2. They saw a lizard.
3. They saw a fish swimming in the water.
4. Todd ate an apple.

LANGUAGE ARTS

118 100 First Grade Skills

Page 118

Skill 56: Articles

Directions: Write **a** or **an** for each noun.

1. an owl
2. a dish
3. a brother
4. an oven
5. a sale
6. an actor

Directions: Write a sentence with **a**.

Answers will vary.

Directions: Write a sentence with **an**.

Answers will vary.

Directions: Write a sentence with **the**.

Answers will vary.

LANGUAGE ARTS

100 First Grade Skills 119

Page 119

Answer Key

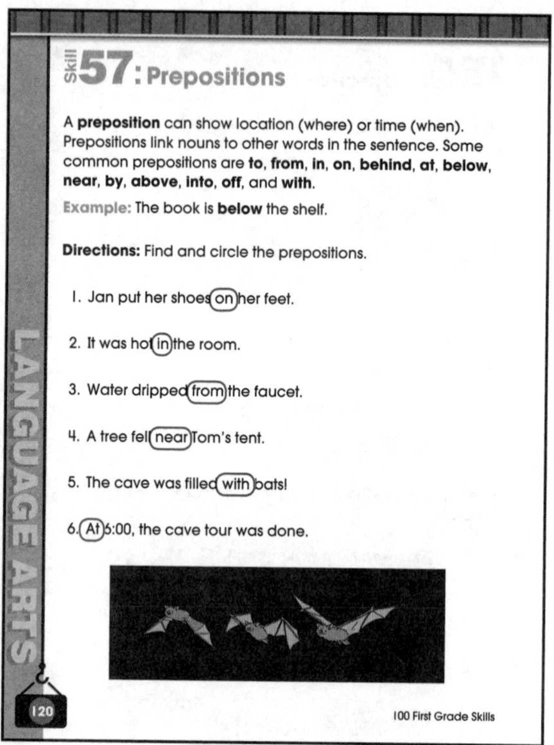

Skill 57: Prepositions

A **preposition** can show location (where) or time (when). Prepositions link nouns to other words in the sentence. Some common prepositions are **to**, **from**, **in**, **on**, **behind**, **at**, **below**, **near**, **by**, **above**, **into**, **off**, and **with**.

Example: The book is **below** the shelf.

Directions: Find and circle the prepositions.

1. Jan put her shoes (on) her feet.
2. It was hot (in) the room.
3. Water dripped (from) the faucet.
4. A tree fell (near) Tom's tent.
5. The cave was filled (with) bats!
6. (At) 6:00, the cave tour was done.

LANGUAGE ARTS

120 100 First Grade Skills

Page 120

Skill 57: Prepositions

Directions: Use the words in the box to complete each item below.

beside	above	in	behind	under

1. Where is the girl?
   under the covers
2. Where is the bear?
   beside the boy
3. Where is the fox?
   in a box
4. Where is the dog house?
   behind the dog
5. Where is the cat?
   above the dog

LANGUAGE ARTS

100 First Grade Skills 121

Page 121

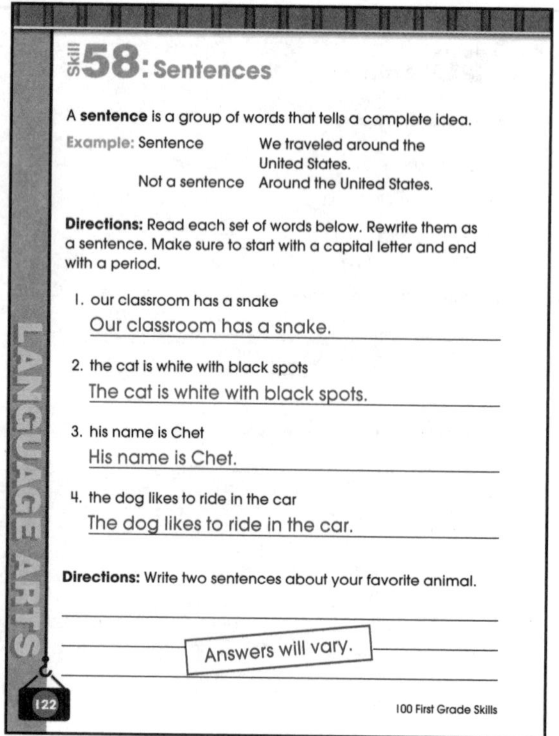

Skill 58: Sentences

A **sentence** is a group of words that tells a complete idea.

Example: Sentence — We traveled around the United States.
Not a sentence — Around the United States.

Directions: Read each set of words below. Rewrite them as a sentence. Make sure to start with a capital letter and end with a period.

1. our classroom has a snake
   Our classroom has a snake.
2. the cat is white with black spots
   The cat is white with black spots.
3. his name is Chet
   His name is Chet.
4. the dog likes to ride in the car
   The dog likes to ride in the car.

Directions: Write two sentences about your favorite animal.

Answers will vary.

LANGUAGE ARTS

122 100 First Grade Skills

Page 122

Skill 58: Sentences

Directions: Write **S** if the words below make a sentence. Write **NS** if they do not make a sentence.

1. S We went to Texas.
2. S Colorado is a beautiful state.
3. NS Tall mountains and cool air.
4. S I would like to live there.
5. S We also saw California.
6. NS The beautiful ocean.

Directions: Write words of your own to complete each sentence.

1. This summer, ______
2. One day, ______

Answers will vary.

LANGUAGE ARTS

100 First Grade Skills 123

Page 123

Answer Key

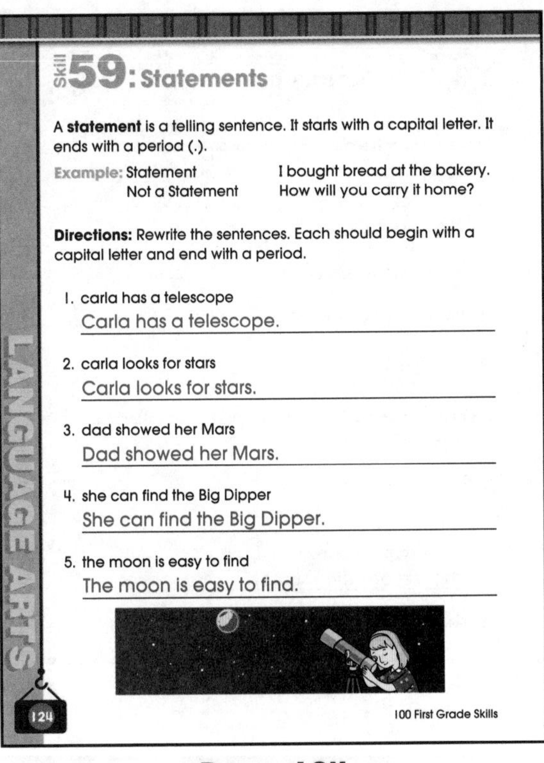

Skill 59: Statements

A **statement** is a telling sentence. It starts with a capital letter. It ends with a period (.).

Example: Statement — I bought bread at the bakery.
Not a Statement — How will you carry it home?

Directions: Rewrite the sentences. Each should begin with a capital letter and end with a period.

1. carla has a telescope
   Carla has a telescope.
2. carla looks for stars
   Carla looks for stars.
3. dad showed her Mars
   Dad showed her Mars.
4. she can find the Big Dipper
   She can find the Big Dipper.
5. the moon is easy to find
   The moon is easy to find.

LANGUAGE ARTS

124 — 100 First Grade Skills

Page 124

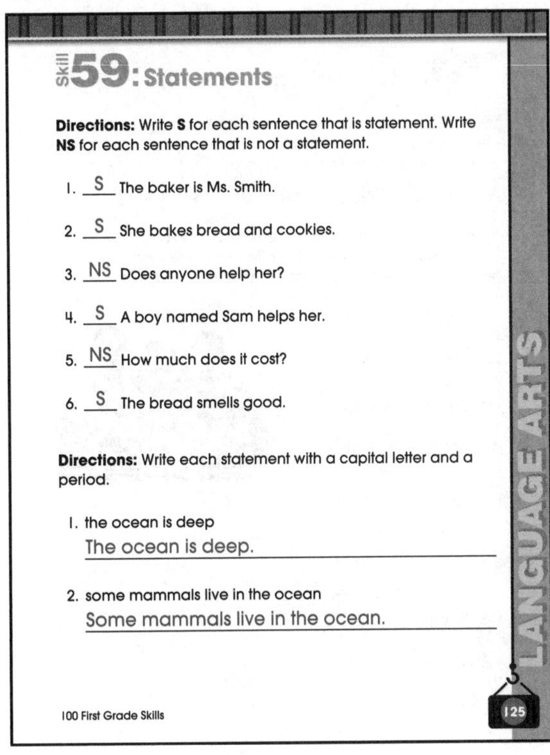

Skill 59: Statements

Directions: Write **S** for each sentence that is statement. Write **NS** for each sentence that is not a statement.

1. S The baker is Ms. Smith.
2. S She bakes bread and cookies.
3. NS Does anyone help her?
4. S A boy named Sam helps her.
5. NS How much does it cost?
6. S The bread smells good.

Directions: Write each statement with a capital letter and a period.

1. the ocean is deep
   The ocean is deep.
2. some mammals live in the ocean
   Some mammals live in the ocean.

LANGUAGE ARTS

100 First Grade Skills — 125

Page 125

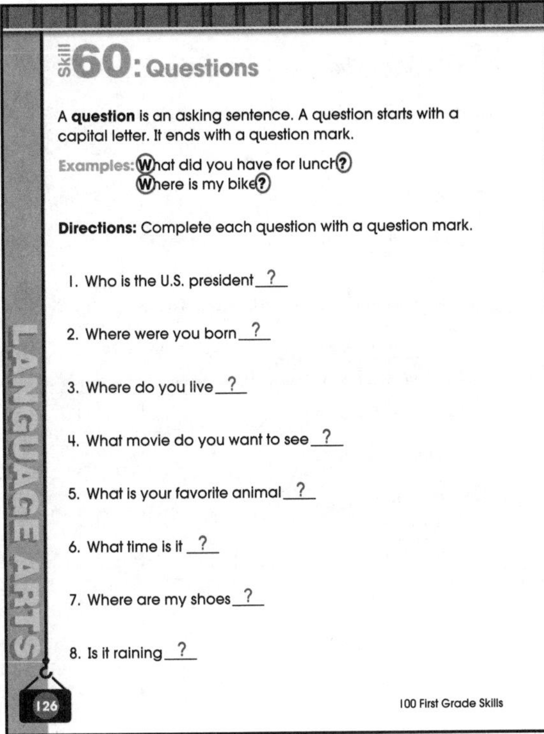

Skill 60: Questions

A **question** is an asking sentence. A question starts with a capital letter. It ends with a question mark.

Examples: What did you have for lunch?
Where is my bike?

Directions: Complete each question with a question mark.

1. Who is the U.S. president ?
2. Where were you born ?
3. Where do you live ?
4. What movie do you want to see ?
5. What is your favorite animal ?
6. What time is it ?
7. Where are my shoes ?
8. Is it raining ?

LANGUAGE ARTS

126 — 100 First Grade Skills

Page 126

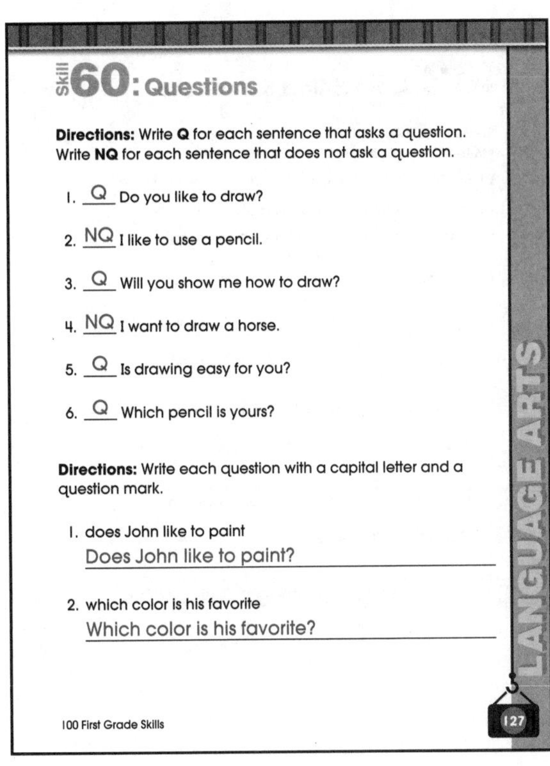

Skill 60: Questions

Directions: Write **Q** for each sentence that asks a question. Write **NQ** for each sentence that does not ask a question.

1. Q Do you like to draw?
2. NQ I like to use a pencil.
3. Q Will you show me how to draw?
4. NQ I want to draw a horse.
5. Q Is drawing easy for you?
6. Q Which pencil is yours?

Directions: Write each question with a capital letter and a question mark.

1. does John like to paint
   Does John like to paint?
2. which color is his favorite
   Which color is his favorite?

LANGUAGE ARTS

100 First Grade Skills — 127

Page 127

Answer Key

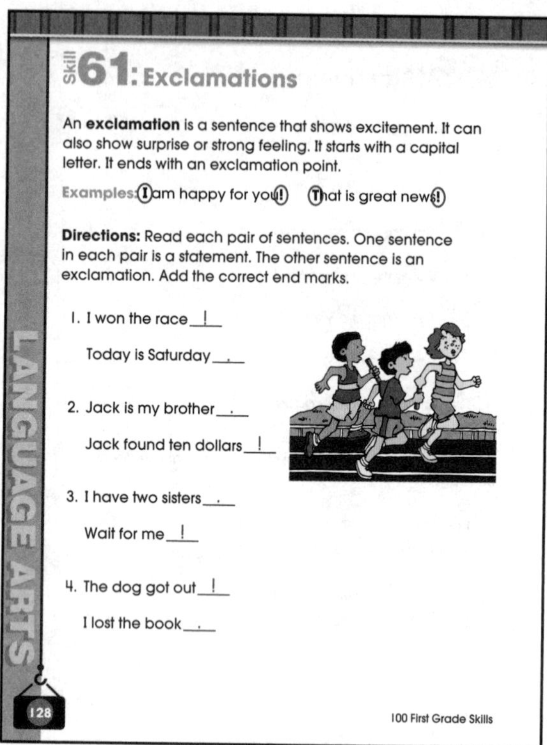

Skill 61: Exclamations

An **exclamation** is a sentence that shows excitement. It can also show surprise or strong feeling. It starts with a capital letter. It ends with an exclamation point.

Examples: I am happy for you! That is great news!

Directions: Read each pair of sentences. One sentence in each pair is a statement. The other sentence is an exclamation. Add the correct end marks.

1. I won the race !
   Today is Saturday .
2. Jack is my brother .
   Jack found ten dollars !
3. I have two sisters .
   Wait for me !
4. The dog got out !
   I lost the book .

LANGUAGE ARTS

128 100 First Grade Skills

Page 128

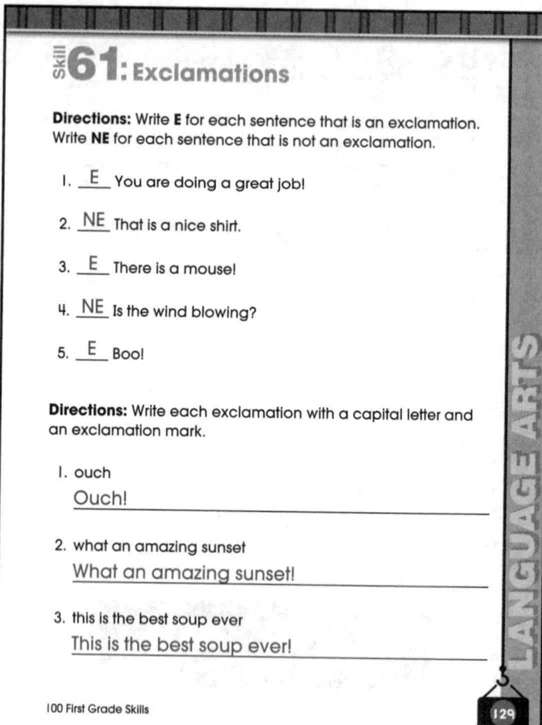

Skill 61: Exclamations

Directions: Write **E** for each sentence that is an exclamation. Write **NE** for each sentence that is not an exclamation.

1. E You are doing a great job!
2. NE That is a nice shirt.
3. E There is a mouse!
4. NE Is the wind blowing?
5. E Boo!

Directions: Write each exclamation with a capital letter and an exclamation mark.

1. ouch
   Ouch!
2. what an amazing sunset
   What an amazing sunset!
3. this is the best soup ever
   This is the best soup ever!

LANGUAGE ARTS

100 First Grade Skills 129

Page 129

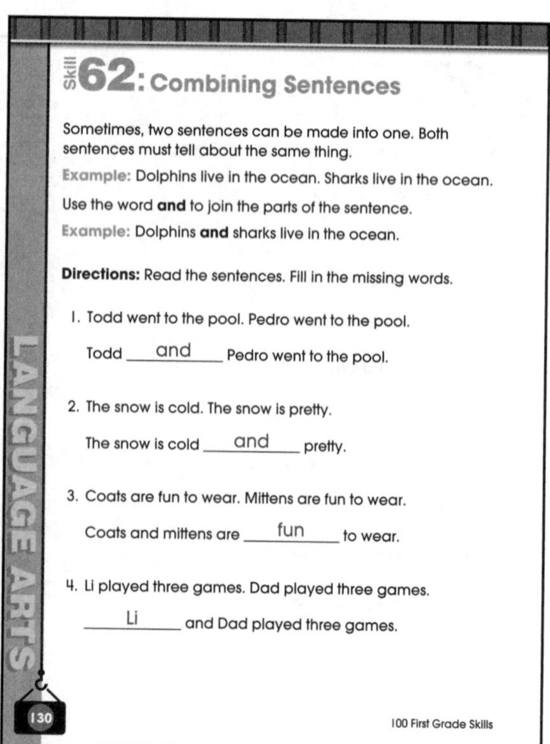

Skill 62: Combining Sentences

Sometimes, two sentences can be made into one. Both sentences must tell about the same thing.

Example: Dolphins live in the ocean. Sharks live in the ocean.

Use the word **and** to join the parts of the sentence.

Example: Dolphins **and** sharks live in the ocean.

Directions: Read the sentences. Fill in the missing words.

1. Todd went to the pool. Pedro went to the pool.
   Todd and Pedro went to the pool.
2. The snow is cold. The snow is pretty.
   The snow is cold and pretty.
3. Coats are fun to wear. Mittens are fun to wear.
   Coats and mittens are fun to wear.
4. Li played three games. Dad played three games.
   Li and Dad played three games.

LANGUAGE ARTS

130 100 First Grade Skills

Page 130

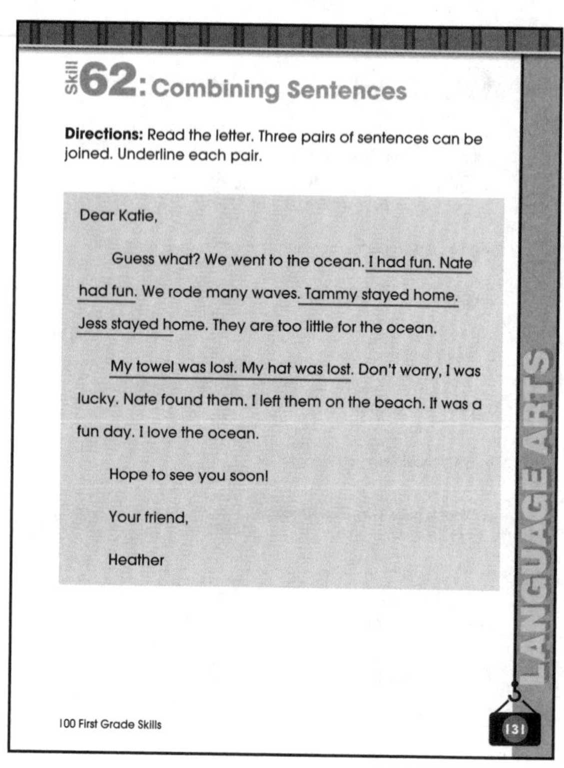

Skill 62: Combining Sentences

Directions: Read the letter. Three pairs of sentences can be joined. Underline each pair.

Dear Katie,

Guess what? We went to the ocean. I had fun. Nate had fun. We rode many waves. Tammy stayed home. Jess stayed home. They are too little for the ocean.

My towel was lost. My hat was lost. Don't worry, I was lucky. Nate found them. I left them on the beach. It was a fun day. I love the ocean.

Hope to see you soon!

Your friend,

Heather

LANGUAGE ARTS

100 First Grade Skills 131

Page 131

Answer Key

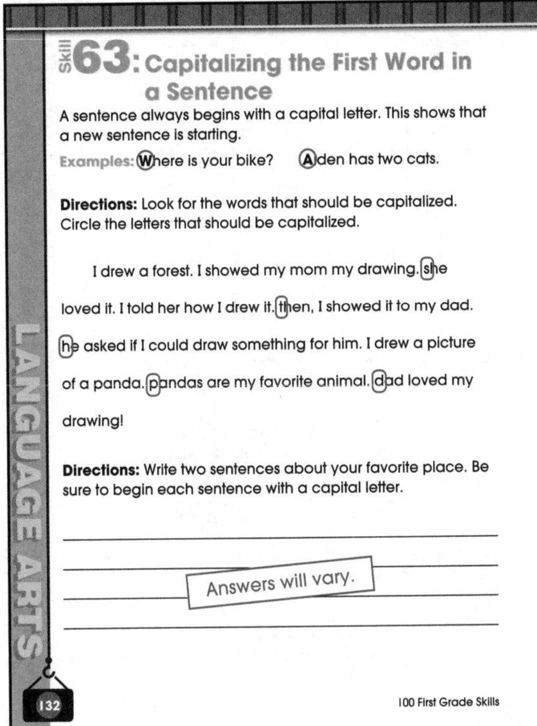

Skill 63: Capitalizing the First Word in a Sentence

A sentence always begins with a capital letter. This shows that a new sentence is starting.

Examples: (W)here is your bike? (A)den has two cats.

Directions: Look for the words that should be capitalized. Circle the letters that should be capitalized.

I drew a forest. I showed my mom my drawing. (s)he loved it. I told her how I drew it. (t)hen, I showed it to my dad. (h)e asked if I could draw something for him. I drew a picture of a panda. (p)andas are my favorite animal. (d)ad loved my drawing!

Directions: Write two sentences about your favorite place. Be sure to begin each sentence with a capital letter.

Answers will vary.

LANGUAGE ARTS

132 100 First Grade Skills

Page 132

Skill 63: Capitalizing the First Word in a Sentence

Directions: Rewrite each sentence. Be sure to begin each sentence with a capital letter.

1. it is time to wake up.
   It is time to wake up.
2. put on your clothes.
   Put on your clothes.
3. breakfast is ready.
   Breakfast is ready.
4. can you be ready in five minutes?
   Can you be ready in five minutes?
5. remember your homework.
   Remember your homework.
6. the bus leaves soon.
   The bus leaves soon.

LANGUAGE ARTS

100 First Grade Skills 133

Page 133

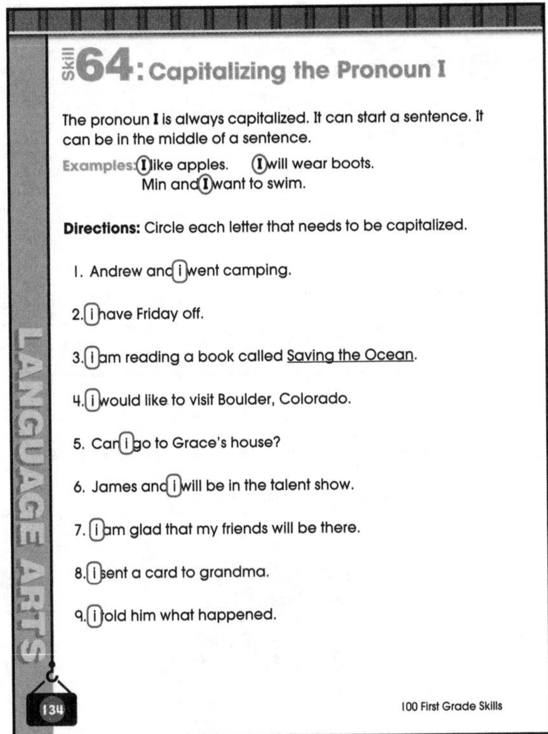

Skill 64: Capitalizing the Pronoun I

The pronoun **I** is always capitalized. It can start a sentence. It can be in the middle of a sentence.

Examples: (I) like apples. (I) will wear boots. Min and (I) want to swim.

Directions: Circle each letter that needs to be capitalized.

1. Andrew and (i) went camping.
2. (i) have Friday off.
3. (i) am reading a book called Saving the Ocean.
4. (i) would like to visit Boulder, Colorado.
5. Can (i) go to Grace's house?
6. James and (i) will be in the talent show.
7. (i) am glad that my friends will be there.
8. (i) sent a card to grandma.
9. (i) told him what happened.

LANGUAGE ARTS

134 100 First Grade Skills

Page 134

Skill 64: Capitalizing the Pronoun I

Directions: Read each sentence below. Write the word **I** in the box. Fill in the other blank with a word that completes the sentence.

1. [I] like the color Answers will vary.
2. Answers will vary and [I] play soccer.
3. [I] like to draw Answers will vary.
4. [I] have a new Answers will vary.
5. My Answers will vary and [I] like to watch movies together.
6. Each weekend, [I] go Answers will vary.

LANGUAGE ARTS

100 First Grade Skills 135

Page 135

Answer Key

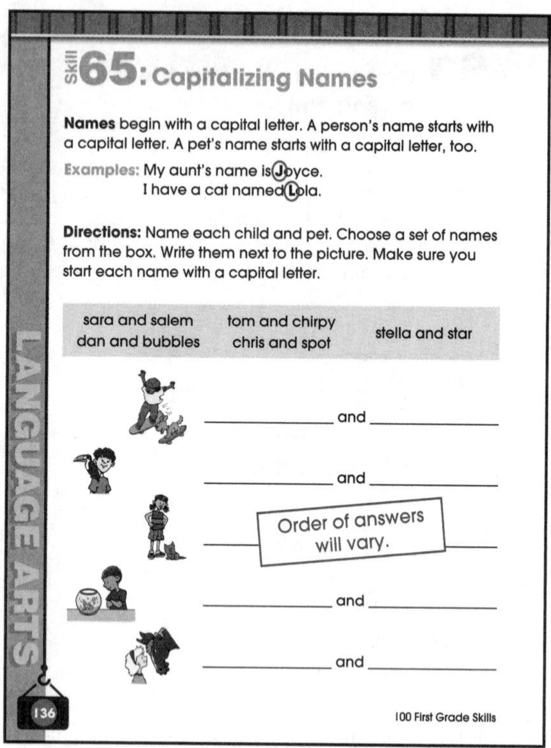

Skill 65: Capitalizing Names

Names begin with a capital letter. A person's name starts with a capital letter. A pet's name starts with a capital letter, too.

Examples: My aunt's name is Joyce.
I have a cat named Lola.

Directions: Name each child and pet. Choose a set of names from the box. Write them next to the picture. Make sure you start each name with a capital letter.

sara and salem dan and bubbles	tom and chirpy chris and spot	stella and star

_____ and _____

_____ and _____

Order of answers will vary.

_____ and _____

_____ and _____

LANGUAGE ARTS

136 100 First Grade Skills

Page 136

Skill 65: Capitalizing Names

Directions: The names below do not start with a capital letter. Find each letter that should be a capital letter. Make three lines below it (≡). Then, write the capital letter above it.

1. luke, jason, and leo are all sam's brothers. (L J L S)
2. paco named the puppies bella and sassy. (P B S)
3. jack saw his friend anita at the store. (J A)
4. tanya got to feed penny and samson at the farm. (T P S)

Directions: Write a sentence about two of your friends. Use their names in the sentence.

Answers will vary.

100 First Grade Skills 137

LANGUAGE ARTS

Page 137

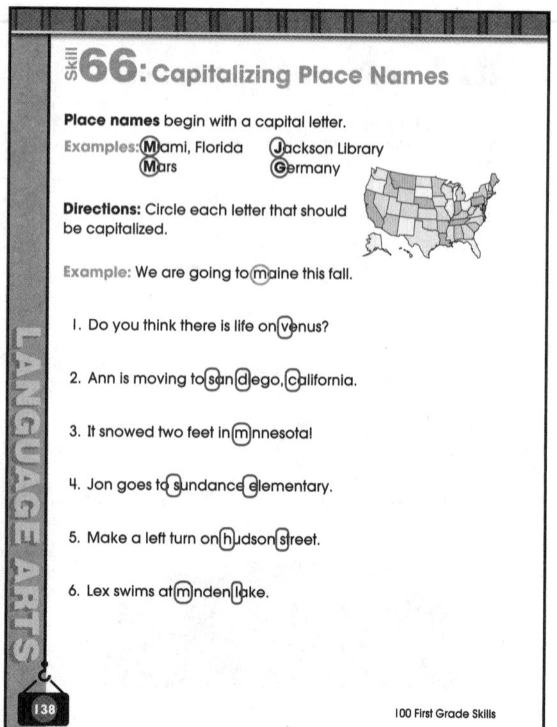

Skill 66: Capitalizing Place Names

Place names begin with a capital letter.

Examples: Miami, Florida Jackson Library
Mars Germany

Directions: Circle each letter that should be capitalized.

Example: We are going to maine this fall.

1. Do you think there is life on venus?
2. Ann is moving to san diego, california.
3. It snowed two feet in minnesota!
4. Jon goes to sundance elementary.
5. Make a left turn on hudson street.
6. Lex swims at minden lake.

LANGUAGE ARTS

138 100 First Grade Skills

Page 138

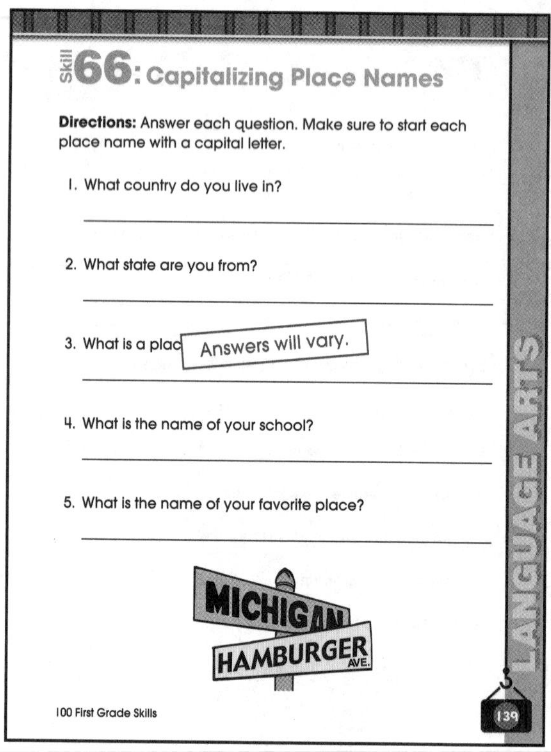

Skill 66: Capitalizing Place Names

Directions: Answer each question. Make sure to start each place name with a capital letter.

1. What country do you live in?
2. What state are you from?
3. What is a plac Answers will vary.
4. What is the name of your school?
5. What is the name of your favorite place?

100 First Grade Skills 139

LANGUAGE ARTS

Page 139

Answer Key

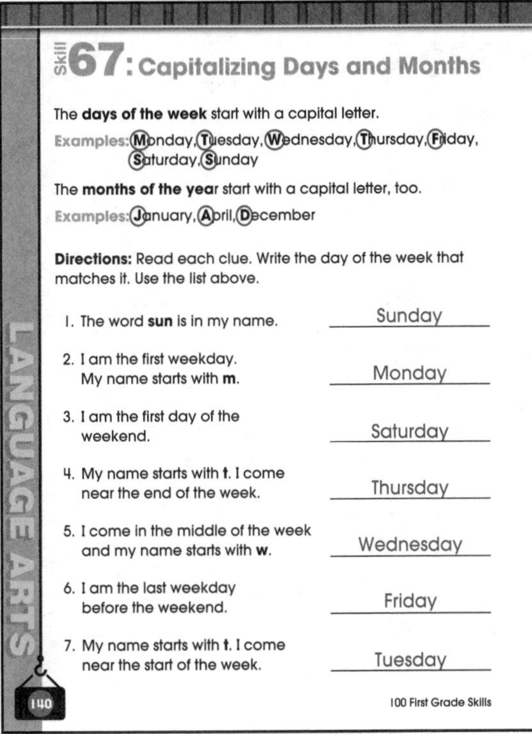

Skill 67: Capitalizing Days and Months

The **days of the week** start with a capital letter.

Examples: Monday, Tuesday, Wednesday, Thursday, Friday, Saturday, Sunday

The **months of the year** start with a capital letter, too.

Examples: January, April, December

Directions: Read each clue. Write the day of the week that matches it. Use the list above.

1. The word **sun** is in my name. Sunday
2. I am the first weekday. My name starts with **m**. Monday
3. I am the first day of the weekend. Saturday
4. My name starts with **t**. I come near the end of the week. Thursday
5. I come in the middle of the week and my name starts with **w**. Wednesday
6. I am the last weekday before the weekend. Friday
7. My name starts with **t**. I come near the start of the week. Tuesday

LANGUAGE ARTS

140 100 First Grade Skills

Page 140

Skill 67: Capitalizing Days and Months

Directions: Fill in the month in each sentence. Make sure to use a capital letter.

1. (january) Nancy's birthday is in January.
2. (august) Pedro likes to swim in August.
3. (december) Jake builds a snowman in December.
4. (march) Mina met Rachel in March.
5. (october) October is my favorite month.
6. (september) School starts in September.

When is your birthday? ________

In what month is your favorite holiday? ________

Answers will vary.

LANGUAGE ARTS

100 First Grade Skills 141

Page 141

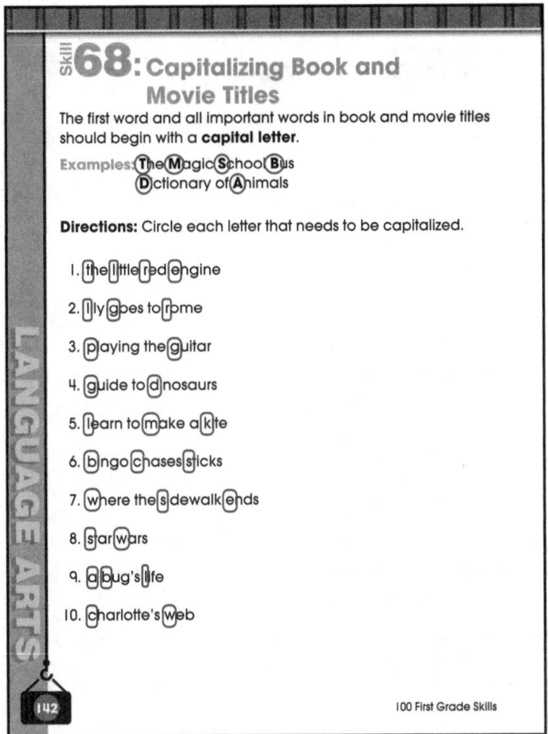

Skill 68: Capitalizing Book and Movie Titles

The first word and all important words in book and movie titles should begin with a **capital letter**.

Examples: The Magic School Bus
Dictionary of Animals

Directions: Circle each letter that needs to be capitalized.

1. the little red engine
2. lily goes to rome
3. playing the guitar
4. guide to dinosaurs
5. learn to make a kite
6. bingo chases sticks
7. where the sidewalk ends
8. star wars
9. a bug's life
10. charlotte's web

LANGUAGE ARTS

142 100 First Grade Skills

Page 142

Skill 68: Capitalizing Book and Movie Titles

Directions: Circle each letter that needs to be capitalized.

1. toy story
2. green eggs and ham
3. frozen
4. ivy and bean

Directions: Answer each question with a book or movie title.

1. What is your favorite book?
2. What is your favorite movie?
3. What book are you reading now?
4. What was the last movie you saw?

Answers will vary.

LANGUAGE ARTS

100 First Grade Skills 143

Page 143

Answer Key

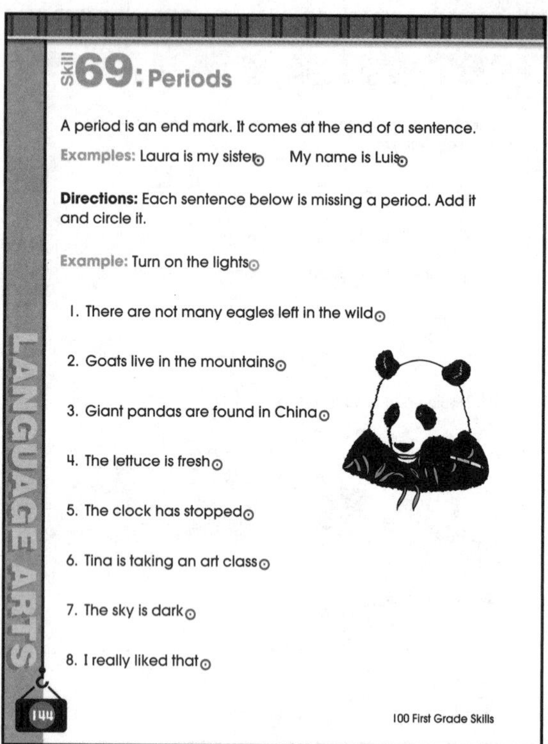
Skill 69: Periods

A period is an end mark. It comes at the end of a sentence.

Examples: Laura is my sister. My name is Luis.

Directions: Each sentence below is missing a period. Add it and circle it.

Example: Turn on the lights.

1. There are not many eagles left in the wild.
2. Goats live in the mountains.
3. Giant pandas are found in China.
4. The lettuce is fresh.
5. The clock has stopped.
6. Tina is taking an art class.
7. The sky is dark.
8. I really liked that.

LANGUAGE ARTS

144

100 First Grade Skills

Page 144

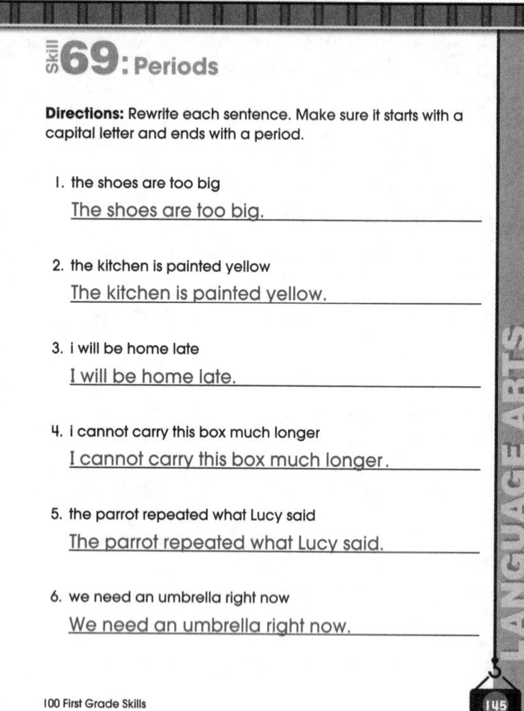
Skill 69: Periods

Directions: Rewrite each sentence. Make sure it starts with a capital letter and ends with a period.

1. the shoes are too big
   The shoes are too big.
2. the kitchen is painted yellow
   The kitchen is painted yellow.
3. i will be home late
   I will be home late.
4. i cannot carry this box much longer
   I cannot carry this box much longer.
5. the parrot repeated what Lucy said
   The parrot repeated what Lucy said.
6. we need an umbrella right now
   We need an umbrella right now.

LANGUAGE ARTS

100 First Grade Skills

145

Page 145

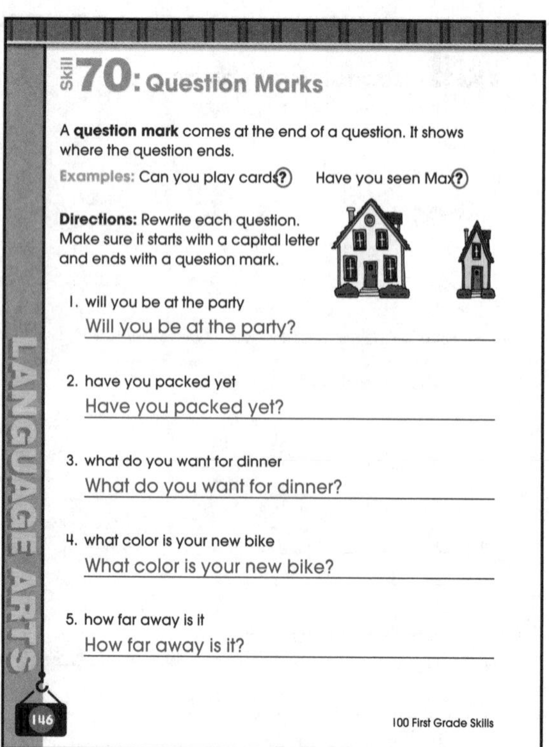
Skill 70: Question Marks

A question mark comes at the end of a question. It shows where the question ends.

Examples: Can you play cards? Have you seen Max?

Directions: Rewrite each question. Make sure it starts with a capital letter and ends with a question mark.

1. will you be at the party
   Will you be at the party?
2. have you packed yet
   Have you packed yet?
3. what do you want for dinner
   What do you want for dinner?
4. what color is your new bike
   What color is your new bike?
5. how far away is it
   How far away is it?

LANGUAGE ARTS

146

100 First Grade Skills

Page 146

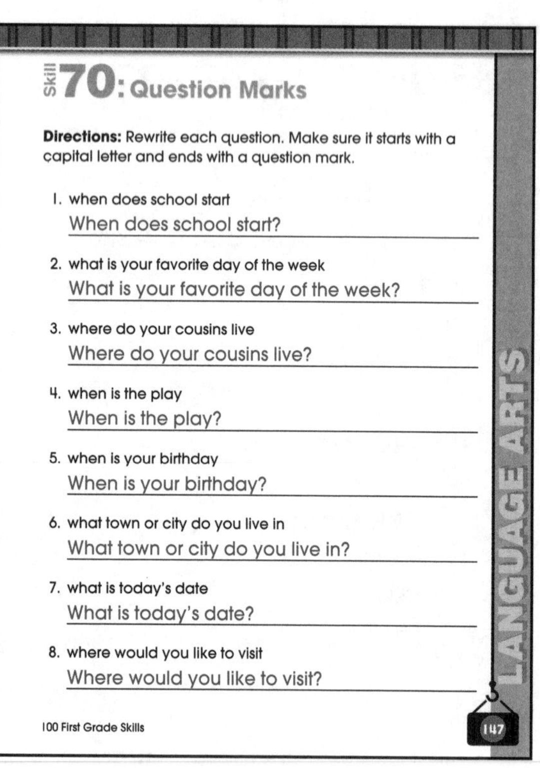
Skill 70: Question Marks

Directions: Rewrite each question. Make sure it starts with a capital letter and ends with a question mark.

1. when does school start
   When does school start?
2. what is your favorite day of the week
   What is your favorite day of the week?
3. where do your cousins live
   Where do your cousins live?
4. when is the play
   When is the play?
5. when is your birthday
   When is your birthday?
6. what town or city do you live in
   What town or city do you live in?
7. what is today's date
   What is today's date?
8. where would you like to visit
   Where would you like to visit?

LANGUAGE ARTS

100 First Grade Skills

147

Page 147

Answer Key

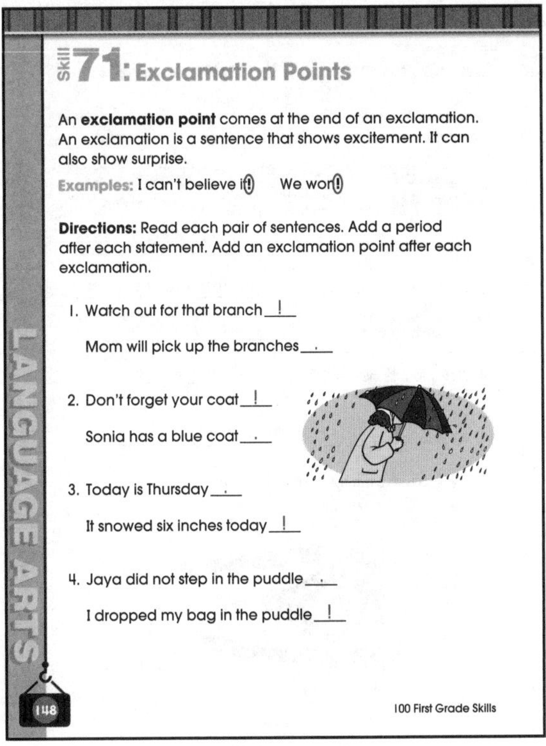

Skill **71: Exclamation Points**

An **exclamation point** comes at the end of an exclamation. An exclamation is a sentence that shows excitement. It can also show surprise.

Examples: I can't believe it! We won!

Directions: Read each pair of sentences. Add a period after each statement. Add an exclamation point after each exclamation.

1. Watch out for that branch __!__

   Mom will pick up the branches __.__

2. Don't forget your coat __!__

   Sonia has a blue coat __.__

3. Today is Thursday __.__

   It snowed six inches today __!__

4. Jaya did not step in the puddle __.__

   I dropped my bag in the puddle __!__

LANGUAGE ARTS

148 100 First Grade Skills

Page 148

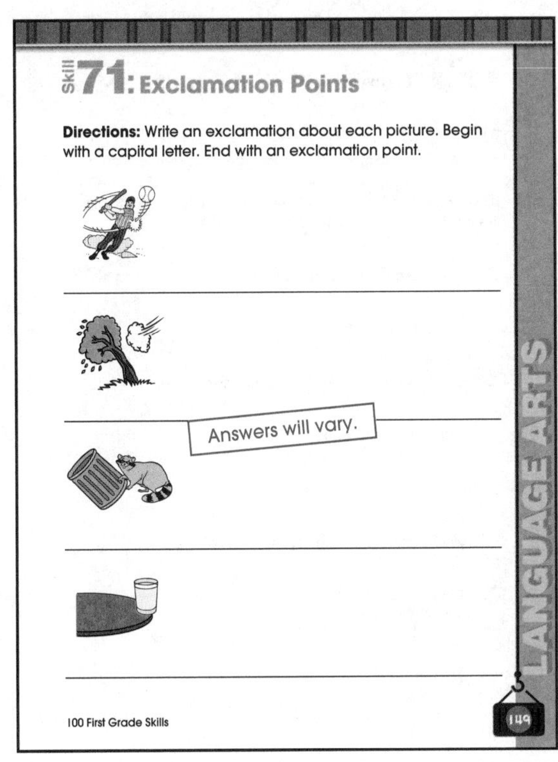

Skill **71: Exclamation Points**

Directions: Write an exclamation about each picture. Begin with a capital letter. End with an exclamation point.

Answers will vary.

LANGUAGE ARTS

100 First Grade Skills 149

Page 149

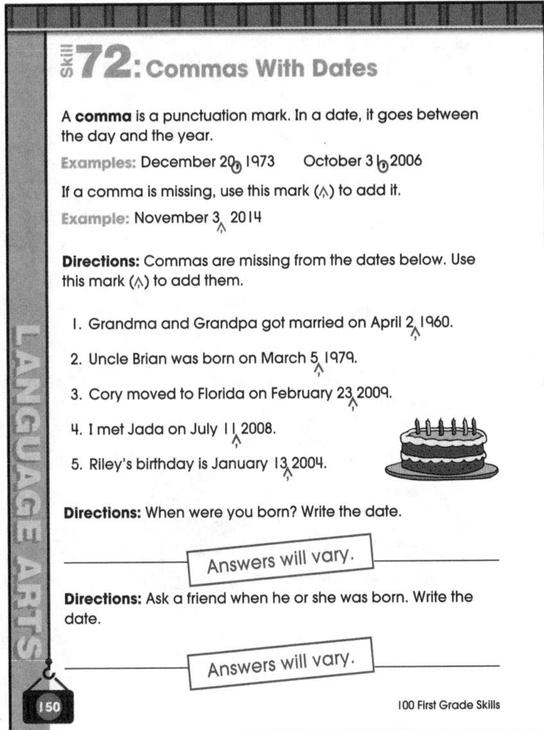

Skill **72: Commas With Dates**

A **comma** is a punctuation mark. In a date, it goes between the day and the year.

Examples: December 20, 1973 October 31, 2006

If a comma is missing, use this mark (^) to add it.

Example: November 3, 2014

Directions: Commas are missing from the dates below. Use this mark (^) to add them.

1. Grandma and Grandpa got married on April 2, 1960.
2. Uncle Brian was born on March 5, 1979.
3. Cory moved to Florida on February 23, 2009.
4. I met Jada on July 11, 2008.
5. Riley's birthday is January 13, 2004.

Directions: When were you born? Write the date.

Answers will vary.

Directions: Ask a friend when he or she was born. Write the date.

Answers will vary.

LANGUAGE ARTS

150 100 First Grade Skills

Page 150

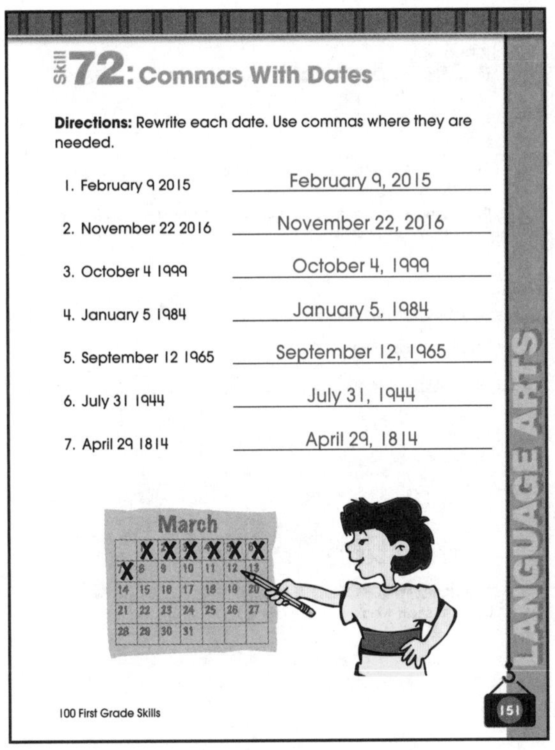

Skill **72: Commas With Dates**

Directions: Rewrite each date. Use commas where they are needed.

1. February 9 2015 — February 9, 2015
2. November 22 2016 — November 22, 2016
3. October 4 1999 — October 4, 1999
4. January 5 1984 — January 5, 1984
5. September 12 1965 — September 12, 1965
6. July 31 1944 — July 31, 1944
7. April 29 1814 — April 29, 1814

LANGUAGE ARTS

100 First Grade Skills 151

Page 151

Answer Key

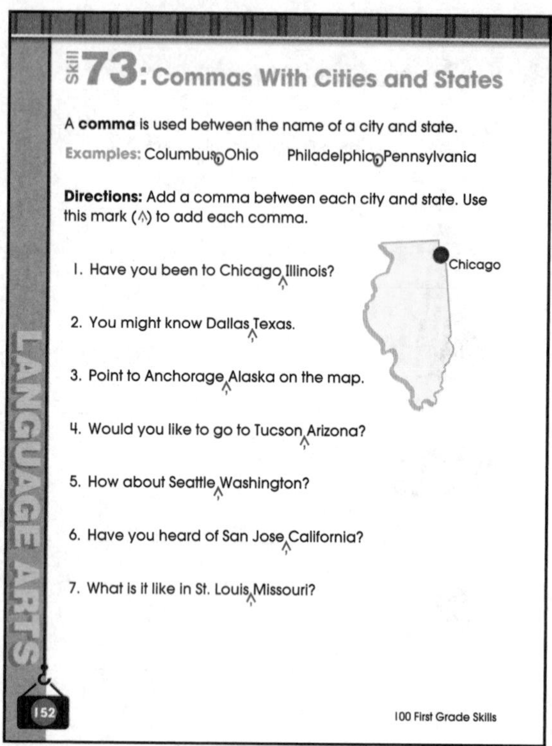

Skill 73: Commas With Cities and States

A **comma** is used between the name of a city and state.

Examples: Columbus, Ohio Philadelphia, Pennsylvania

Directions: Add a comma between each city and state. Use this mark (^) to add each comma.

1. Have you been to Chicago, Illinois?
2. You might know Dallas, Texas.
3. Point to Anchorage, Alaska on the map.
4. Would you like to go to Tucson, Arizona?
5. How about Seattle, Washington?
6. Have you heard of San Jose, California?
7. What is it like in St. Louis, Missouri?

LANGUAGE ARTS

152 100 First Grade Skills

Page 152

Skill 73: Commas With Cities and States

Directions: Finish each sentence with a city and state from the box. Use commas where they are needed.

Lima Ohio ... Austin Texas
Macon Georgia ... Miami Florida

Order of answers will vary.

1. Jordan's uncle lives in Lima, Ohio.
2. In March, Liz will go to Macon, Georgia.
3. Ashley is moving to Reno, Nevada.
4. Stefanie has lived in Portland, Maine for 9 years.
5. Angela found Austin, Texas on the map.
6. It will take Cassie three days to drive to Miami, Florida.

Ohio State Flag

LANGUAGE ARTS

100 First Grade Skills 153

Page 153

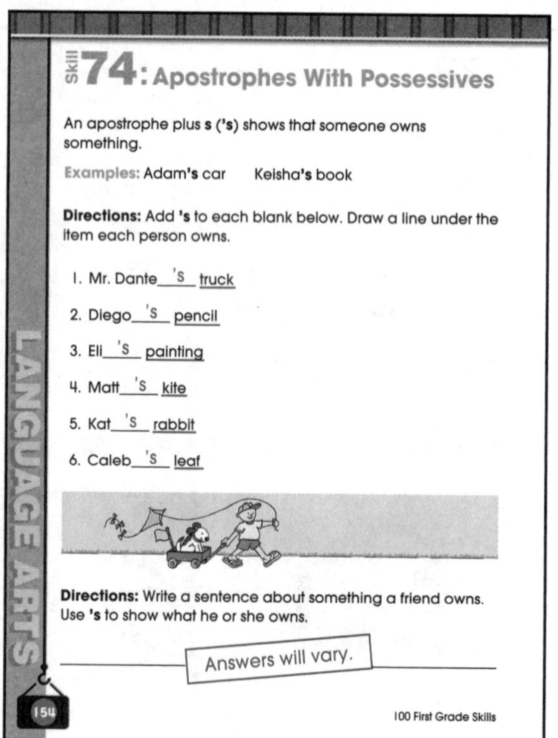

Skill 74: Apostrophes With Possessives

An apostrophe plus **s ('s)** shows that someone owns something.

Examples: Adam**'s** car Keisha**'s** book

Directions: Add **'s** to each blank below. Draw a line under the item each person owns.

1. Mr. Dante's truck
2. Diego's pencil
3. Eli's painting
4. Matt's kite
5. Kat's rabbit
6. Caleb's leaf

Directions: Write a sentence about something a friend owns. Use **'s** to show what he or she owns.

Answers will vary.

LANGUAGE ARTS

154 100 First Grade Skills

Page 154

Skill 74: Apostrophes With Possessives

Directions: Read each pair of sentences. Make a check mark (✓) next to the one that is correct.

1. ✓ John's scarf
   ___ Johns scarf
2. ___ Amys snake'
   ✓ Amy's snake
3. ✓ Amad's boots
   ___ Amads boots
4. ___ Noels cookie
   ✓ Noel's cookie
5. ___ Kims bird
   ✓ Kim's bird

LANGUAGE ARTS

100 First Grade Skills 155

Page 155

Answer Key

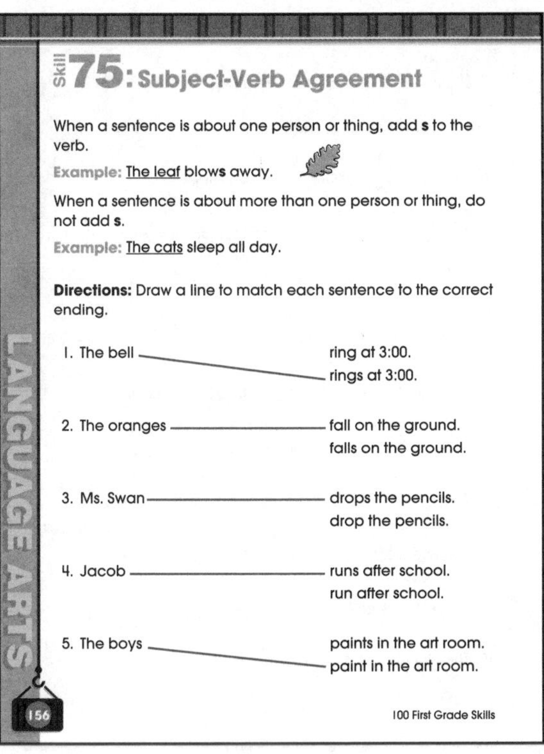

Skill 75: Subject-Verb Agreement

When a sentence is about one person or thing, add **s** to the verb.

Example: The leaf blows away.

When a sentence is about more than one person or thing, do not add **s**.

Example: The cats sleep all day.

Directions: Draw a line to match each sentence to the correct ending.

1. The bell — ring at 3:00. / rings at 3:00.
2. The oranges — fall on the ground. / falls on the ground.
3. Ms. Swan — drops the pencils. / drop the pencils.
4. Jacob — runs after school. / run after school.
5. The boys — paints in the art room. / paint in the art room.

LANGUAGE ARTS

156 100 First Grade Skills

Page 156

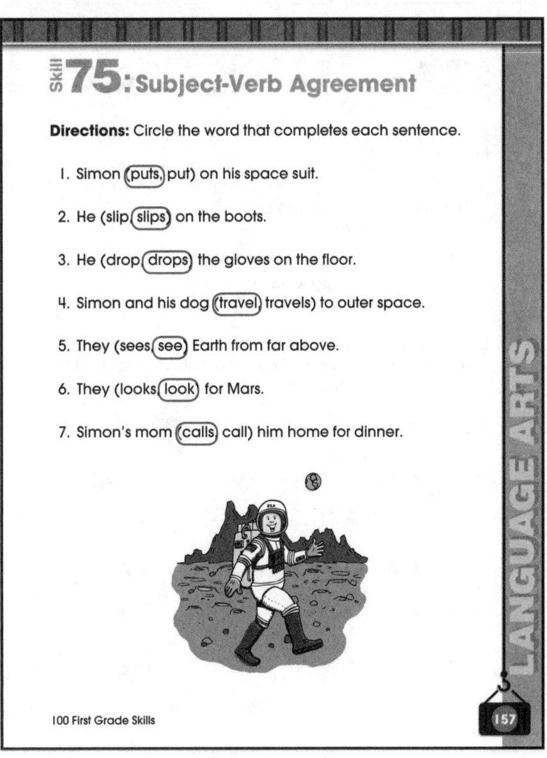

Skill 75: Subject-Verb Agreement

Directions: Circle the word that completes each sentence.

1. Simon (puts, put) on his space suit.
2. He (slip, slips) on the boots.
3. He (drop, drops) the gloves on the floor.
4. Simon and his dog (travel, travels) to outer space.
5. They (sees, see) Earth from far above.
6. They (looks, look) for Mars.
7. Simon's mom (calls, call) him home for dinner.

LANGUAGE ARTS

100 First Grade Skills 157

Page 157

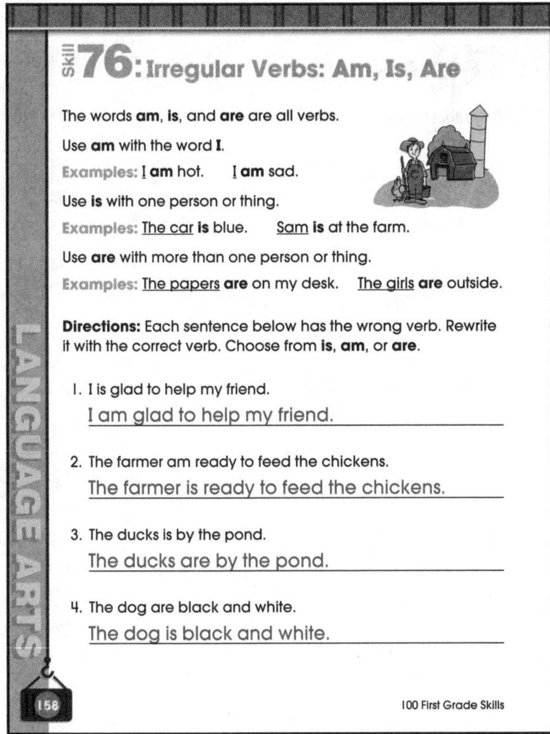

Skill 76: Irregular Verbs: Am, Is, Are

The words **am**, **is**, and **are** are all verbs.

Use **am** with the word **I**.

Examples: I **am** hot. I **am** sad.

Use **is** with one person or thing.

Examples: The car **is** blue. Sam **is** at the farm.

Use **are** with more than one person or thing.

Examples: The papers **are** on my desk. The girls **are** outside.

Directions: Each sentence below has the wrong verb. Rewrite it with the correct verb. Choose from **is**, **am**, or **are**.

1. I is glad to help my friend.
   I am glad to help my friend.
2. The farmer am ready to feed the chickens.
   The farmer is ready to feed the chickens.
3. The ducks is by the pond.
   The ducks are by the pond.
4. The dog are black and white.
   The dog is black and white.

LANGUAGE ARTS

158 100 First Grade Skills

Page 158

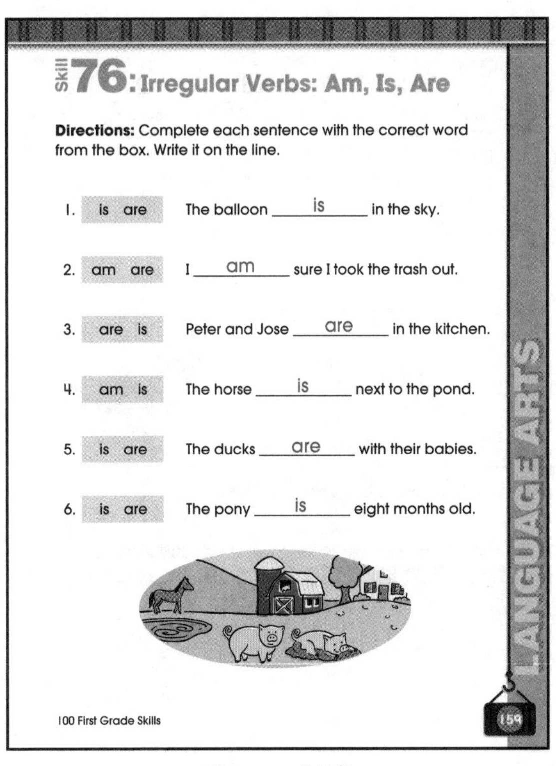

Skill 76: Irregular Verbs: Am, Is, Are

Directions: Complete each sentence with the correct word from the box. Write it on the line.

1. is are — The balloon ___is___ in the sky.
2. am are — I ___am___ sure I took the trash out.
3. are is — Peter and Jose ___are___ in the kitchen.
4. am is — The horse ___is___ next to the pond.
5. is are — The ducks ___are___ with their babies.
6. is are — The pony ___is___ eight months old.

LANGUAGE ARTS

100 First Grade Skills 159

Page 159

Answer Key

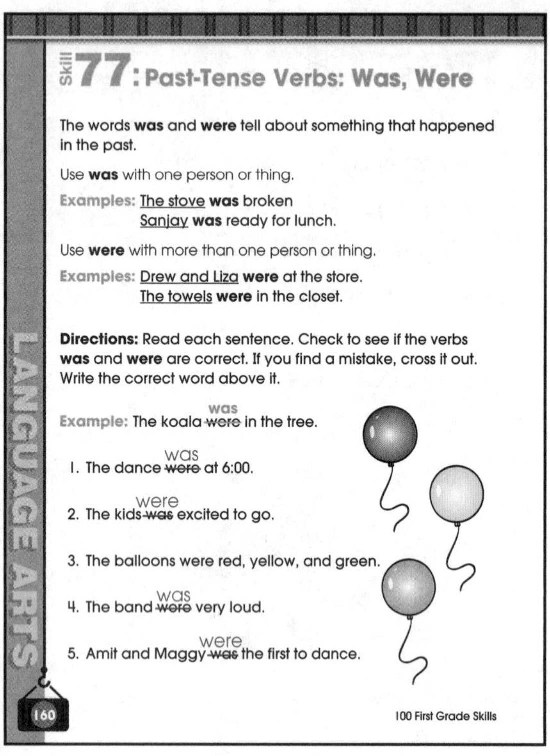

Skill 77: Past-Tense Verbs: Was, Were

The words **was** and **were** tell about something that happened in the past.

Use **was** with one person or thing.

Examples: The stove **was** broken
Sanjay **was** ready for lunch.

Use **were** with more than one person or thing.

Examples: Drew and Liza **were** at the store.
The towels **were** in the closet.

Directions: Read each sentence. Check to see if the verbs **was** and **were** are correct. If you find a mistake, cross it out. Write the correct word above it.

Example: The koala ~~were~~ was in the tree.

1. The dance ~~were~~ was at 6:00.
2. The kids ~~was~~ were excited to go.
3. The balloons were red, yellow, and green.
4. The band ~~were~~ was very loud.
5. Amit and Maggy ~~was~~ were the first to dance.

LANGUAGE ARTS

160 100 First Grade Skills

Page 160

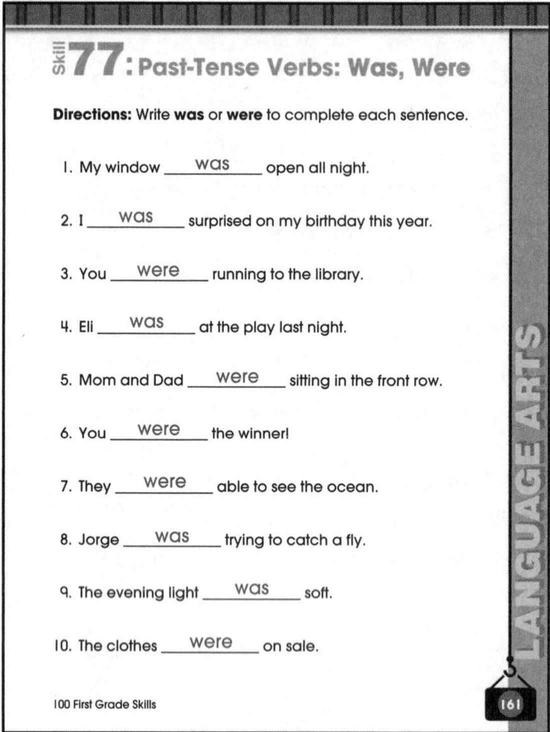

Skill 77: Past-Tense Verbs: Was, Were

Directions: Write **was** or **were** to complete each sentence.

1. My window was open all night.
2. I was surprised on my birthday this year.
3. You were running to the library.
4. Eli was at the play last night.
5. Mom and Dad were sitting in the front row.
6. You were the winner!
7. They were able to see the ocean.
8. Jorge was trying to catch a fly.
9. The evening light was soft.
10. The clothes were on sale.

LANGUAGE ARTS

100 First Grade Skills 161

Page 161

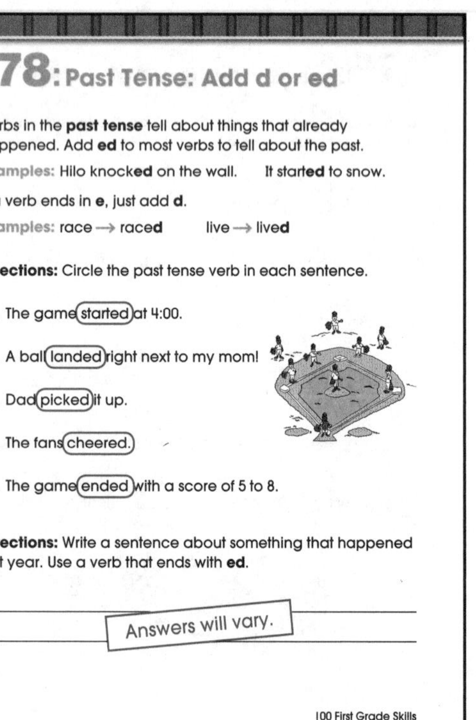

Skill 78: Past Tense: Add d or ed

Verbs in the **past tense** tell about things that already happened. Add **ed** to most verbs to tell about the past.

Examples: Hilo knock**ed** on the wall. It start**ed** to snow.

If a verb ends in **e**, just add **d**.

Examples: race → race**d** live → live**d**

Directions: Circle the past tense verb in each sentence.

1. The game (started) at 4:00.
2. A ball (landed) right next to my mom!
3. Dad (picked) it up.
4. The fans (cheered.)
5. The game (ended) with a score of 5 to 8.

Directions: Write a sentence about something that happened last year. Use a verb that ends with **ed**.

Answers will vary.

LANGUAGE ARTS

162 100 First Grade Skills

Page 162

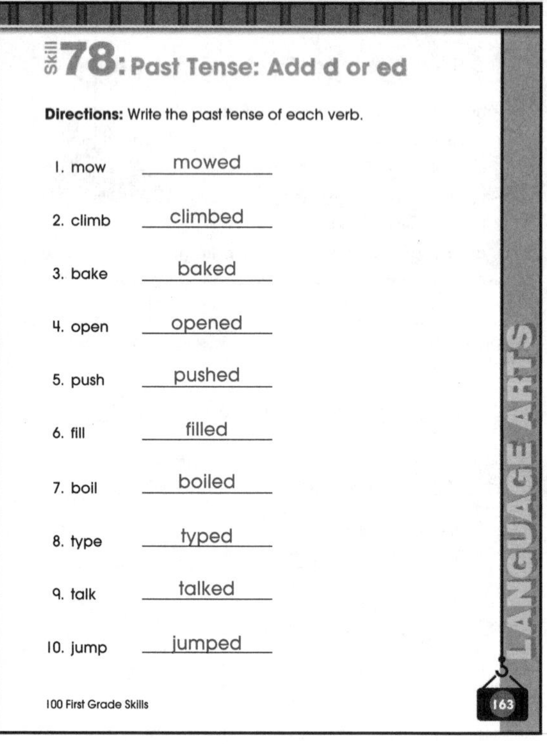

Skill 78: Past Tense: Add d or ed

Directions: Write the past tense of each verb.

1. mow mowed
2. climb climbed
3. bake baked
4. open opened
5. push pushed
6. fill filled
7. boil boiled
8. type typed
9. talk talked
10. jump jumped

LANGUAGE ARTS

100 First Grade Skills 163

Page 163

Answer Key

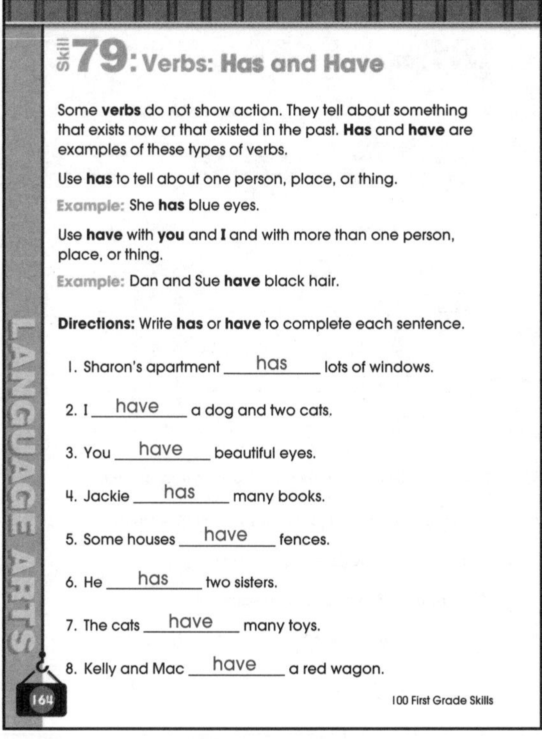

Skill 79: Verbs: Has and Have

Some **verbs** do not show action. They tell about something that exists now or that existed in the past. **Has** and **have** are examples of these types of verbs.

Use **has** to tell about one person, place, or thing.

Example: She **has** blue eyes.

Use **have** with **you** and **I** and with more than one person, place, or thing.

Example: Dan and Sue **have** black hair.

Directions: Write **has** or **have** to complete each sentence.

1. Sharon's apartment ___has___ lots of windows.
2. I ___have___ a dog and two cats.
3. You ___have___ beautiful eyes.
4. Jackie ___has___ many books.
5. Some houses ___have___ fences.
6. He ___has___ two sisters.
7. The cats ___have___ many toys.
8. Kelly and Mac ___have___ a red wagon.

LANGUAGE ARTS

164 100 First Grade Skills

Page 164

Skill 79: Verbs: Has and Have

Directions: Write **has** or **have** to complete each sentence.

1. We ___have___ fun plans for this summer.
2. The school ___has___ Friday off.
3. My dad ___has___ three fishing poles.
4. The girl ___has___ a hat.
5. Lia and I ___have___ tomatoes on our sandwiches.
6. The doghouses ___have___ new roofs.
7. His sister ___has___ dance shoes.
8. The zoo ___has___ many animals.

Directions: Write a sentence with the word **has**.

Answers will vary.

Directions: Write a sentence with the word **have**.

Answers will vary.

LANGUAGE ARTS

100 First Grade Skills 165

Page 165

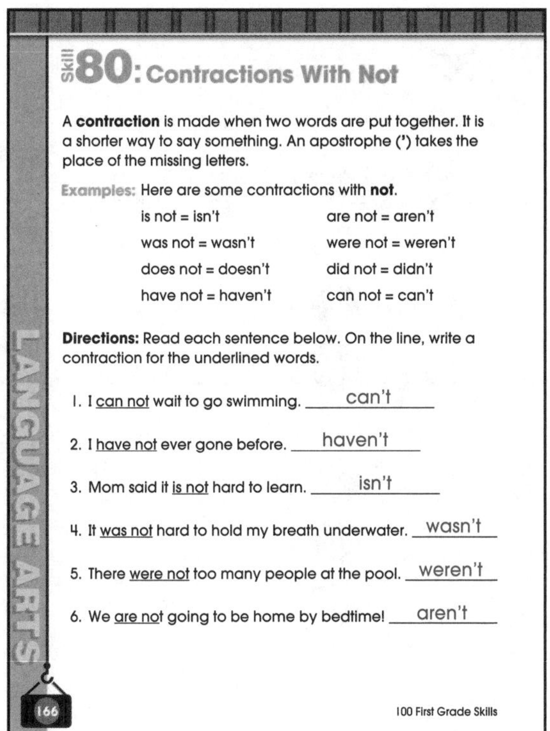

Skill 80: Contractions With Not

A **contraction** is made when two words are put together. It is a shorter way to say something. An apostrophe (') takes the place of the missing letters.

Examples: Here are some contractions with **not**.

is not = isn't	are not = aren't
was not = wasn't	were not = weren't
does not = doesn't	did not = didn't
have not = haven't	can not = can't

Directions: Read each sentence below. On the line, write a contraction for the underlined words.

1. I can not wait to go swimming. ___can't___
2. I have not ever gone before. ___haven't___
3. Mom said it is not hard to learn. ___isn't___
4. It was not hard to hold my breath underwater. ___wasn't___
5. There were not too many people at the pool. ___weren't___
6. We are not going to be home by bedtime! ___aren't___

LANGUAGE ARTS

166 100 First Grade Skills

Page 166

Skill 80: Contractions With Not

Directions: Write the contraction for each group of words

1. is not = ___isn't___
2. does not = ___doesn't___
3. would not = ___wouldn't___
4. have not = ___haven't___
5. can not = ___can't___

Directions: Write a contraction to complete each sentence.

1. We ___haven't___ seen the movie. (have not)
2. Ryan ___wasn't___ able to visit Aunt Anne. (was not)
3. He said he ___can't___ be there at 2:00 p.m. (can not)

Directions: Write a sentence using each contraction.

1. isn't:
2. didn't:

Answers will vary.

LANGUAGE ARTS

100 First Grade Skills 167

Page 167

Answer Key

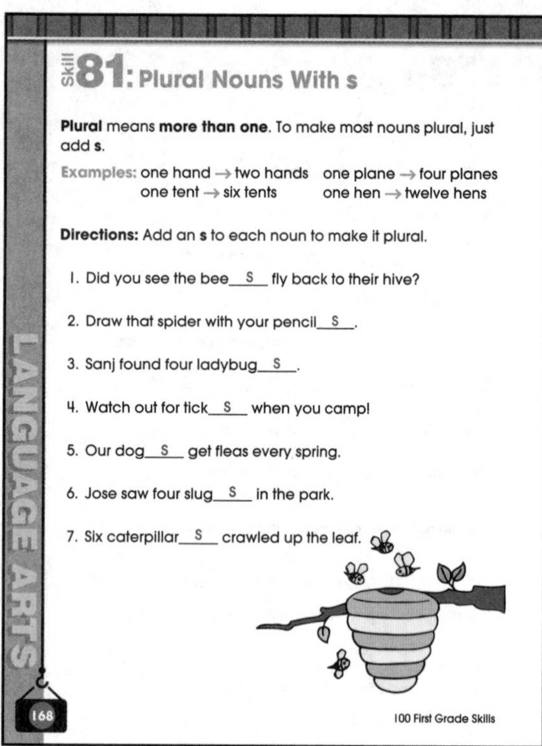

Skill **81: Plural Nouns With s**

Plural means **more than one**. To make most nouns plural, just add **s**.

Examples: one hand → two hands one plane → four planes
one tent → six tents one hen → twelve hens

Directions: Add an **s** to each noun to make it plural.

1. Did you see the bee__s__ fly back to their hive?
2. Draw that spider with your pencil__s__.
3. Sanj found four ladybug__s__.
4. Watch out for tick__s__ when you camp!
5. Our dog__s__ get fleas every spring.
6. Jose saw four slug__s__ in the park.
7. Six caterpillar__s__ crawled up the leaf.

LANGUAGE ARTS

168 100 First Grade Skills

Page 168

Skill **81: Plural Nouns With s**

Directions: Write each noun in the correct column.

peanut	toes	crickets	guitar	swing
band	shirts	letters	keys	pond

Singular	Plural
peanut	toes
band	shirts
guitar	crickets
swing	letters
pond	keys

Directions: Circle the correct word to finish each sentence.

1. Andrea fed each elephant one (peanut/peanuts).
2. There were three (guitar/guitars) at the store.
3. All of the (swing/swings) in the park were full.
4. Mark likes to swim in a (pond/ponds) in the summer.

100 First Grade Skills 169

LANGUAGE ARTS

Page 169

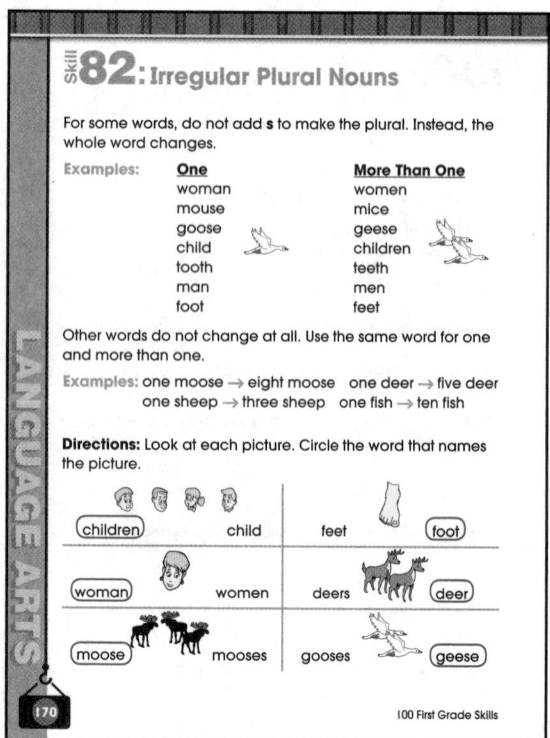

Skill **82: Irregular Plural Nouns**

For some words, do not add **s** to make the plural. Instead, the whole word changes.

Examples:

One	More Than One
woman	women
mouse	mice
goose	geese
child	children
tooth	teeth
man	men
foot	feet

Other words do not change at all. Use the same word for one and more than one.

Examples: one moose → eight moose one deer → five deer
one sheep → three sheep one fish → ten fish

Directions: Look at each picture. Circle the word that names the picture.

(children) child	feet (foot)
(woman) women	deers (deer)
(moose) mooses	gooses (geese)

LANGUAGE ARTS

170 100 First Grade Skills

Page 170

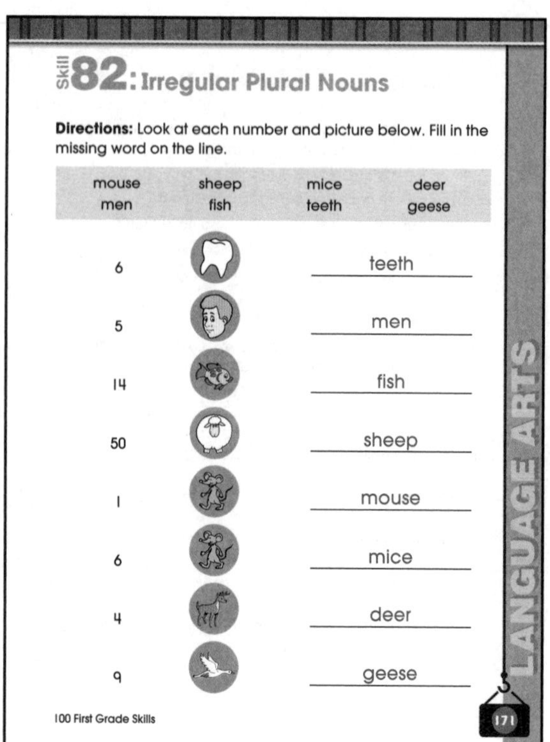

Skill **82: Irregular Plural Nouns**

Directions: Look at each number and picture below. Fill in the missing word on the line.

mouse	sheep	mice	deer
men	fish	teeth	geese

6	teeth
5	men
14	fish
50	sheep
1	mouse
6	mice
4	deer
9	geese

100 First Grade Skills 171

LANGUAGE ARTS

Page 171

Answer Key

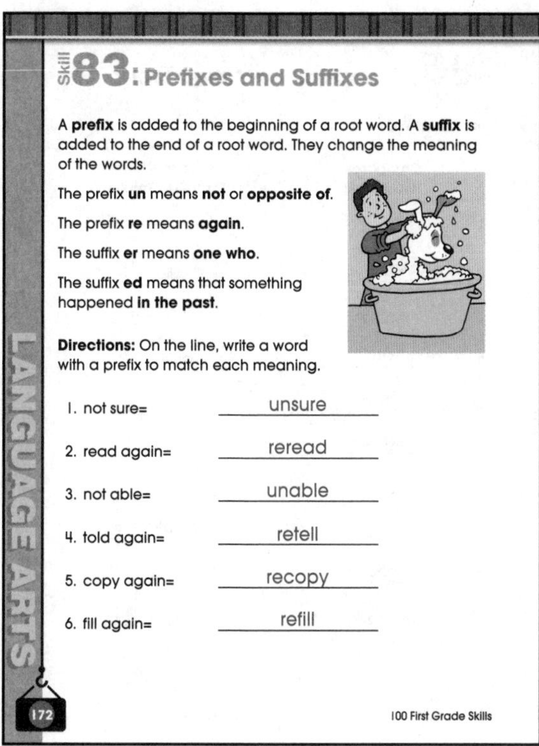

Skill 83: Prefixes and Suffixes

A **prefix** is added to the beginning of a root word. A **suffix** is added to the end of a root word. They change the meaning of the words.

The prefix **un** means **not** or **opposite of**.

The prefix **re** means **again**.

The suffix **er** means **one who**.

The suffix **ed** means that something happened **in the past**.

Directions: On the line, write a word with a prefix to match each meaning.

1. not sure= unsure
2. read again= reread
3. not able= unable
4. told again= retell
5. copy again= recopy
6. fill again= refill

LANGUAGE ARTS

172 100 First Grade Skills

Page 172

Skill 83: Prefixes and Suffixes

Directions: Each **bold** word is missing a suffix. Add the suffix **er** or **ed**. Use the meaning of the sentence to decide which one to add.

1. Lin **tuck**_ed_ her doll into bed.
2. Kendra **smile**_d_ at the baby.
3. Alyssa wants to be a **paint**_er_ one day.
4. Grandpa handed a check to the **bank**_er_.

Directions: Write the words under the correct headings.

unhurt	reuse	unfair
liked	farmer	singer

Words With Prefixes	Words With Suffixes
unhurt	liked
reuse	farmer
unfair	singer

LANGUAGE ARTS

100 First Grade Skills 173

Page 173

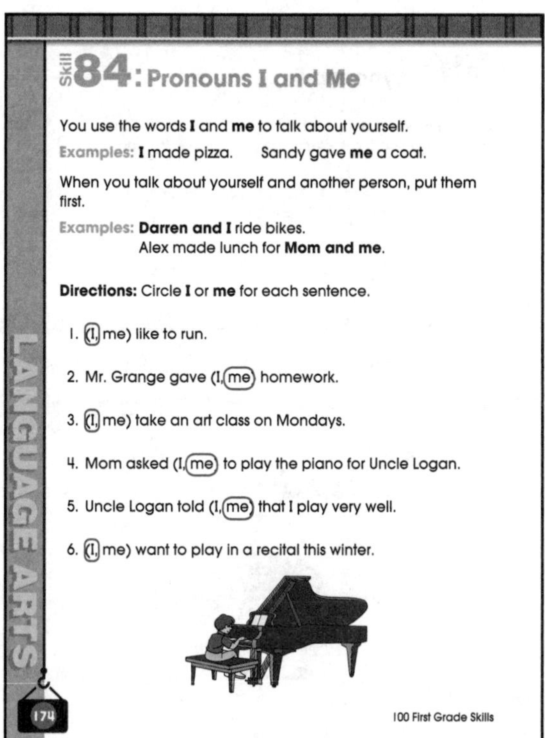

Skill 84: Pronouns I and Me

You use the words **I** and **me** to talk about yourself.

Examples: **I** made pizza. Sandy gave **me** a coat.

When you talk about yourself and another person, put them first.

Examples: **Darren and I** ride bikes.
Alex made lunch for **Mom and me**.

Directions: Circle **I** or **me** for each sentence.

1. (I, me) like to run. [I circled]
2. Mr. Grange gave (I, me) homework. [me circled]
3. (I, me) take an art class on Mondays. [I circled]
4. Mom asked (I, me) to play the piano for Uncle Logan. [me circled]
5. Uncle Logan told (I, me) that I play very well. [me circled]
6. (I, me) want to play in a recital this winter. [I circled]

LANGUAGE ARTS

174 100 First Grade Skills

Page 174

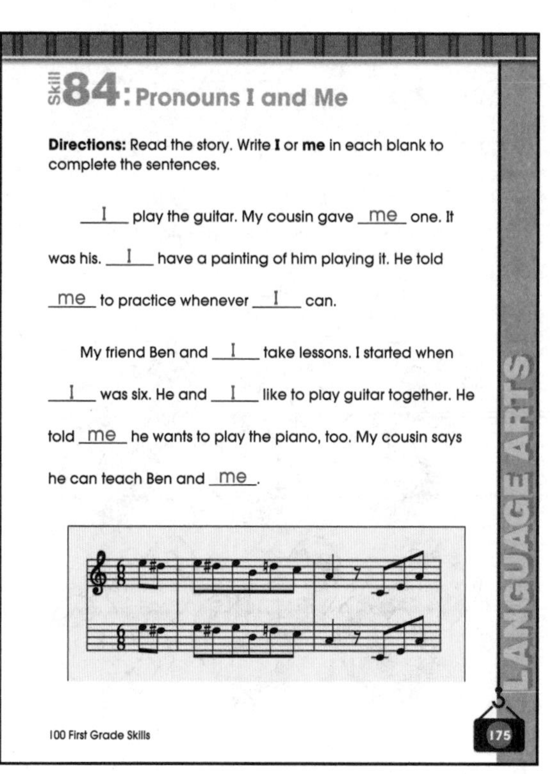

Skill 84: Pronouns I and Me

Directions: Read the story. Write **I** or **me** in each blank to complete the sentences.

_I_ play the guitar. My cousin gave _me_ one. It was his. _I_ have a painting of him playing it. He told _me_ to practice whenever _I_ can.

My friend Ben and _I_ take lessons. I started when _I_ was six. He and _I_ like to play guitar together. He told _me_ he wants to play the piano, too. My cousin says he can teach Ben and _me_.

LANGUAGE ARTS

100 First Grade Skills 175

Page 175

Answer Key

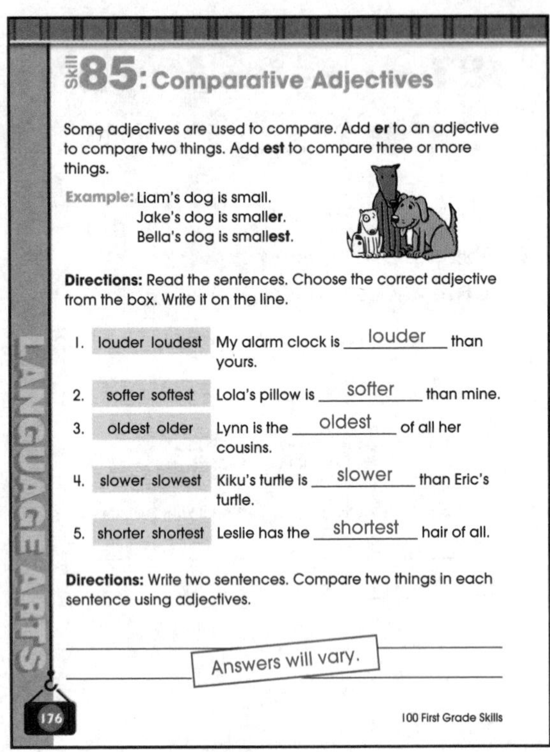

Skill 85: Comparative Adjectives

Some adjectives are used to compare. Add **er** to an adjective to compare two things. Add **est** to compare three or more things.

Example: Liam's dog is small.
Jake's dog is small**er**.
Bella's dog is small**est**.

Directions: Read the sentences. Choose the correct adjective from the box. Write it on the line.

1. louder loudest — My alarm clock is louder than yours.
2. softer softest — Lola's pillow is softer than mine.
3. oldest older — Lynn is the oldest of all her cousins.
4. slower slowest — Kiku's turtle is slower than Eric's turtle.
5. shorter shortest — Leslie has the shortest hair of all.

Directions: Write two sentences. Compare two things in each sentence using adjectives.

Answers will vary.

176 — 100 First Grade Skills

Page 176

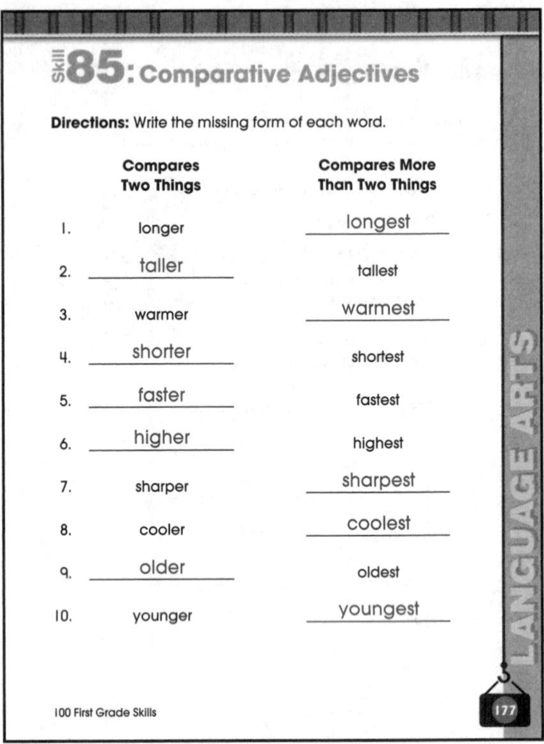

Skill 85: Comparative Adjectives

Directions: Write the missing form of each word.

	Compares Two Things	Compares More Than Two Things
1.	longer	longest
2.	taller	tallest
3.	warmer	warmest
4.	shorter	shortest
5.	faster	fastest
6.	higher	highest
7.	sharper	sharpest
8.	cooler	coolest
9.	older	oldest
10.	younger	youngest

100 First Grade Skills — 177

Page 177

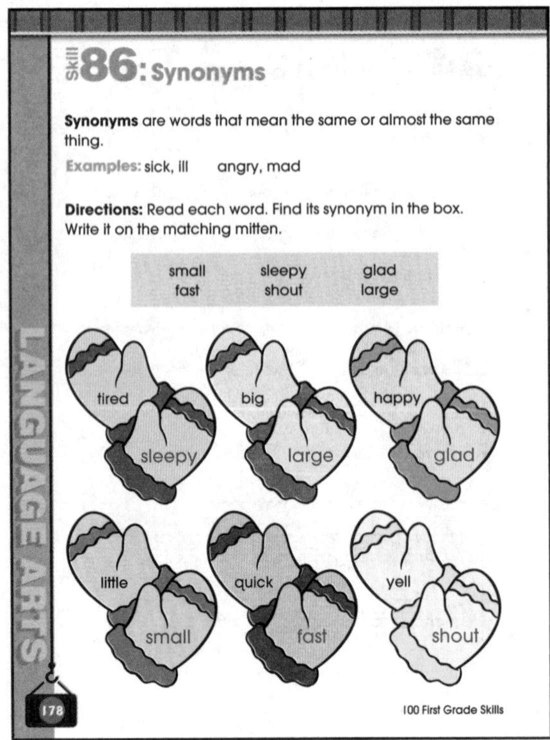

Skill 86: Synonyms

Synonyms are words that mean the same or almost the same thing.

Examples: sick, ill   angry, mad

Directions: Read each word. Find its synonym in the box. Write it on the matching mitten.

small	sleepy	glad
fast	shout	large

tired — sleepy
big — large
happy — glad
little — small
quick — fast
yell — shout

178 — 100 First Grade Skills

Page 178

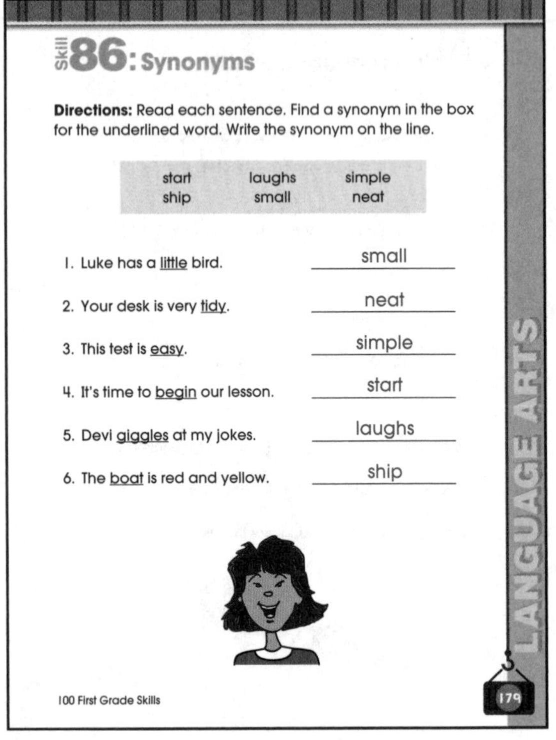

Skill 86: Synonyms

Directions: Read each sentence. Find a synonym in the box for the underlined word. Write the synonym on the line.

start	laughs	simple
ship	small	neat

1. Luke has a little bird. — small
2. Your desk is very tidy. — neat
3. This test is easy. — simple
4. It's time to begin our lesson. — start
5. Devi giggles at my jokes. — laughs
6. The boat is red and yellow. — ship

100 First Grade Skills — 179

Page 179

Answer Key

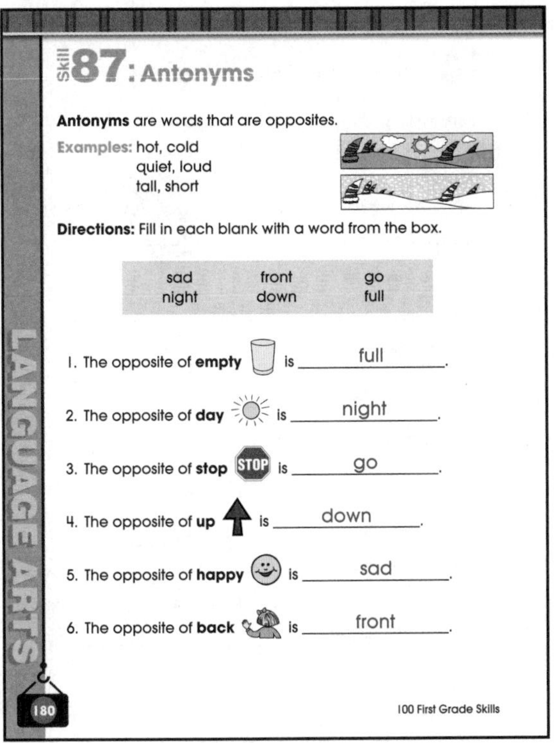

Skill 87: Antonyms

Antonyms are words that are opposites.

Examples: hot, cold
quiet, loud
tall, short

Directions: Fill in each blank with a word from the box.

sad	front	go
night	down	full

1. The opposite of **empty** is full.
2. The opposite of **day** is night.
3. The opposite of **stop** is go.
4. The opposite of **up** is down.
5. The opposite of **happy** is sad.
6. The opposite of **back** is front.

LANGUAGE ARTS

180 100 First Grade Skills

Page 180

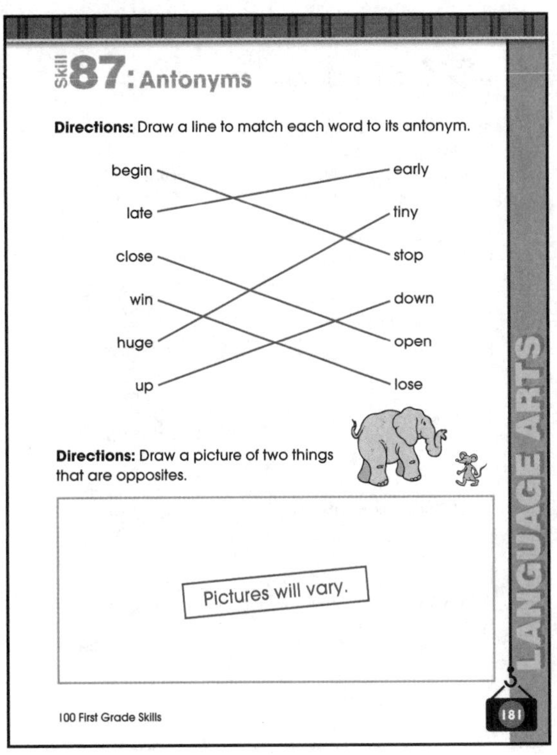

Skill 87: Antonyms

Directions: Draw a line to match each word to its antonym.

begin	early
late	tiny
close	stop
win	down
huge	open
up	lose

Directions: Draw a picture of two things that are opposites.

Pictures will vary.

LANGUAGE ARTS

100 First Grade Skills 181

Page 181

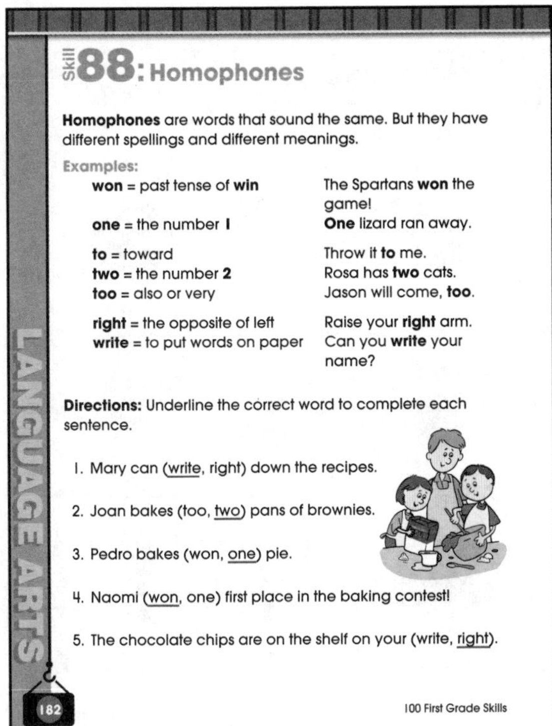

Skill 88: Homophones

Homophones are words that sound the same. But they have different spellings and different meanings.

Examples:

won = past tense of **win**	The Spartans **won** the game!
one = the number **1**	**One** lizard ran away.
to = toward	Throw it **to** me.
two = the number **2**	Rosa has **two** cats.
too = also or very	Jason will come, **too**.
right = the opposite of left	Raise your **right** arm.
write = to put words on paper	Can you **write** your name?

Directions: Underline the correct word to complete each sentence.

1. Mary can (write, right) down the recipes.
2. Joan bakes (too, two) pans of brownies.
3. Pedro bakes (won, one) pie.
4. Naomi (won, one) first place in the baking contest!
5. The chocolate chips are on the shelf on your (write, right).

LANGUAGE ARTS

182 100 First Grade Skills

Page 182

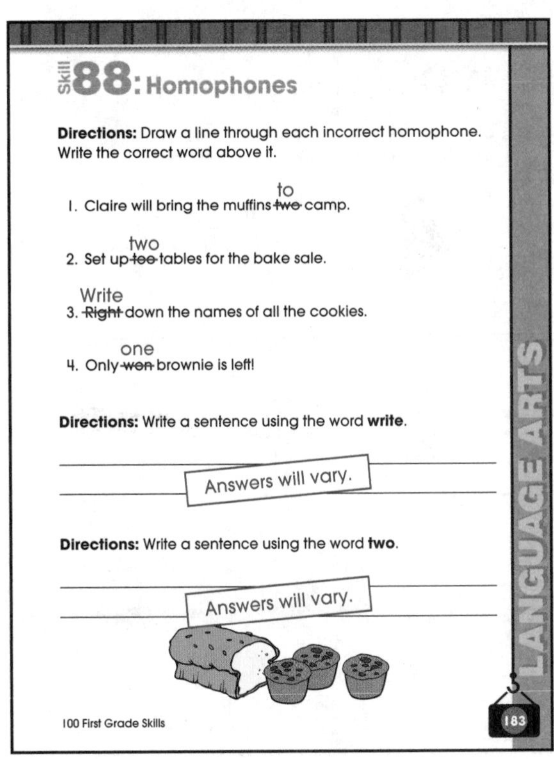

Skill 88: Homophones

Directions: Draw a line through each incorrect homophone. Write the correct word above it.

1. Claire will bring the muffins ~~two~~ to camp.
2. Set up ~~too~~ two tables for the bake sale.
3. ~~Right~~ Write down the names of all the cookies.
4. Only ~~won~~ one brownie is left!

Directions: Write a sentence using the word **write**.

Answers will vary.

Directions: Write a sentence using the word **two**.

Answers will vary.

LANGUAGE ARTS

100 First Grade Skills 183

Page 183

Answer Key

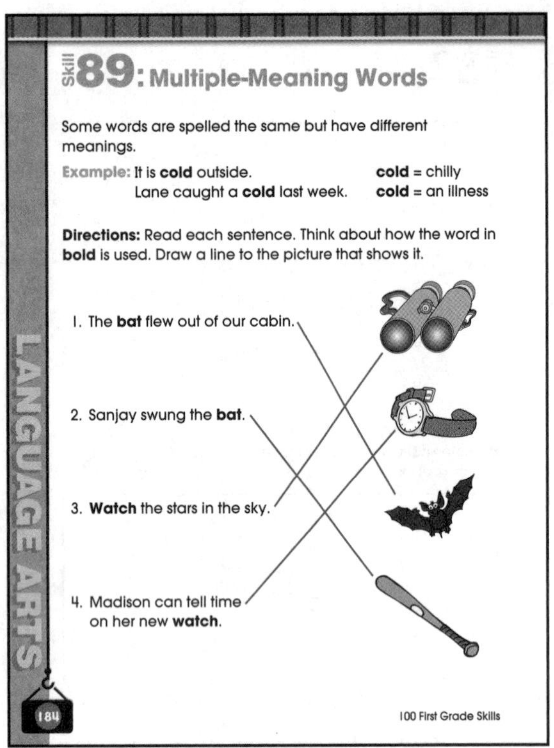

Skill **89: Multiple-Meaning Words**

Some words are spelled the same but have different meanings.

Example: It is **cold** outside. — **cold** = chilly
Lane caught a **cold** last week. — **cold** = an illness

Directions: Read each sentence. Think about how the word in **bold** is used. Draw a line to the picture that shows it.

1. The **bat** flew out of our cabin.
2. Sanjay swung the **bat**.
3. **Watch** the stars in the sky.
4. Madison can tell time on her new **watch**.

LANGUAGE ARTS

184 — 100 First Grade Skills

Page 184

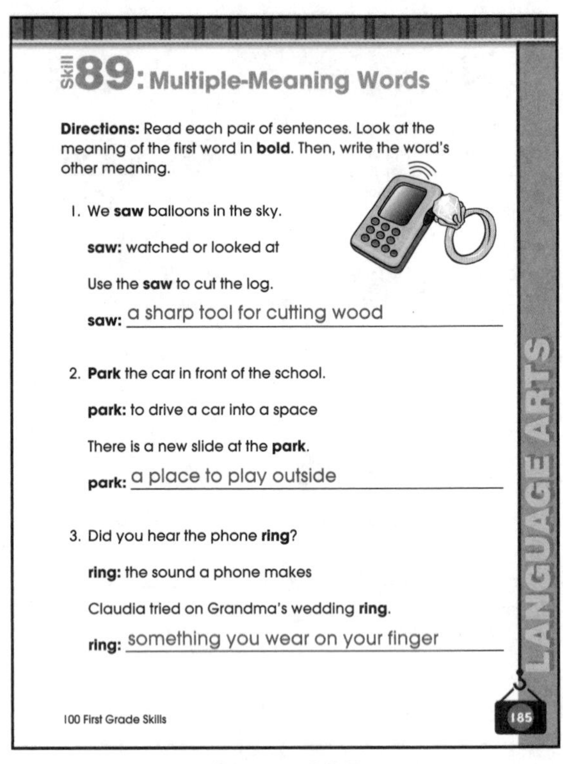

Skill **89: Multiple-Meaning Words**

Directions: Read each pair of sentences. Look at the meaning of the first word in **bold**. Then, write the word's other meaning.

1. We **saw** balloons in the sky.

   saw: watched or looked at

   Use the **saw** to cut the log.

   saw: a sharp tool for cutting wood

2. **Park** the car in front of the school.

   park: to drive a car into a space

   There is a new slide at the **park**.

   park: a place to play outside

3. Did you hear the phone **ring**?

   ring: the sound a phone makes

   Claudia tried on Grandma's wedding **ring**.

   ring: something you wear on your finger

LANGUAGE ARTS

100 First Grade Skills — 185

Page 185

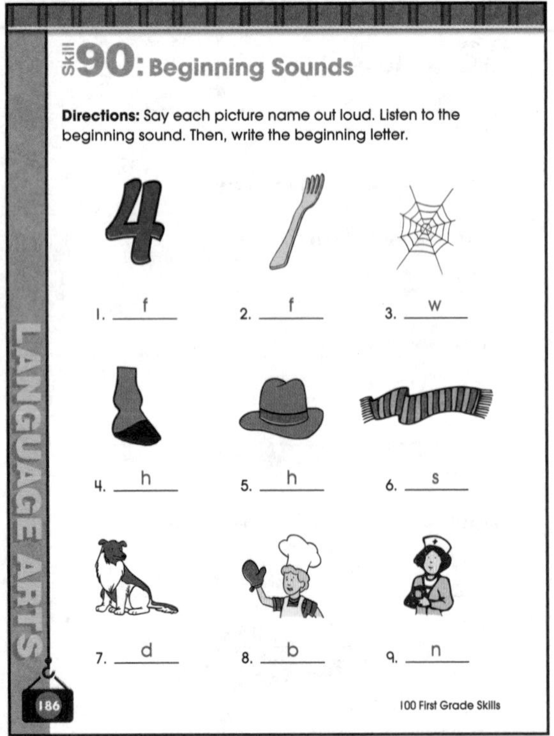

Skill **90: Beginning Sounds**

Directions: Say each picture name out loud. Listen to the beginning sound. Then, write the beginning letter.

1. f
2. f
3. w
4. h
5. h
6. s
7. d
8. b
9. n

LANGUAGE ARTS

186 — 100 First Grade Skills

Page 186

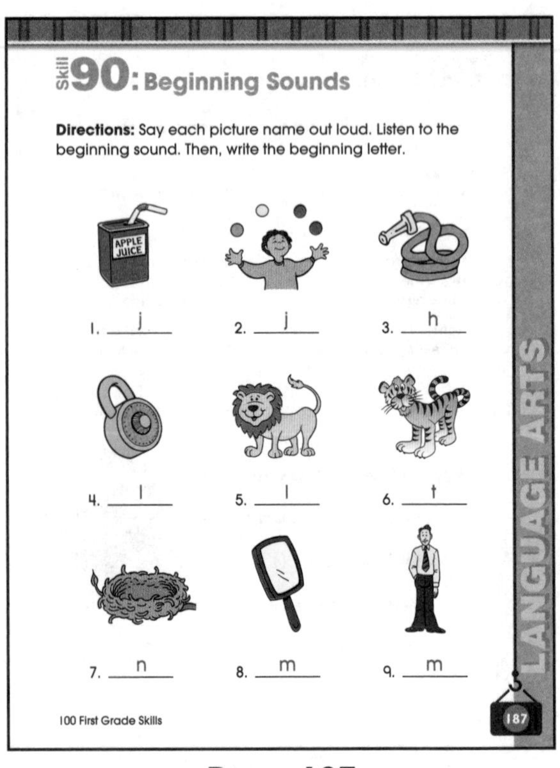

Skill **90: Beginning Sounds**

Directions: Say each picture name out loud. Listen to the beginning sound. Then, write the beginning letter.

1. j
2. j
3. h
4. l
5. l
6. t
7. n
8. m
9. m

LANGUAGE ARTS

100 First Grade Skills — 187

Page 187

Answer Key

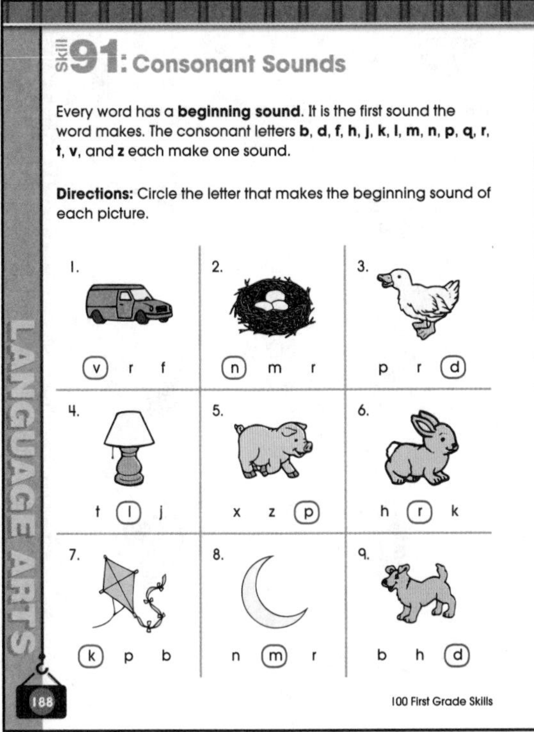

Skill **91: Consonant Sounds**

Every word has a **beginning sound**. It is the first sound the word makes. The consonant letters **b**, **d**, **f**, **h**, **j**, **k**, **l**, **m**, **n**, **p**, **q**, **r**, **t**, **v**, and **z** each make one sound.

Directions: Circle the letter that makes the beginning sound of each picture.

1. (v) r f
2. (n) m r
3. p r (d)
4. t (l) j
5. x z (p)
6. h (r) k
7. (k) p b
8. n (m) r
9. b h (d)

LANGUAGE ARTS

188 100 First Grade Skills

Page 188

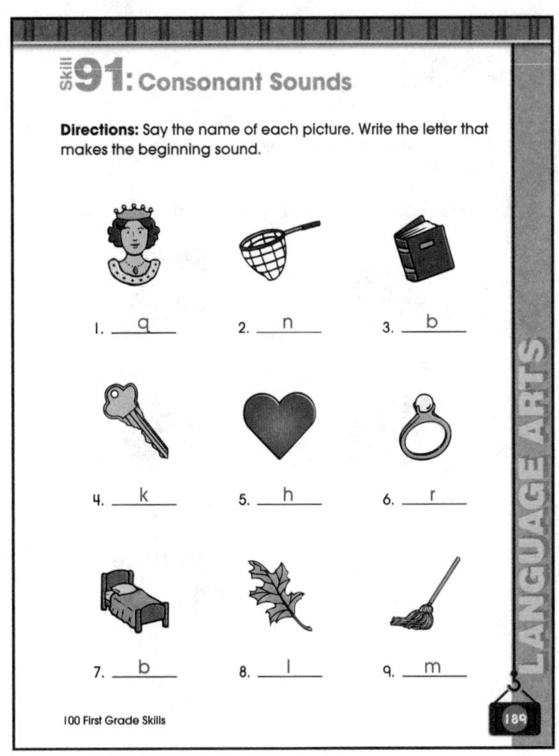

Skill **91: Consonant Sounds**

Directions: Say the name of each picture. Write the letter that makes the beginning sound.

1. q
2. n
3. b
4. k
5. h
6. r
7. b
8. l
9. m

LANGUAGE ARTS

100 First Grade Skills 189

Page 189

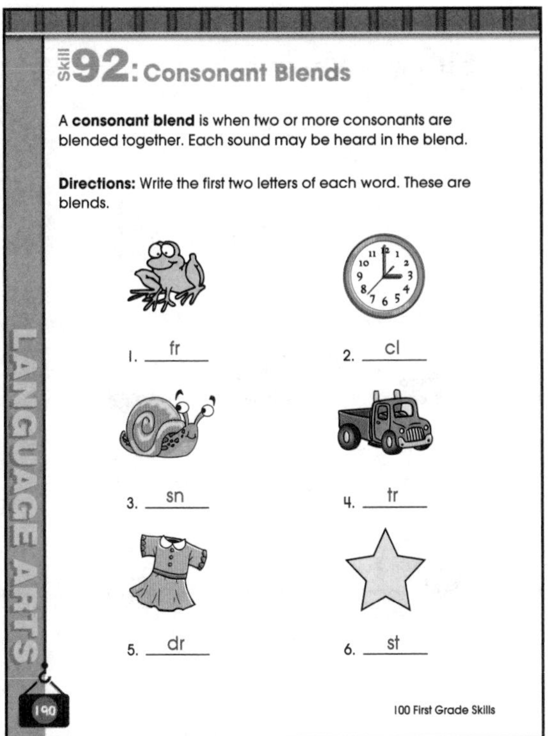

Skill **92: Consonant Blends**

A **consonant blend** is when two or more consonants are blended together. Each sound may be heard in the blend.

Directions: Write the first two letters of each word. These are blends.

1. fr
2. cl
3. sn
4. tr
5. dr
6. st

LANGUAGE ARTS

190 100 First Grade Skills

Page 190

Skill **92: Consonant Blends**

Directions: Write the first two letters of each word. These are blends.

1. fl
2. bl
3. sl
4. pl
5. sl
6. tr

LANGUAGE ARTS

100 First Grade Skills 191

Page 191

Answer Key

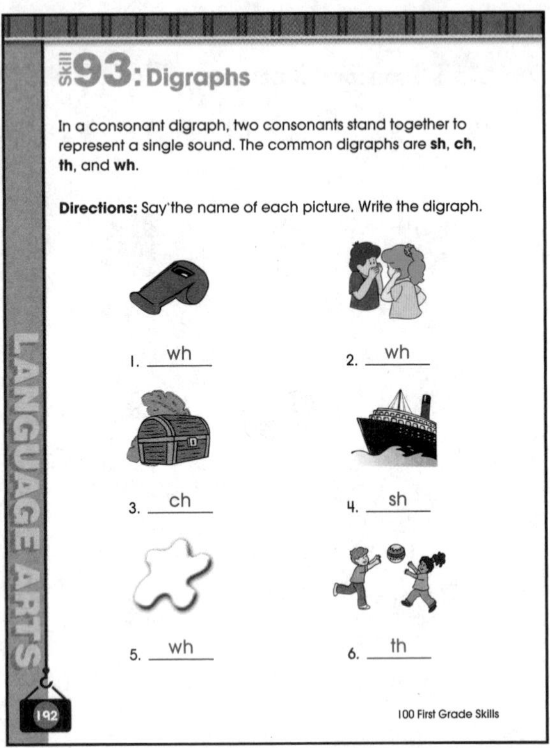

Page 192

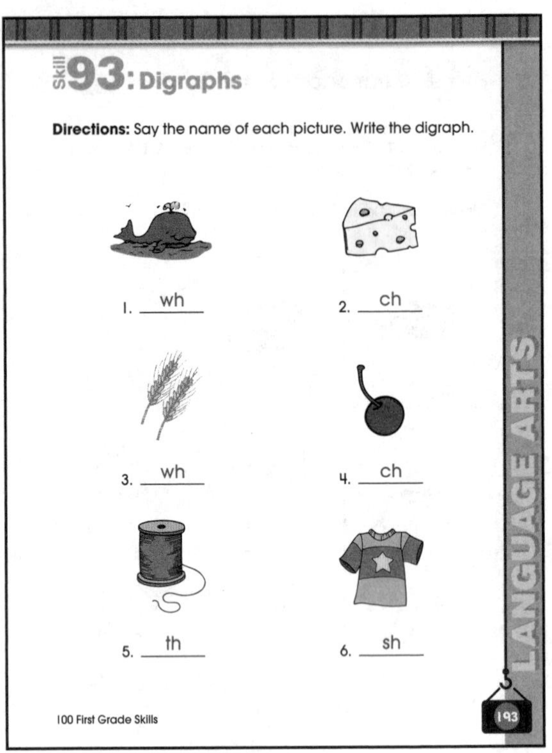

Page 193

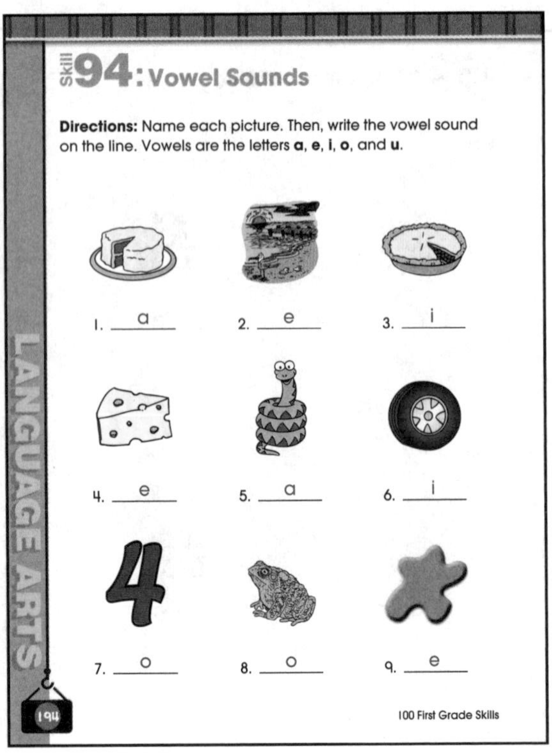

Page 194

Page 195

Answer Key

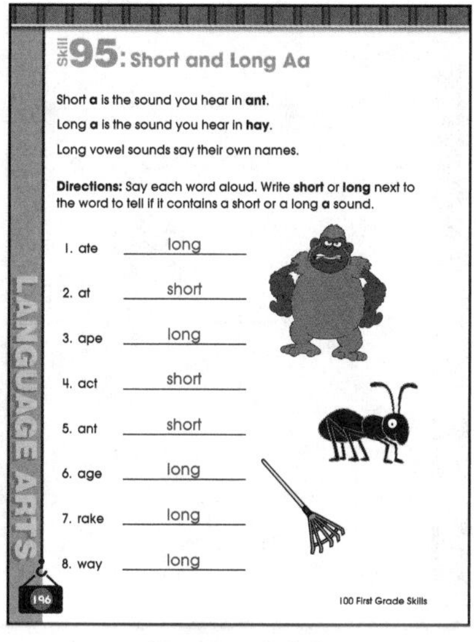

Skill **95: Short and Long Aa**

Short **a** is the sound you hear in **ant**.

Long **a** is the sound you hear in **hay**.

Long vowel sounds say their own names.

Directions: Say each word aloud. Write **short** or **long** next to the word to tell if it contains a short or a long **a** sound.

1. ate long
2. at short
3. ape long
4. act short
5. ant short
6. age long
7. rake long
8. way long

LANGUAGE ARTS

196 100 First Grade Skills

Page 196

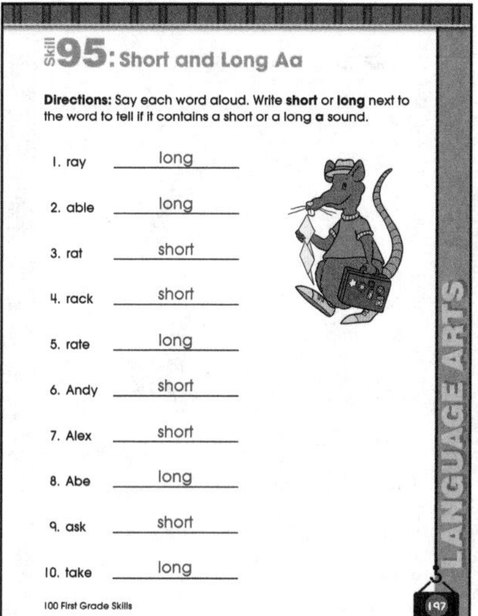

Skill **95: Short and Long Aa**

Directions: Say each word aloud. Write **short** or **long** next to the word to tell if it contains a short or a long **a** sound.

1. ray long
2. able long
3. rat short
4. rack short
5. rate long
6. Andy short
7. Alex short
8. Abe long
9. ask short
10. take long

LANGUAGE ARTS

100 First Grade Skills 197

Page 197

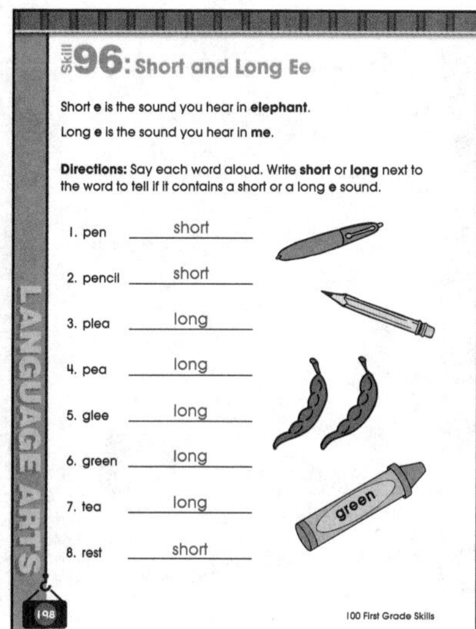

Skill **96: Short and Long Ee**

Short **e** is the sound you hear in **elephant**.

Long **e** is the sound you hear in **me**.

Directions: Say each word aloud. Write **short** or **long** next to the word to tell if it contains a short or a long **e** sound.

1. pen short
2. pencil short
3. plea long
4. pea long
5. glee long
6. green long
7. tea long
8. rest short

LANGUAGE ARTS

198 100 First Grade Skills

Page 198

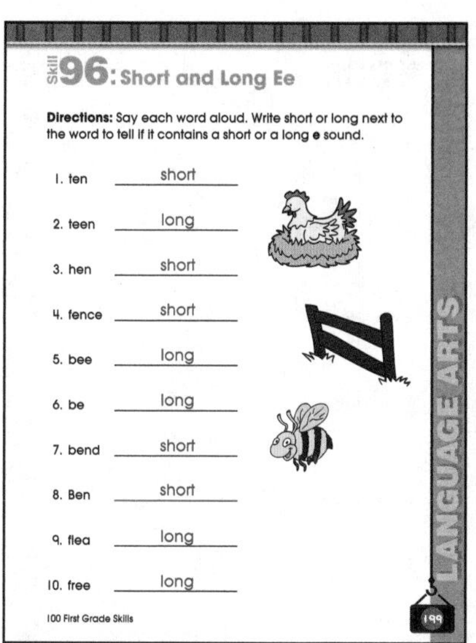

Skill **96: Short and Long Ee**

Directions: Say each word aloud. Write short or long next to the word to tell if it contains a short or a long **e** sound.

1. ten short
2. teen long
3. hen short
4. fence short
5. bee long
6. be long
7. bend short
8. Ben short
9. flea long
10. free long

LANGUAGE ARTS

100 First Grade Skills 199

Page 199

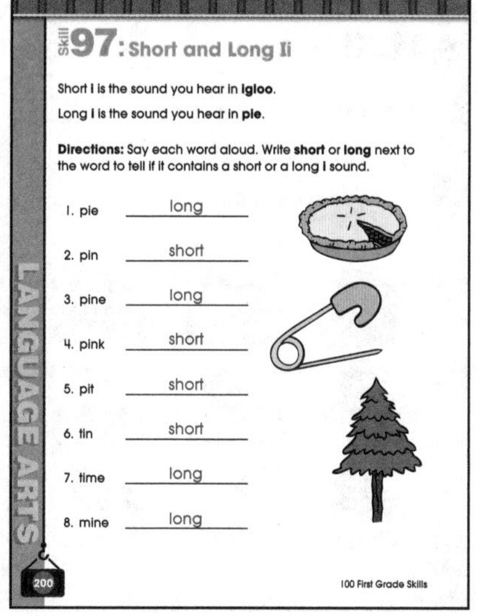

Skill **97: Short and Long Ii**

Short **i** is the sound you hear in **igloo**.

Long **i** is the sound you hear in **pie**.

Directions: Say each word aloud. Write **short** or **long** next to the word to tell if it contains a short or a long **i** sound.

1. pie long
2. pin short
3. pine long
4. pink short
5. pit short
6. tin short
7. time long
8. mine long

LANGUAGE ARTS

200 100 First Grade Skills

Page 200

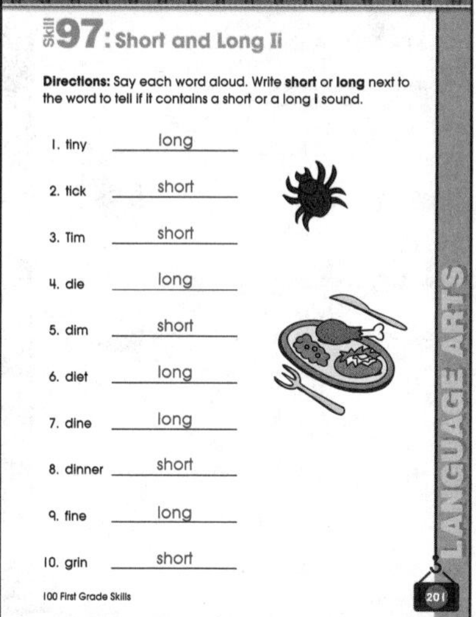

Skill **97: Short and Long Ii**

Directions: Say each word aloud. Write **short** or **long** next to the word to tell if it contains a short or a long **i** sound.

1. tiny long
2. tick short
3. Tim short
4. die long
5. dim short
6. diet long
7. dine long
8. dinner short
9. fine long
10. grin short

LANGUAGE ARTS

100 First Grade Skills 201

Page 201

Answer Key

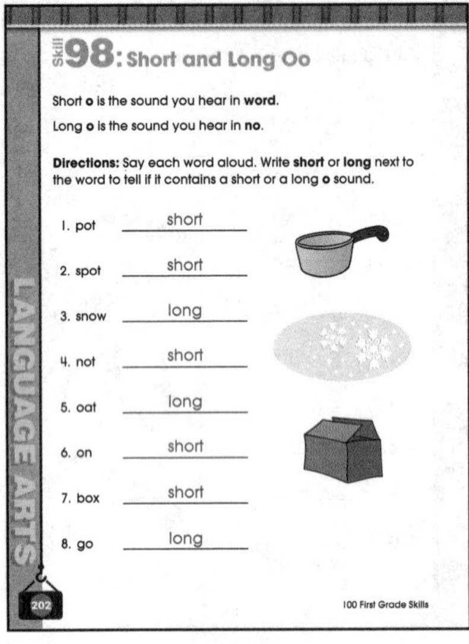

Skill **98: Short and Long Oo**

Short **o** is the sound you hear in **word**.

Long **o** is the sound you hear in **no**.

Directions: Say each word aloud. Write **short** or **long** next to the word to tell if it contains a short or a long **o** sound.

1. pot short
2. spot short
3. snow long
4. not short
5. oat long
6. on short
7. box short
8. go long

LANGUAGE ARTS

202 100 First Grade Skills

Page 202

Skill **98: Short and Long Oo**

Directions: Say each word aloud. Write **short** or **long** next to the word to tell if it contains a short or a long **o** sound.

1. mop short
2. rope long
3. Oliver short
4. show long
5. shop short
6. store short
7. stop short
8. slope long
9. flow long
10. row long

PET STORE

STOP

LANGUAGE ARTS

100 First Grade Skills 203

Page 203

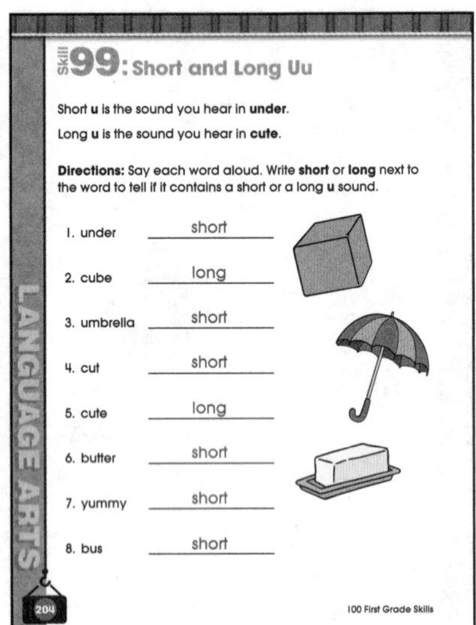

Skill **99: Short and Long Uu**

Short **u** is the sound you hear in **under**.

Long **u** is the sound you hear in **cute**.

Directions: Say each word aloud. Write **short** or **long** next to the word to tell if it contains a short or a long **u** sound.

1. under short
2. cube long
3. umbrella short
4. cut short
5. cute long
6. butter short
7. yummy short
8. bus short

LANGUAGE ARTS

204 100 First Grade Skills

Page 204

Skill **99: Short and Long Uu**

Directions: Say each word aloud. Write **short** or **long** next to the word to tell if it contains a short or a long **u** sound.

1. mule long
2. club short
3. duck short
4. dune long
5. tuck short
6. tune long
7. run short
8. funny short
9. suit long
10. truck short

LANGUAGE ARTS

100 First Grade Skills 205

Page 205

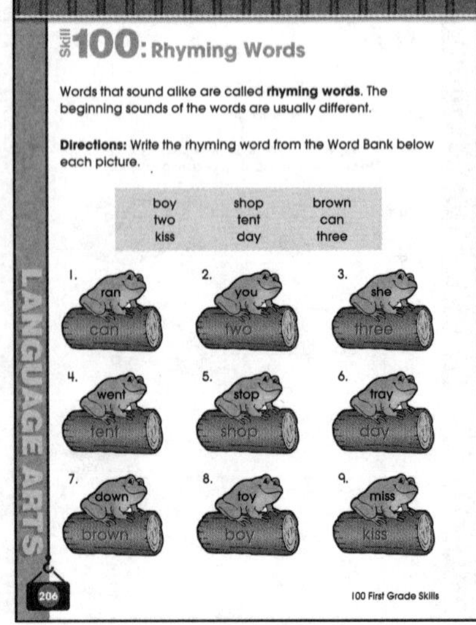

Skill **100: Rhyming Words**

Words that sound alike are called **rhyming words**. The beginning sounds of the words are usually different.

Directions: Write the rhyming word from the Word Bank below each picture.

boy	shop	brown
two	tent	can
kiss	day	three

1. ran — can
2. you — two
3. she — three
4. went — tent
5. stop — shop
6. tray — day
7. down — brown
8. toy — boy
9. miss — kiss

LANGUAGE ARTS

206 100 First Grade Skills

Page 206

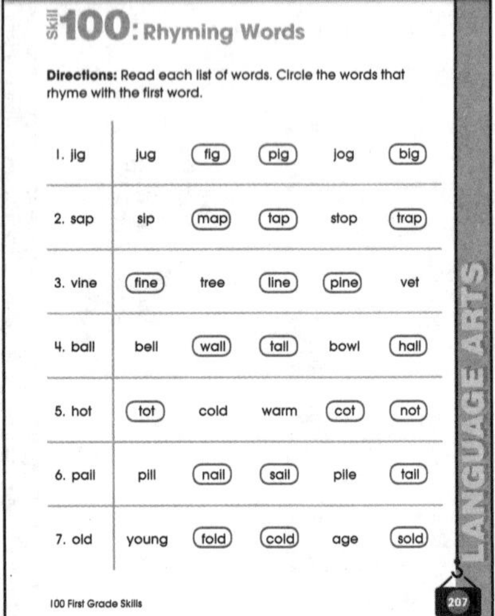

Skill **100: Rhyming Words**

Directions: Read each list of words. Circle the words that rhyme with the first word.

1. jig	jug	(fig)	(pig)	jog	(big)
2. sap	sip	(map)	(tap)	stop	(trap)
3. vine	(fine)	tree	(line)	(pine)	vet
4. ball	bell	(wall)	(tall)	bowl	(hall)
5. hot	(tot)	cold	warm	(cot)	(not)
6. pail	pill	(nail)	(sail)	pile	(tail)
7. old	young	(fold)	(cold)	age	(sold)

LANGUAGE ARTS

100 First Grade Skills 207

Page 207